Refresh

'project review.

Dear Edouard,

Many thanks for making sure that it all happens.

ASSOCIATION

erBook G4

Ken-hin Teo, Social Condenser, Intermediate Unit 3

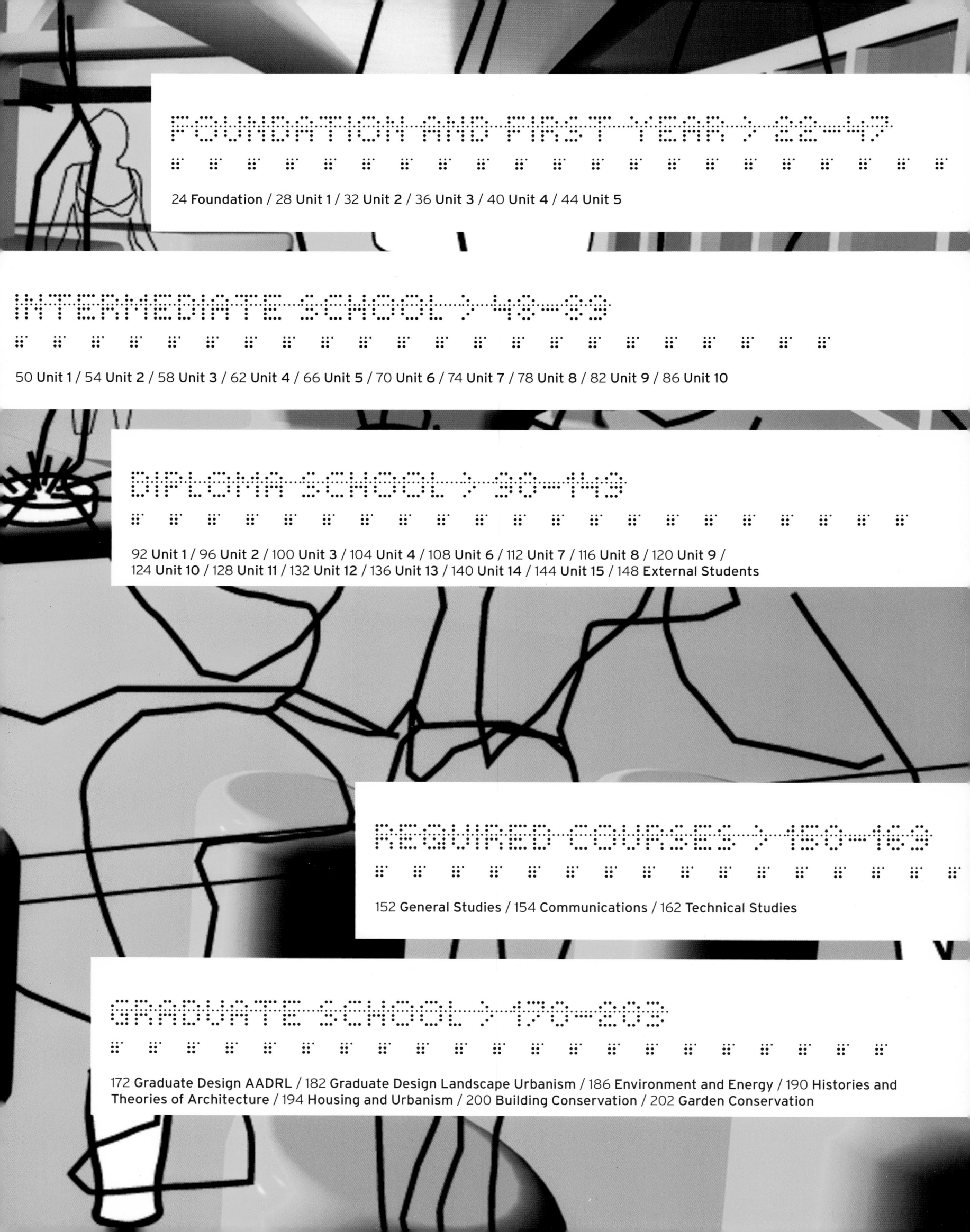

The work of the AA is a dynamic process that is constantly evolving. This is in part a result of the academic structure of the School: from the Foundation to the Graduate programmes, AA students and teachers have a greater degree of autonomy than is the case in most other schools of architecture. Yet this greater autonomy and freedom needs to be debated, negotiated and developed in relation to the work and practices of other students and teachers in the School. It is this active and often conflicting space, in between individual work and collective project, that best defines the AA.

The introduction of new academic co-ordinators in the First Year, Intermediate and Diploma Schools (Tony Swannell, Charles Tashima, and Peter Beard respectively) has played a significant role in helping to articulate the relationship between the teaching units. At the same time their involvement has aided the interactions of the units and their students with the School's other programmes and requirements. These changes are intended to enhance the connections throughout the different parts of the School and to ensure that student architects are exposed to a greater diversity of ideas and practices. When it comes to architectural projects it is not always possible to see progress on a daily or sometimes even a weekly basis. For a student of architecture, having to build a relationship between the various elements of the course of study, this can seem to be even more the case.

How does studio work benefit in any measurable sense from the teaching of architectural history and theory? How does the teaching of technical subjects help articulate the design project? Establishing these connections is something that takes time. Nevertheless, many of our debates during the past year have been concerned with raising and responding to such questions in a systematic and pragmatic manner. Our goal has been to realise a vision of architectural education that, as it continues to cover a range of disciplines, emphasises the relational rather than the accumulative aspect of learning. For example, the balance between the autonomy of a discipline such as architectural history and the instrumental role it can play in design is in need of continuous updating. But it is this process of updating that enables the work to continue to make new contributions to the discourses of architecture.

The proliferation of models, objects, structures and prototypes throughout the different parts of the School demonstrates the commitment of the AA and its students to directly addressing and confronting the space between concept and realisation. In a recent lecture at the School, Frei Otto provided an exemplary demonstration of an architect's long and consistent search for this form of material imagination. Similarly, the works presented in this review, from Foundation to Graduate School, entwine the virtual and the actual, the political and the physical. These projects invariably balance the recovery and recognition of fragments of an earlier material culture with the projection and construction of new futures. In doing so, they recognise the simultaneous presence of the conceptual and the physical in the project of architectural imagination.

Mohsen Mostafavi June 2001

Aya Maeda, Intermediate Unit 10: Body Suit project.
Photograph by Goswin Schwendinger.

On 20 December 1999 a catastrophe almost occurred at a publicity event for the 'Mediatheque' then under construction in Sendai. The event in question, 'SENDAI Calling', was organised by a local advertising agency. The idea was to have a crowd of young people assemble in front of the construction site, facing a tree-lined boulevard decorated for Christmas, and have their friends call them all at precisely the same time, so that they could get 'high' on the ringers going off in harmony. Needless to say, the IT specialists were not pleased. While neither this incident nor those previously described caused any serious damage, there is no doubt that mistakes in organising communications and communities will inevitably generate panic in the information system.

These stories illustrate the parallels between the technologies of the mobile phone and the internet. Both make efficient use of existing, small-scale infrastructures, circumventing the need for a consolidated infrastructure. In other words, they present a dispersed infrastructure operation technology.

Such technology can be described in terms of urban infrastructure. Taking narrow back roads rather than congested main arteries allows you to get where you're going faster. But if you find the back road blocked by construction or a bunch of kids playing football you'll have to duck into a side road. And if everyone starts using these little back roads they will immediately overload – a single big Mercedes with the air-conditioning on full blast has the potential to cause a tailback when the connecting routes are so small. This is what happened with the seijinshiki in Yokohama. Users can't afford to ignore the fact that even brief phone calls can destroy the whole infrastructure when the traffic is too dense.

Akira Suzuki, *Do Android Crows Fly Over the Skies of an Electronic Tokyo?* (AA Publications, 2001)
www.aaschool.ac.uk/publications

The AA's public events have always featured an international cast of lecturers and exhibitors, and this year was no exception. Two nationalities, however, were particularly strongly represented in the 2000/01 programme. From January to February, the AA Gallery was home to *Droog+Do Create*, an installation featuring a range of objects designed by the Dutch collective (whose name, Droog, translates as 'dry'). These objects, which might find a place in any home, are remarkable in that they require owner interaction to achieve their final form. As an opening-night demonstration, Mohsen Mostafavi (bravely filling a role played by a female bodybuilder wearing a pink bikini in the Paris production) flexed his muscles and took a sledgehammer to *Do Hit*, a steel cube that is to be bludgeoned into an armchair. Following the hitting, framing, scratching, adding, swinging and breaking (to which those present needed little exhortation) Renny Ramakers and Gijs Bakker, founders of Droog, described their careers in the context of their nationality. This entertaining dialogue covered topics ranging from the travel arrangements of Holland's royal family to the nutritive requirements of tulip bulbs (they need no manure), and characterised the Dutch as an unorthodox mixture of the conservative and the wilfully unusual.

A series of lectures on Dutch design tended to emphasise the latter aspect of the national character. Speakers included artist Joep van Lieshout, landscape architect Michael van Gessel and book designer Irma Boom.

Many of those who come to lecture at the AA also involve themselves in the wider activities of the School. Boom was no exception, designing this year's public events posters – with their instantly recognisable chequerboard of tear-off diaries. Boom has also collaborated with AA Publications to design Akira Suzuki's *Do Android Crows Fly Over the Skies of an Electronic Tokyo?* Available this autumn, the book provides an elegantly written and idiosyncratic analysis of current and future aspects of urban life in Japan.

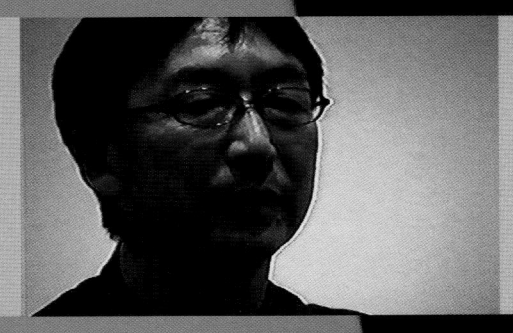

A series of essays covers everything from national infrastructures and telephone networks to the design of the smallest of family spaces and, indeed, of families themselves. Suzuki describes a landscape that is invisible but not virtual, 'it is a substantive landscape made of electromagnetic waves. Most importantly it is not monopolised by an exclusive information elite': schoolchildren can collapse a mobile phone network, the toilette of young girls defines the structure of family apartments. 'This may seem a strange kind of urban theory. But the cities of today and tomorrow only exist within the twisted relations between the physical community and its network counterpart. We should think of it as a soft landscape that is constantly being updated by its users...'

The Sendai Mediatheque became the focus of attention over Easter. Toyo Ito's recently inaugurated building represents a new type of public architecture, one that remains open to the kind of updating championed by Suzuki. As Ito, who presented the work in a lecture at the AA, states: 'the local government enjoined us to make Sendai Mediatheque "barrier-free", meaning free of barriers obstructing access by the weak or handicapped. I took "barrier-free" to mean also freedom from administrative constraints... many people are no doubt wondering what exactly its purpose is... even those of us involved in its design entertain different images of the facility, and even as the opening approaches many discussions on its character continue... we have still not arrived at a consensus'.
The structure of the building, which, in a manner similar to Le Corbusier's 'Domino System', contains no walls or braces, is based around a system of seven layers of flat floors supported by 13 tree-like tubes; its construction was documented by almost 100 photographs by Naoya Hatakeyama, exhibited in the AA Gallery.

2001 was Japan year, and in keeping with this Tadashi Kawamata arrived at the AA to conduct the third Maeda Artist Workshop. Like Krzysztof Wodiczko before him, Kawamata chose to develop an investigation of public space, which began in November 2000 when students conducted a series of field works in London. These tested means by which to create new types of space that are a direct response to the context and materiality of a given area of existing public space, but that allow for a private experience akin to that of daydreaming in a busy café. This concept of 'lodging' was developed during further work in Tokyo. While many of the constructions in London had incorporated a barrier or protective quality, in Tokyo these aspects were replaced by an engagement with the network of social relationships that made up the local community. In May 2001 the results of the workshops in London and Tokyo were exhibited in the AA Gallery, and the experience gained from these projects was put to the test during a 72-hour lodging project in London.

The work of the last three Maeda Artist Workshops (including projects by Richard Wilson, Krzysztof Wodiczko, and Tadashi Kawamata) is featured in *AA Files 43*, available in July.

Design in its broadest sense was another of this year's themes. In the Autumn Term fashion designer Hussein Chalayan came to talk at the AA about his work and career. Although he only graduated seven years ago, Chalayan's designs have earned him a reputation as a visionary and he has twice been named British Fashion Designer of the Year. He discussed the use of experimental materials (from rusted fabrics to washable paper) and unorthodox techniques, as well as the great sense of drama in his work. Among the works he showed were a remote control dress, and the furniture-wear collection – in which a coffee table transforms into a skirt and dresses are made from fitted chair covers. As Chalayan revealed, his practice has much to do with architecture, particularly in his use of CAD and furniture technologies and his fascination with materials and technique. Another leading designer to visit the AA was Marc Newson. His lecture highlighted the diversity of his work – from commercial designs for Alessi to watches, cars and more unusual commissions such as the interior of a Dassault

Q: Your exhibition at the AA will take place both inside the Exhibition Gallery and in a Portakabin located on the paved area of Bedford Square directly opposite it. Can you explain how this will work?

We will use the gallery and the portakabin to exhibit document of the workshops conducted in London and Tokyo in November 2000 and January 2001 respectively. The portakabin will house an estate agency named Lodging London/Tokyo, which will introduce lodgings made by teams of students and myself via video, maps and other documentation. In the gallery, we will show 'left-over' structures, which could be read as display houses in a Home Show. Finally, on the day after the show opens, the students and myself will begin a 72-hour lodging project in London.

Q: How do you imagine these spaces will be perceived by visitors to the show?

I guess that people might be puzzled as they stand in the Gallery amongst all the left-over structures. Although, seen on their own, these resemble the discarded skins of absent bodies, by visiting the Portakabin viewers may recognise the relationship between them and their original locations. These skins indicate the volume of lodgings. I hope that people will view them not as a series of fragments, but as a series of temporary states within the two cities.

Q: Usually a Home Show is an exhibition of volumes that have yet to be inhabited. In this case the Gallery contains spaces that have already been inhabited...

A: Perhaps this should be a Second-hand Home Show.

Tadashi Kawamata, interviewed by Shin Egashira, from AA Files 43. Available late July. www.aaschool.ac.uk/publications

Top row (left to right): Hussein Chalayan; Marc Newson; Victor Burgin. Video stills by Joel Newman.

Main image: Tania Rodriguez, Intermediate Unit 4: a 'sleeping vitrine' in Trafalgar Square, from the 'Lodging London/Tokyo' project with Tadashi Kawamata.

Nietzsche never visited Paris. The more I read during the summer the stranger this seemed. He was familiar with many European cities. He was especially enthusiastic in his admiration for French culture. French was the only language he knew well apart from his own. The city must have occupied a privileged place in his imagination. The reason why Nietzsche never visited Paris is suggested in his corresponcdence with Paul Rée and Lou Salomé. In April 1882, while in Rome, Nietzsche met, and apparently fell in love with, Salomé. During that same spring Nietzsche, Salomé and their mutual friend Paul Rée made plans to set up an intellectual ménage à trois. The idea of living together came from Salomé and originally concerned only herself and Rée. But the two readily agreed that Nietzsche be included. Nietzche suggested that they should live in Paris. He set about contacting friends who might find a suitable apartment. The three were still discussing their Paris plans while they met again, in Leipzig, in November. Then quite abruptly Salomé and Rée left the city, without warning anyone, or leaving any indication of where they had gone. The abandoned Nietzsche assumed, incorrectly, that they were in Paris.

Victor Burgin, Nietzsche's Paris, from Shadowed (AA Publications, 2000). www.aaschool.ac.uk/publications

Falcon private aircraft. Other designers who visited the AA included Mike Phillips, (the creative director of AKA Design, designers of the Ducati MH900e) and Bruce Mau (designer of OMA's *S,M,L,XL* book).

Tony Oursler, Jemima Stehli, shez 360, Jochen Gerz, Langlands and Bell, Reich and Szyber, Ori Gersht and Nathan Coley were added to the growing list of people – both established and up-and-coming – who have taken part in the AA's long-running Friday night Artist's Talk series.

'In these movies that are not true movies, these panoramas that are not true panoramas, turned towards buildings that are not, as simulacra of their originals, true buildings, Burgin has succeeded in inventing a new kind of space...' (Anthony Vidler)

The exhibition of *Nietzsche's Paris*, a specially commissioned video work by Victor Burgin, brought this space to the AA. The work, an intrication of physical and psychical space, draws on correspondence between Friedrich Nietzsche, Lou Salomé and Paul Rée to explore a very particular conjunction of terms – Nietzsche, architecture, Paris – in a single space. The exhibition was accompanied by an AA publication, *Shadowed*, which documents Burgin's video work of the last five years.

Luce Irigaray, one of the leading exponents of philosophical feminism, came to the AA during the Autumn Term to answer the question of 'Comment vivre durablement ensemble?' During the talk she brought her long-standing investigations into symbolisation, language and alterity to bear on the construction of apartment blocks and the material encounters of day-to-day co-habitation. This theme found a response in a lecture by Joseph Rykwert, one of the pioneers of the study of the history and theory of architecture. He discussed his latest publication, *The Seduction of Place* – an analysis of the late-twentieth-century city. Like Irigaray, he looked at metropolitan values, at what it means to be, and live, in a city today, and celebrated what

he perceived to be the pluralism, tolerance and cultural vitality of
the modern city. A response was given by the eminent sociologist
Richard Sennett. Other speakers this year have included
James Ackerman, Hilde Heynen, Andrew Benjamin, Norman Bryson
and Kenneth Frampton.

Theoretical and historical issues were also covered by the various
conferences and exhibitions held at the AA. In the Spring Term
scholars from both the UK and Germany gathered at the School to
examine the difficult issue of German architecture and its changing
past. This focused on the continuing controversy surrounding
representations of the Holocaust, and the problems arising out of
reunification. A conference on performative notation in the Summer
Term looked at the ways in which change, movement and time can be
described and analysed across a range of disciplines, from dance to
cinema, from architecture to music. Le Corbusier received a great
deal of exposure this year, through a lecture given by Charles Jencks,
a conference, and an exhibition in the Front Members' Room.
The conference and exhibition examined the role of publishing in the
development of Le Corbusier's œuvre, drawing on recent research by
Jencks and the AA's Design Research Laboratory (AADRL). This work
aimed at demonstrating the influence of Corb's publishing efforts on
his methods and processes. The themes of this exhibition will be
expanded upon in a forthcoming AA publication.

One of the most eagerly anticipated events this year was the visit
of Frei Otto, the renowned German architect. A pioneer of tensile
structures, he lectured to an overflowing audience about the
relationship between architecture and the natural sciences, and the
inspiration that he has drawn from nature over the past half century.
Nature, and 'green' issues, are an equally important part of the work
of Laurie Baker, the subject of an exhibition in the Front Members'
Room. Originally from Birmingham, Baker has lived in Kerala,
southern India for more than fifty years. During this time he has

shown little interest in international architectural trends, instead arguing for sustainability, economic and social viability. The exhibition demonstrated that Baker is one of architecture's true humanists.

Two more practices came to the AA from the Netherlands – NL Architects (who worked with Droog on the Mandarina Duck shop in Paris) and Lars Spuybroek. The latter discussed the work of his practice, NOX, and his investigations into the relationship between architecture and media, particularly computing. Other architects who visited this year included Terry Farrell, David Chipperfield (who were both discussing recent international projects), Valerio Olgiati (recently featured in *AA Files 42*), the Irish architect Shane de Blacam (whose work will appear in a future issue of *AA Files*) and former AA tutor Elia Zenghelis, who had just won the first Annie Spink prize for excellence in architectural teaching. The AA's excellence of teaching (and the excellence of its students) was also recognised in the RIBA President's Medals, with the Silver Medal (for Part 2 students) shared between three AA students – Takuya Onishi, Ole Scheeren and Henrik Rothe. The Bronze Medal (for Part 1 students) was awarded jointly to another AA student, Jordi Pagés Ramon.

So, thank you for listening. This was half a century's work, half a century's research, half a century of sculpting forms. I hope it was not too much to shoot through. Are there any questions?

Q: At the beginning of the lecture you mentioned your training as a mason, working with heavy materials, and then you moved very quickly on to lightweight structures. Could you describe to us how this shift came about?

For that, I need to tell you a bit of biography. After school I started training as a stonemason. This was natural for me: my father was a sculptor, my grandfather too. But at the same time I had a hobby – building gliders. Then in the war, when I was 17 or 18, I trained as a pilot, and was given the chance to design planes – motor planes too. At 19 I was in a Russian prisoner-of-war camp holding 40,000 people. In 1945 many of the prisoners died and it was necessary to build a cemetery, and of course we held an architectural competition to design it. I took a little piece of paper that I'd found and I started to make a sketch. Half a year later – without even a single semester of training – I found myself the leader of the team that was building the cemetery, responsible for about 200 of the best craftsmen of all different kinds, including some very good architects. I was only made responsible because I was the youngest – the leader could not go home right away, but had to stay until the end of 1947, to complete the work. So I had these different kinds of background – lightweight structures from the gliders, and building with stone – which I mixed together. I was 'chief engineer and architect' of this cemetery, but I had practically no materials, apart from the steel rails that were lying around. How could we build with no materials? So I wrote a scientific paper about how to make structures with the least materials. I didn't know then that this was an original paper ...

Q: You work in a very unusual area, between architecture and engineering, which is not a 'profession' as such. Could you say something about the place of technique in your work? How do you try it out? How do you learn it? Through books, through architectural models, or though sculpture?

My way of thinking differs from that of most engineers. It is, in fact, the way of stonemasons or woodworkers – it involves bringing things together and studying them in reality, without any complicated equations. (I know of only two, three, four equations that are necessary for dimensioning buildings.) This other way of thinking also leads to other forms. Of course, sometimes I accuse my friends – engineers – of being unscientific. A scientist, when he has a theoretical model, must usually prove it with an experiment. When the building engineer has a theoretical model, he cannot prove it before he builds his building. And most concrete and stone buildings are very difficult to prove – to know that the forces and stresses that you have calculated are really right. So I chose another way, inventing forms and proving them through models. Up till now this was a good link. There's only one problem – many engineers don't make these models any more. They say it's too much work, the computer gets the same results. But who controls the computer? If you only look at the screen, have you really understood the building? One thing is true: when you've made the model with your own hands, like a craftsman, then you know the building.

Frei Otto, lecture at the AA, May 2001

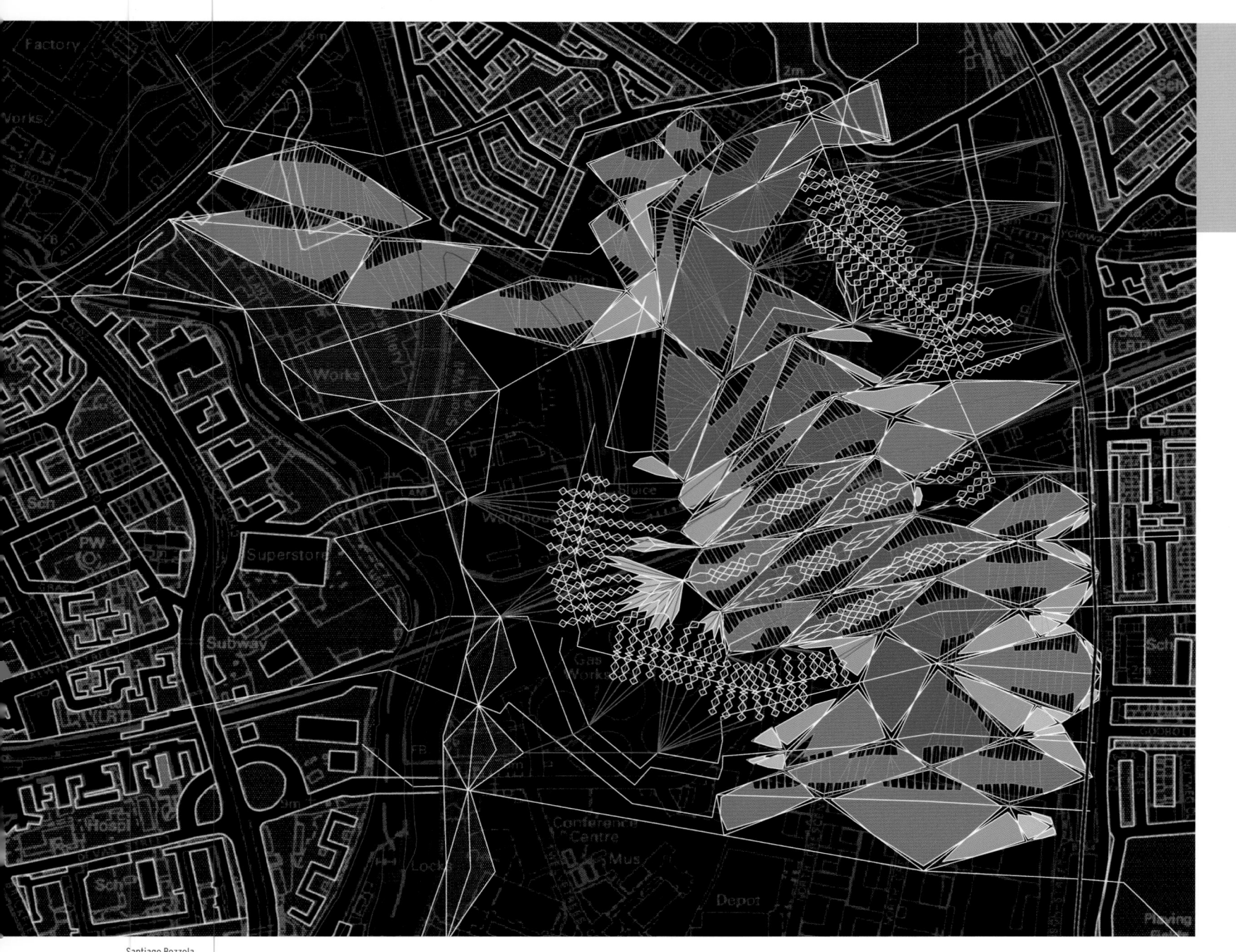

Santiago Bozzola
Changing Structures: tectonic performances between
a leisure park and a productive land *See p. 182*

GRADUATE SCHOOL > LANDSCAPE URBANISM

Valerie Bennett

INTERMEDIATE SCHOOL > UNIT 4

Montage by Henry Leung
Capsule Hotel unloading in Bedford Square Gardens.
Intermediate Unit 4 project
See p. 62

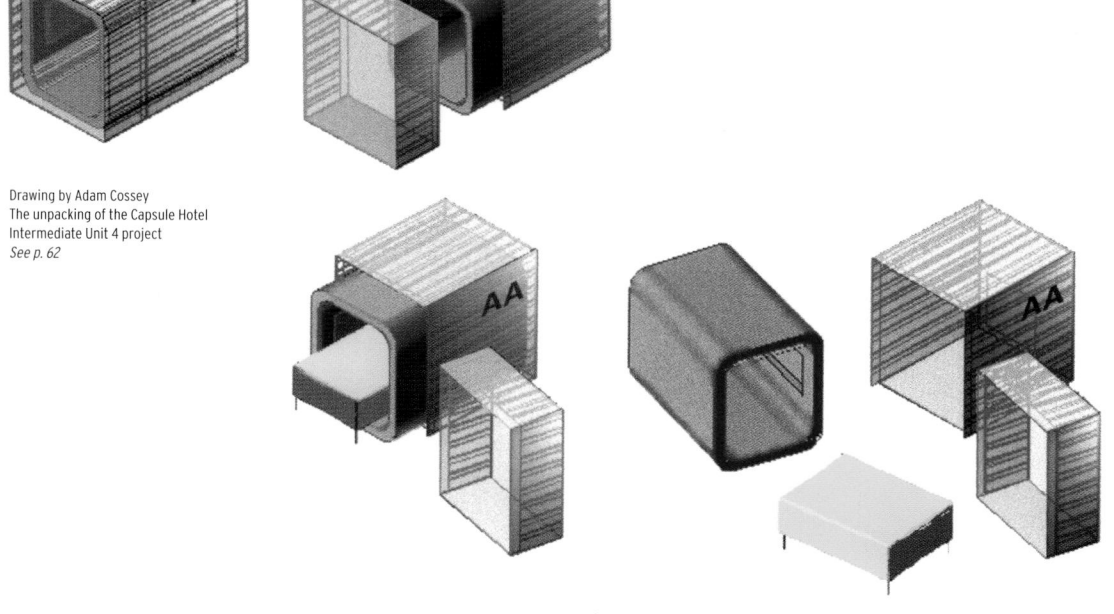

Drawing by Adam Cossey
The unpacking of the Capsule Hotel
Intermediate Unit 4 project
See p. 62

Valerie Bennett

INTERMEDIATE SCHOOL > UNIT 10

Assaf Zuker
Body suit project *See p. 86*

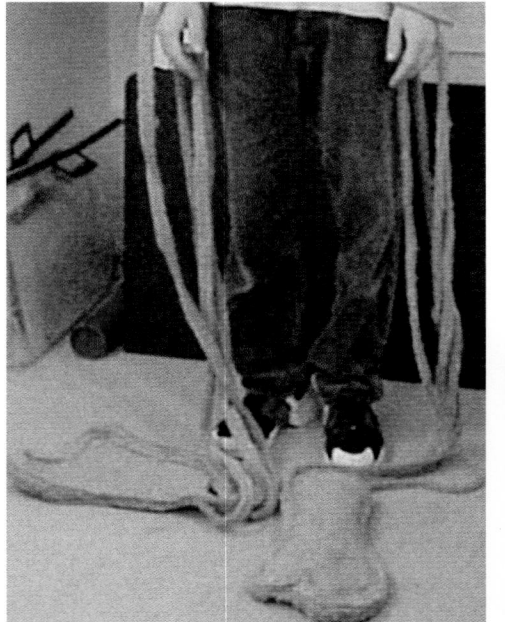

Naoko Yamada
Body suit project *See p. 86*

Hoi Chi Ng
Bridge model
See p. 86

Anthony Fairhurst
Child Rehabilitation Unit, Southwark (both images)
See p. 108

DIPLOMA SCHOOL > UNIT 6

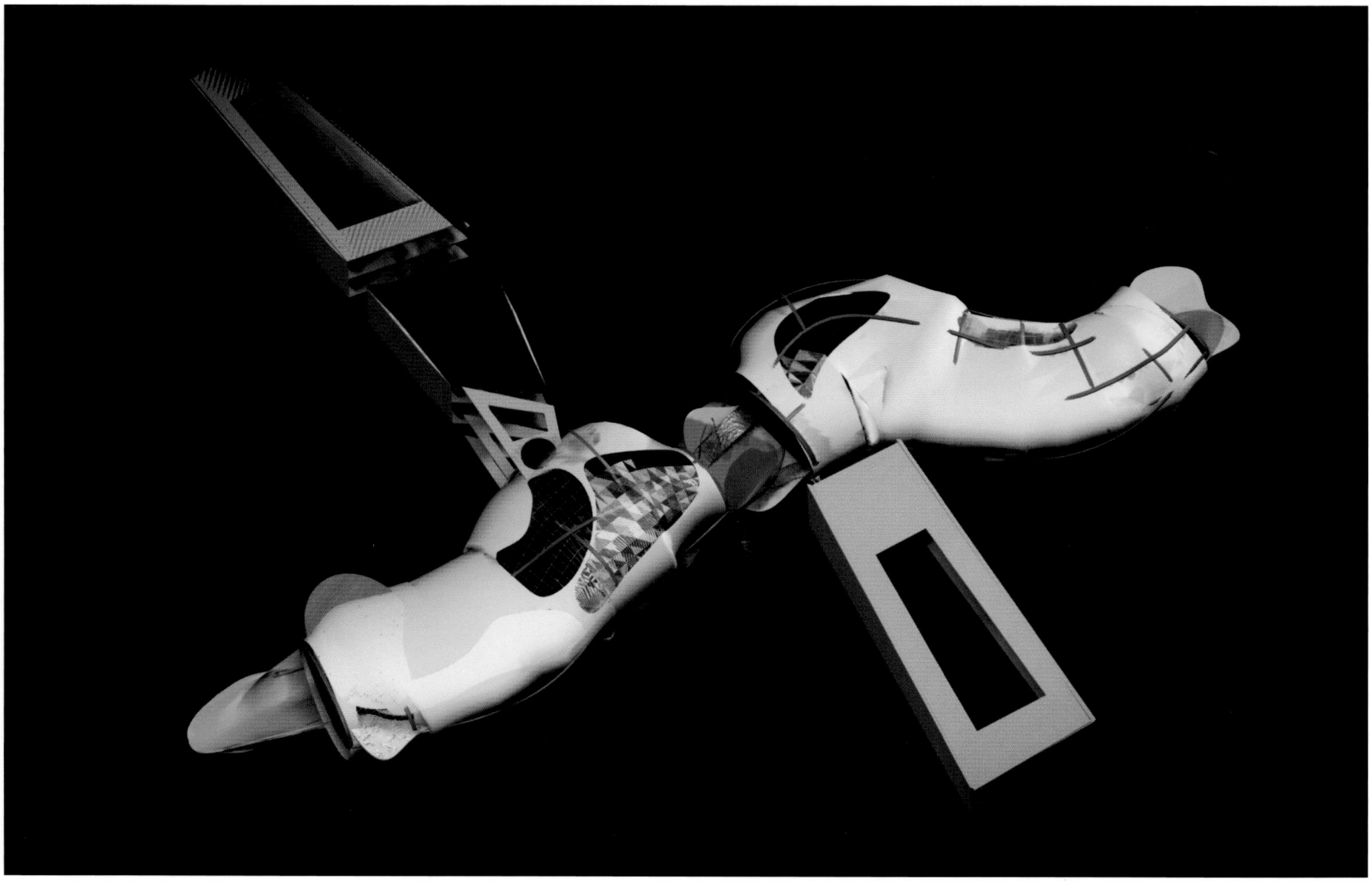

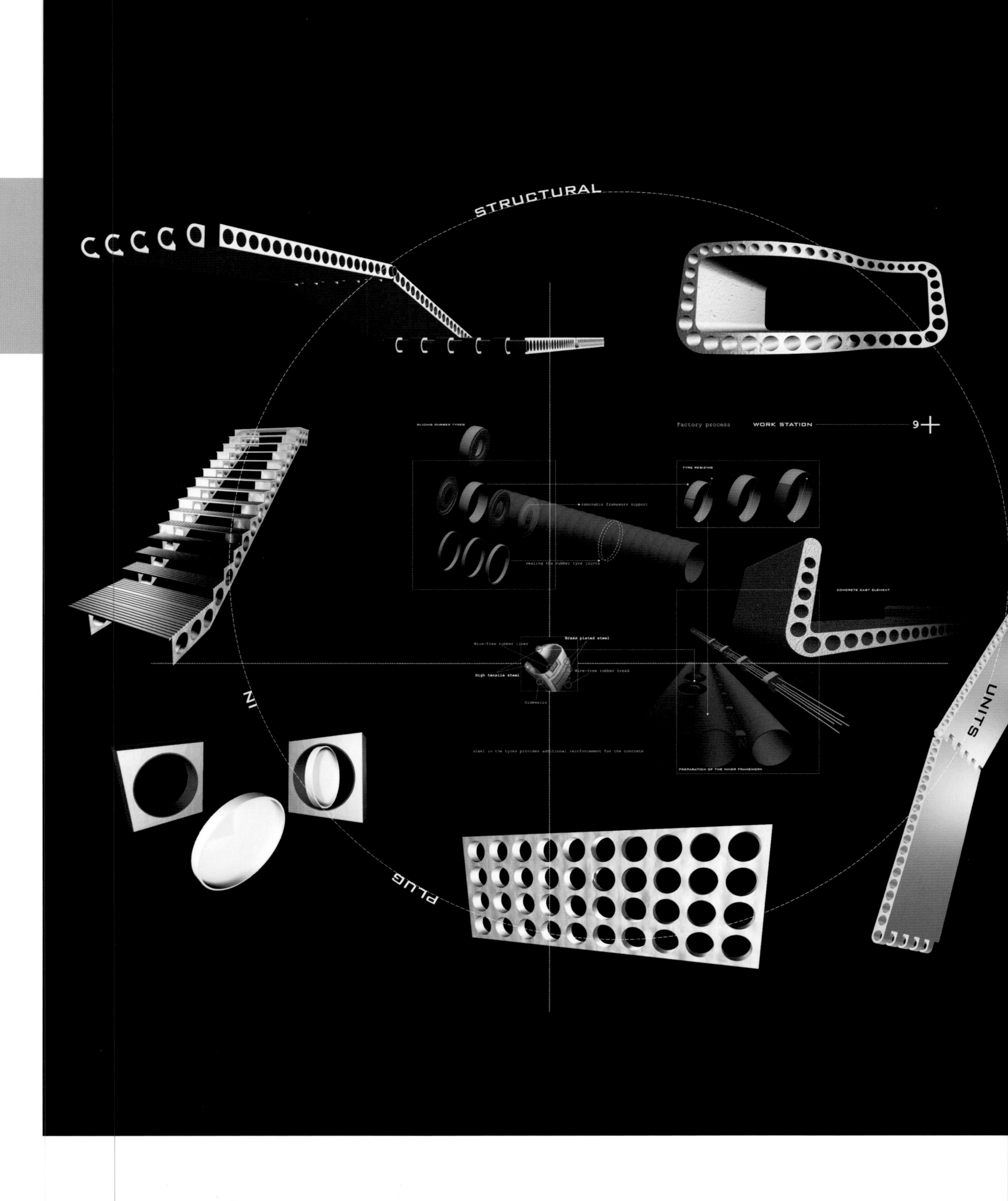

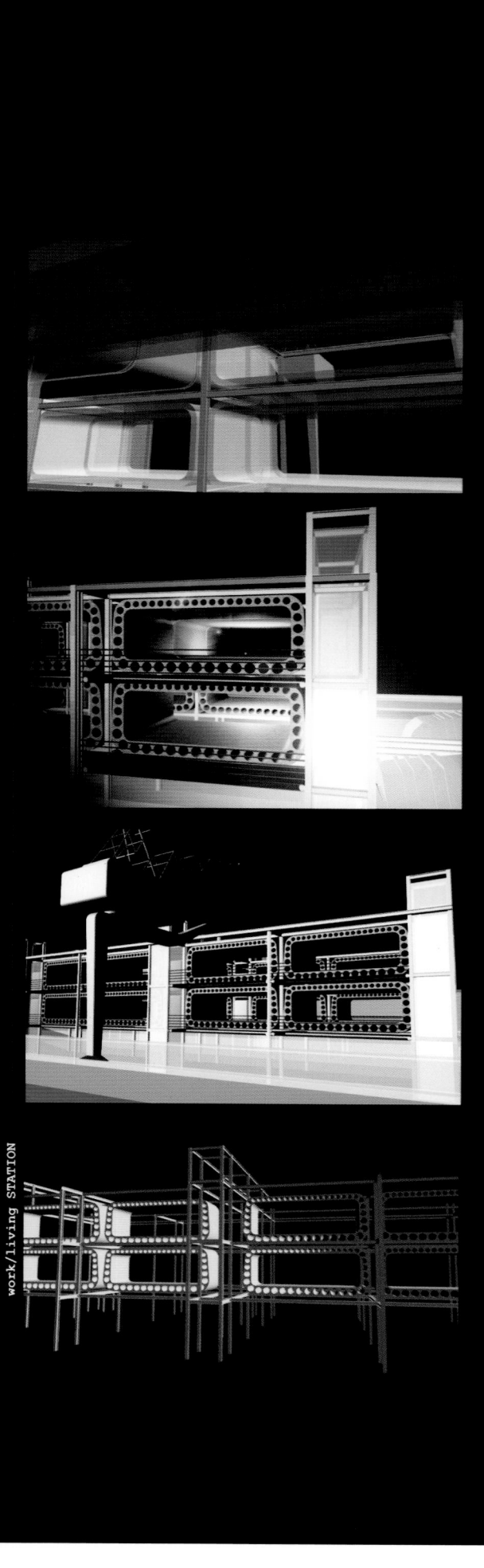

work/living STATION

DIPLOMA SCHOOL > UNIT 2

Siniša Rodić
Refugee housing in Belgrade (made from scrap tyres)
See p. 116

Christina Leung and Nobuyuki Tabata
Skateboard Track
See p. 32

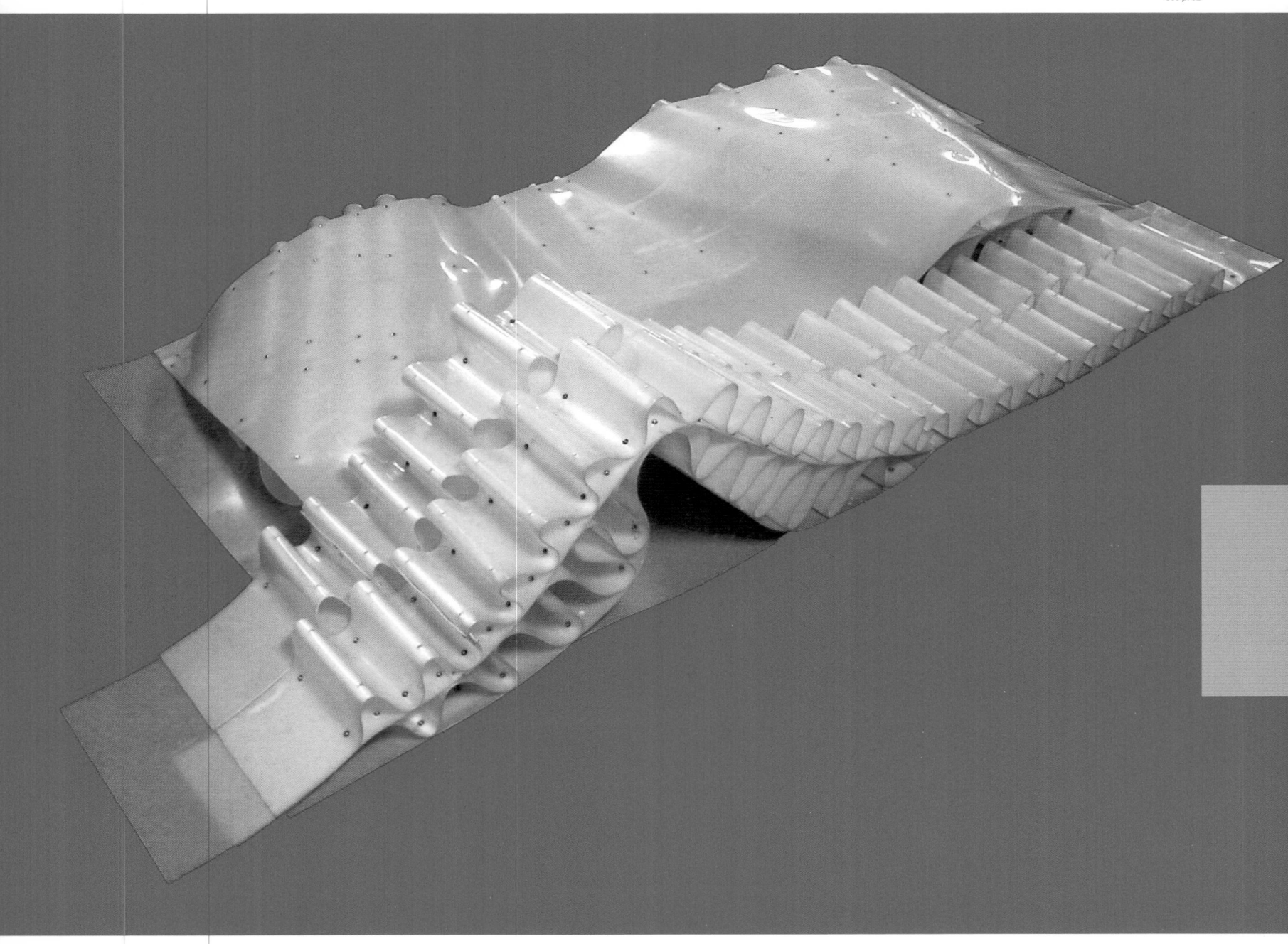

AADRL Phase II thesis design project by
P. Bavadekar, L. Pereira Miguel, Y. Nagumo, V. Shankar
Mass Customization study diagrams: 'Urbanets'
See p. 172

GRADUATE SCHOOL > AA DRL

AA DRL

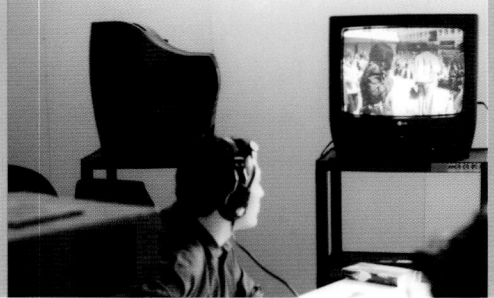

Valerie Bennett

INTERMEDIATE SCHOOL > UNIT 3

Ken-Hin Teo
Section: tube/street/lobby/bar/art
See p. 58

Stefan Rydin
Infrastructural redevelopment for Stockholm Slussen
View 1 (above): towards the bus terminal
View 2 (below): towards public amenities and shopping facilities
See p. 104

DIPLOMA SCHOOL > UNIT 4

Jimmy Wan, Fumiko Sakata, Indoor Play-Scape, First Year Unit 2

Foundation

Unit Staff Julia Wood, Veronika Schmid, Valentin Bontjes van Beek, David Max Phillips
Students Fahad Al-Ayoubi, Zainab Ali-Reza, Irene Astrain, Anastasia Boutsika, Edward Carter, Jake Choi, Farah Diab Ghanim, Sarah Fadhili, Rasha Farsi, Carl Leigh Fraser, Benjamin Jones, Andrea Marini, Beza Mbeboh, Otilia Portillo

Special thanks to guest tutors and jurors Gaby Agis, Louisa Auletta, Sue Barr, Gianni Botsford, Karola Dierichs, Oliver Domeisen, Alistair Gill, Brian Hatton, Mark Hemel, Gunther Koppelhuber, Torange Khonsari, Carolina de Lannoy, Andreas Lang, Michael McNamara, Ciro Najle, Chris Pauling, David Racz, Kay Roberts, Spela Videcnik, Gary Woodley and the Workshop

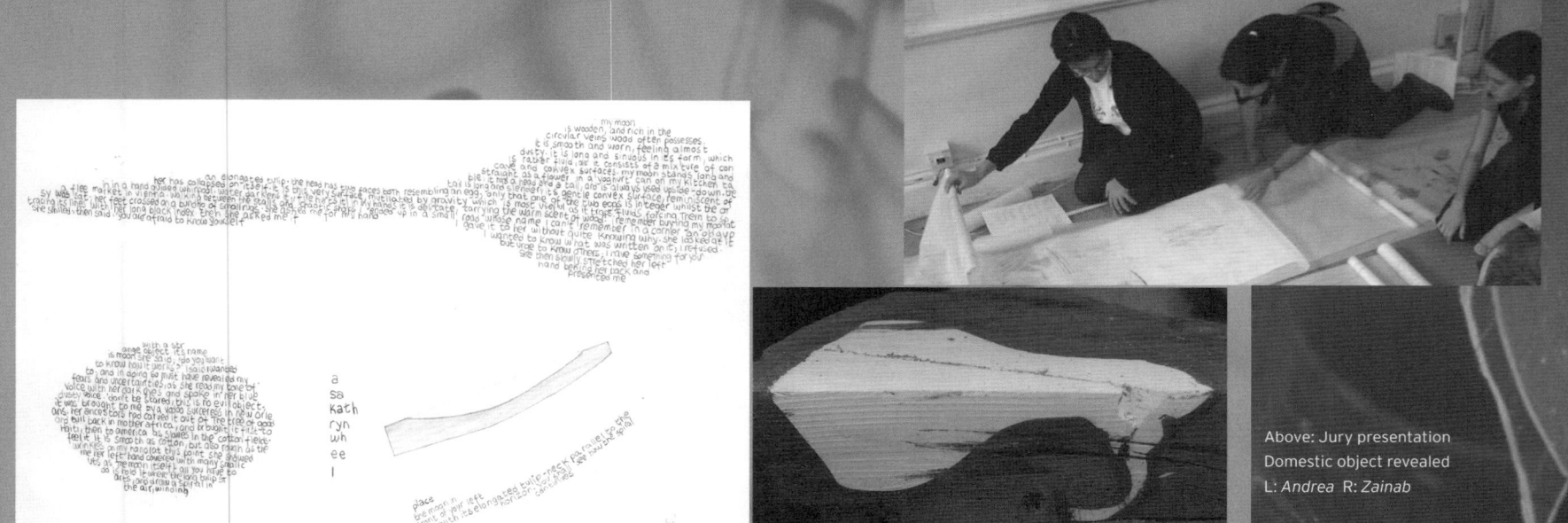

Above: Jury presentation
Domestic object revealed
L: *Andrea* R: *Zainab*

What is architecture? What is space? We began the year asking these fundamental questions. What is memory? What is public and private? What is mapping? What is designing? We continued to ask questions and explore the answers. What is reproduction in 2D and 3D? What is notation? What are plan and section? How can we use these both as creative process tools and as informative means of representation? How can we learn from the everyday, the given, the fashionable and the historic, without numbing our senses but instead triggering our inquisitive minds to research, draw and construct?

We entered Foundation as tourists, familiar with facade, monument, street map and souvenir. We are leaving as designers participating in an interactive world, with a physical and mental sense of space, with powers to define and manipulate space at different scales, to play games of strategy with control and chance, knowing we can set and break our rules to allow our passion and imagination to lead us onto the next project.

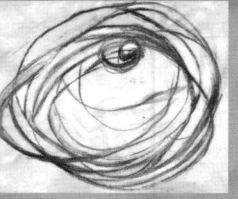

As soon as I looked up I was amazed by the framed sky. ...was it a projection? a large photograph or painting? was there a glass screen between the room's space and the outside space? I finally decided that it was an opening in the ceiling. In order to appreciate the experience to its fullest, I lay down on the carpet and looked up through the opening. The sky was out of context; I had never seen it framed so before. The sky was beautiful and..this new way of seeing it was incredible. Later it started to drizzle and I could not see the raindrops until they were very close to my face.. I began to question the difference between outdoor and indoor space and what defines them. James Turrell's *Sky Spaces* created an extension of space by making us feel outside yet we were still inside. *Farah*

Doodles: scaled and projected. 2D-3D TL: *Anastasia* TR: *Jake* BL: *Beza* BR: *Irene*

Background: Ink study: *Andrea*

Architect's Pilgrimage to New York: Where Hell meets Heaven
Brooklyn was the illest experience. I was lost in the darkness of this dark place, where at night the streets are more desert than the desert. There is a feeling of insecurity there. Even the simplest things like the payphones are held against the wall by big metal bars. Everything is barred....similar to Cameroon but the difference is when you look into the eyes of these people you see a sudden rush to release all their agony. The buildings are run down but the cars are incredible... lex jeeps, mercs, cadillacs...

Playing the City
As I play on my musical instrument the base-like 'tong' that resounds from my plucking of the strings creates a sudden rush in the heart of the pole and gradually travels through the ground. Playing my instrument turns me into the pole which controls and listens to the reverberating soundwaves that control the entire city. My negative brothers, which are situated everywhere in the five neighbourhoods, receive and project the base line across the city. The heavy thump slowly makes its way into the bodies and structures and explores individual minds. As I vibrate through each organism I feel their joys and agony. Many people in Astor Place feel comfortable but seem to have no sense of direction... I can feel the agitation for change...   *Beza*

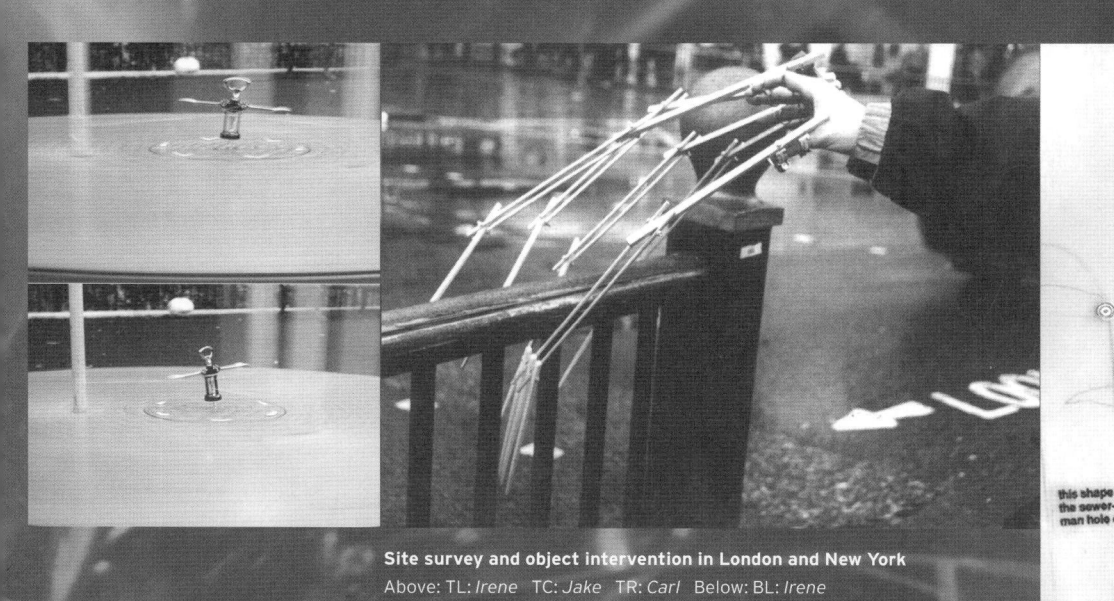

Site survey and object intervention in London and New York
Above: TL: *Irene*   TC: *Jake*   TR: *Carl*   Below: BL: *Irene*

Cell domestic bodyspace BR: *Andrea*

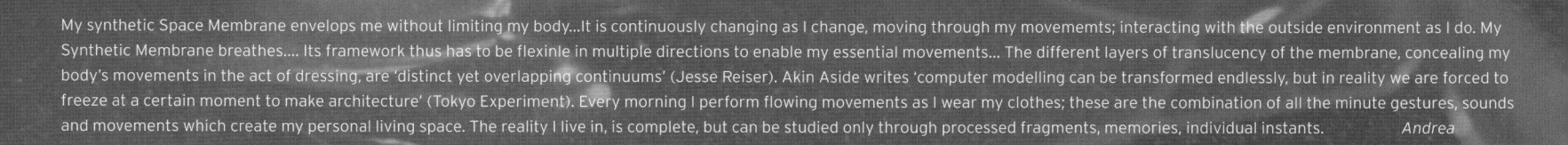

My synthetic Space Membrane envelops me without limiting my body...It is continuously changing as I change, moving through my movememts; interacting with the outside environment as I do. My Synthetic Membrane breathes.... Its framework thus has to be flexinle in multiple directions to enable my essential movements... The different layers of translucency of the membrane, concealing my body's movements in the act of dressing, are 'distinct yet overlapping continuums' (Jesse Reiser). Akin Aside writes 'computer modelling can be transformed endlessly, but in reality we are forced to freeze at a certain moment to make architecture' (Tokyo Experiment). Every morning I perform flowing movements as I wear my clothes; these are the combination of all the minute gestures, sounds and movements which create my personal living space. The reality I live in, is complete, but can be studied only through processed fragments, memories, individual instants.   *Andrea*

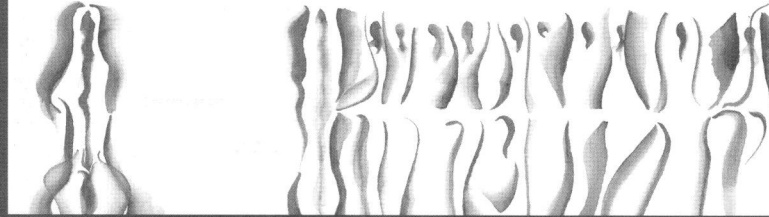

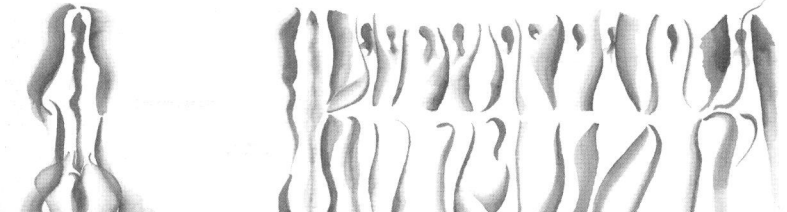

Background: Cell model : *Irene*

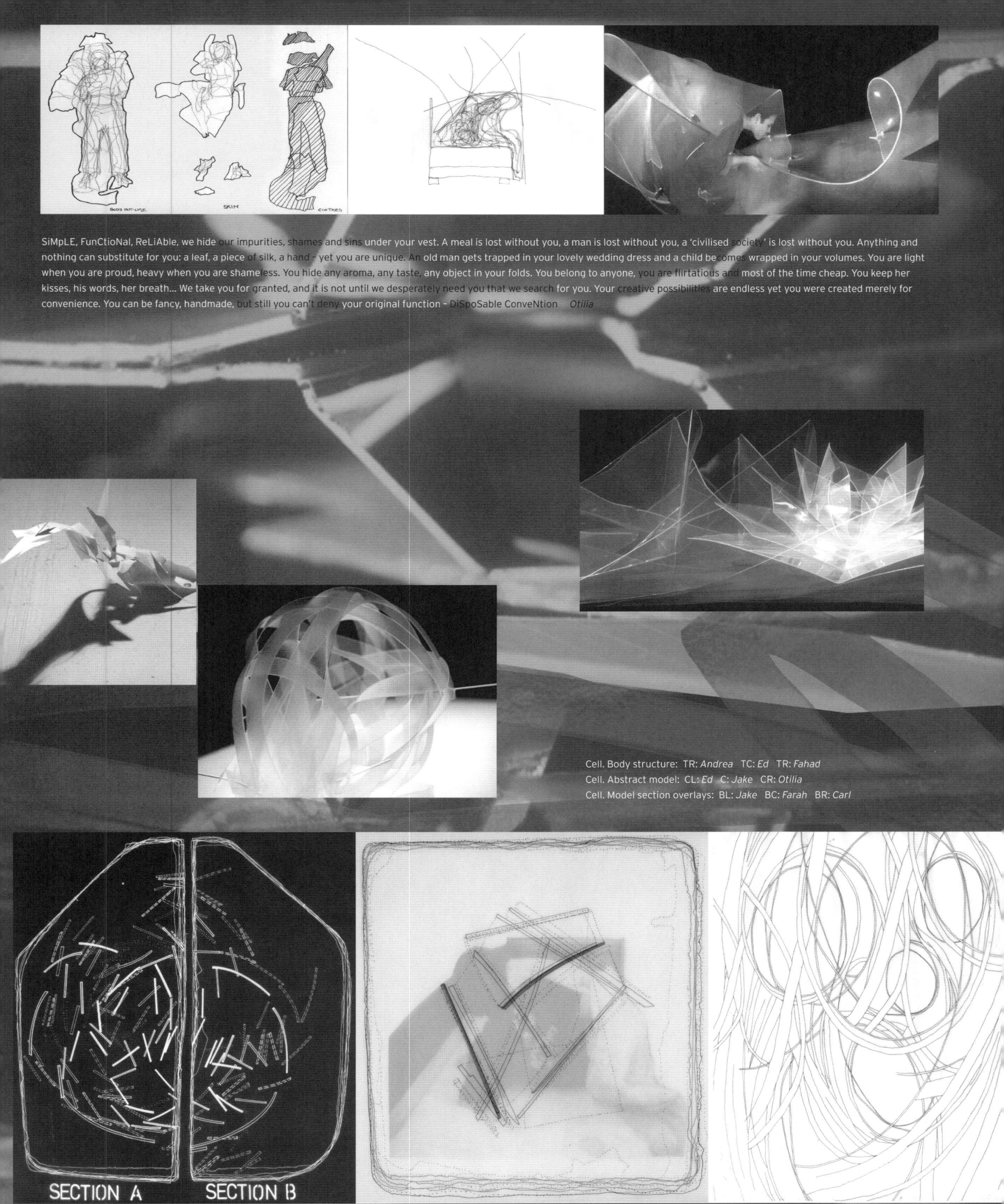

SiMpLE, FunCtioNal, ReLiAble, we hide our impurities, shames and sins under your vest. A meal is lost without you, a man is lost without you, a 'civilised society' is lost without you. Anything and nothing can substitute for you: a leaf, a piece of silk, a hand - yet you are unique. An old man gets trapped in your lovely wedding dress and a child becomes wrapped in your volumes. You are light when you are proud, heavy when you are shameless. You hide any aroma, any taste, any object in your folds. You belong to anyone, you are flirtatious and most of the time cheap. You keep her kisses, his words, her breath... We take you for granted, and it is not until we desperately need you that we search for you. Your creative possibilities are endless yet you were created merely for convenience. You can be fancy, handmade, but still you can't deny your original function - DiSpoSable ConveNtion   *Otilia*

Cell. Body structure: TR: *Andrea*   TC: *Ed*   TR: *Fahad*
Cell. Abstract model: CL: *Ed*   C: *Jake*   CR: *Otilia*
Cell. Model section overlays: BL: *Jake*   BC: *Farah*   BR: *Carl*

SECTION A   SECTION B

Background: Cell. Underground race track and flossing ground: *Beza*

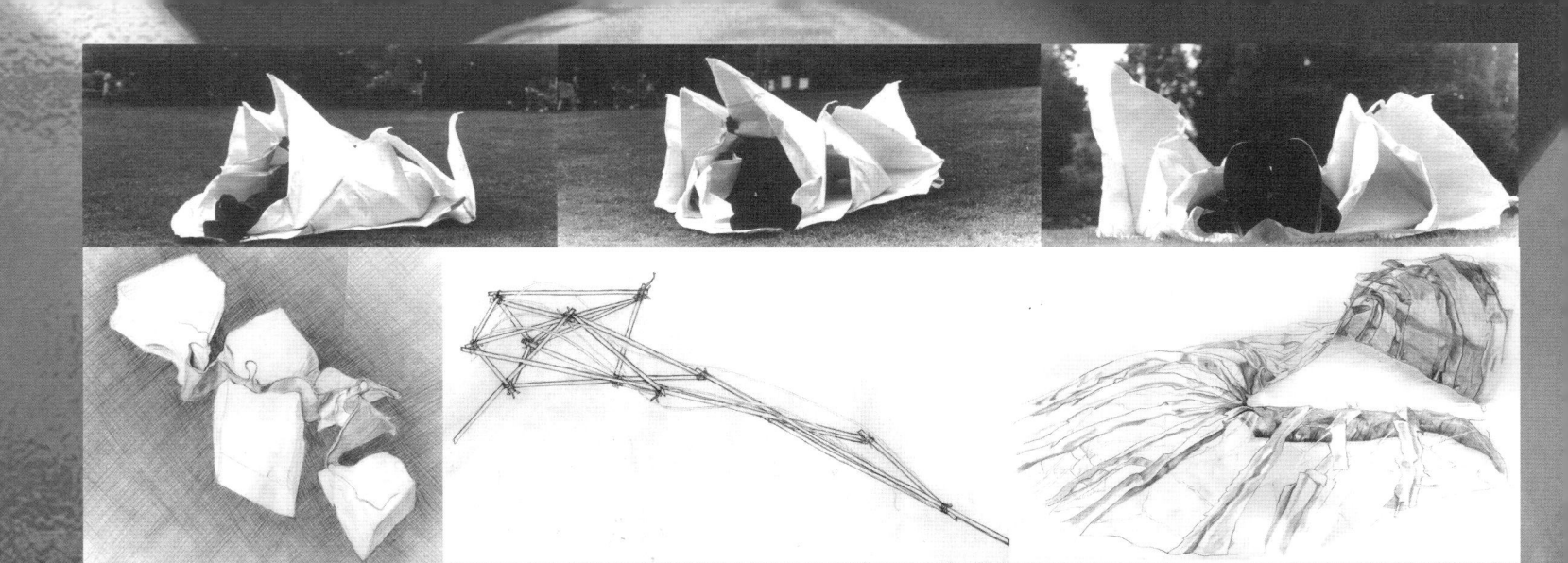

Above: Top: Cell body structure: *Otilia*   Centre: Cell development drawings: CL: *Anastasia*   C: *Beza*   CR: *Irene*
Below: Multicell Water Garden: TL: *Farah, Irene, Otilia*   TR: *Andrea*   BL: *Farah, Irene, Otilia*   BR: *Jake*

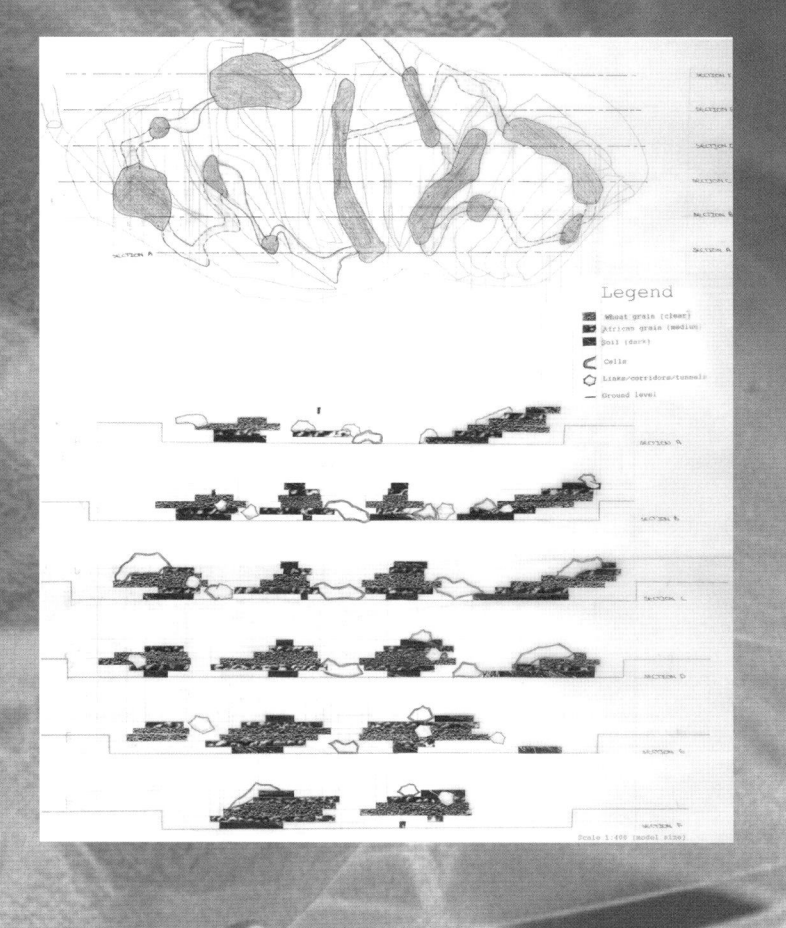

Liquid Vertigo Programme. There must be circulation within the casino; mainly axial, along the south–north line. This could be indicated through the flow of water beneath a clear ground, along the sides of the casino, and through the use of lighting, indicated by the 'tails' of my cells. They are shaped by external directionalities (car, pedestrian and train traffic) but simultaneously shape the internal ones (human circulation in the landscape). There have to be nodes, nexuses, turbulences along which the circulation can flow; gambling tables, slot machines, night-club rooms, bars.
Andrea

Background: Cell Aquatic Garden: *Carl*

First Year Unit 1

Ruth: in the city, Nov 00

The unit work this year began by looking at the idea of the city as the sea. How can we design a vessel for the city, a boat that has the flexibility to dock in one or many locations – a portable enclosure that provides not only shelter but also the possibility to adapt the existing fabric of the city?

We investigated the techniques and methods of boat construction by visiting both timber and fibre-glass boatyards. The different processes were documented to allow us to make a series of full-size details testing the

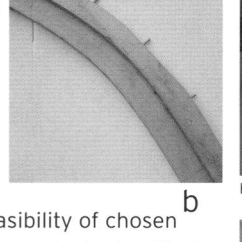

materials and the techniques that individuals wanted to use in their own designs. This process of making

a

b

not only questioned the feasibility of chosen materials but also allowed us to look at critical details and joints in the construction.

Then, working in groups, we set up our own boatyard. After making 1:1 working drawings in the form of plans, sections and elevations, we were able to begin the construction of our boats. Throughout the construction process the design was adapted to deal with construction restraints and issues of materiality.

Daniel: lost in Camber Sands, April 01

Vessel for the City, #1 (Alex, Ruth, William)

Vessel for the City, #1, testing in Dungeness

Light planking detail (William)

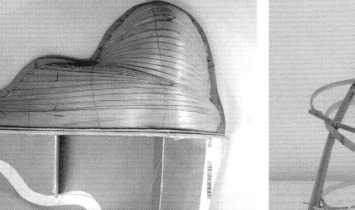
Initial model #1 (William)

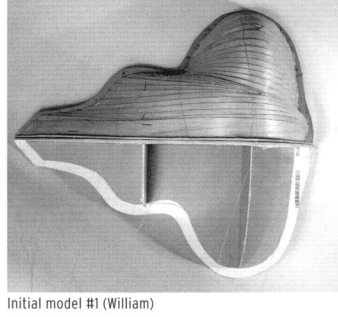
Initial model #2 (Ruth)

Key wood for planking (William)

Keel/planking detail (Alex)

Keel/hog detail (Daniel)

Interior skin (Martin)

c

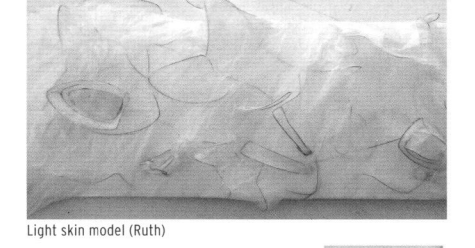
Light skin model (Ruth)

d

e

f

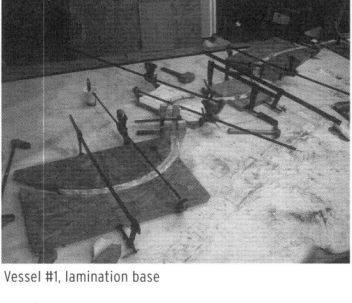
William in Bedford Square, Nov 00

Vessel #1, lamination base

Bamboo arch construction

Tailoring the volume of light

Vessel for the City #2. Testing gravity in Dungeness (Chloe, Daniel, Martin, Stefania)

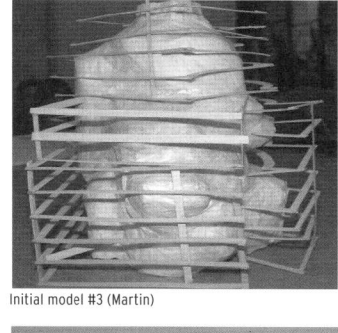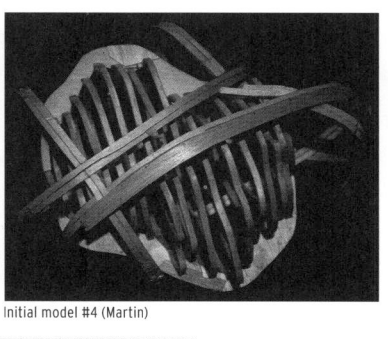

Initial model #3 (Martin)

Initial model #4 (Martin)

Interior view for sea ...Vessel #2

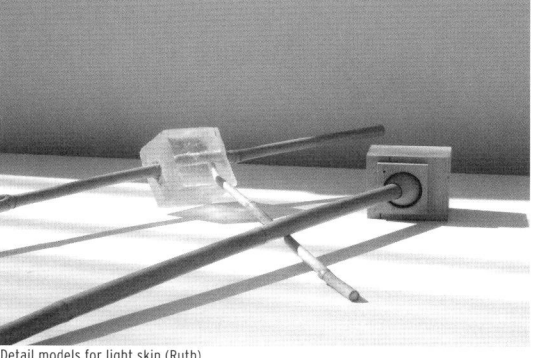

Detail models for light skin (Ruth)

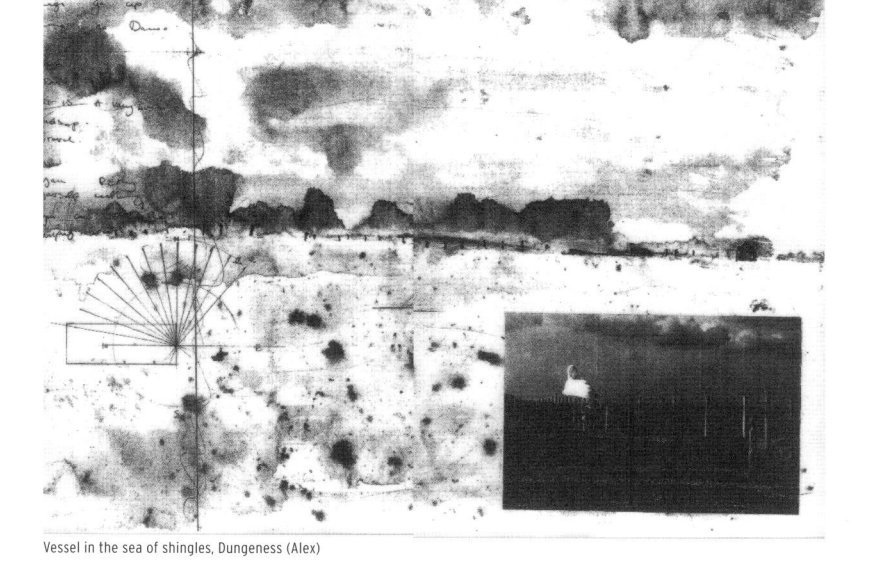

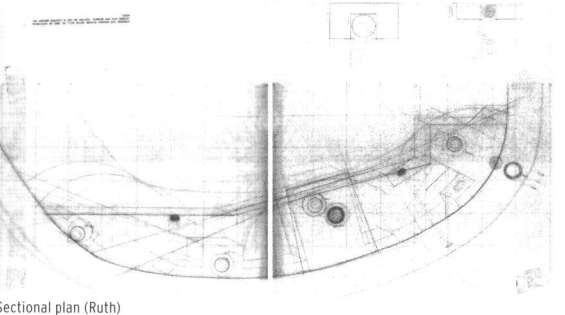

Sectional plan (Ruth)

Vessel in the sea of shingles, Dungeness (Alex)

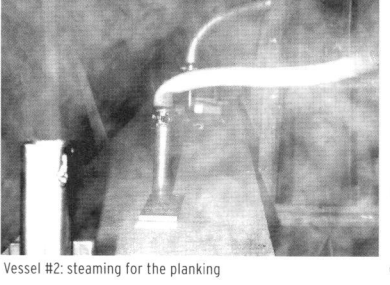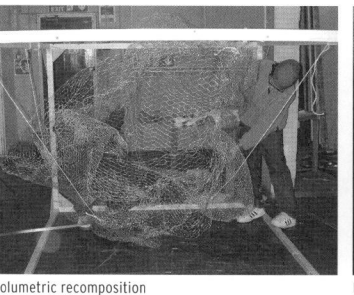

Vessel #2: steaming for the planking

Cast-off wire mesh skin

Volumetric recomposition

Laminated sections with jig

The vessels were taken out of the city environment and tested in three different landscapes: Dungeness, Camber Sands and Hastings. We were interested in how we could adapt the boats to deal with their new

Ami on the road, Nov. '00

locations, ground conditions and surroundings.

Returning to London, our final project was to design a room for

the city – a room that was unstable yet stable, a room both to view and to view from, a room for measuring. Our mapping of the conditions of the previous testing grounds

Security for the hidden

provided points of reference that influenced our positions once back in the city. Individual projects researched a room for a camera

to measure below the surface of the ground; an observatory for viewing stars; a solar measurement room; a listening room and new ground for left-over market produce.

Unit Staff

Shin Egashira and Lucy Tilley

Students

Stefania Batoeva, Daniel Castella, Alex Chalmers, William Hai Liang Chen, Ruth Kedar, Chloe Kobayashi, Edward Martin Roderick Wells

Alex in Camber Sands, April 01

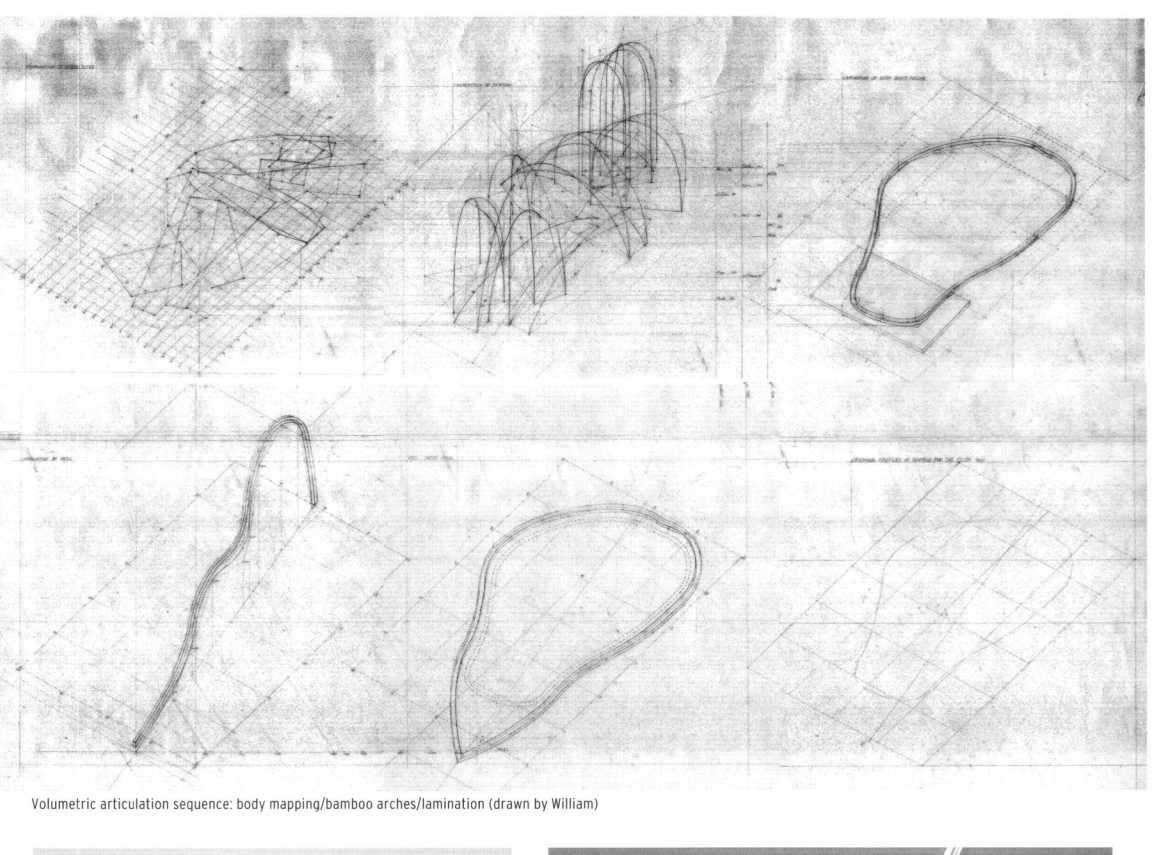

Volumetric articulation sequence: body mapping/bamboo arches/lamination (drawn by William)

Sound score prototype (Martin)

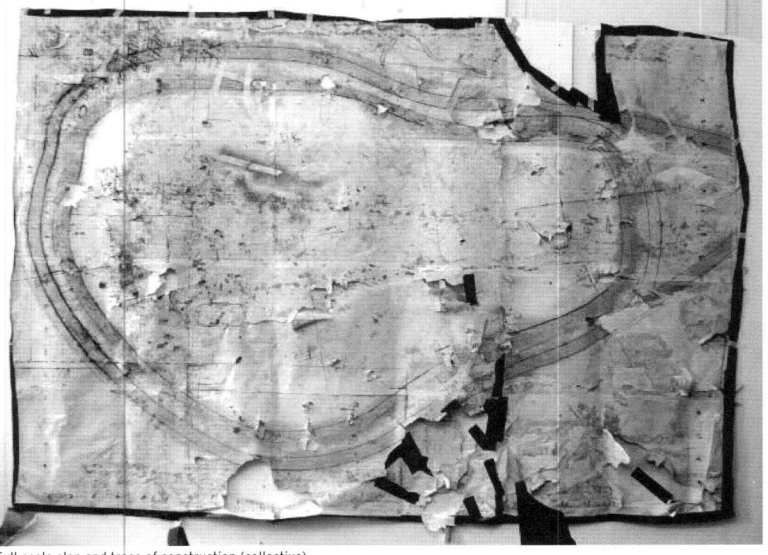

Full-scale plan and trace of construction (collective)

A sound room in Prince's Circle (Martin)

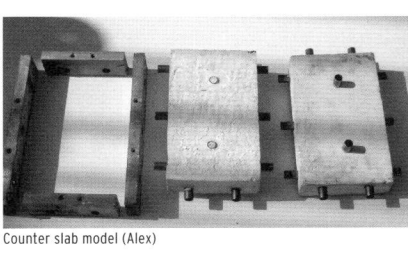

Counter slab model (Alex)

New fabric for Berwick Street Market

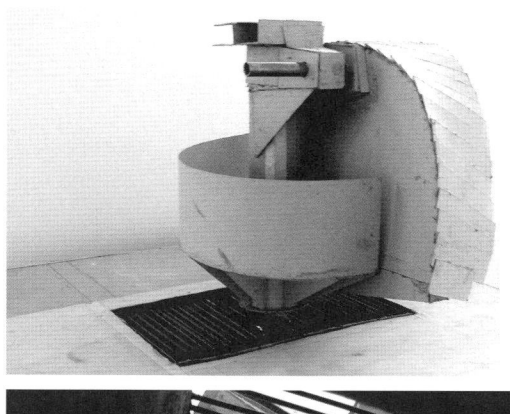

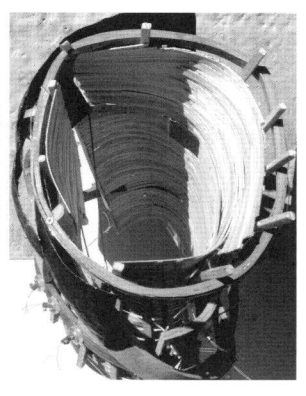

A room for detecting the depth of the city (Alex)

Intersectional observatory model (Stefania)

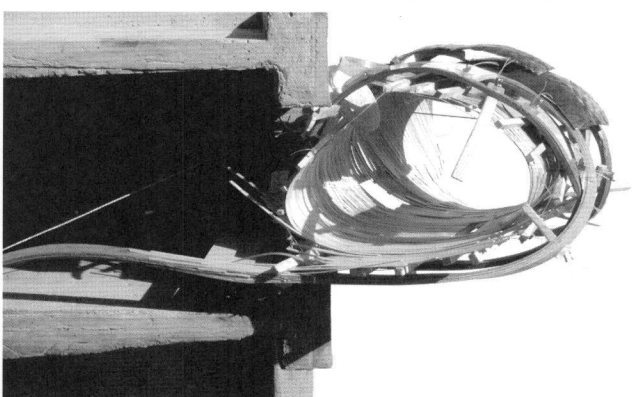

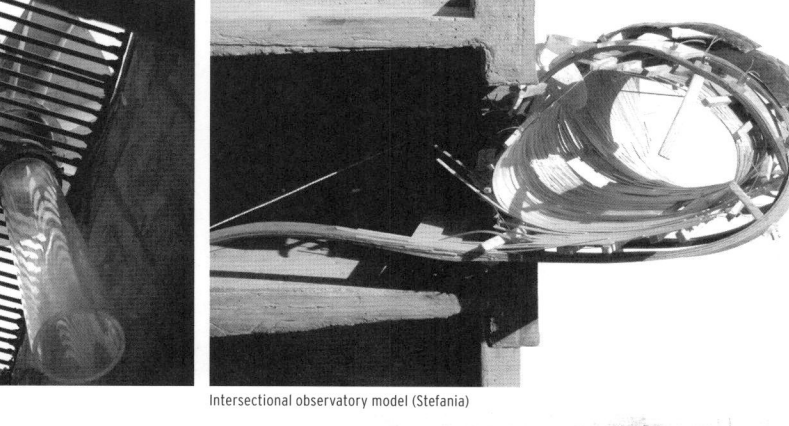

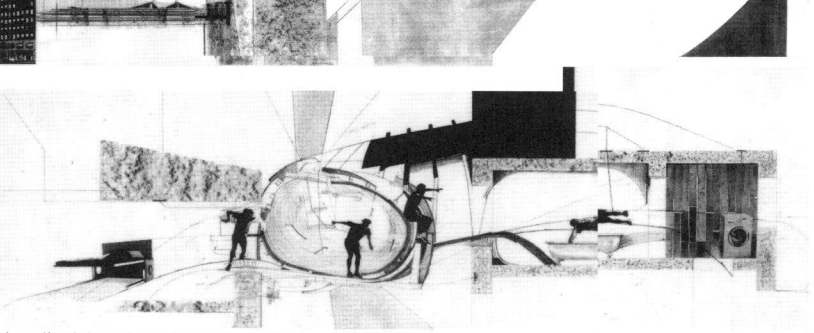

Multidirectional recording device (Alex)

Intersectional observatory collage section (Stefania)

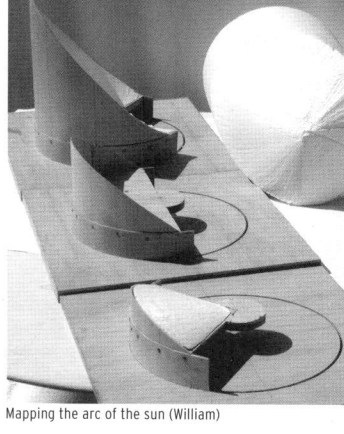

(Ruth)

Mapping the arc of the sun (William)

A room for the winter sunset at the edge of Little Venice (WIlliam)

First Year Unit 2

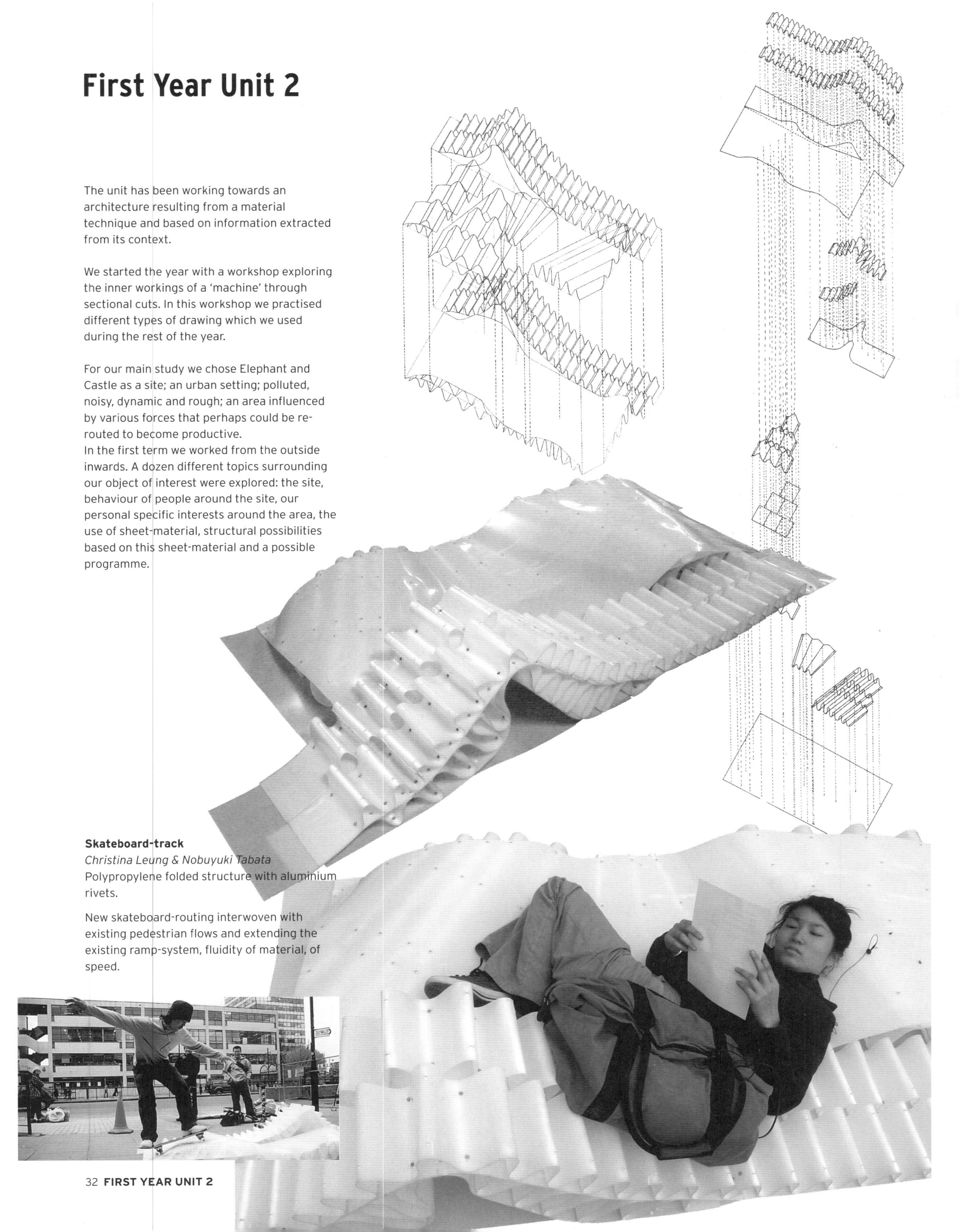

The unit has been working towards an architecture resulting from a material technique and based on information extracted from its context.

We started the year with a workshop exploring the inner workings of a 'machine' through sectional cuts. In this workshop we practised different types of drawing which we used during the rest of the year.

For our main study we chose Elephant and Castle as a site; an urban setting; polluted, noisy, dynamic and rough; an area influenced by various forces that perhaps could be re-routed to become productive.
In the first term we worked from the outside inwards. A dozen different topics surrounding our object of interest were explored: the site, behaviour of people around the site, our personal specific interests around the area, the use of sheet-material, structural possibilities based on this sheet-material and a possible programme.

Skateboard-track
Christina Leung & Nobuyuki Tabata
Polypropylene folded structure with aluminium rivets.

New skateboard-routing interwoven with existing pedestrian flows and extending the existing ramp-system, fluidity of material, of speed.

In the second and third terms we worked from the inside outwards. We started with a workshop investigating folding techniques based on origami. The technique was brought back to our projects at different scales. The structural possibilities were further explored and investigated in relation to the projected programme and intended use on site. This eventually resulted in a full-scale prototype, which was tested on location.

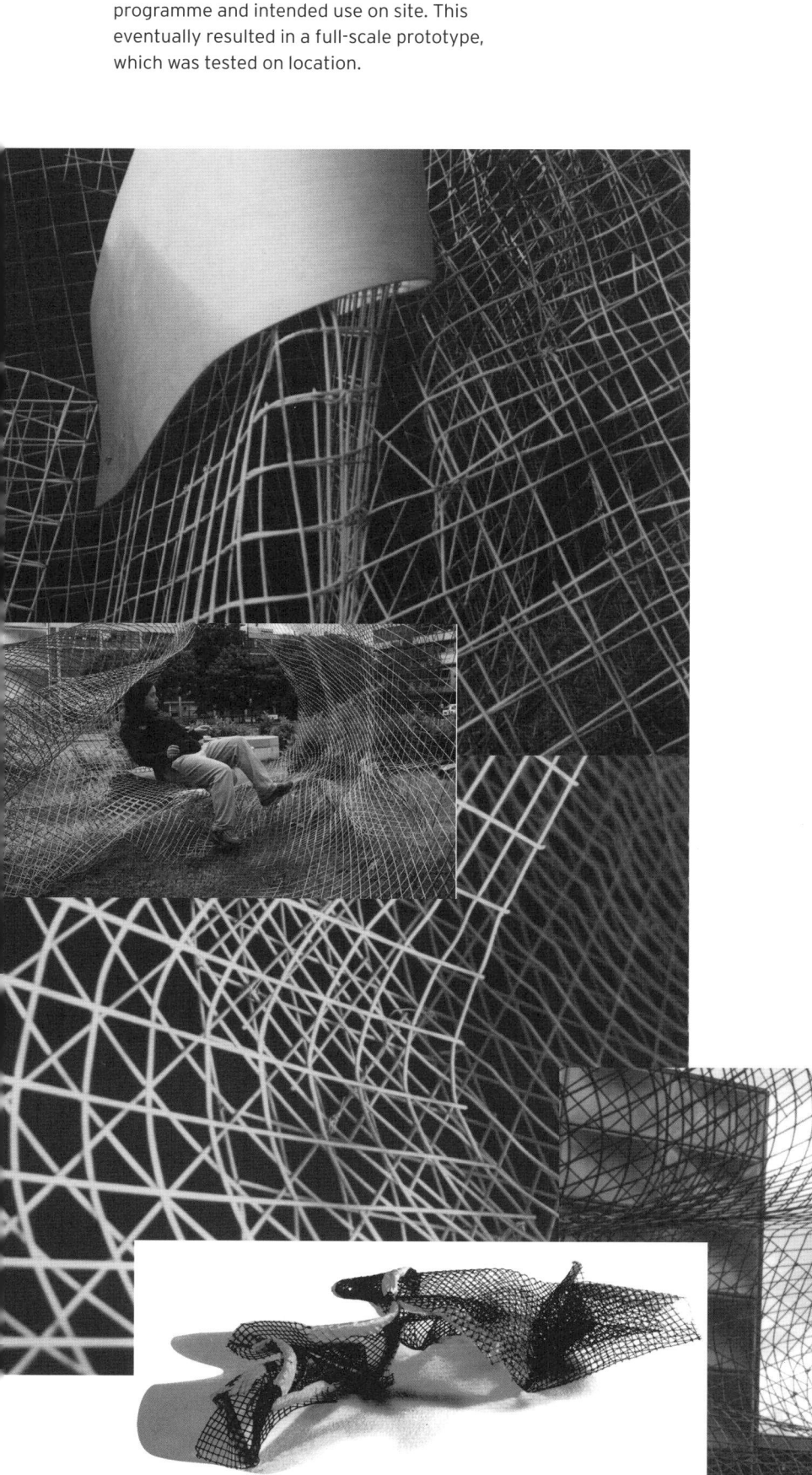

Open-air projection-supported exhibition space
Vanessa Poon & Christos Malekos
Partially painted copper-coated mesh with iron knots, seats of plywood.

Fluidity of folds that smoothly entice the passing public to explore; mesh densities and projection-screen are controlled by the structural system of folded mesh.

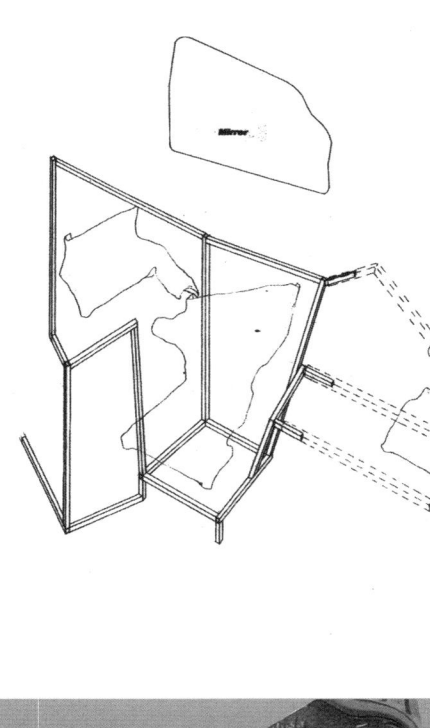

Students
Robert Gluckman, Hadiza Gwadabe, Amir Hamzah, SoonTak Joo, Christina Leung, Christos Malekos, Vanessa Poon, Fumiko Sakata, Nobuyuki Tabata, Jimmy Wan

Unit Staff
Mark Hemel, Denis Balent, Gianni Botsford

Thanks to
Shin Egashira, Michael Hensel, Nathaniel Kolbe, Barbara Kuit, Moshen Mostafavi, Ciro Najle, Michael McNamara, Garin O'Aivazian, Mark Prizeman, Teresa Stoppani, Tony Swannell, Jeff Turko, Caroline Voet, Brendan Woods, Andrew Yau, S333, AA DRL

Mirror-supported viewing structure
SoonTak Joo & Hadiza Gwadabe
Welded steel frame with perspex seating and acrylic mirrors.

Valuable views are endorsed, invaluable ones suppressed; fluidity of different positions varying between sitting, leaning and standing.

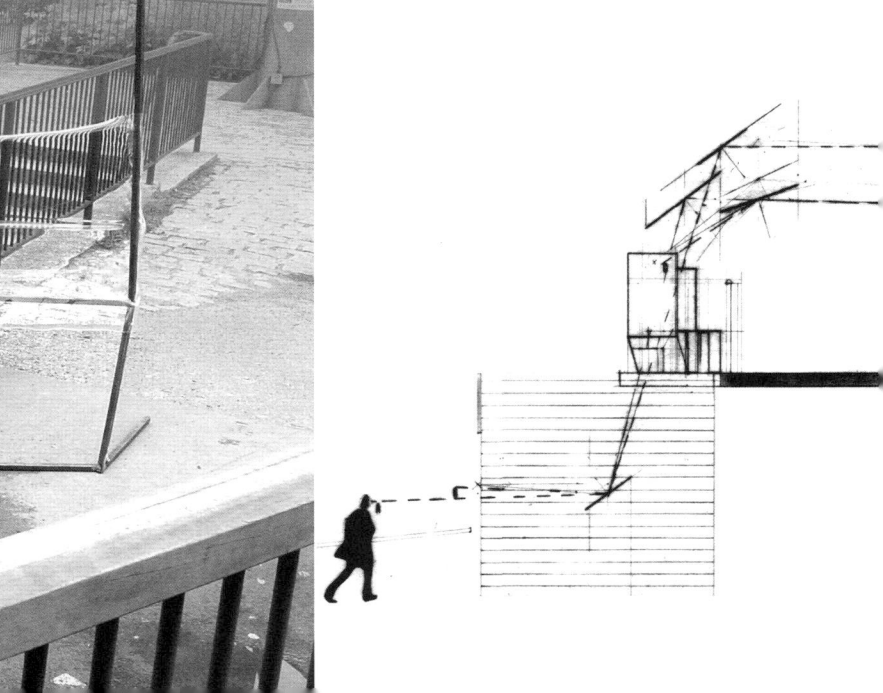

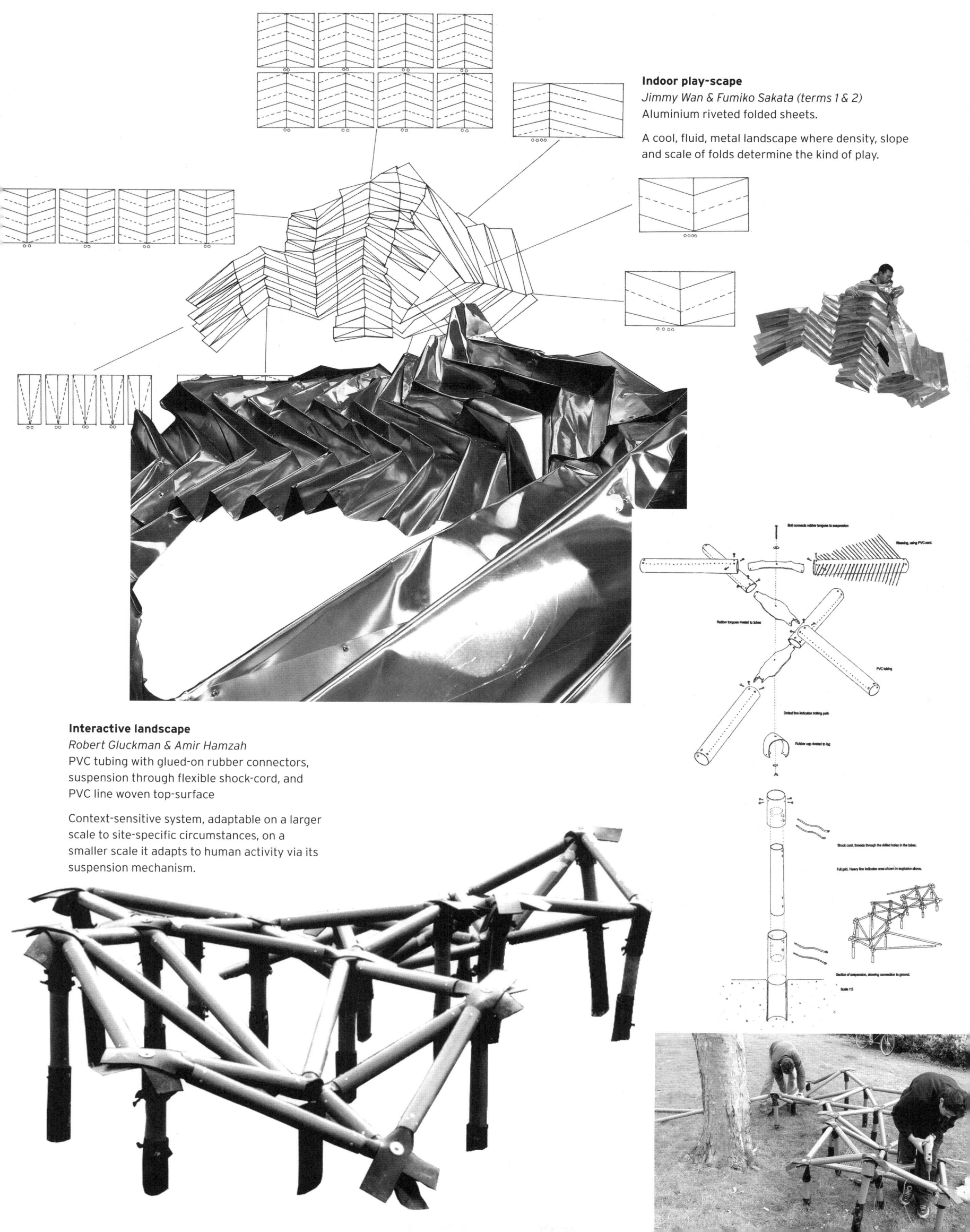

Indoor play-scape
Jimmy Wan & Fumiko Sakata (terms 1 & 2)
Aluminium riveted folded sheets.

A cool, fluid, metal landscape where density, slope and scale of folds determine the kind of play.

Interactive landscape
Robert Gluckman & Amir Hamzah
PVC tubing with glued-on rubber connectors, suspension through flexible shock-cord, and PVC line woven top-surface

Context-sensitive system, adaptable on a larger scale to site-specific circumstances, on a smaller scale it adapts to human activity via its suspension mechanism.

First Year Unit 3

daniel coll i capdevila

kazuhiro murayama antonis karides

krasimir kotsinov charles peronnin

Enter Venice

The unit used Venice as a theoretical site of spatial interventions. We explored ways to enter Venice and developed ways to coexist with(in) it. The water-body of the city was investigated as a mirror of ourselves: a body whose precarious survival relies on a delicate balance of control and lack of control, of the necessarily natural and the elaborately artificial, on micro-adjustments rather than revolutions. The main objective of this experience was to define and articulate questions on space and the making and inhabiting of it.

The unit's work is articulated in three inter-linked sections whose common issue is the notion of the body: the body in space (singular), the body's relations with and occupation of space (plural), the body of the city (singular/plural).

Body 1: Sectional Die

The devising of a spatial tool to develop and unfold the process of space-making, before approaching Venice. The sectional die is the student's body inscribed; a volume which is questioned, manipulated and eventually dissolved; a non-homogeneous folded surface; an object whose boundaries are deformed, exploded, implied; an ambiguous device which is at first the object of design and then becomes a tool for space reading/making. The inscription of the body in the volume of the cube questions its geometry, deforms it, dissolves and explodes it. The die questions the opposition of plan/section and operates as a 3D cutting tool. It questions vertical/horizontal, above/below, balanced/precarious. The die is not homogeneous; it is porous, (im)permeable, has weight, materiality, texture, light; it experiences (de)formation(s). The exploration of the difference between the specific (individual) body and abstract geometries exposes the issues of movement, time, variation, control and lack of control.

ioanna ioannidi

pavlos sideris eduardo ardiles

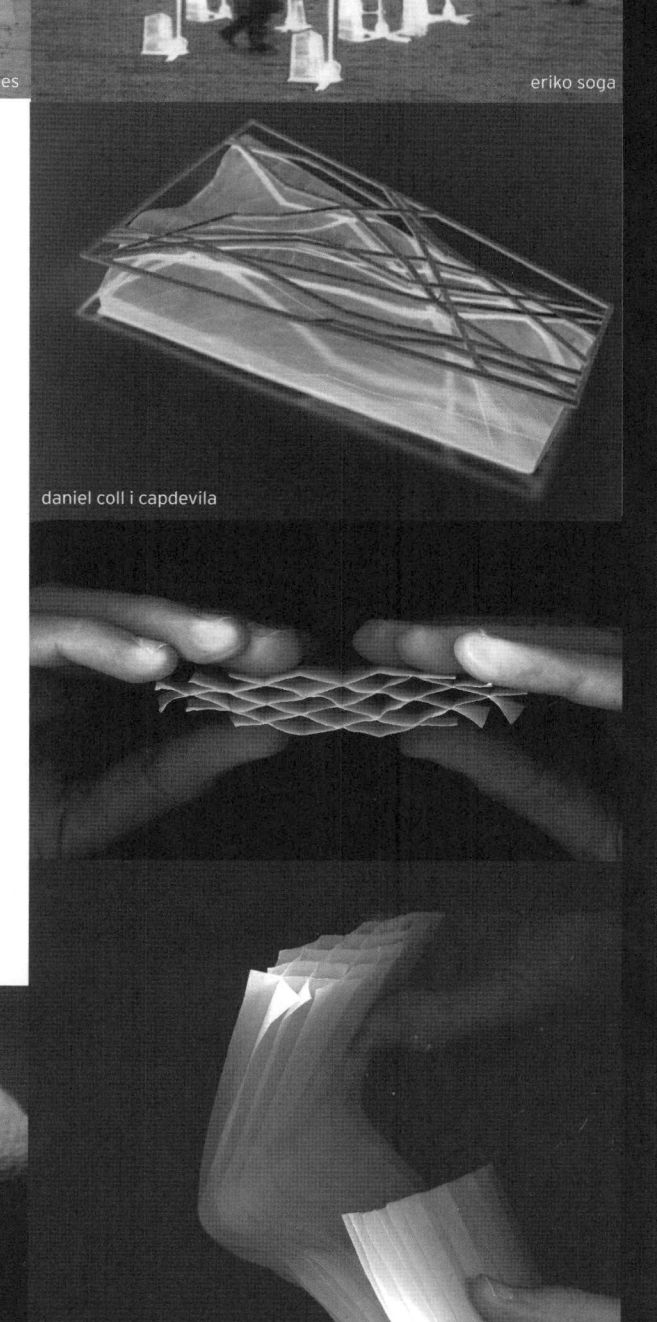

kazuhiro murajama

eduardo ardiles

eriko soga

daniel coll i capdevila

Body 2: Rolling Dice

The individual sectional dice, already compromised by materiality and transformations, are brought to interact with the space of the city: from singular (body in space) to plural space of negotiation (multiple bodies), the projects produce interferences with the already established uses of the site and expose the potential violence embedded in the process of intrusion.

Venice is explored as a body inside which we move, a 3D context that imposes modifications on our own bodies. Venice becomes the paradigm of our being in the world, of a contemporary notion of inhabitation, of a non-invasive site by playing with (not against) the available elements and the given conditions.

The sectional die is brought to interact with the space of the city, it becomes the sampler of the urban condition and the object of (re)-design. The city imposes its conditions on the new (imported) element: the never neutral process of insertion requires the devising of a strategy of painful/painless smooth insinuation into the mobile space of Venice. The process of insertion/ assimilation into the city operates a mutual transformation that leads to the dissolution of the sectional die. The issue of urban space is addressed with a permanent/ temporary structure. Eleven individually designed market stands question and reinvent the informal neighbourhood market of Campo Santa Margherita. The layout of the new market-place derives from an *in situ* study of the Campo's activities and a negotiation process initiated in Venice with a marketplace workshop. The market stands are lightweight removable structures which occupy a specific negotiated site in the square during the day and are stored in a nearby building at night. Ephemeral but permanent, they are allowed to mark their territory and leave traces on the urban ground (pavement). Details and technical drawings were developed as part of the Technical Studies submission.

antonis karides   eduardo ardiles

kazuhiro murayama

Body 3: The City

The water-body of Venice provides a continuous variation and redefinition of site conditions and the coincidence of building and site-making in an indissoluble process of growth and destruction. The physical form of the water-body is neither natural nor artificial, but the product of a compromise - a-formity; it exists not in the representation but in the performance and the (re)enactment of an agreement. Venice is the place of the hyperpresent, where the 'dignity of the moment' (Manfredo Tafuri) dissolves opposing categories of time and space, and contains conflicts without destroying them. In this sense Venice operates in the absence of definitive enclosures and through surfaces of resistance (water, facades).

The project takes place between land and water, between the island of the dead (San Michele) and the island of production and craft (Murano), and is inserted as an open system wedged in between two closed ones (convent and cemetery). How to occupy a site which is potentially non-existent, which formally does not belong to any of the existing established systems, which physically is extremely fragile and vulnerable, and yet is overcharged with meaning and historical significance? How to intrude, by playing with, rather than against, the given conditions? How to use architecture to reveal the complexities of a site which has always been (re)defined by the containment and storage of bodies (convent and cemetery) and the movement and circulation of ideas (cultural circle)?

The projects for a small cultural centre and scholar/artist residence propose to reactivate the marginal site as a place of collection, elaboration, production and spreading of knowledge. Isolation - in *insula* - in this case does not mean to be cut off from the world; on the contrary, the interventions on the island aim at opening up (re-opening) its space to visitors and travellers.

The different proposals derive from considerations on the workings of the body of the city, and address the issues of margin, outside/inside/in between. The presence of the water, the changing relationships of island/water, wall/water are explored. Variation, protection, fragility, movement, exposure to the elements (rising waters) are emphasised. Accessibility and secrecy, display and invisibility, privacy and public access coexist in the proposed schemes.

eriko soga   eduardo ardiles

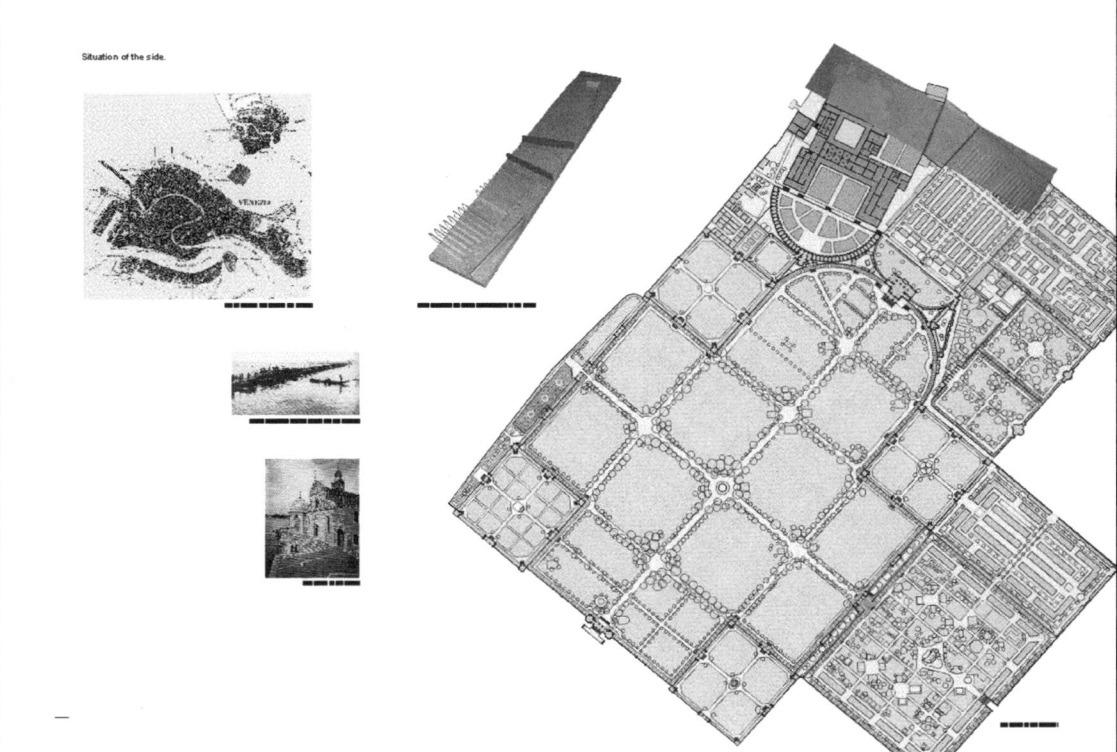

Situation of the side.

daniel coll i capdevila

daniel coll i capdevila

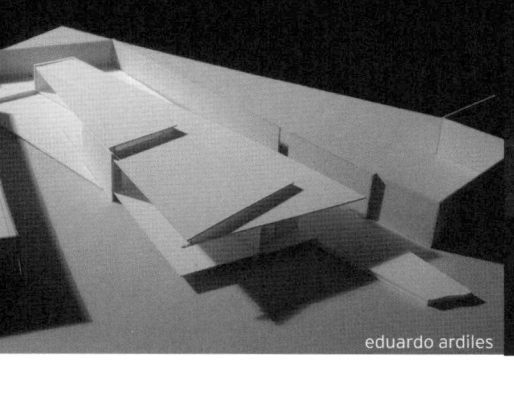

eduardo ardiles

kazuhiro murayama

antonis karides

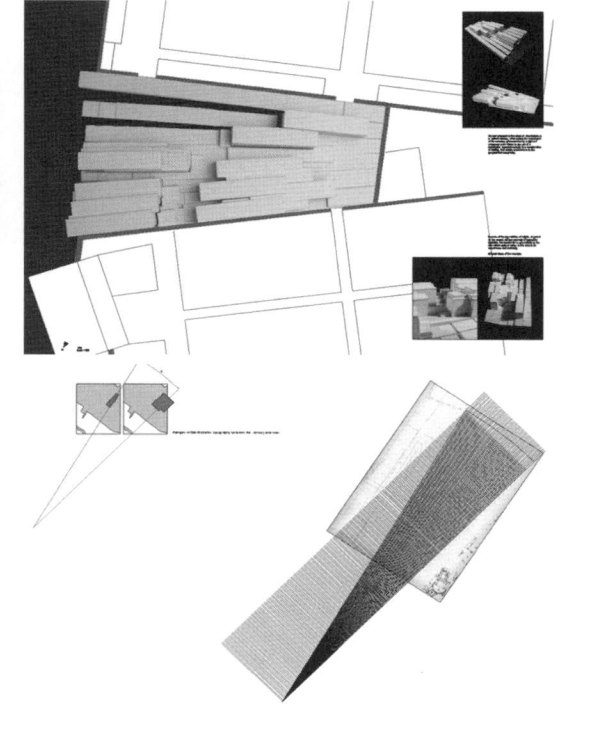

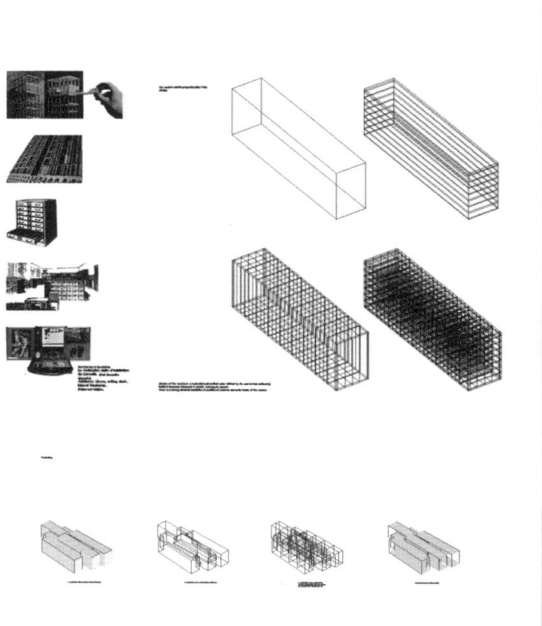

pavlos sideris

Unit Staff
Teresa Stoppani, Rainer Hofmann

Students
Eduardo Ardiles, Daniel Coll I Capdevila,
Diego Garcia Scaro, Ioanna Ioannidi,
Antonis Karides, Moritz Klatten,
Krasimir Kotsinov, Kazuhiro Murajama,
Charles Peronnin, Pavlos Sideris, Eriko Soga

Thanks to
Thordis Ahrrenius, Shumon Basar,
Peter Beard, Rinio Bruttomesso,
Tom Emerson, Simon English,
Piero Falchetta, Cody Gaynor, Mark Hemel,
Katrin Lahusen, Billie Lee, Mohsen Mostafavi,
Marianne Mueller, Ciro Najle,
Natasha Nicholson, Claire Racine,
Stefano Rocchetto, Irénée Scalbert,
Marisa Scarso, Tony Swannell,
Charles Tashima, David Whitehead,
Ivana Wingham, Brendan Woods

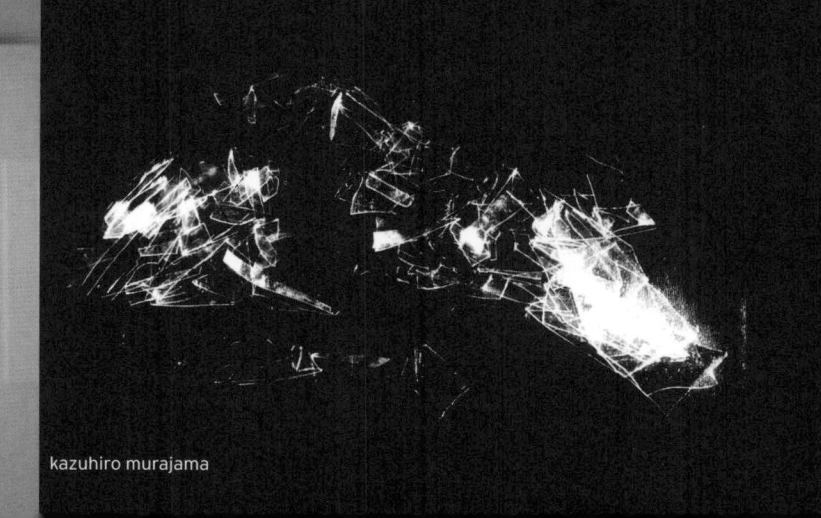

diego garcia scaro

kazuhiro murajama

First Year Unit 4

MATERIALITY + FILM

Film as a highly constructed imaginary world of its own.
Materiality as the essence of the physical world.

Unit 4 has challenged this duality through careful watching + making + extracting of spatial qualities latent in the narrative details of films and constructed processes towards the fabrication of material things.

Two main projects –
one dealt with conditions of intense interiority
the other with the openness of the street

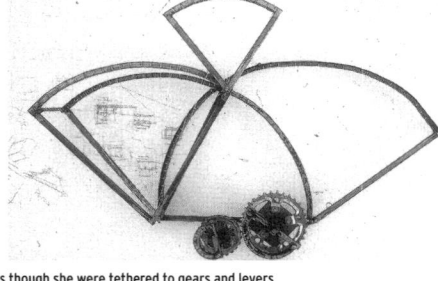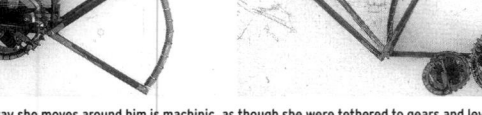

CHARLIE   The way she moves around him is machinic, as though she were tethered to gears and levers.

ESI   Paul and Camille's flat laid out like a colour-coded game of objects.

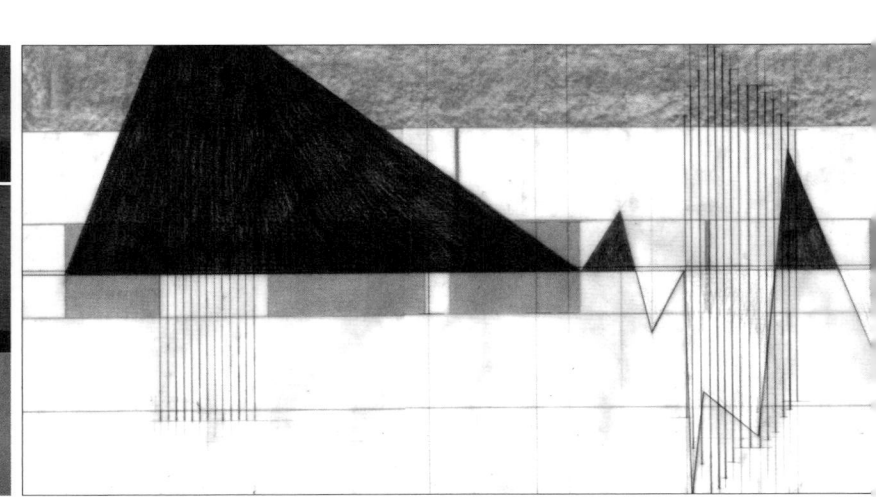

BACO   Tensions between a man and a woman lead to a surge of anxiety, and a climax of reflection.

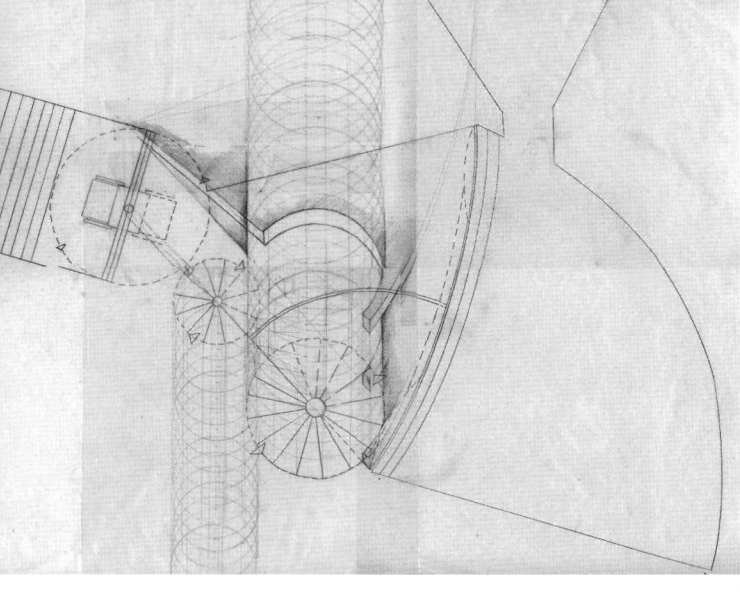

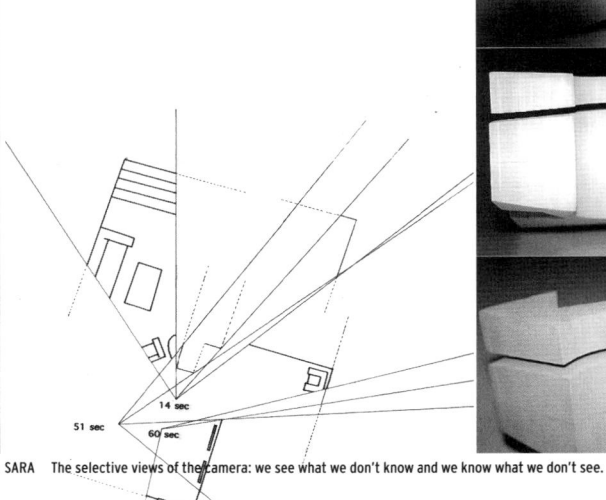

SARA   The selective views of the camera: we see what we don't know and we know what we don't see.

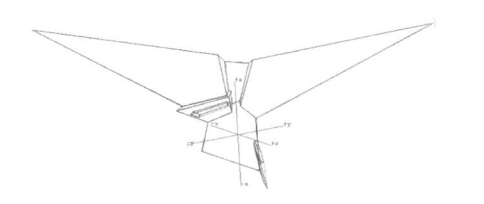

ANUK   There is a parallax between the perspective of the room and the screen we watch. A complex geometry of exact misalignments.

1 0:00 looking directly at mirror image
2 0:05 looking along wall - into darkness
3 0:13 staring at floor - thinking
4 0:16 leaning shoulder to shoulder with
        mirror image - looking into mirror
        from side - views cross

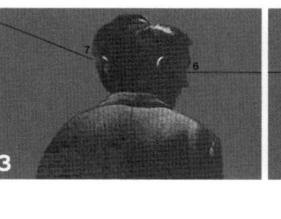

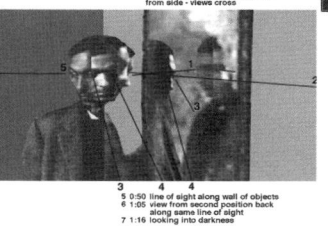

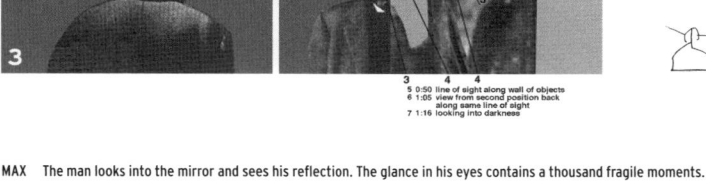

3
5 0:50 line of sight along wall of objects
6 1:05 view from second position back
        along same line of sight
7 1:16 looking into darkness

MAX   The man looks into the mirror and sees his reflection. The glance in his eyes contains a thousand fragile moments.

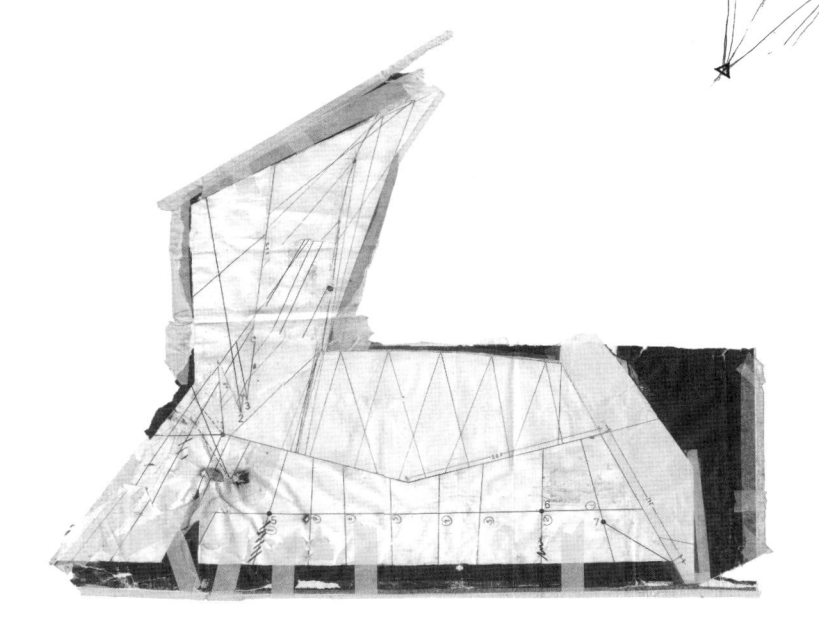

A ROOM FROM A FILM
One-minute film clips from *Le mépris* (1), *L'éclisse* (2), *Nostalgia* (3) and *Lost Highway* (4), all containing instances of heightened consciousness where the characters' conflicts are played out via their surroundings.

The students started with the clips and devised their own techniques of zooming in on an event within the event. At the end of the process a physical version of the event was built – abstract but tactile, often a fleeting moment frozen into a new scale, these 'rooms' were evolutions from the found 'rooms' captured in the films.

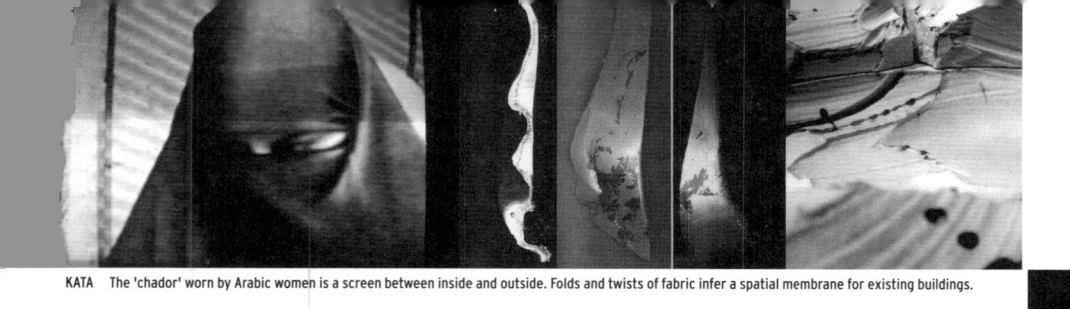

KATA The 'chador' worn by Arabic women is a screen between inside and outside. Folds and twists of fabric infer a spatial membrane for existing buildings.

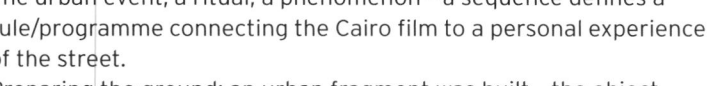
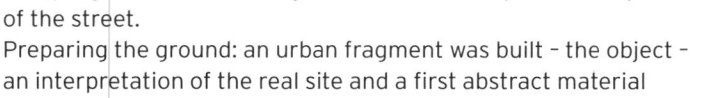

EGYPT: CARVED-OUT SPACE AND URBAN FRENZY
Four two-minute films describing four very different viewpoints/
positions from within the extreme urban spatial/political context
of Cairo.

FROM CAIRO TO EDGWARE ROAD – THE STREET
Overlaying the Cairo experience (a detail from the film) with
the reality of Edgware Road led to a moment of collision and
rediscovery. Memories and contradictions, beginnings for a
process of construction...

The urban event, a ritual, a phenomenon – a sequence defines a
rule/programme connecting the Cairo film to a personal experience
of the street.
Preparing the ground: an urban fragment was built – the object –
an interpretation of the real site and a first abstract material
manifestation.
The addition: through additive and transformative building
processes the object was questioned in terms of its spatial/urban
potential and redefined in the form of a proposal for a public space.

GABRIEL Peeling away the ground creates a new connection to the lower level: a shifting set of relationships over time.

ESI Sheesha Bar Library, somewhere to escape to, spiralling downwards, in a maze of stairs.

PHOIVOS The way we live has to be reflected in the houses we dwell in: temporary, made to order and available everywhere.

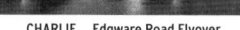

CHARLIE   Edgware Road Flyover

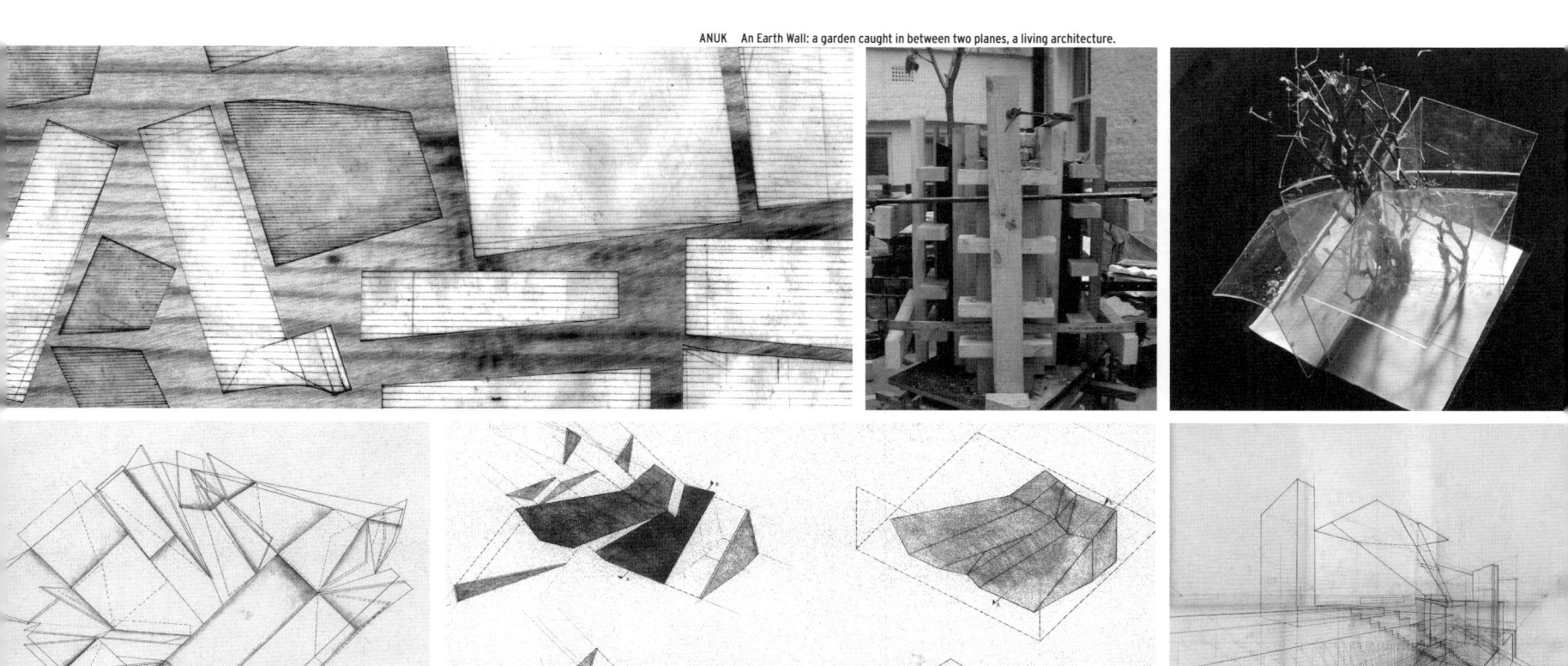

ANUK   An Earth Wall: a garden caught in between two planes, a living architecture.

PANOS A folding shed in a housing estate: in the summer it provides a meeting place for all the residents, whilst in the winter it curls up to provide a common storage space.   CHARLIE Vertical labyrinth perspective

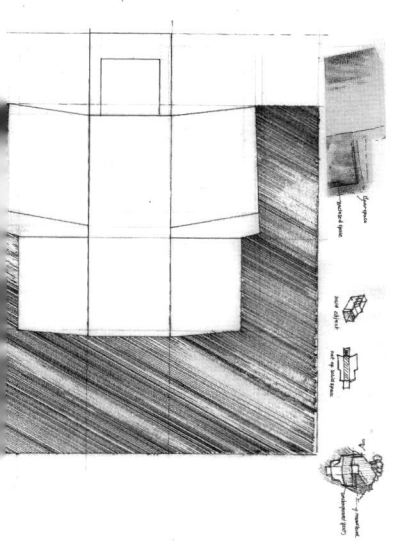

MASHA   A hidden baroque labyrinth made with glass hedges mediates between the street and a gárden.

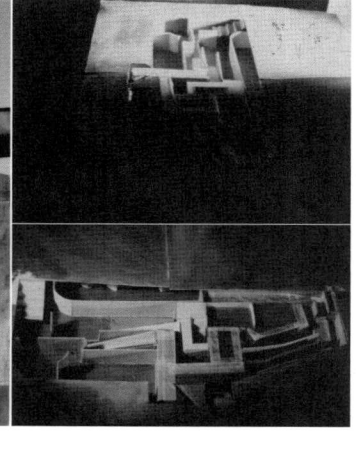

Unit Staff Katrin Lahusen, Shumon Basar

Students
Baco Beaujolin, Esi Carboo, Sara Castilho, Anuk Chanyapak, Kata Eliasdottir, Masha Gonopolskaja, Charles Hui, Panos Panayiotis, Gabriel Sanchez Garin, Phoivos Skroumbelos, Max Von Werz

Thanks to
Miraj Ahmed, Pierre d'Avoine, Peter Beard, Oliver Domeisen, Tom Emerson, Mark Hemel, Michael Hensel, Gillian Horn, Helmet Kinzer, Andreas Lang, Marcellus Letang, Peter Lewis, Petra Marguc, Mohsen Mostafavi, Joel Newman, Chris Pauling, Mark Prizeman, David Racz, Irénée Scalbert, Trys Smith, Tony Swannell, Charles Tashima, Lucy Tilley, Julia Wood, Brendan Woods

First Year Unit 5

Term 1 began with Inventory. The inventory offers not only the happiness of knowing but also the knowledge of having ordered one's knowledge. The inventory was an invitation to use ludic and irrational means of bringing together the imaginary and the real in the same space. The inventory was used as the brief for the design of a personal domestic space in a 250-cubic-metre volume. Students were asked to reassess their 'house' in the process of siting it in Brunswick Square Gardens. The point of contact between building and site was viewed as a charged moment and followed a careful measured and level survey using improvised equipment. We visited the tailor, Timothy Everest, in Spitalfields to learn about pattern-cutting and the way in which full-size drawings are used to make complex 3D

Angela Cheung

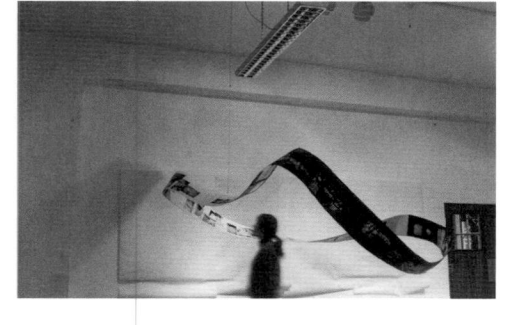

Federico Ferrari

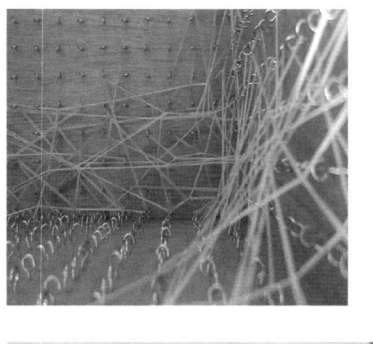

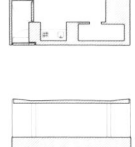

Nausica Gabrielides

Andrew Heid

Jun Kawamata

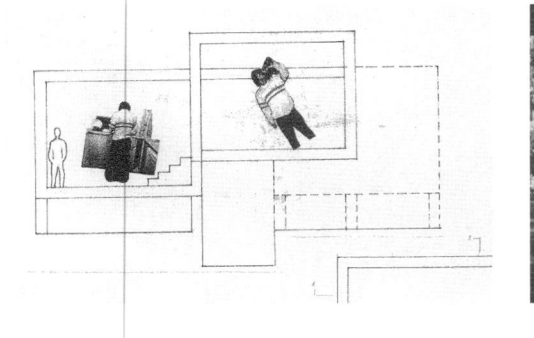

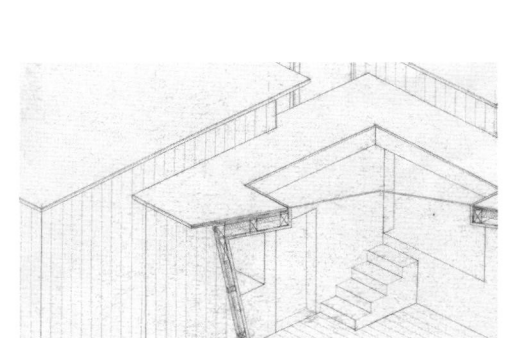

objects. We also visited the Sugden House in Watford by Alison and Peter Smithson – a tailormade house and also 'the ugliest house in Britain', according to Derek Sugden's mother-in-law.

In Term 2 we investigated how the individual becomes a player in the city and how in turn the city responds. The Routines in Term 2 were about finding ways of seeing and representing as a means of analysing the urban condition. Some of the issues with which we have been concerned include the body in public space, producing the city, consuming the city, globalisation and the body and the body politic.

In Term 3 the Routines were related to the design and making of an object in a public space at the Brunswick Centre. They invited an examination of the relationship we have with objects, and of how objects add another layer to our experience within the city.

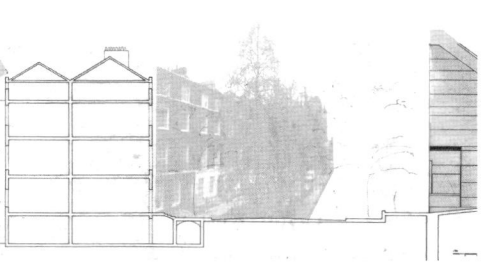

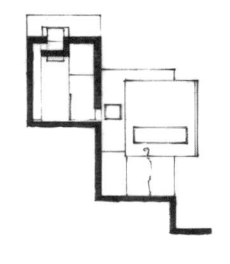

Routines

Project work was developed as a series of Routines. The Routine became an invitation to rehearse, practise and improvise, to exercise one's imagination, to take chances and take control, and to perform (think and act simultaneously) using one's own body to negotiate a broad cultural context – architectural, social, economic, physical, global, personal. Some Routines lasted a day, most a few weeks. We were interested in thinking on our feet and finding the means of recording the significant moment, but also wanted to have time to develop an idea over a longer period. The pacing of the programme and the unit dynamic has, we hope, given space for each unit member to begin the process of finding an individual voice.

Utopia

The unit discussed architecture in terms of the ideal and the contingent and examined the potential for transformation and mutability. We contemplated architecture as a game where rules and constraint become a vehicle for the imagination.

Kuniaki Mogami

Tiffany Ogden

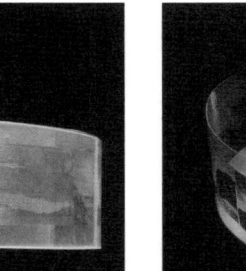

Tom Smith

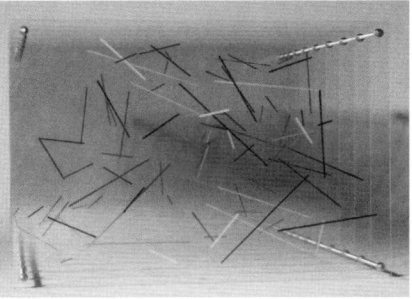

Serafina Sama

Mark Tynan

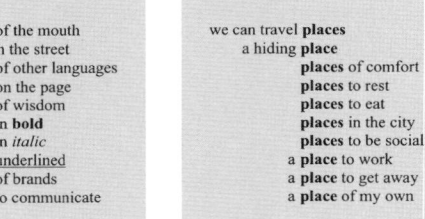

words of the mouth
the word on the street
the words of other languages
the words on the page
words of wisdom
words in **bold**
words in *italic*
words underlined
words of brands
we use words to communicate

we can travel **places**
a hiding **place**
places of comfort
places to rest
places to eat
places in the city
places to be social
a **place** to work
a **place** to get away
a **place** of my own

Reading

Selected reading included Georges Perec – *Species of spaces*, David Harvey – *Spaces of hope*, Manfredo Tafuri – *Architecture and utopia*, Thomas More – *Utopia*, Leslie Martin – *The grid as generator*, Susie Orbach – *The payoff: on how the market induced our moral panic*. This fuelled our research into utopian thinking in the context of architecture and beyond, and actively encouraged looking back and looking sideways as an essential aspect of looking forward.

Sites

The Brunswick Centre by Patrick Hodgkinson was the principal site of our investigation. This was complemented by the unit trip to Savannah, Georgia. Savannah is a product of eighteenth-century enlightenment thinking – an arcadia, a pioneer settlement, its grid layout suggestive of the game and its individual houses alluding to the monad – the elemental dwelling. The Brunswick Centre, in contrast, is a heroic attempt to include all the ingredients of the city within a single building.

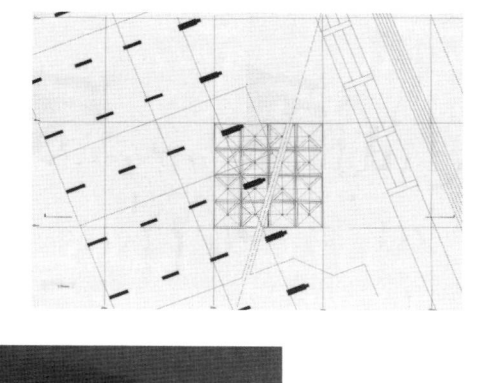

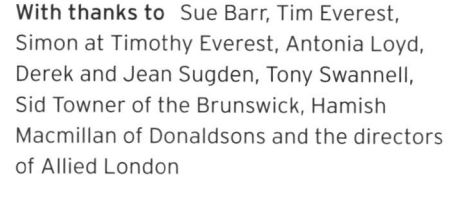

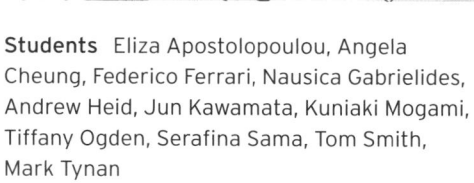

Students Eliza Apostolopoulou, Angela Cheung, Federico Ferrari, Nausica Gabrielides, Andrew Heid, Jun Kawamata, Kuniaki Mogami, Tiffany Ogden, Serafina Sama, Tom Smith, Mark Tynan

Guests David Grandorge, Mark Hemel, Patrick Hodgkinson, Mike Ingall, Clare Melhuish, Mohsen Mostafavi, Nic Rhode, John Southall, Teresa Stoppani, Tony Swannell, Brendan Woods

With thanks to Sue Barr, Tim Everest, Simon at Timothy Everest, Antonia Loyd, Derek and Jean Sugden, Tony Swannell, Sid Towner of the Brunswick, Hamish Macmillan of Donaldsons and the directors of Allied London

Unit Staff Miraj Ahmed, Pierre d'Avoine, Tom Emerson

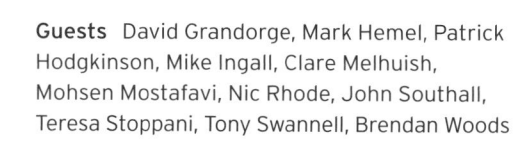

INTERMEDIATE SCHOOL→

Hiromasa Makino, Portable Summer Resort, Intermediate Unit 4

Intermediate Unit 1

Unit Staff
Andrew Houlton and Stephen Taylor

Students
Lucienne Leung
Aram Martirossian
Asako Mogi
Roberto Garcia-Monzón
Suzanne Ting

Visiting Critics
Patrick Lynch, Peter Beard, Andrew Stone,
Steve Bowkett, Christoph Grafe,
Irina Davidovici

Technical Input
Paul Hardman

The unit has centred its studies upon Deptford
in southeast London using exploratories:

CAMOUFLAGE

CHEST

FORD

Deptford High Street

Deptford Creek

CHEST

'a box, usually large and sturdy, used for storage or shipping'

Modest structures were proposed which collected the aspirations of chosen interest groups, their relationship to Deptford, and their activity or presence within the community. An expedient to identify local interests or representation, pivotal in promoting change in the area.

The 'chest' as an idea oscillates between introverted containment and the external declaration of an object as locator within an urban fabric. A narrative image of a chest excites us with the mystery of its contents. Yet in terms of ownership, the notion of 'chest' suggests a private and privileged knowledge of the contents: we can only peruse at the owner's invitation. This oscillating position between protection and invitation proved a difficult ground for making objects as interventions within Deptford as a community.

An outcome was that many proposals became muted after initial attemptsto achieve an overt extremity and visibility amongst the embedded characteristics of this neighbourhood.

The persistent memory of camouflage recurs.

CAMOUFLAGE

'a device or expedient designed to conceal or deceive'

The unit began the year by contemplating the act of extreme concealment and anonymity within two distinct landscapes: the Deptford High Street and the riverside frontage at Watergate steps.

Investigations proposing implants and graftings were spliced into locations using expedients such as the manipulation of a surface or edging or the translation of a sign. These were installed in their respective locations and recorded and observed.

To conceal an object or a characteristic requires a clear understanding of the background conditions from which concealment begins. Proposed outcomes for 'camouflage' have haunted later projects, tempering more overtly interventionist programmes.

Deptford Creek

Roberto Garcia-Monzón Camouflage

Aram Martirossian Chest

FORD

'a place where water may be crossed on foot'

The name Deptford is a corruption of the old English 'deep ford', referring to the ancient strategic ford over the river Ravensbourne at Deptford Creek.

On our unit visit to Amsterdam we saw examples of structured urban regeneration from the 'super block' to the reinterpretation of the row house. All reflected an apparent confidence in advocating strong urban strategies that engage the contemporary needs of the city and embrace a history of infrastructural provision.

We began our next project in London by visiting the London Docklands around Canary Wharf and making comparative observations between the area and Amsterdam's Eastern Dock development. Initial observations were made about the culture of competition – the corporation set against self-interest.

The area of study was the tract of land sandwiched between the new elevated DLR railway and Deptford Creek. This is a landscape of industrial decline. Though light industrial units occupy some of the pockets of land, the wharves along the creek are now largely derelict. The unit observed trends in current consultation schemes submitted to the planning authorities, as strategies for regeneration in the area. Many of these seemed to be based upon the speculative notion that there is a cultural preference for suburban settings, for four-storey dwellings dressed as suburban villas. There was a curious reluctance to acknowledge the urban condition of the city; riverside developments are often walled communities, orientated to the river whilst turning their backs on the fabric of Deptford.

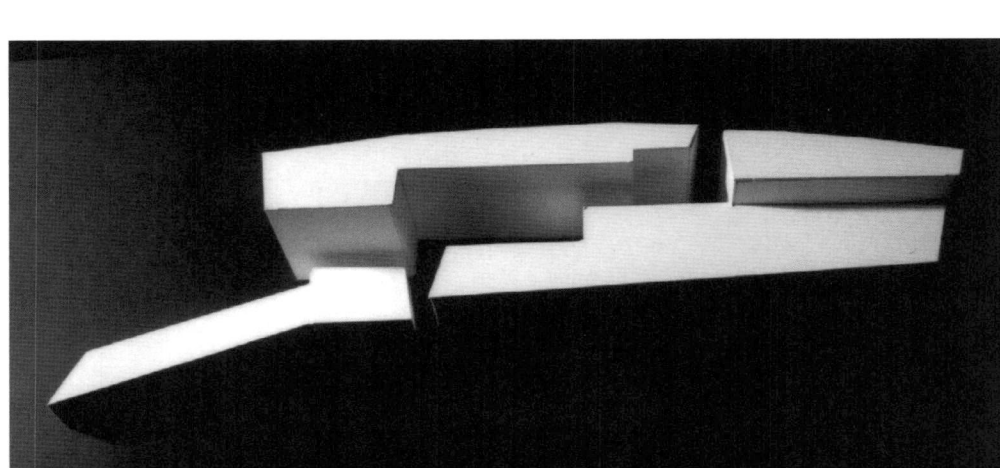

Roberto Garcia-Monzón Section through housing blocks

Asako Mogi Vestibule

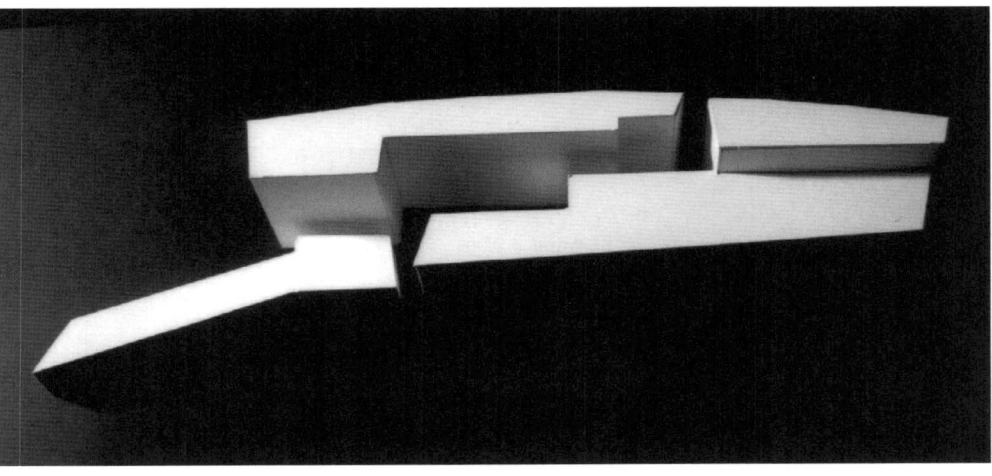

Asako Mogi Camouflage

Lucienne Leung Ford project

Each member of the unit chose a pocket of land for appraisal, being conscious of existing structures, marks... histories. The project began with the intention of investigating methods of weaving and grafting these open landscapes, seeking inherent responses towards the intensification of the area's fabric. This gave rise to a process of negotiation questioning the nature of boundary conditions and the appropriate response to neighbours' declarations regarding demarcation. The shifting of place and territory was recorded.

Docklands Lightrailway Undercroft

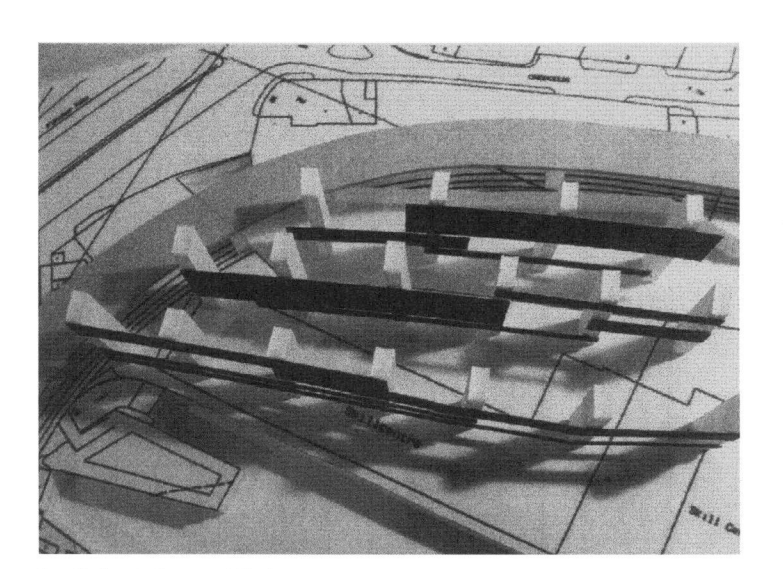

Aram Martirossian Process model ford

Aram Martirossian Process model ford

Roberto Garcia-Monzón Housing and public space

Intermediate Unit 2

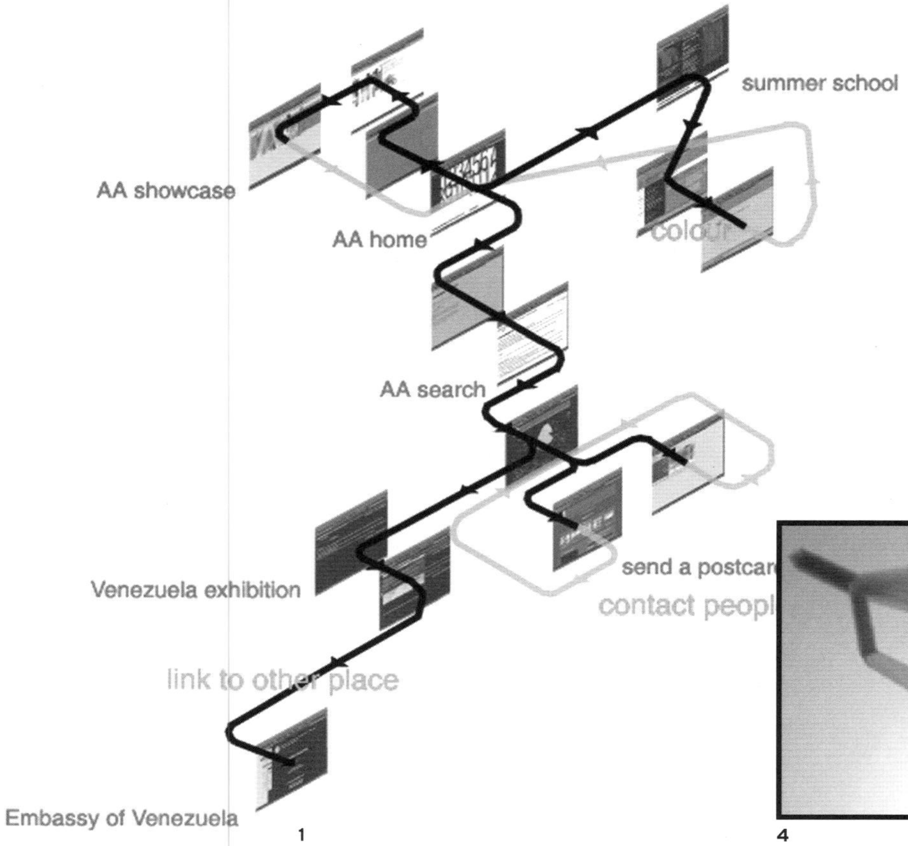

summer school

AA showcase

AA home

colour

AA search

Venezuela exhibition

send a postcard

contact people

link to other place

Embassy of Venezuela

1

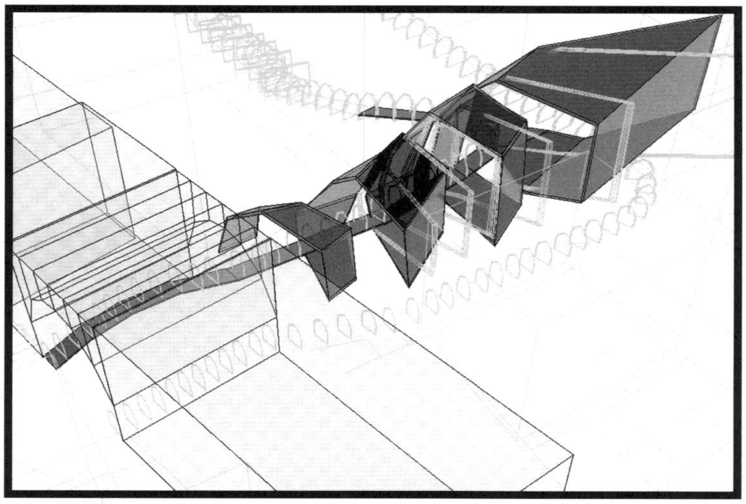

3

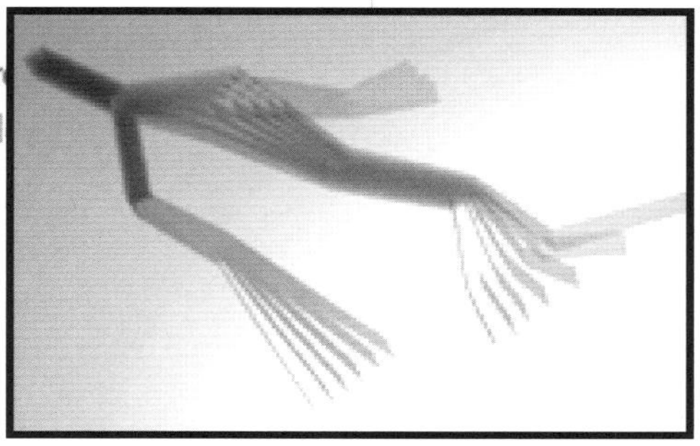

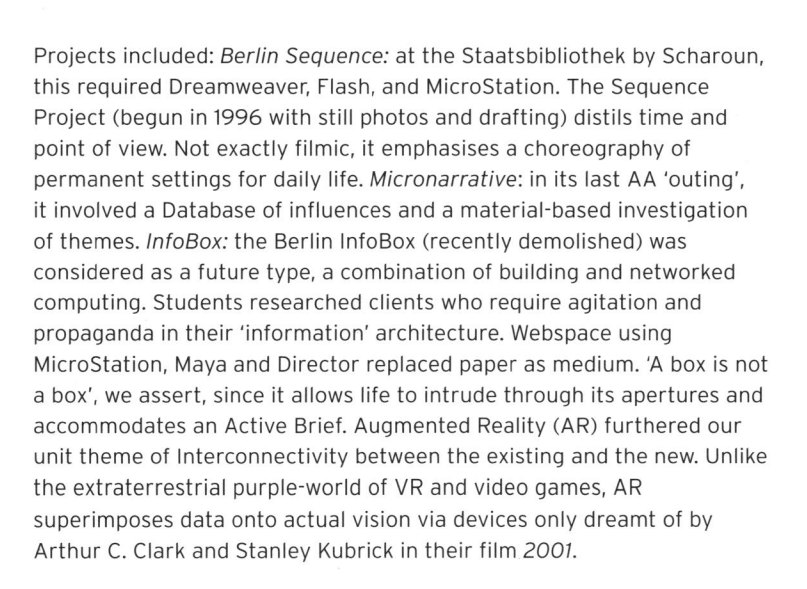

4

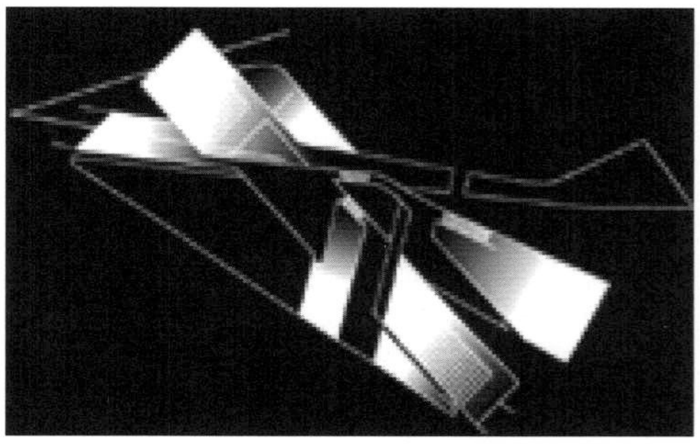

5

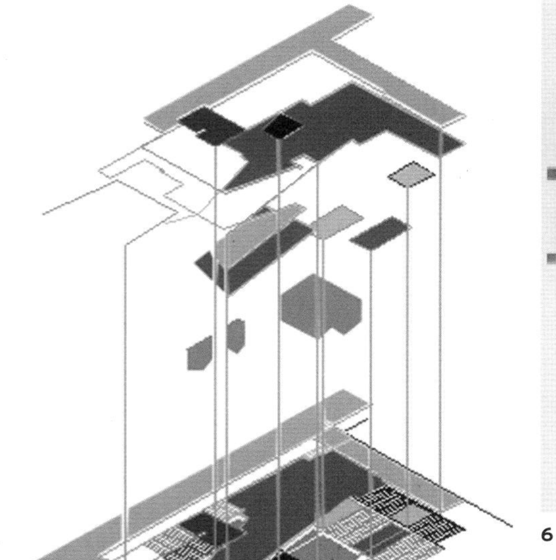

2

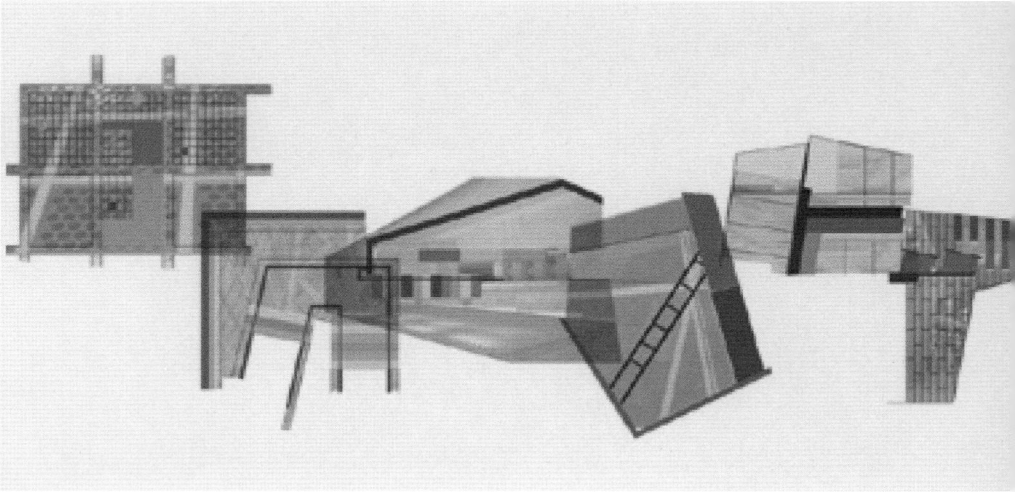

6

'*Ingres is said to have created an artistic order out of rest; I should like to create an order from feeling and, going still further, from motion.*'
Paul Klee, September 1914

Our farewell year concludes with the Commonplace and Active Brief interacting with the Web and critical CAD use. Klee's ambition thrives as web software that facilitates urbanism in lively mobile models. The Unit has completed a five-year plan of concept materialisation and computerisation, willingly enmeshing itself in the paradigm shift now affecting architecture and the society it springs from. Urban and IT networks are as significant to us as cathedrals were to medieval Europeans; our aspirations for work and leisure focus on their emerging potential. New software can show space and activity measured in time at least as much as in material. Material is nonetheless fundamental; the Micronarrative project emphasises workshop tests in respect of student themes. The individual's Database of influences identifies interests from which the most pressing emerge. In a time of rapid change, the Database sources what Hejduk called a 'spirit of renewal' in architecture.

Projects included: *Berlin Sequence:* at the Staatsbibliothek by Scharoun, this required Dreamweaver, Flash, and MicroStation. The Sequence Project (begun in 1996 with still photos and drafting) distils time and point of view. Not exactly filmic, it emphasises a choreography of permanent settings for daily life. *Micronarrative:* in its last AA 'outing', it involved a Database of influences and a material-based investigation of themes. *InfoBox:* the Berlin InfoBox (recently demolished) was considered as a future type, a combination of building and networked computing. Students researched clients who require agitation and propaganda in their 'information' architecture. Webspace using MicroStation, Maya and Director replaced paper as medium. 'A box is not a box', we assert, since it allows life to intrude through its apertures and accommodates an Active Brief. Augmented Reality (AR) furthered our unit theme of Interconnectivity between the existing and the new. Unlike the extraterrestrial purple-world of VR and video games, AR superimposes data onto actual vision via devices only dreamt of by Arthur C. Clark and Stanley Kubrick in their film *2001*.

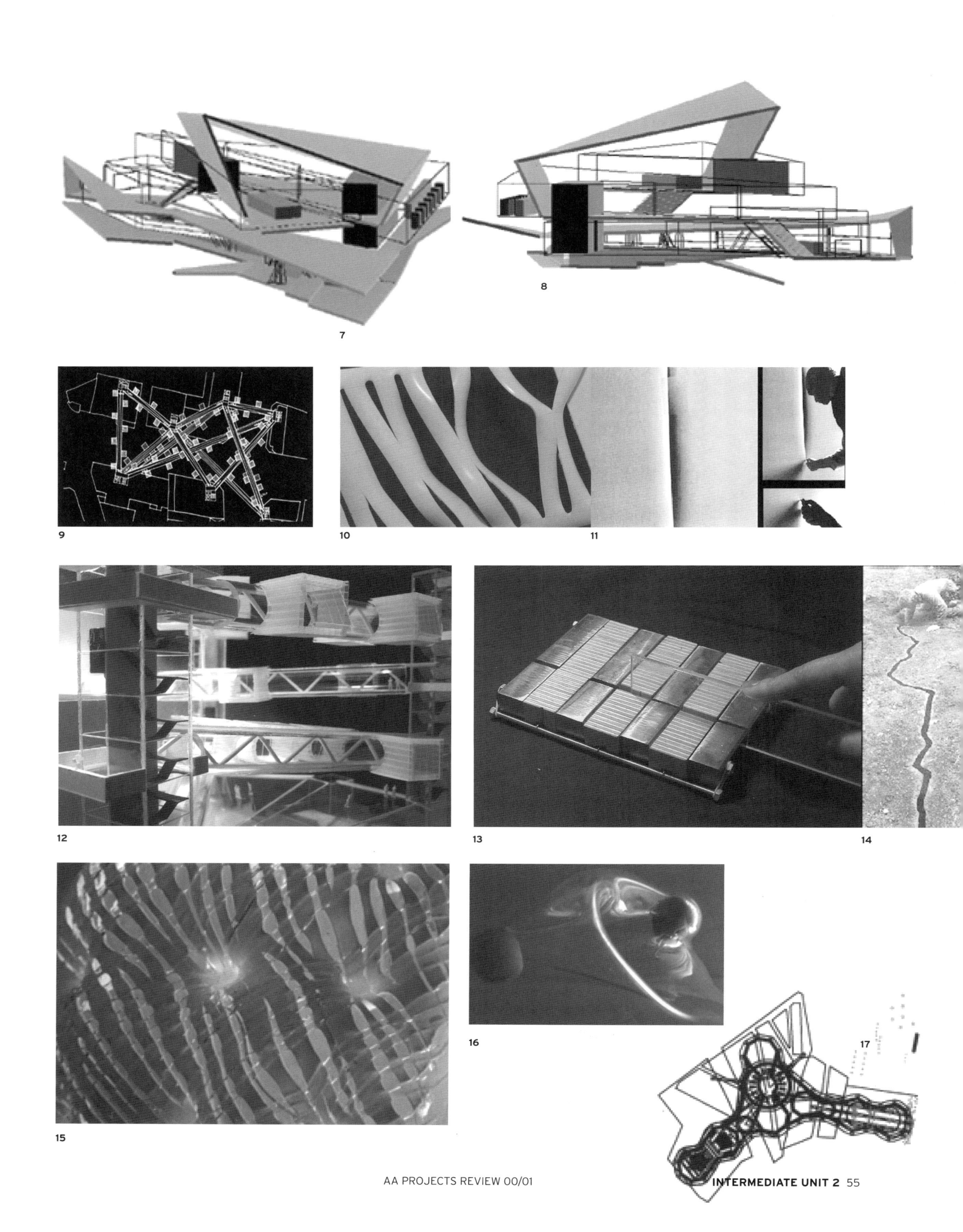

7

8

9

10

11

12

13

14

15

16

17

STUDENTS

(remember: 1 Assumption 2 Question 3 Investigation 4 Synthesis 5 Proposal)

Kelvin Chu **1** The AA website navigation diagram contrasts with the AA premises. **2** Berlin Axo: a Sequence to the upper library level.
3 InfoBox: the streetspace from Southwark Underground Station to Tate Modern as a continuous void for the Macromedia software InfoBox. Comprising a public roofspace and a cavernous arcade below, Macromedia position Augmented Reality elements along the route.

Itay Gershi **4** Micronarrative: pressurised moments are shown by timber in tension tested to its limits. **5** InfoBox: the international organisation 'Seeds for Peace' strives for reconciliation among the youth of cultures in conflict, such as Israel and Palestine. Branching from the railway as timber shell spaces, the geometry derives from glulam structure and overlapping surfaces. **6** Berlin Sequence: a multi-projection drawing investigates the relationship between orthograph projection and building experience.

Elvira Softic **7, 8** InfoBox: Borough Market develops itself by displaying its history, products and services on a ramped surface. The folded structure

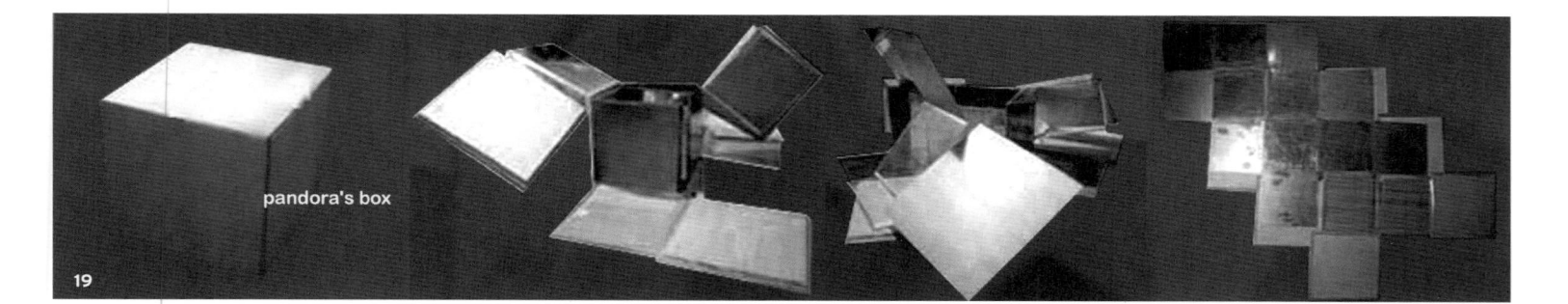

18

pandora's box

19

20

21

22

includes a bookshop and offices. The new construction is immediately adjacent to the market, forming a foil for the Victorian glass roofs.

Ho-Min Kim **9, 12** InfoBox: Southwark Street is revamped as a multi-level megasystem plus network of advertising displays (an IT Piccadilly Circus) with new vertical infrastructure. An elevated, transparent 'street' is the focus of living pods in the sky.

Joo-Eun Sung **11** Micronarrative: Lucio Fontana slices the canvas (in a Flash recreation) violating the ground of painting. (New software idea: 'Slash') This became the basis for a series of cutting experiments in canvas and plastic. **10** The cutting experiments were continued in plywood and steel. **14** Another kind of cut: Andy Goldsworthy cuts a jagged trench in ground.

Hikaru Kitai **15, 16** Micronarrative: 'Zebra Space', 'Klein Space' – made by vacuum-forming opaque and transparent plastic layers. **17** Biodiversity Info Box at the Borough Market site expands the scale of the Micronarrative 'fluidity' investigations, becoming a greenhouse of hydroponic plants grown in a sustainable envelope. Bulbous timber lattices are tuned to sunlight and suggest new enclosed routes in a great horticultural city.

Omar Al-Omari **18, 22** InfoBox: Nortel Networks served as client for an

interactive corporate display using Augmented Reality to overlay data on window views of the City from Bankside. Proportion and Sequence of an Information Space are based on previous music study.

Teresa Cheung **19** Micronarrative: An unfolding 'box' suggests an infinite labyrinth. Danger is hidden within an anodyne exterior. Overlayed meanings and elaborate hierarchies form a series of structural repetitions.

Yiu Fai Poon **20** InfoBox: Process artists such as Christo will be housed in an institutional/industrial or 'industutional' space. Visitors will tour studio space; huge roof apertures allow them to peer at work in progress without interrupting.

Joana Pacheco **21** Amnesty International propose to renovate and augment Southwark railway arches for electronic human rights reports.

Michael Shevel **23,24** InfoBox: Curving pathways through the site form the basis of an architecture based on spheres. The site is devoted to presenting developers' proposals, as at Berlin Info Box. The proposal uses networked IT and Hollopro glass screens to display projects and illustrate debates. The box above street level contains offices and serves as display to the roads and rail.

Francesco Brenta **25, 26** Micronarrative: The 'hook' is a critique of a

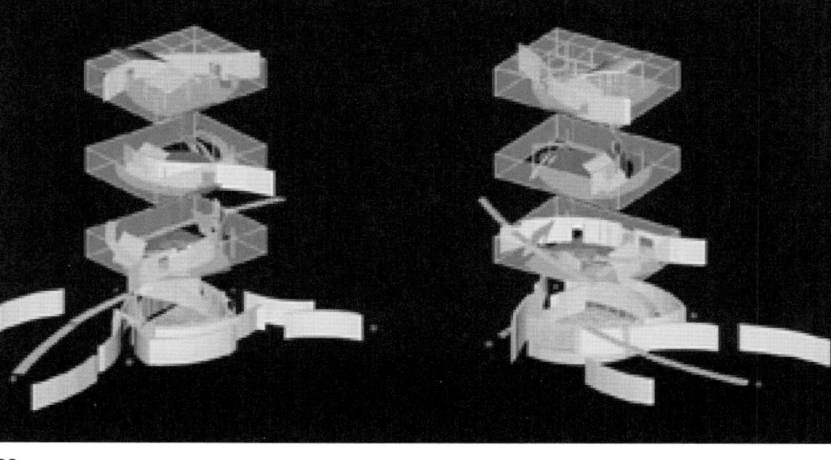

23

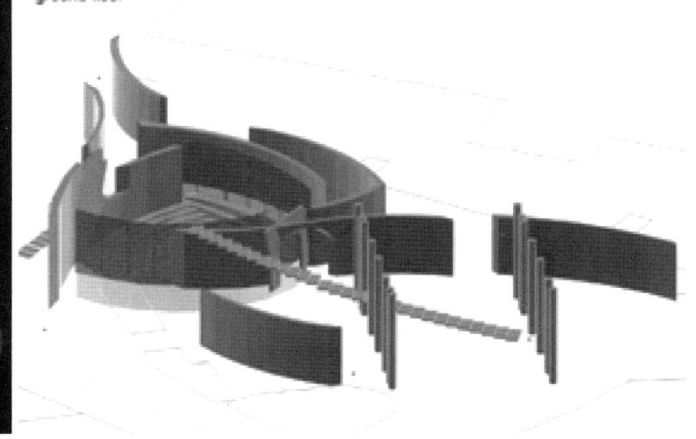

ground floor

24

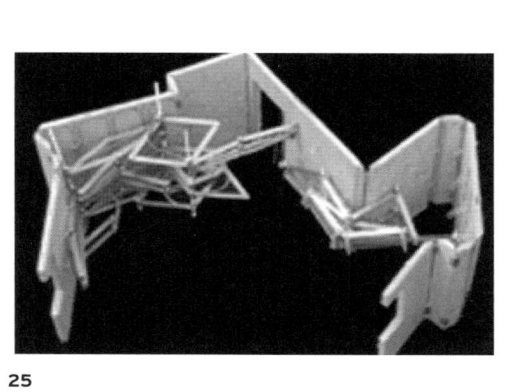

25

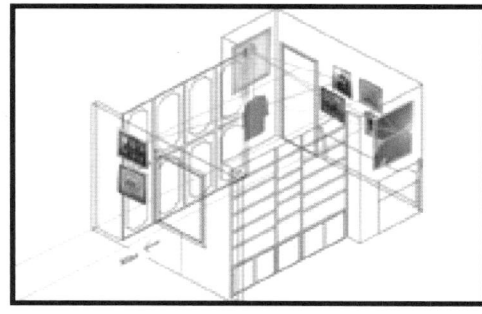

26

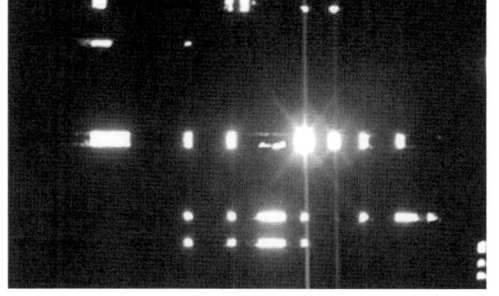

27

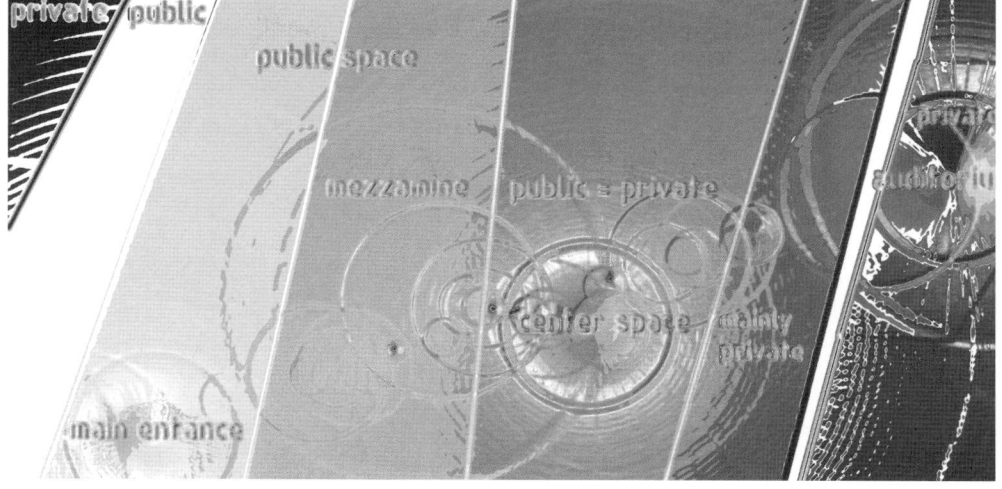

28

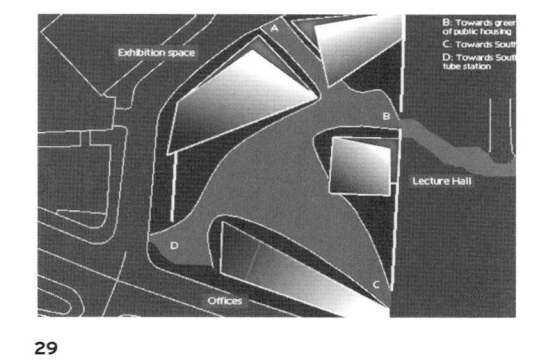

29

childhood bedroom. The project 'unfolded' as juxtapositions of various artefacts. As in Broodthaers' collections, the placement of objects records family history and trauma.

Marina Antsaklis **27**, **29** Micronarrative: Eroded layers of plywood developed emergent properties in layers and light (e.g. a moiré pattern) InfoBox: CABE (the Commission for Architecture and the Built Environment) plans to showcase itself: 'Ace Park with building attached'.

Kristine Bisgaard **28** InfoBox: Vanishing Point, an experimental theatre group, sponsor an InfoBox for young talent. The site's existing striations become identified with programmatic variation in spaces for rehearsal and impromptu presentation.

Goodbye to the AA

The Unit would like to thank all the people who have helped us during our many years at the AA; we will miss you all most frightfully! This year's work, in particular, would have been impossible without the energy, insight, and hard work of our two talented teaching assistants, Veronica Schmid and Ludwig Abache, and without the generous participation of Matthias Reese and Renzo Vallebuona on site during the Berlin Unit Trip in November 2000.

We would also like to thank Bentley Systems for their time and software. In addition, we are eternally grateful to Martin Akpoveta, Pascal Babeau, Philippe Barthélémy, Sue Barr, David Bass, Peter Beard, John Bell, Christian Bodhi, Edward Bottoms, Mary Bowman, Derek Brampton, Ott Chawapong, Darko Calina, Javier Castañon, Charlotte Coudrille, Sheep Dalton, TS Master Ros the Diamond, Anna Douglas, Marilyn Dyer, Belinda Flaherty, Jamie Fobert, Julia Frazer, Pete Gomes, Liz Griffiths, Mark Hemel, Chris Hight, Johannes Kaeferstein, Philip King, Gordana Korolija, Andreas Lang, Marcellus Letang, Antonia Loyd, Mohsen Mostafavi, Ciro Najle, Joel (Rock n' Roll) Newman, Marie Nicolas, Chris Pauling, Diana Periton, John Place, Christine Petters, David Petters, Kim Quasi, Nicola Quinn, David Racz, Kevin Rowbotham, Pascal Schoening, Aileen Smith, Goetz Stoeckmann, Mole Wernick, Mike Weinstock, Julia Wood, Simos Yannas. Thanks also for the continued support of former students Yanko Apostolov, Chaing Tat Lee, Sylvia Ng, Henrik Lonberg, Sinisa Rodic and Irina Velkova.

Martha LaGess is the new Dean of University of Texas at Arlington Architecture. She and Michael McNamara will run a visiting studio at the Harvard GSD in Fall 2001-2 with tutor Veronika Schmid.

Intermediate Unit 3

Brandmark & Brandscape

Cities are increasingly seen as landscapes where each building markets itself as a distinct sign or billboard representing the corporate identity of brands that have less to do with socio-political contexts than with the globalisation of brand values. Inter 3 investigates the relationship between branding and architecture. Design proposals are developed as part of a year-long investigation that leads to the design of a new typology, the Brandmark.

Students identify a brand strategy that is specific to their chosen brand. They research building typologies and structural methodologies appropriate to their final proposal. What are the consequences for the built environment when powerful corporate conglomerates have the facility to territorialise large areas of the central districts of major cities?

The unit studies the notion of the branded landmark (Brandmark) and investigates its programmatic configuration and its relationship to the city. These buildings provide a globalised, tele-visual urbanism, a global tele-city presenting chosen brand identities. Brandmark explores the end of specific local identity and contextual formalism. It replaces localised strategy with a global value vocabulary. Brandmark is the creation of a new typology and its consequent impact on urbanism.

Brands are no longer products; they are concepts. Brand values are conceptual terms that allow brands to territorialise the materials or the ethic that suit their desire for increased commerce, status and power. What role will we have in this game, as brands increasingly turn to architects to transform their export into something experiential and spatialised, on an urban scale? Brands operate by actively structuring identity, defining terms that enable conditions and objects to be distinguished from one another. In the marketplace, for instance, how might we distinguish one pair of trousers from another? On a global scale, how might one nation distinguish itself from another?

Cities, regions and nations that are increasingly engaged in privatising what was once considered public are capitalising on this identity-formation mechanism. How might we use what we know about branding to articulate aspects of our culture, and what new strategies might we employ to wake up the city in the process?

In student projects, brands take over existing buildings such as Centrepoint, the Westway Building, and Trafalgar Square. They strategically place new forms to transform the urban environment. We imagine how a brand might spatialise and materialise itself on an architectural and an urban scale, developing and testing spatial strategies based upon each student's identification and analysis of their brand's values.

Project One/Branded object
The collision of an everyday object (no larger than a shoe) and a brand, with the purpose of extending the brand's values into new territory. How might the brand's 2D values materialise three-dimensionally? Scale: 1:1

Project Two/Branded retail unit
A modular, prefabricated, component system (such as a cargo container, portable cabin, greenhouse or garden shed), where the brand's values and a high-street retail programme meet.

In January, we visited Los Angeles and Las Vegas. We studied Los Angeles precisely because it is a sprawling, horizontal landscape, a continuous field with few built monuments or markers. Las Vegas is diametrically opposed. It is an instant city, a series of fabricated landmarks that are agglomerations of memories of other places, concentrations of other fields. Las Vegas casinos are first-generation multi-programmed typologies.

Project Three/EasyEverything™
Each student transforms two floors of

Centrepoint to accommodate a given retail programme, to 'brand' the tower for EasyEverything™. Student proposals reconfigure the hi-rise internally and externally, in service of the brand.

Final Project/Brandmark & Brandscape
A brand headquarters that accommodates existing and appropriated programmes suitable FOR each brand. It gives the brand a new architectural and urban presence, combining public and private space in its bid to create a 3D experience of its values.

The work from this studio was generated for educational purposes. The work is not intended to have any commercial value. Proposals for brands are developed as conceptual strategies, without consent from any brand.

Staff
Kim **Colin**
Kevin **Rhowbotham**
Clive **Sall**

Students
1   Bosmat **Brants** (Absolut™)
2   Alex **Catterall** (Guinness™)
3   Manu **Grosso** (Swatch™)
4   Antonia **Josten** (Disney™)
5   Ashley **Littlewood** (Madonna)
6   Ayako **Mizuma** (Pokemon™)
7   Kenzo **Osuga** (Muji™)
8   Spencer **Owen** (McDonalds™)
9   Isabel **Pietri** (Nike™)
10 Paris **Sargologos** (EasyEverything™)
11 Chie **Shimizu** (Nike™)
12 Michelangelo **Spinelli** (Apple™)
13 Ken-Hin **Teo** (Rolex™)
14 Tav **Thanadsaang** (Playboy™)
15 Su-Cheng **Wang** (G-Shock™)

We thank the following for their support: Yousif Albustani, Alphaville, Dave Beech, John Buck, Bump, Ros Diamond, Angus Fairhurst, Paul Khera, Malcolm McGregor, David Panos, Richard Scott and Stuart Smith

2

12

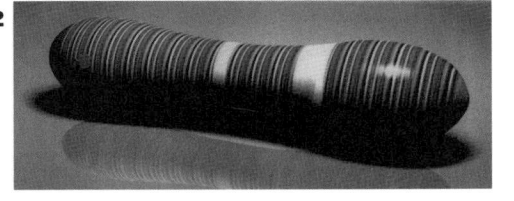

13

13

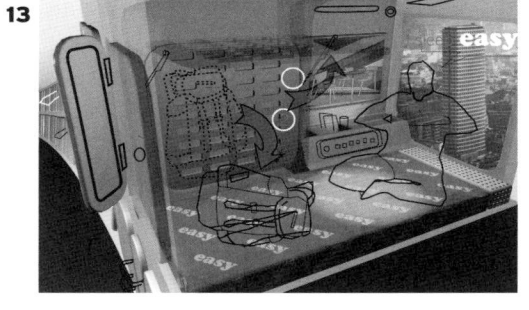

5

14

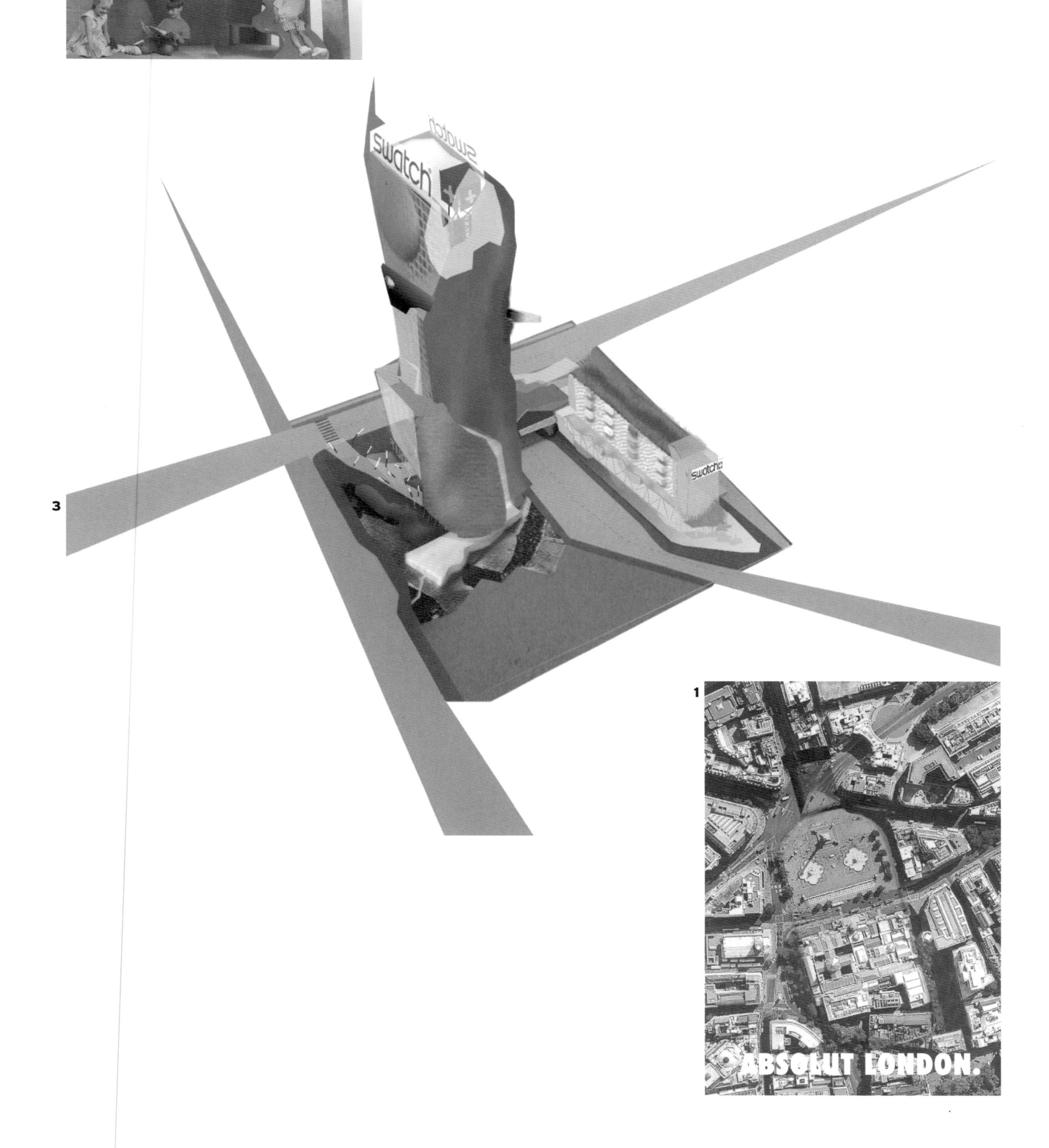

6

3

1

ABSOLUT LONDON.

7

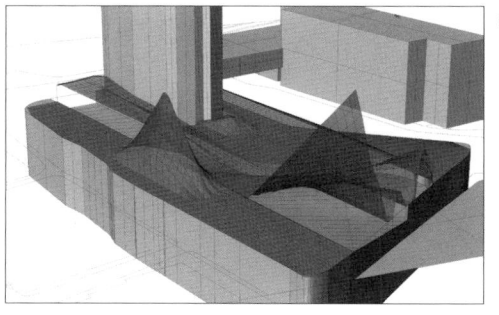

9

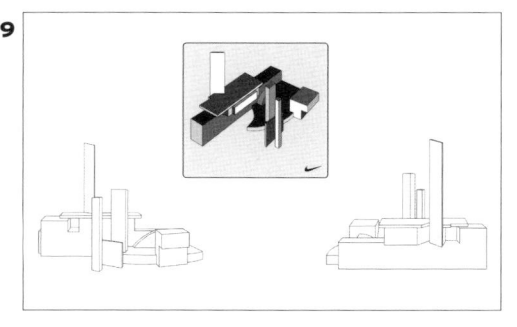

4

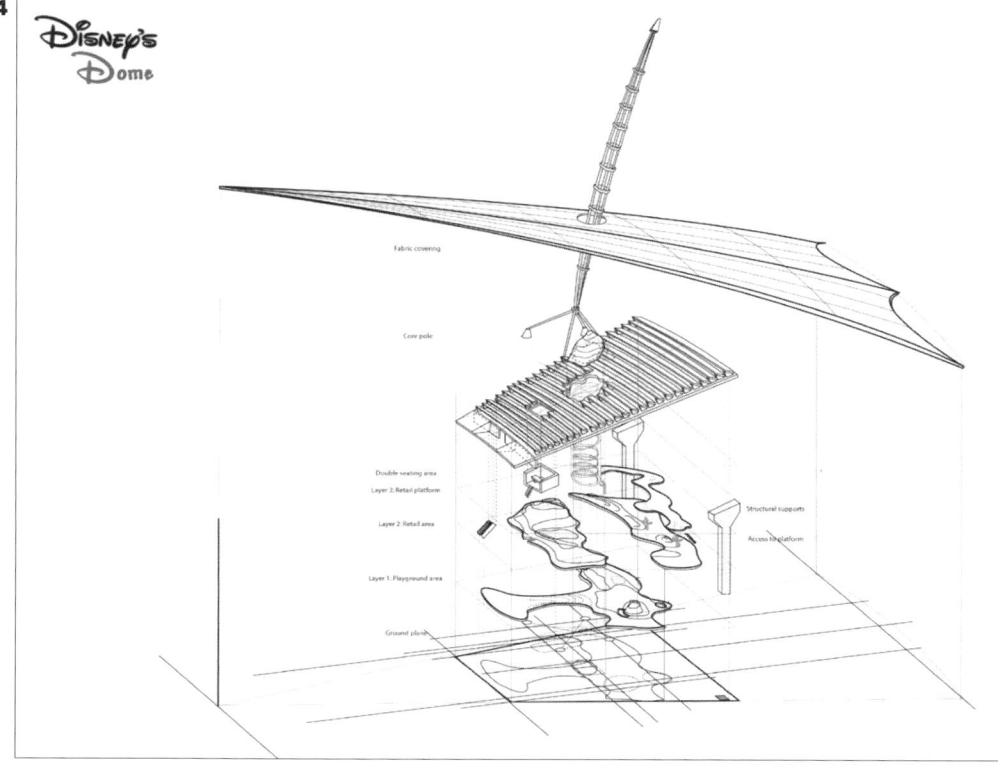

Disney's
Dome

Fabric covering

Core pole

Double seating area
Layer 2: Retail platform

Layer 2: Retail area

Layer 1: Playground area

Ground plush

Structural supports

Access to platform

8

15

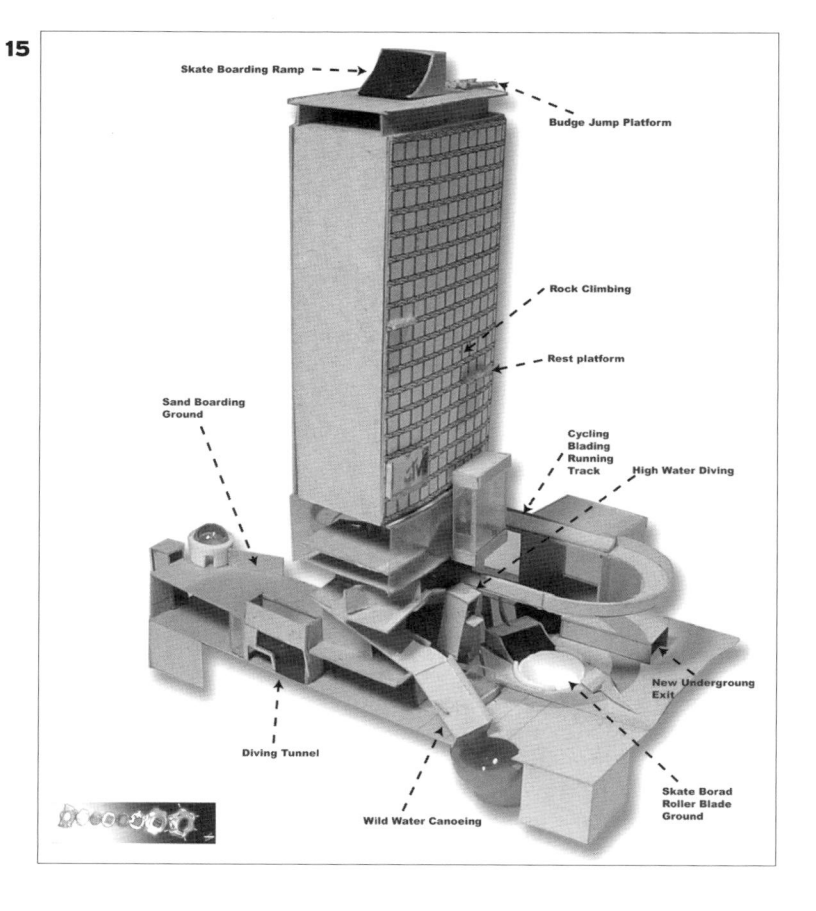

Skate Boarding Ramp

Budge Jump Platform

Rock Climbing

Rest platform

Sand Boarding
Ground

Cycling
Blading
Running
Track

High Water Diving

New Undergroung
Exit

Diving Tunnel

Wild Water Canoeing

Skate Borad
Roller Blade
Ground

15

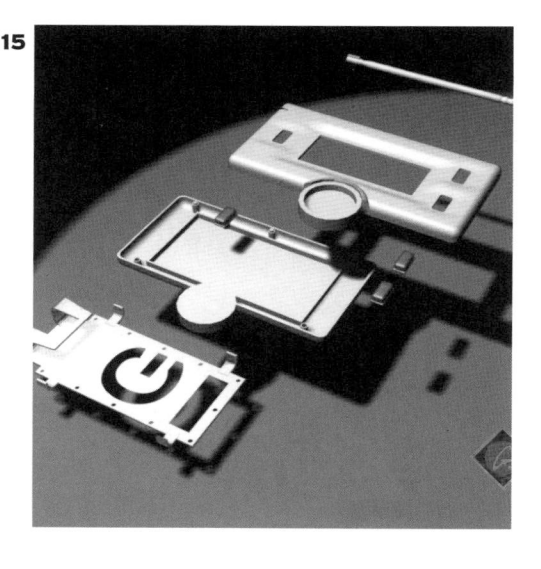

Intermediate Unit 4

Unit Staff
Alex de Rijke
Philip Marsh
Sadie Morgan

'capsule hotel'

The late Robin Evans defined architects as people who make drawings and models, not buildings. This year, Inter 4 students actually made a building: a full-size prototype for a 'capsule hotel'. While drawings and scale models informed the product, they were not conclusive in its realisation. The process of making, even on the initial level of vac-formed plastic prototypes, demanded answers to questions that not even a computer had required to be asked. The objective of the capsule-making project was to learn about the parameters of mass production, the properties and limits of materials, and the requirements of teamwork: the architect as co-ordinator and production line rather than simply an issuer of drawings. According to the unit methodology, we have worked extensively from catalogues and samples of new building materials. This year the capsule design and build embodies research into three types of lightweight self-finished structures: 1) various polycarbonate sheet cladding profiles used as hybrid structure 2) expanded foam-bonded plywood as monocoque 3) resin-coated sheet polystyrene (AVL handbook method) as monocoque.

The results of this work will be fully explained and documented in a forthcoming AA publication on the capsule hotel construction, titled *How much does your building weigh?*

Individual project work has exploited knowledge gained from the collaborative construction experience, pushing further and separate hypotheses for nomadic architectures via issues of cultural/environmental climate, infrastructure, services and form.

In this unit no distinction is made between design and technical explorations, on the basis that in architecture there can be no imagination that is not technical. Conceptual clarity has been insisted upon and anything extraneous has been challenged to the point of its eradication. In the context of this hardworking atmosphere of production, the tutors have had the unusual task of asking whether designs could be better reduced or even eliminated. No excess: just a building, a process and a product. This must be a first for the AA.

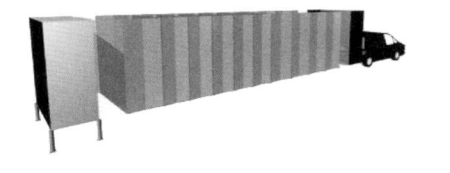

We would like to thank the the following contributors and critics to the capsule hotel programme: Cedric Price, Joep van Lieshout, Nic Pople, Mohsen Mostafavi, Michael Hadi, Fred Scott, Mike Weinstock, Dominic Papa.

Hiromasa Makino

Adam Cossey

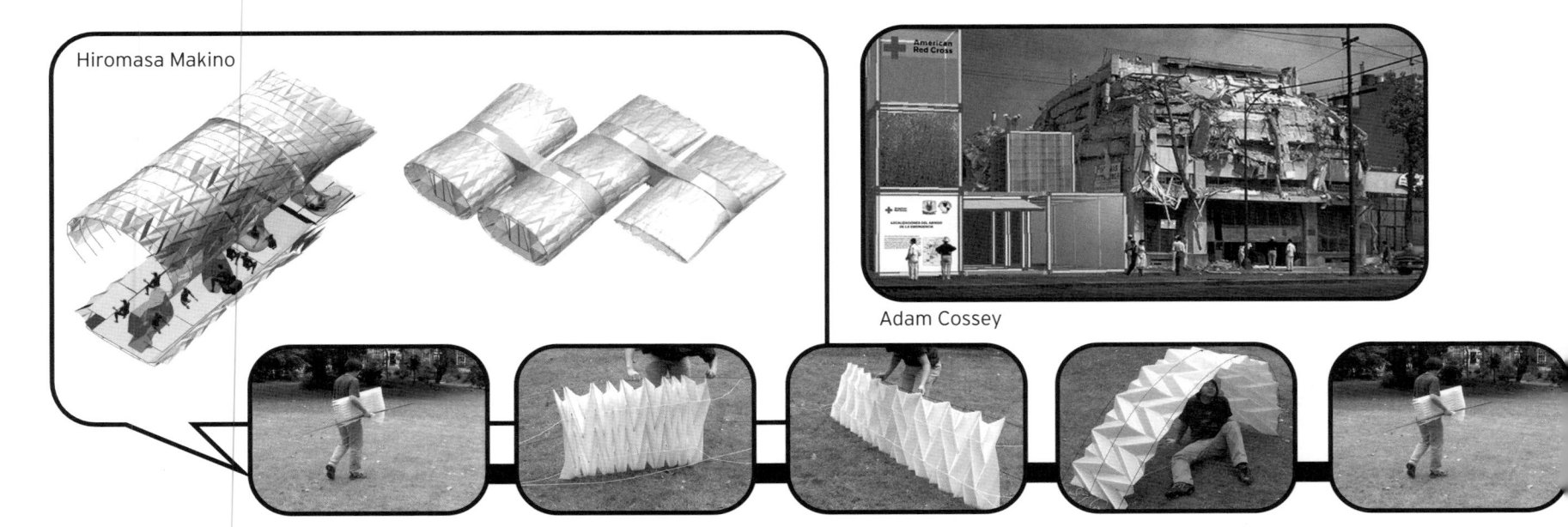

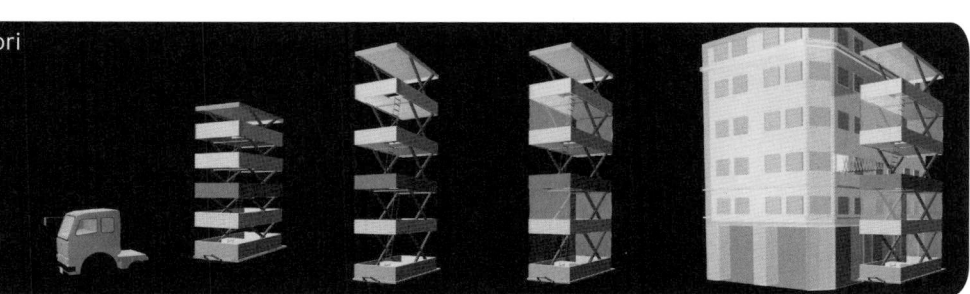

Hikaru Hattori

Adrian Priestman

Igor Gottschalk

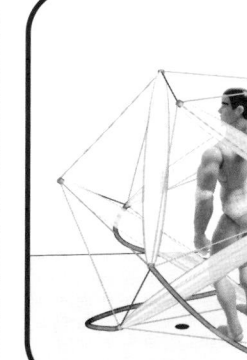

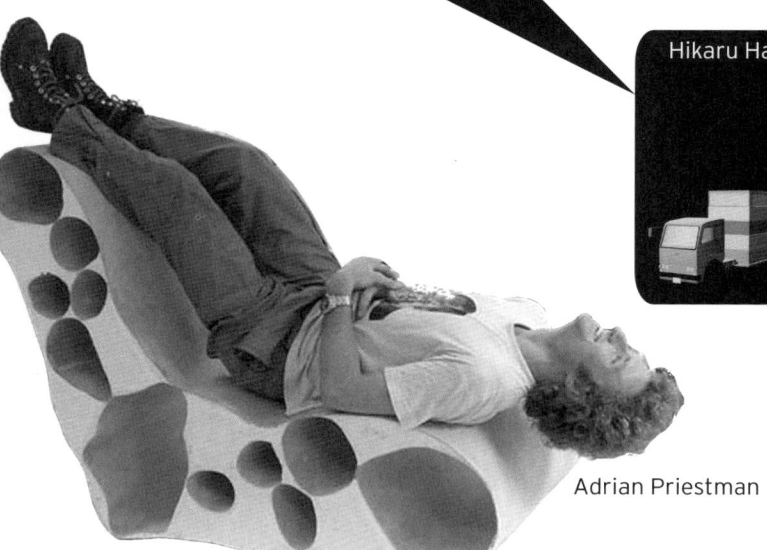

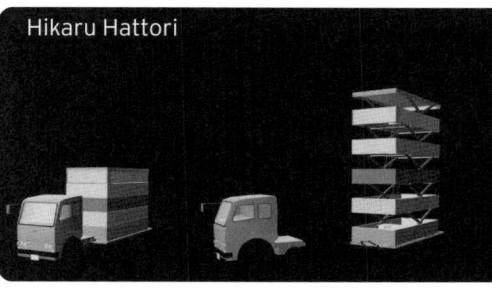

Junko Yanagisawa

Suk-Kyu Hong

Alastair Townsend

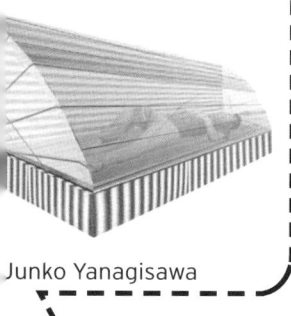

Tania Rodriguez

inter 4our capsule hotel

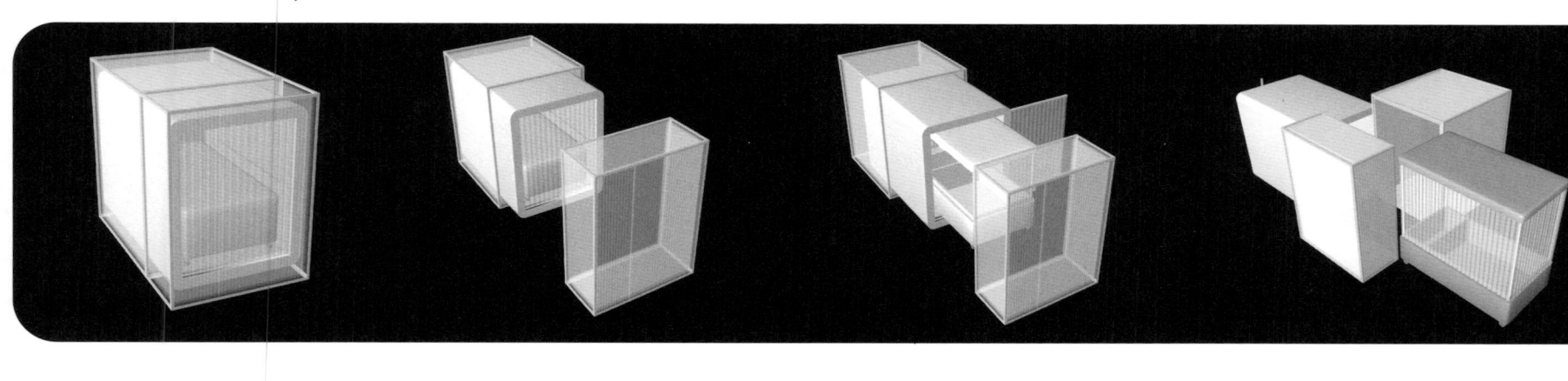

exhibitor/social capsule
laminated multi-wall sheet polycarbonate

group 1

Adam Cossey, Hikaru Hattori, Maria Martin,
Tania Rodriguez, Junko Yanagisawa

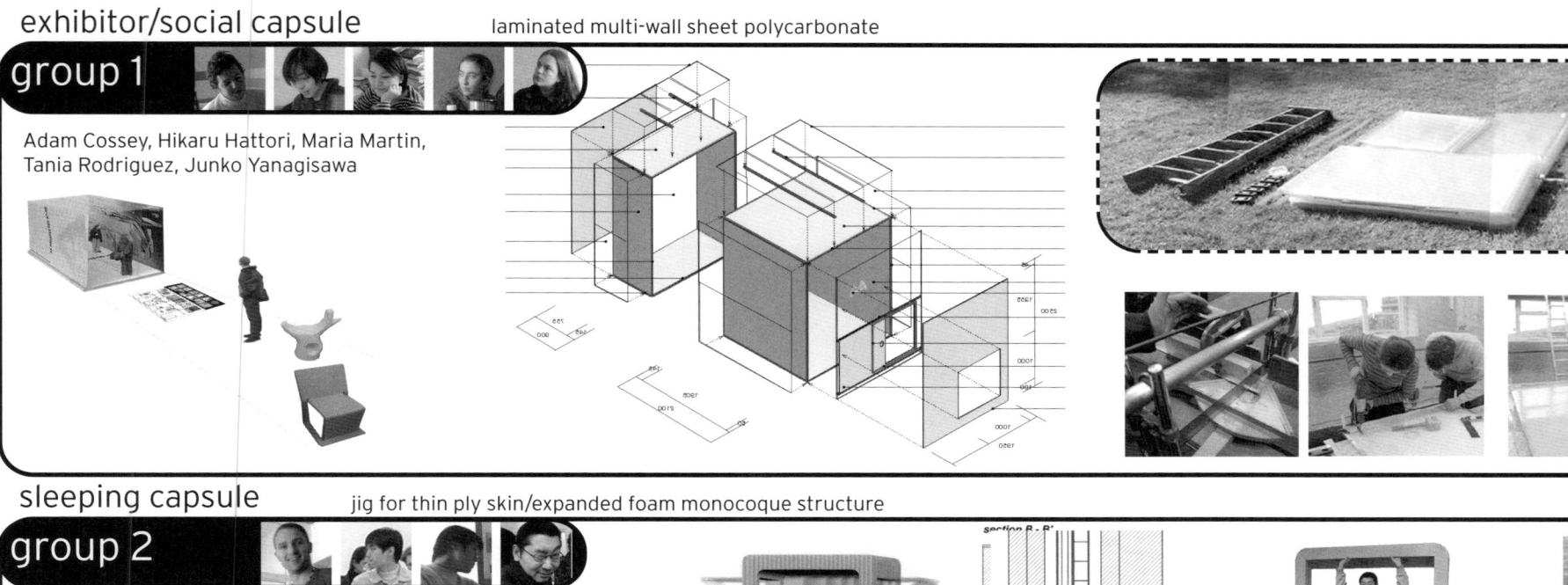

sleeping capsule
jig for thin ply skin/expanded foam monocoque structure

group 2

Adrian Priestman, Henry Leung,
Hiromasa Makino, Suk-Kyu Hong

bathing capsule
sheet-foam/-glass reinforced resin structure

group 3

Tom Dulke, Igor Gottschalk,
Beatriz Minguez de Molina, Alastair Townsend

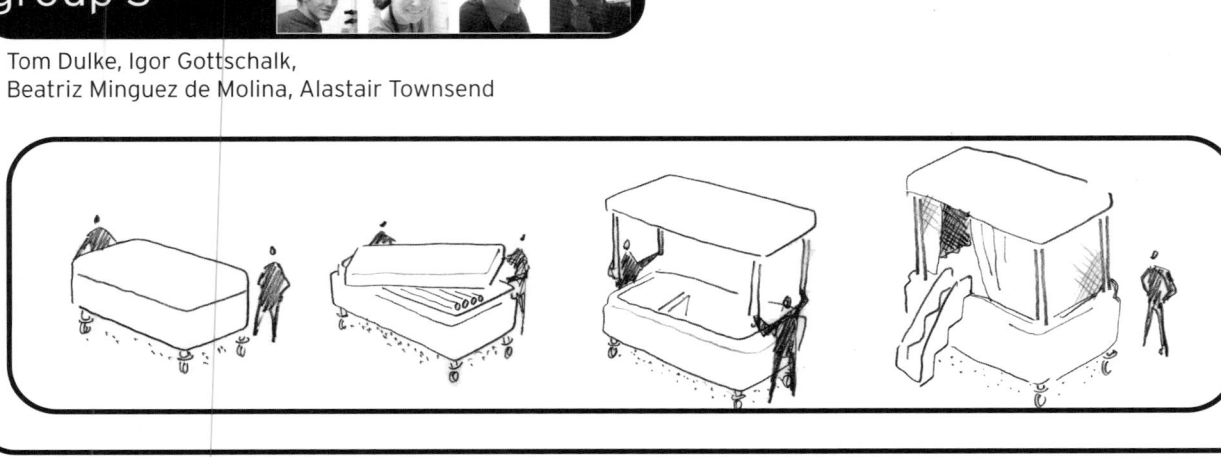

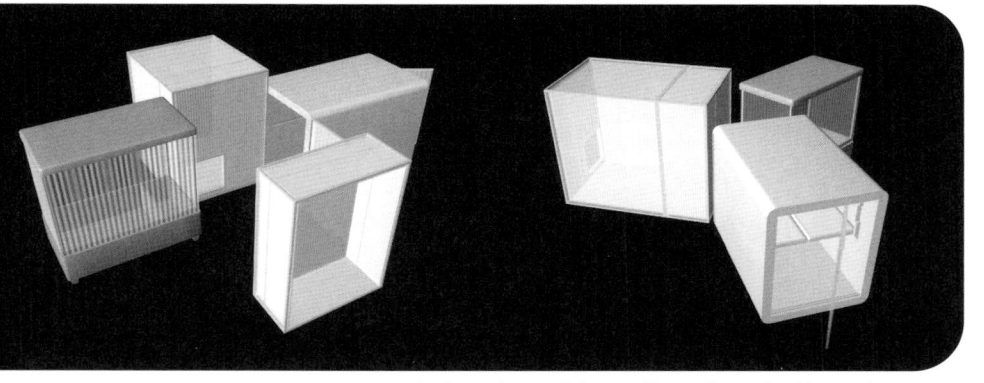

rendering of possible configurations by Henry Leung

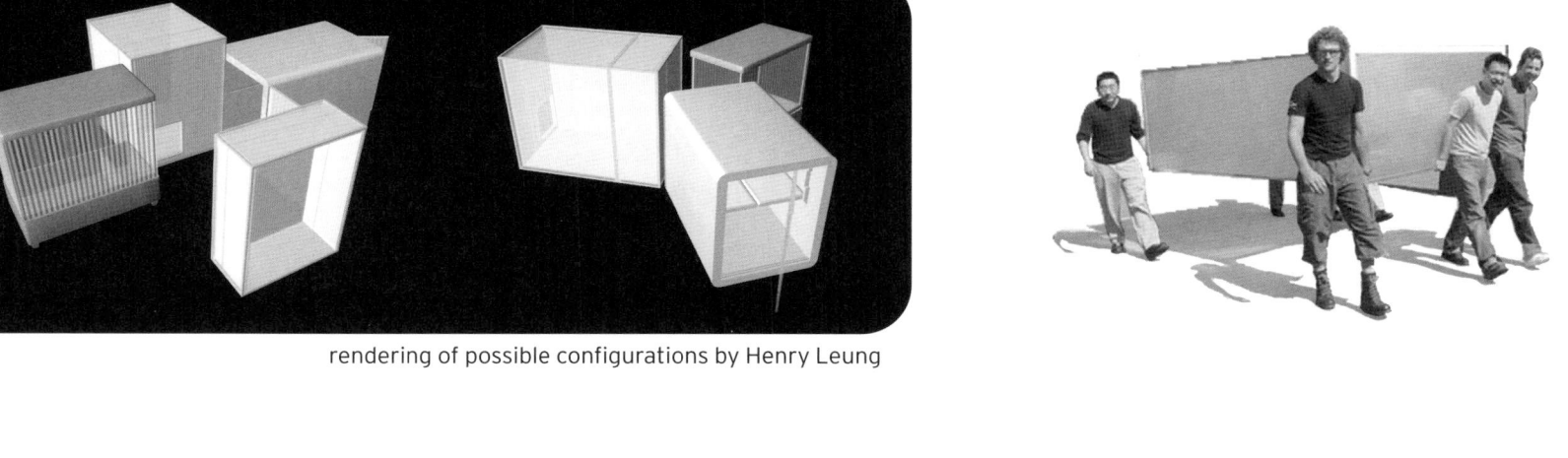

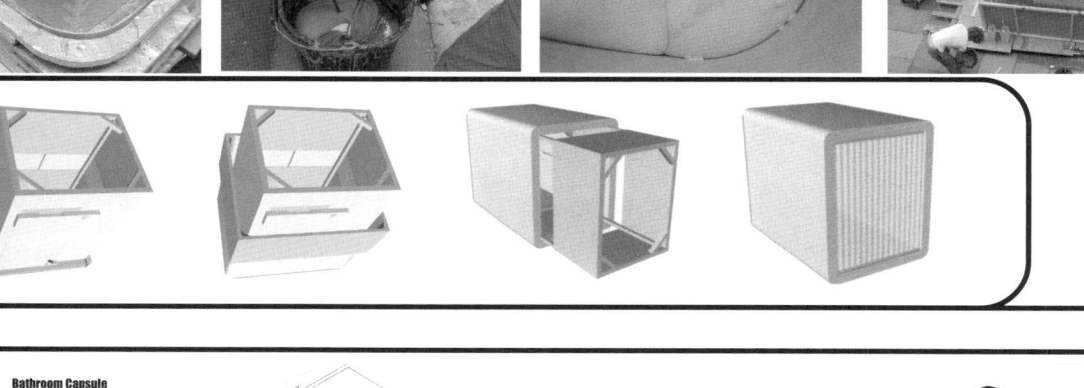

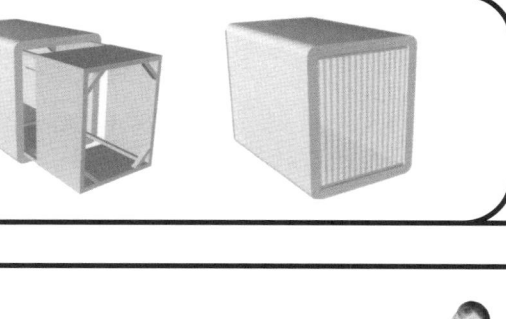

Bathroom Capsule

Building components

Polyurethane Insulating Foam
Kingspan (110) 240:130:5 cm

Roof lip with handles, foam
240:15:5 cm

Curved corners to accomodate
corner supports.

Join in foam structure

Plastic drainage tube
Height 79cm; Diameter 6cm

Plastic drain "collar" glued

Wooden corner piece
2cm deep

Floor template

Corner support

Aluminium scaffolding pole

Slices cut out of foam for
corner templates

Polyurethane Base Two layers
230:120:10 cm

Groove cut in foam to seat corner support
20:20:2 cm

Exploding Isometric 1:10

Bathroom Capsule £1,90.00

Key to materials and functions
1. Kingspan Polyurethane foam FIS. Used in the
building trade as a wall insulator,
prefabricated in 5cm deep boards.

2. The foam is easy to work with and smooth
finishes can be obtained. The foam used for
the base has a thin layer if fibreglass matt on each side.

3. The corner supports are made from
plastic piping of two different
diameters 6cm and 7cm. The larger
pipe acts as a collar and locks the
wooden templates in place.

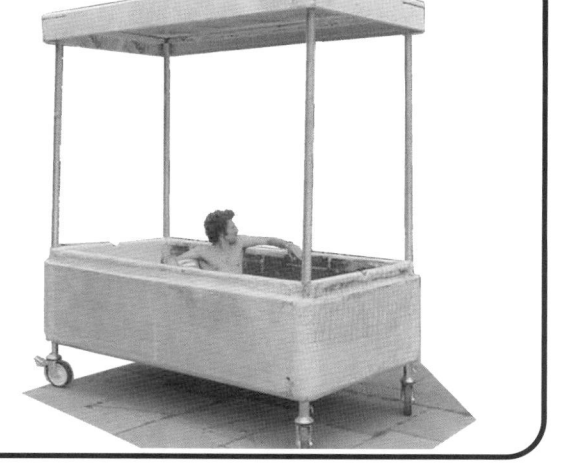

Intermediate Unit 5

Dan Narita   Hyun Jung Jung

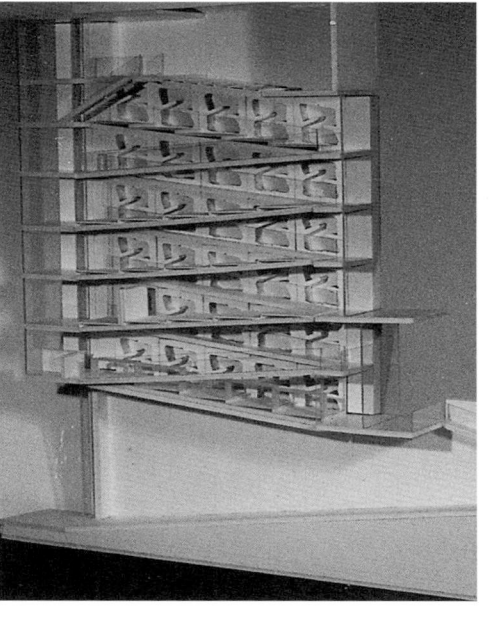

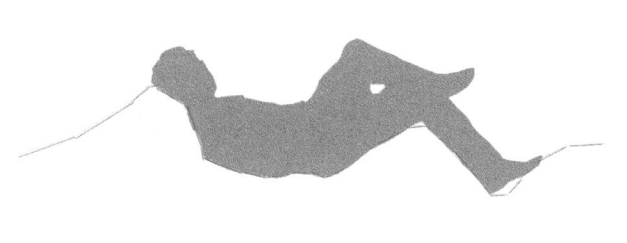

Specificity and Materiality

The Arènes de Lutece in Paris is the focus for the two projects developed by Intermediate Unit 5. Located in the Latin Quarter, near Jussieu University, the site reveals layers of Paris' architectural history: Gallo-Roman ruins, medieval and Hausmannian structures and contemporary buildings. The brief for the first half of the year was to investigate the physical and historical context of the site as the generator for the design of a small building or architectural intervention. The work revealed several 'families' of projects which validate and reveal the specificity of the site. Some of the projects looked at re-establishing the function and original purpose of the Arena while others proposed a 'museographical' or exhibition device, which allows the history of the arena to be understood. Others offered a new perception of the ruins initiated by a specific reading of the topography, the urbanism and the history of the site, and looked at developing new relationships with the city.

In the second half of the year, the unit looked at a site slotted between two existing buildings along the rue Linné. One side of the building faces the street and the other faces the gardens of the Arènes de Lutece overlooking the Square Capitan. The development of the brief for the second site focused on proposals which would respond to the specific character of the local community within the wider context of Paris. The work of the unit aims to focus on the substance and material quality of building.

Rita Lee   Natalie Waters

 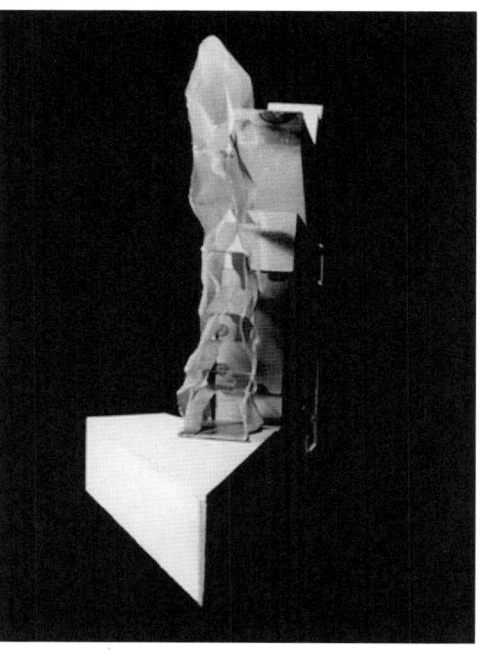 

Unit Master
Philippe Barthélémy

Unit Tutor
Mary Bowman

Technical Tutor
Neil Thomas

Students
Athanassios Economou
Sharon Givony
Hyun Jung Jung
Woo-Young Kim
Rita Lee
Niccolo Montesi
Dan Narita
Christiana Palmiris
Sarifah Anisah Wan Madzihi
Ana Saboia
Natalie Waters
Amilia Zainudin
Oriel Zinaburg

Special thanks to
Antonia Loyd
Michael McNamara
David Racz
Cindy Walters

Ana Saboia   Sharifah Anisah Wan Madzihi   Sharon Givony

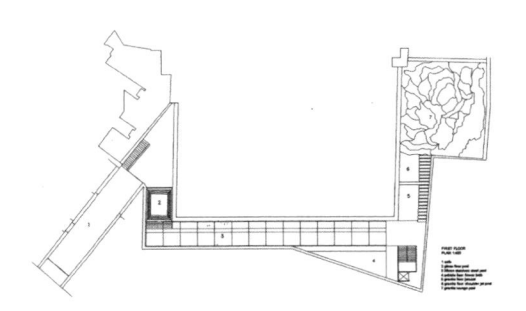

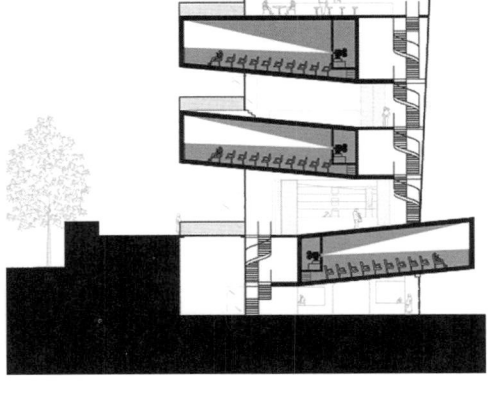

Athanassios Economou developed a museographical or exhibition platform along the wall of the entrance corridor to the south, which establishes the level of the ground during the first two centuries.

Hyun Jung Jung re-establishes the nineteenth-century entry sequence imposed by the Sainte-Genevieve hill. In her second project she developed a community centre which responds both to the garden and the city with interlinking spaces.

Rita Lee's project looks at 'cleaning up' a site that has been carved up and made especially banal by unsuitable landscape treatment. Her project is a piece of urban furniture which reappears in the second project for a dual-aspect restaurant.

Sharon Givony has taken the opportunity offered by the creation of a new development along the rue des Boulangers to invent a new relationship with the nearby campus of Jussieu. In the second project she developed an independent cinema club linked to the university.

Woo-Young Kim looked at repositioning the stage and has regrouped and developed the support spaces for the theatre and garden in an underground building. The second building becomes an underground performance space.

Niccolo Montesi looked at reconstructing the internal concentric passageways for the seating in the Arena. He re-establishes continuity by recreating the upper level platforms with bridges that straddle the entrance galleries. The bridges reinterpret stone construction in a modern way.

Athanassios Economou   Oriel Zinaburg   Amilia Zainudin

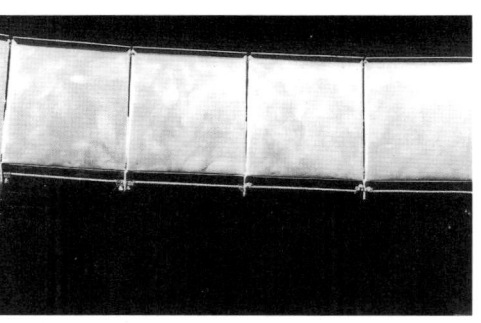

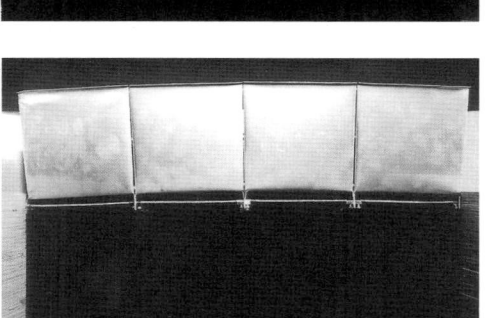

Dan Narita affirms the public character of the arena and opens it up in a more radical way to the rue Monge. The second project becomes a reading space for students, accessed by a series of stepped ramps containing library, video and internet facilities.

Sharifah Anisah Wan Madzihi appropriates part of the metro station and locates in it an exhibition space, creating a link with the upper level. In her second project she takes as a starting point the limits of the old water tank, to create a new spa.

Amilia Zainudin re-establishes the organisation of the arena by completing the seating area and access. The folded steel structure becomes a platform, bridge and stair. This exploration of folded metal is continued in her second project, a children's library.

Ana Saboia re-establishes the limits of the site and superimposes the traces of the original geometry by proposing a gallery space which can recount the history of the arena.

Natalie Waters reveals the original foundations of the 'cavea' by creating an exhibition hall under the seating. Her second project creates an 'after-school club with fencing, climbing, chess, modelmaking, video and news rooms stacking together like a child's toy.

Oriel Zinaburg uses the upper existing level to the south to invent a new entrance which reveals the brutality of the Haussmann intervention. His second project is a library and information space which reveals the history of the arena site.

Intermediate Unit 6

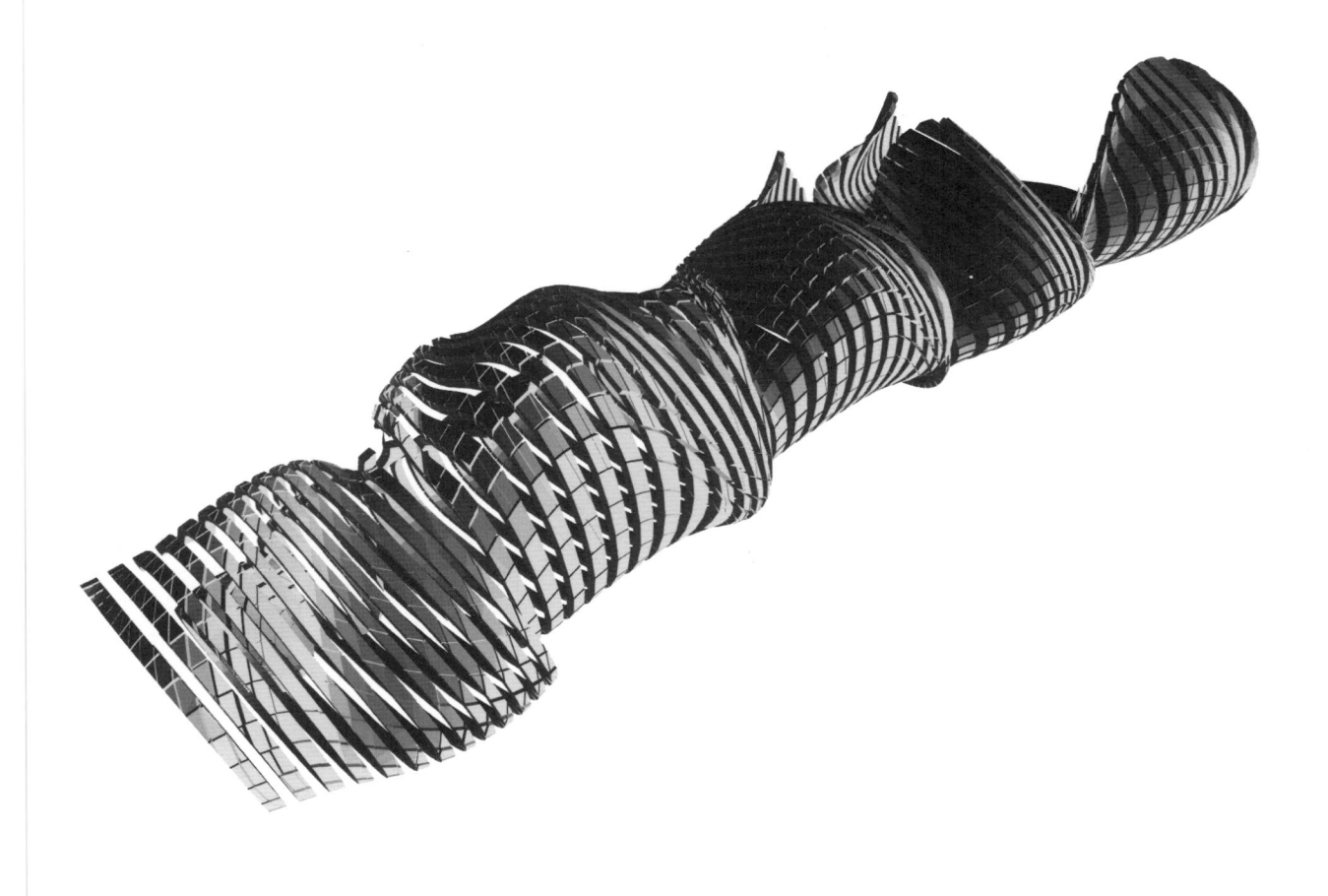

Justin Lau

Co-location/Augmentation

Unit Master
John Bell

Tutor
Theo Lorenz

Technical Support
Aran Chadwick

Students
Chi-Kit Cheung
Hani Fallaha
Hideyuki Kishimoto
Justin Lau
Raymond Lau
Andy Meira
Paula Nascimento
Ifeanyi Oganwu
Marin Sawa
Peter Staub
Alicia Tan

The unit would like to thank:

Russell Brown, Adam Covell, Aran Chadwick,
Jon Goodbun, Jason Griffiths, Lorens Holm, Nate
Kolbe, Gunther Koppelhuber, Mohsen Mostafavi,
Ciro Najle, Benedict O'Looney, Stephen Perrella,
David Racz, Kevin Rhowbotham, Joe Robson,
Natascha Sandmeier, Patrik Schumacher,
Charles Tashima, Kim Thornton,
Ben Van-Bruggen, Filip Visnjic, Paul Wahba

How to begin?

A little light polemic. Alfred Jarry who, among
other accomplishments, was Pablo Picasso's
weapon-supplier, wrote:

*Pataphysics will examine the laws governing
exceptions, and will explain the universe
supplementary to this one; or, less ambitiously,
will describe a universe which can be – and
perhaps should be – envisaged in the place of
the traditional one.*

Whether cloaked in facticity or proceeding from
convenient fictions, the place of most
architectural production is perennially elsewhere,
the act of making conducted against a continually
evoked, proleptic surface or ground. To proceed in
such a manner is to begin from externalities; this
might be seen as consonant with archetypal,
extensive notions of site, affording certain
apparent advantages, principally those born of
remote operation from a comfortable distance.

Direct engagement with real immediacies may
then be safely deferred until the possibility of
their articulation has been elided by, in the
broadest sense, 'site conditions'. Whether these
conditions are formal, programmatic or
geographic, they remain external.

What if there were another site, a site more
immanent, replete with intensive qualities,
continually and simultaneously present in every
moment of the design process; a counter or para-
site exerting at least equal force on the
conception of architecture – a pataphysical
equivalent?

Of course, there is;
this year we went looking for it.

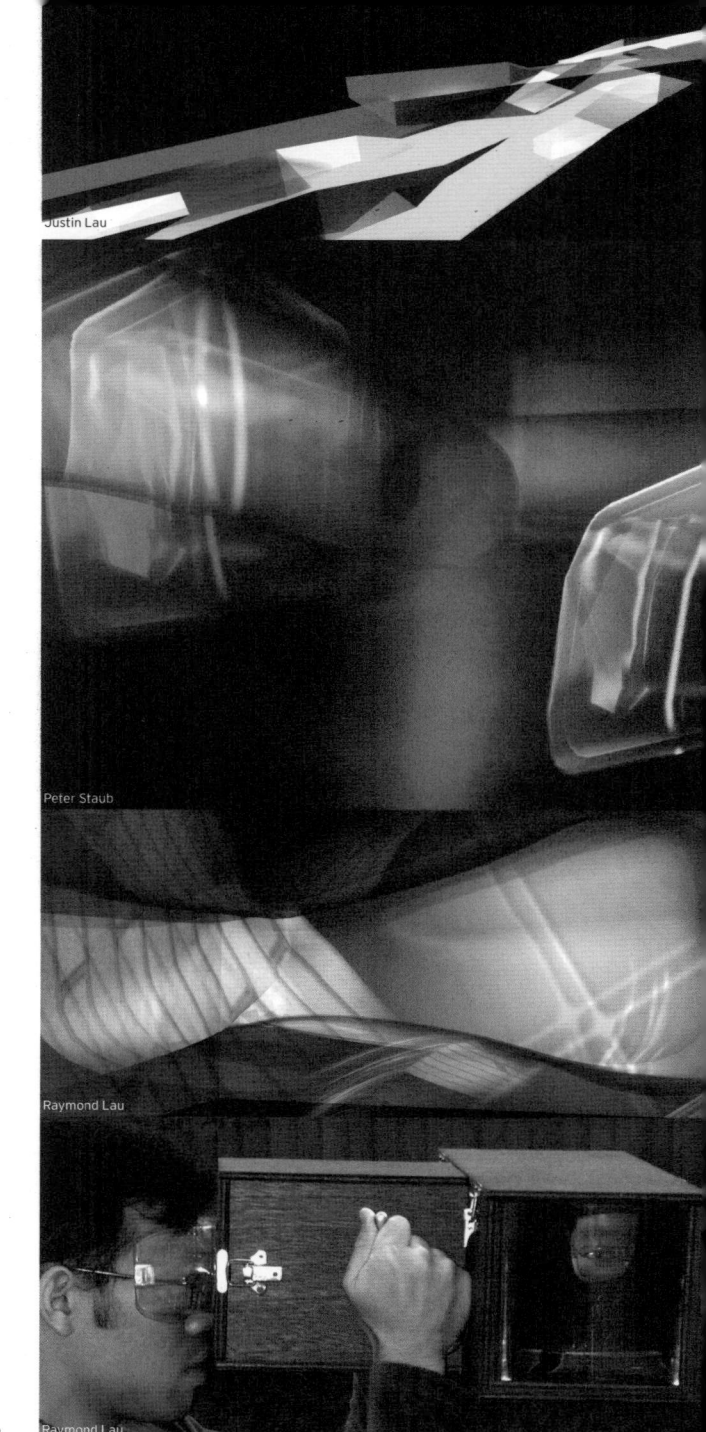

Justin Lau

Peter Staub

Raymond Lau

Raymond Lau

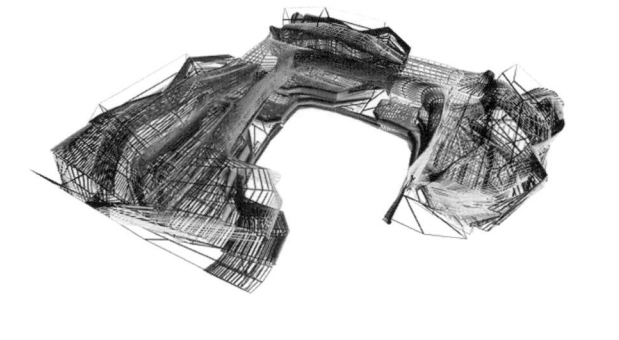

Alicia Tan

Project 1

Camera Lucida: a device for seeing two things simultaneously

Normative and tedious modes of architectural representation seek to reduce the wonder of a sliding moment to the deadly sclerosis of convention. In an attempt to avoid this dismal prospect, we considered a number of approaches which refused the hubristic certainties of conventional programmatic development.

Concerned with fragments; tectonic, ergonomic, conceptual, generated using different media - the only absolute requirement was that one piece was modelled in the workshop and one piece was modelled in the computer. The motivation was to begin a new and constructive dialogue regarding the vicissitudes and opportunities afforded by these supposedly polar conditions and begin considering how we move between them.

Project 2

Iterations/irritations: testing remoteness

Unit members chose a short piece of text by any published author which in some way pertained to architecture and sent it by ftp, along with a 3D model of a primitive form, to a randomly selected and anonymous partner from a group at the TU Graz, Austria. The Graz partner was then to modify the object with respect to the appended text and send the result back, accompanied by another piece of writing for the AA partner to work on.

The use of an unknown, remote partner, without any form of contact other than the (monitored) ftp server, ensured that the text fragments and evolving 3D model were the only cues for operation, avoiding so far as possible other vectors of mutation or contamination.

This process was carried through a minimum of ten iterations with 24 hours turnaround time per object/text couple. The series was conceived to open up questions which could be summarised as:

If the written word exerts influence on the creation of architecture, how might we begin to open up and assess some aspects of this influence?

The problem of a single-stage elaboration of a simple 3D form with respect to a short piece of writing (most students chose critical theory or philosophy, although this was not a requirement) provided a clear focus and limited ambit, which promoted polemical debate. The exercise was interesting and provocative, opening possibilities which we hope to pursue in the coming year.

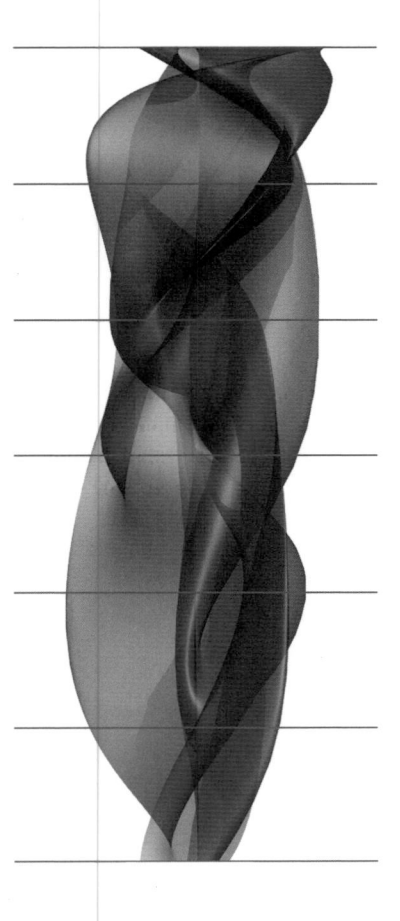

Hani Fallaha

Raymond Lau

Project 3

An exhibition: is it me?

What if the spaces we construct modify our sense of self?

Students were asked to design an exhibition for their own earlier work. The only given was the dimensions of the space for occupation. Thematic concerns were folded into a variety of designs, which took curation as their cognate object.

Project 4

GVNY: pretext

We are absorbed into the media spectacle as both consumers and producers of products, we inhabit two territories simultaneously, co-extensive and interpenetrating.

Introduction

2001 began with a unit trip to New York, concentrating on Greenwich Village. A variety of data-gathering techniques were employed to form a unit resource including photography, video, audio, drawing and found objects.

GVNY: context

The unit continued its attempt to develop new processes of design and production, employing modern techniques and technologies. The first multimedia generators were developed out of the group research material.

These software machines were designed to organise and present edited data in a dynamic and interactive form. Critical evaluation of each student's interests then proceeded in parallel with the production of spatial diagrams: we sought to conflate formal and programmatic development. The next phase of the Greenwich Village project

was to construct the 3D digital doubles of the multimedia piece: emergent programme becoming spatial diagram.

Using digital site models and their already constructed multimedia pieces, unit members were invited to construct spatial diagrams of the material they had chosen within the dimensional confines of each chosen site. Students were asked to consider activity, form, material, colour.

Project 5

GVNY:GVUK

Greenwich Village, New York versus Greenwich Millennium Village, London: two locations – one has maintained its identity as a nexus for avant-garde cultures for more than a century; the other is a new consumerscape© development.

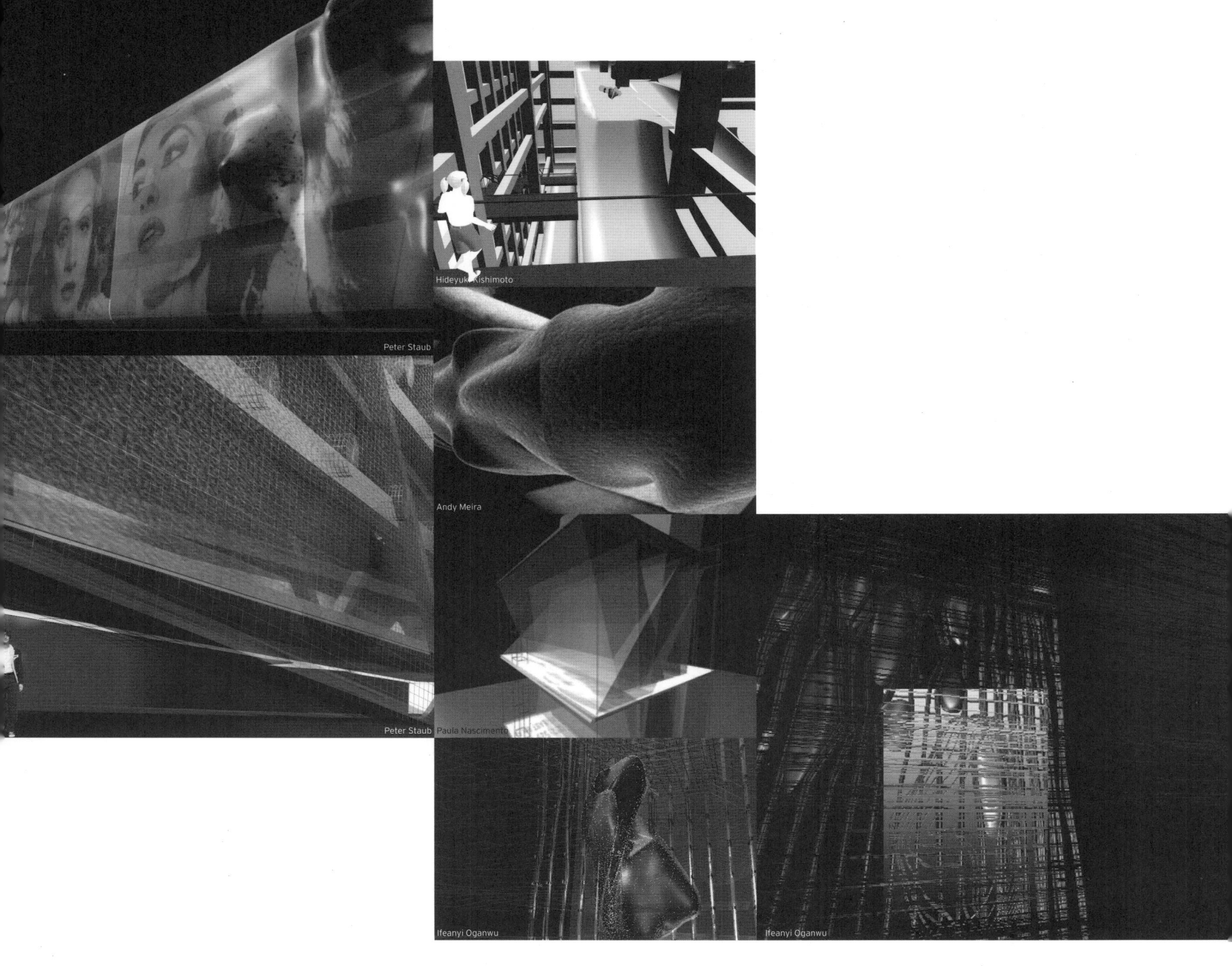

Hideyuki Kishimoto

Peter Staub

Andy Meira

Peter Staub Paula Nascimento

Ifeanyi Oganwu

Ifeanyi Oganwu

Research

Site visits and a guided tour by one of the area's planning officers provided background and political context to the current development. Comparative studies with other major metropolitan areas and an introductory workshop addressing pertinent aspects of contemporary urbanism allowed students to begin to identify areas of interest.

Tactics

Pictographic procedures, such as the familiar cartographic regime of legends, were given slight adjustments in order to function as agents for ludic operations. Websites were downloaded and modified. Advertising material and sales brochures were gathered, critiqued and detourned. Photomontage and planimetric superimpositions were made of diverse locations – including GVNY of course.

Innoculation

The project sought to engage with some ephemeral, unconstituted, peripheral, incidental, overlooked, unsanctioned fragments of GVNY urban life as generative influences for 'low-impact' architectural and urban proposals for GVUK. Architectural responses initially developed as proposals for GVNY infill sites were imported as first moves in the unfolding of urban interventions in GVUK.

Conclusion

Proposals ranged from a drive-in cosmetic surgery clinic with holistic therapy and retail playground to a distributed signage system for occasional churches.

The unit will, hopefully, continue to have a dialogue with Greenwich Planning Department.

Intermediate Unit 7

Students developed and articulated a central issue that focused the different elements in their work and connected the concerns of two projects on two scales. The pursuit of an independent direction within the overall unit framework was strongly encouraged.

The year started with a close look at a small world. 'Cities and Desire 5', a story from Italo Calvino's *Invisible Cities,* was used to alter an existing boardgame and open up an exploration of various materials and techniques of construction. The process of construction was used to translate the narrative concern into a physical investigation, and vice-versa.

A *dérive* was the starting point for our exposure to the city, as we observed how the issues raised through the gameboard resurface on a larger scale. The architectural proposition was used as a tool for anchoring these personal concerns within the common ground of the city. The spaces that were created manifest the negotiation of scales in the process of articulation. Each exercise was an excuse to develop the issue, and each project was an opportunity to ask a more precise question.

Takashi Nishibori

Speculating on the behaviour of different moments of extreme unpredictability as a type of definition. Desire as an uncontrollable emotion controlling actions (the city is created); actions by the body controlled by simple restraints (the city is experienced); the action of the city controlled by the unexpected action of one person within the predictable movement of many (the city is changed). A 'wall' of traffic in London becomes the site for the proposal to create moments which articulate and emphasise the experience of particular behaviours at those points of the site – the sound of the cars, the position of the sun, the movement of people – in this way making a new definition for the Wall within the city.
1a, b, c, d, e, f

Alexia Petridis

'There are parallels between myth and our inner psyche.' (Nietzsche)
A strategy is developed by identifying 'Gates' of transition between these two elements, dissolving their boundaries and merging them together. A series of pavilions are created in a park: dual and ephemeral in nature, they are transitional mechanisms that undergo a stage of metamorphosis, accommodating two different programmes – a theatre and a recreational boating facility. Each programme sets its own parameters influencing the evolution of the other one on site.
2a, b, c, d

Kyoko Kobayashi

The moment of eclipse: two elements come together to make us aware of an invisible existence: moon covering sun makes a shadow on earth – we see stars in the dark blue sky. Searching for this moment in our daily life in the city, a threshold is revealed toward the moment of eclipse. This threshold exists only through ourselves, evoking a particular emotion, the echo of our past. An informal, floating auditorium consists of a sequence of smaller thresholds that interact with the tidal movement of the river, re-opening the threshold between the city and the river. The eclipse becomes defined as the moment when all the thresholds become open to be experienced.
3a, b, c, d

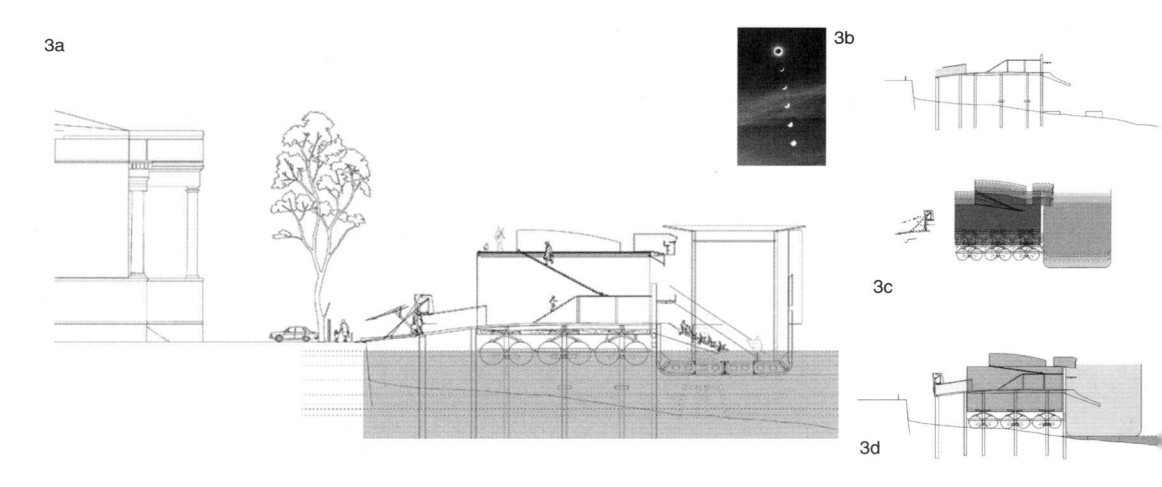

1b

1a

1c

2a

2b

2c

2d

3a

3b

3c

3d

1e

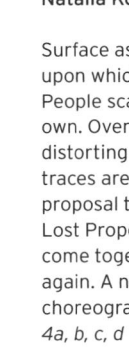
4b

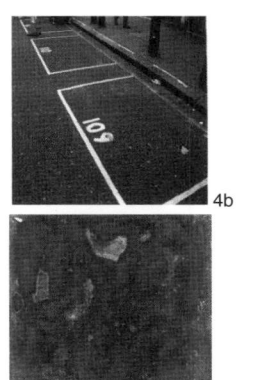
4c

4d

Natalia Kokotos

Surface as a reading of activity, a layer of the city upon which individual narratives are inscribed. People scatter traces that denote the city as their own. Over time, the traces become weathered, distorting the tale of their existence. Observing how traces are inscribed on surfaces in London, this proposal takes Bermondsey Square as the site of a Lost Property Market. Objects from around the city come together momentarily, only to be dispersed again. A new surface is inscribed with carefully choreographed traces.
4a, b, c, d

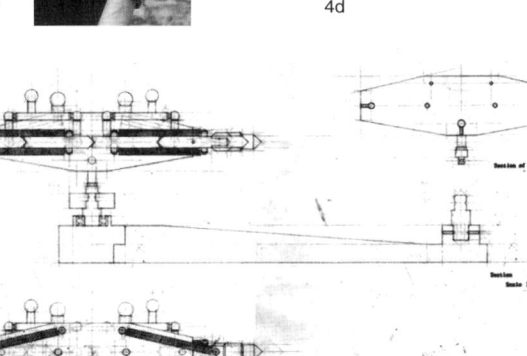

5a

Anastassis Economou

Swallows always return to the same nest. They return in March, the month of Aries, the start of the zodiac circle. Ancient Romans, to remember a speech, placed objects in the zodiac circle, or in a particular route through a house. Likewise I place memories through a house. The positions of the memories are related to the star sign of Aries on a particular day. The angle of the cuts through the house relate to the constellation at a specific moment in time, just as the memories relate to a specific moment in my past.
5a

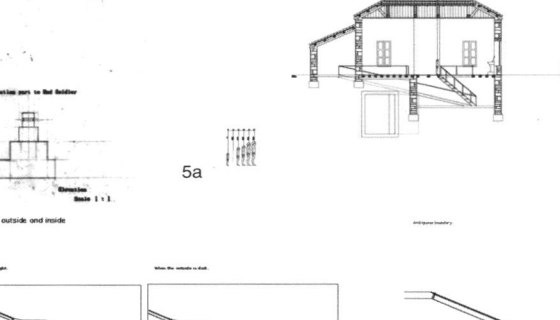

6a

7a

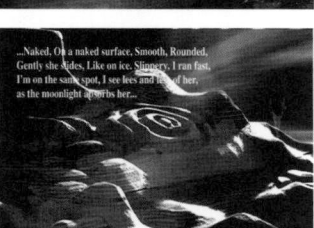
7b

7c

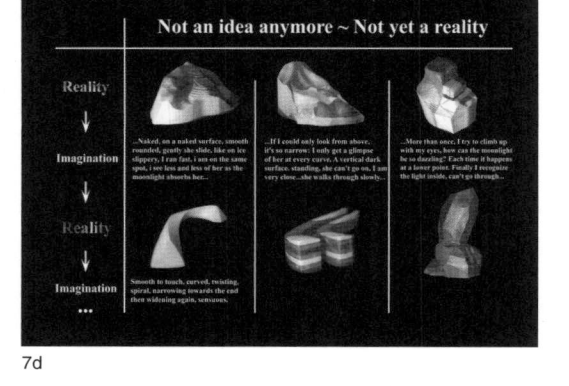
7d

Yuka Suganami

The boundaries of the library are no longer so much physical as electronic, and the distinction between the outside world and the inside is becoming less and less. My project is about creating boundaries whose qualities of sound and light construct a library that is experienced through the senses, from the point of entry to the moment of opening a book. The main material of the building is glass and water, treated in terms of reflection, refraction, distortion and transmission of light, sound and images.
6a, b

6b

Ran Ankory

Intangible to tangible: three stages of transformation. Two versions of a wooden puzzle game identify the moment transforming idea to physical manifestation. Dreams describing the first puzzle become a construction script for the second. Two journeys to particular locations in London confront expectations with experience. Slow accumulated creation of an object as a third design process. 2001 years ago, someone saw Jesus touching a wall on the Via Crucis and, deciding it was important to touch the same spot, began the transformation of this intangible moment into a physical phenomenon. This idea is used to build up a look out point to the sea, Rothschild Avenue, Tel-Aviv.
7a, b, c, d

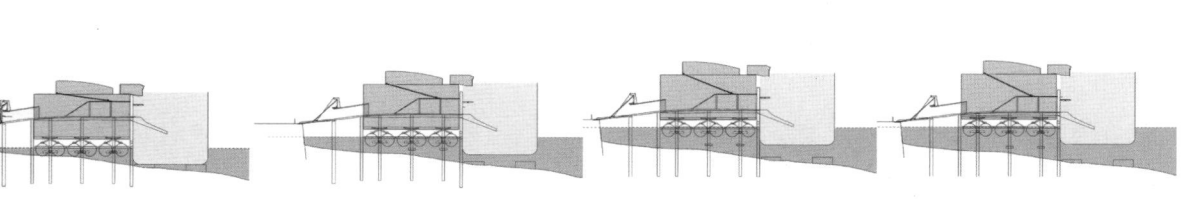

Yeo Joong Yang

A series of speculations on the occupation of territory within a specific period of time. The starting point is Conquer, an outdoor game played on the asphalt of a carpark. The game generates the moment of conflict between different Conquerors whose territories overlap or interact. Two scales of speculations on place and time: occupation, with the body claiming territory and making shelter; and casting areas of ground to demonstrate aspects of time in my act of Conquest. The occupation of empty sites provides a home park for people and their mobile shelters in between places, in between times of building or usage of the sites.
8a, b, c, d, e

8a

8b

8c

8d

8e

Nicolas Durr

A fold is a complex form of mutation and modulation. It gathers upon itself, but at the same time reduces. This dual nature of the fold is my interest. With the *dérive*, I had made a claim that suicide was a mortal fold. My programme consists in generating a break in a wall that separates a Christian and a Jewish cemetery, so providing a resting place for suicide victims while uniting the cemeteries. Using the narrative of the Jewish ceremony and Dante's conception of purgatory, I establish a series of fold lines on the site which generate the wall.
9a, b, c

9a

9b

9c

Bart Schoonderbeek

Experiences making three personal spaces in London define my proposal for a weekend house in the city. Arrival and departure into existing activities identified critical moments where one activity meets another and showed how they influence each other on different scales. The principle of a keel allows my weekend house to be three metres above ground level, between a long-term storage wharf and studio wharf, between the main road and a goods-receiving/shipping pier, above a passageway to the Thames and a temporary open storage site.
Entering and leaving the house, opening and closing it up, is timed with the immediate activities of the site, while at the same time speculating how the definition of this physical and mental space within the larger context of city offers a different way to view and act toward existing spaces and movements.
10a, b, c, d

10a

10b

10c

10d

Alex Papadakis

The ideology of the Flat Earth Society, Islanders, informs the architecture that operates at a series of scales in Hyde Park, as a way of establishing flatness in the world. The society interweaves itself into the many layers of the park, offering external points of contact to the public. On the surface, the programme appears isolated, yet it forms part of a larger underworld network. At the largest scale, it assumes total control over the park water, causing the water table to sink or rise above the ground and creating a new datum from which to measure the depth of the earth. Slow appropriation is its method, imposing a new layer of references relating to flatness.
11a, b, c, d, e

11a

11b

11c

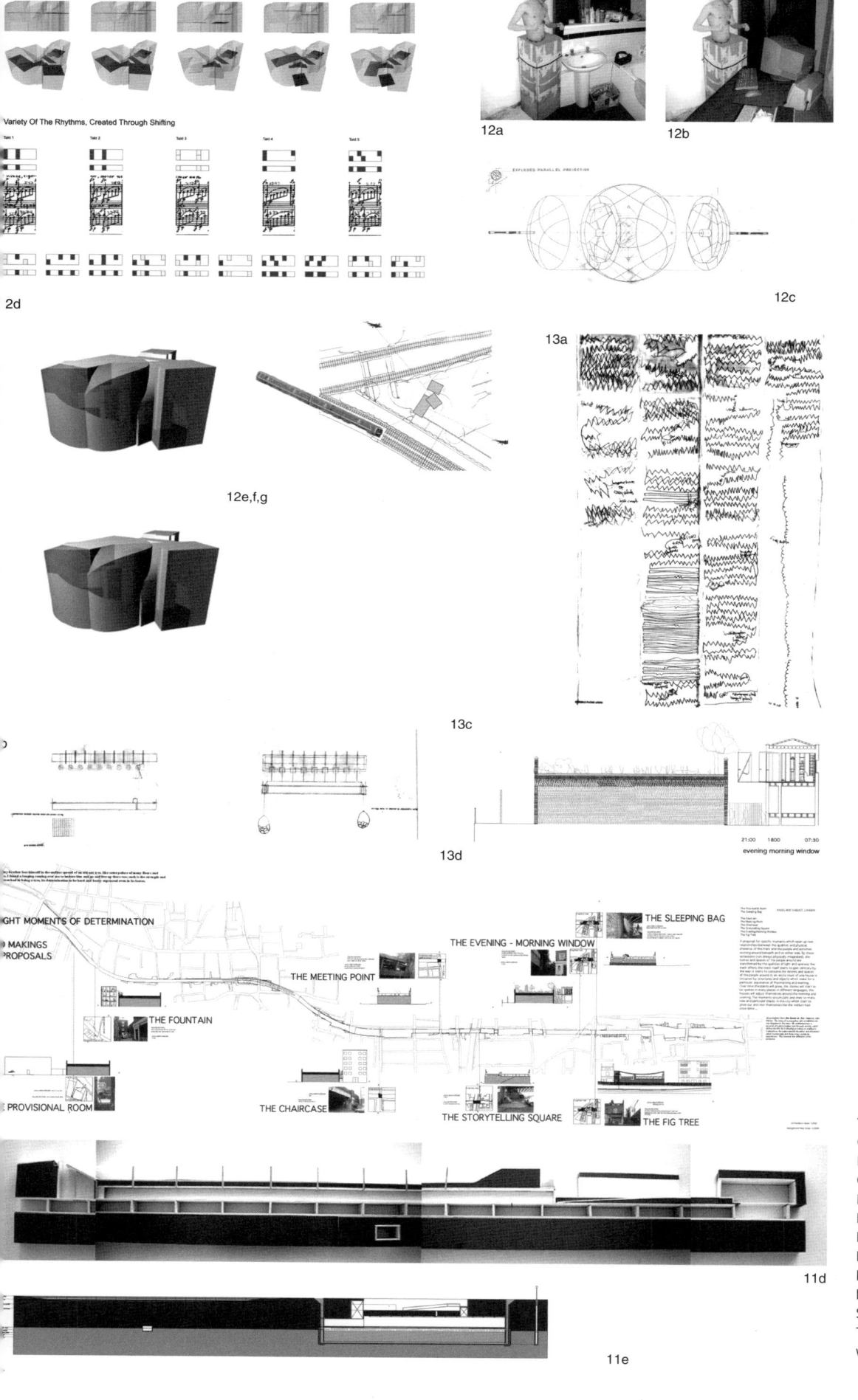

Variety Of The House, Created Through Shifting

Variety Of The Rhythms, Created Through Shifting

2d

12a

12b

12c

12e,f,g

13a

13c

13d

21.00   18.00   07:30
evening morning window

IGHT MOMENTS OF DETERMINATION

MAKINGS
PROPOSALS

THE SLEEPING BAG

THE EVENING - MORNING WINDOW

THE MEETING POINT

THE FOUNTAIN

PROVISIONAL ROOM

THE CHAIRCASE

THE STORYTELLING SQUARE

THE FIG TREE

11d

11e

Christoph Klemmt

A shift is the movement of two pieces against each other resulting in a change of relation between them. An analysis of rhythmic shifts in Ligeti's music informed the proposal of a house for train and plane spotters. The house shifts to give perfect views of the passing trains and planes. The large-scale movements of the city play out the composition of the house.
12a, b, c, d, e, f, g

Ema Bonifacic

Eight Moments of Determination: Two Makings, Six Proposals. Sound as a subconscious moment of access to a forgotten dream or a game strategy. Accumulation of sounds creates something in itself. The disused, elevated Kingsland Viaduct in East London becomes a testing ground: The Provisional Room and The Sleeping Bag are 1:1 makings opening a new relation with the track. Six Proposals offer the activities, places and people around and under the track access to the qualities of the property. The accumulation of proposals changes the presence of the track in the city as it begins to enter and occupy whole volumes, of buildings and bodies, around itself.
13a, b, c, d

Students
Ran Ankory, Ema Bonifacic, Nicholas Durr, Anastassis Economou, Christoph Klemmt, Kyoko Kobayashi, Natalia Kokotos, Takashi Nishibori, Alex Papadakis, Alexia Petridis, Bart Schoonderbeek, Yuka Suganami, Yeo Joong Yang

Unit Staff
David Racz, Andreas Lang

The unit would like to thank:
Carolina Bartram, Don Bates, John Bell, Valentin Bontjes van Beek, Mary Bowman, Jean Michel Crettaz, Celine Conderelli, Simon De Grussa, Sandra Denicke, Padmini Durr, Oliver Domeisen, Jamie Fobert, Osnat Harlap, Michael Hensel, Takuro Hoshino, Johannes Käferstein, Torange Khonsari, Kristina Krotov, Martha LaGess, Marcellus Letang, Petra Marguc, Michael McNamara, Gioia Meller Marcovicz, Mohsen Mostafavi, Diana Periton, Irénée Scalbert, Pascal Schöning, Trystram Smith, Charles Tashima, Michael Weinstock
www.aaschool.ac.uk/inter7

Intermediate Unit 8

Unit Master Charles Tashima

This year's unit work has sought to develop a diverse set of architectural projects that emerge from the interaction of two 'spatial structures' or sites: a particular, real one, **Bairro Lopes, Lisbon**, and an abstract one, **Topographical Fiction**. Both have evolved through cumulative processes and have encompassed terms including elaboration, adaption, emergence and transformation. The time-scale of each site has been relative: the first has involved *speeds* typically found in urban structures and the second has encompassed *speeds* that are more closely related to design processes. The work simultaneously addresses the larger scale of an urban system (1:1000/1:500), the structural, material and spatial scale of a fragment (1:100/1:50) as well as the non-scalar of programmatic and abstract spatial relations.

Fragments and Fields: Engaging Topographical Fictions
The first stage in the development of the work has been the construction of a topographical fiction – variously described as an artificial site, a city of contiguous rooms, a game board, or the continuous project. The terms *topography* and *fiction* are coupled in order to identify two salient conceptions involved in its fabrication. The first describes the importance of a pattern or 'field of inter-dependent relations' to discern a consistent strategy or system, while the other regards the importance of fiction (the compilation of de-situated facts) in cultivating innovation. Growing out of a series of incremental operations onto a 'memory surface' (a pre-existing condition upon which subsequent additions inflect or are inflected), this abstract project is a laboratory for architectural invention. New sites, invented within the construct of our mental and physical environments, are seen as archetypes: constructions of numerous like conditions. The making of the topographical fiction evolved during a period of two weeks in a sequence of exchanges of eight layered A2 panels among seven paired groups. Over time, each of the panels comprising a part of the whole was worked on by all groups. The rules of each group were simple ones and complexity was achieved via the coincidence of multiple operations. New spaces actively and passively responded along the structure of subsequent markings. The proposition here is that all forms of discovery and so-called invention arise out of combinatorial activity – placing things, ideas, events, and materials in new, unpredictable and unforeseen constellations. 'To create consists precisely in not making useless combinations but in making those which are useful and which are only a small minority. Invention is discernment, choice.' (H. Poincaré) The topographical fiction is one such inventive territory comprised of the re-ordering of elements to reveal unexpected relationships between facts, long known, but wrongly believed to be incompatible with each other.

Bairro Lopes, Lisbon and the Programme of Temporary Living
This second site was introduced in the latter half of the year and was presented as an integral part of a continuous line of a single process. Bairro Lopes, located at a periphery, is a large abandon area, a tattered seam in the dense fabric of the city of Lisbon. It is a lost space trapped between the historic centre and more recent peripheral developments, including housing projects and most notably Expo '98. Predominantly filled with illegal housing (favelas) and uncultivated vegetation, it is one of the last remaining pockets of un-built land within walking distance of the centre, and will play an important role in the city's revitalisation. Similar to that of the 'topographical fiction', the current condition has been the result of the coincidence of a series of independent developments that has evolved via a legacy of heterogeneous change. The area includes a highly modulated topography, a wide mix of housing, a range of public functions such as a fish market, sports fields, shops, and a military communications centre. All of these elements have been incrementally added according to need, availability and economy. As the topographical fiction, this site was used as a Petri dish to explore potential strategies for urban development. Our approach to the site places importance on urban densification as a critical element in the maintenance and confirmation of the historical heritage of the city as well as the cultural and social qualities inherent in urban density. Most projects have included the element of time and were projective of future developments. The given programme of temporary living was left conceptually open to include hotels, demountable architecture and housing for short, medium and long-term use. The specificity of this programme was further defined by additional public programmes including sports facilities, markets, parks and gardens.

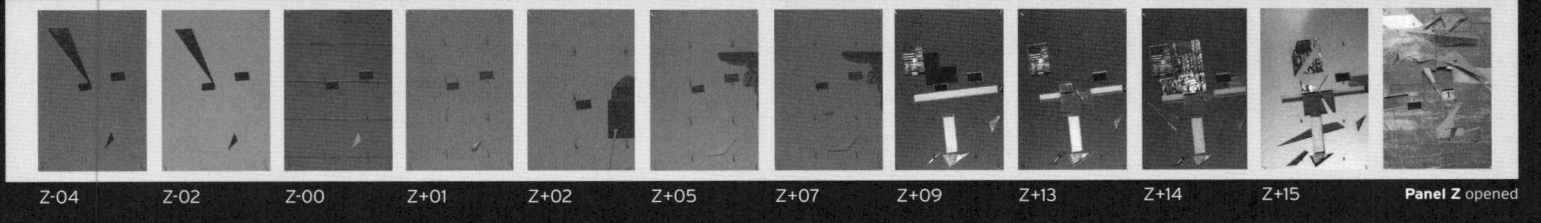

| Z-04 | Z-02 | Z-00 | Z+01 | Z+02 | Z+05 | Z+07 | Z+09 | Z+13 | Z+14 | Z+15 | **Panel Z** opened |

Students
Tiffany Beriro, Edouard Cabay, Andrea di Stefano,
Amanda Friedman, Charu Gandhi, Therese Hegland,
Aleksandra Jaeschke, Philippa Jelfs, Anna Kubelik,
Nazila Maghzian, Julia Mauser, Anna Ohlin, Nazaneen Schaffaie,
Andreas Stahre, Stephanie Talbot, Jin Bok Wee

Visiting Critics
Peter Beard, John Bell, Valentin Bontjes van Beek, Paula Cadima,
Javier Castañon, Eva Castro, Jean Michel Crettaz, Oliver
Domeissen, Zvi Efrat, Hanif Kara, Homa Farjadi, Jane Harrison,
Michael Hensel, Takuro Hoshino, Gillian Horn, Andrew Houlton,
Johannes Käferstein, Holger Kehne, Martha LaGess, Andreas Lang,
Marina Lathouri, George Liaropoulos-Legendre, C.J. Lim, Morten
Ludviksen, Raul Moura, Mohsen Mostafavi, Ciro Najle, David Racz,
Pascal Schöning, Stephen Taylor, Stephan Truby, Erik Wegerhoff,
Mike Weinstock, Eyal Weizman

Special thanks to
Miguel Branco, Paula Cadima, Douglas Gauthier, Ines Lobo,
Jose Paulo dos Santos, Matthias Reese

Group Work **Topographical Fiction** (12-31 October 2000) eight A2 panels

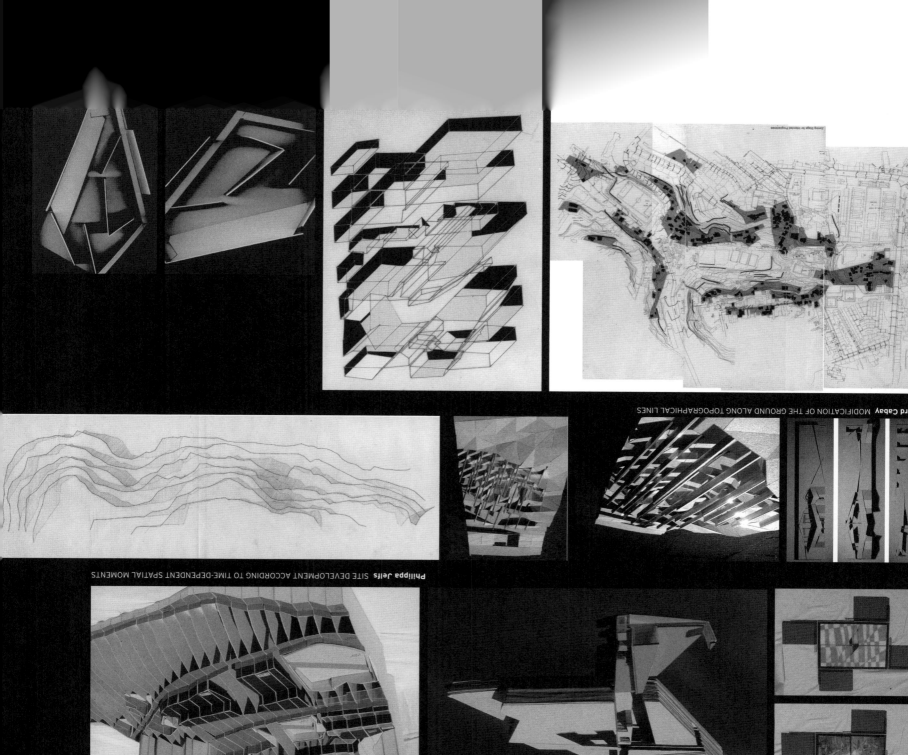

...rd Cabay MODIFICATION OF THE GROUND ALONG TOPOGRAPHICAL LINES

Philippa Jelfs SITE DEVELOPMENT ACCORDING TO TIME-DEPENDENT SPATIAL MOMENTS

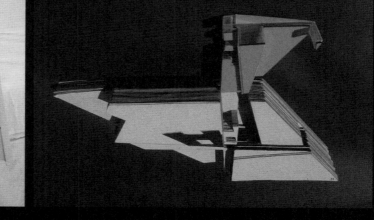

Aleksandra Jaeschke EMERGING R[oo]MS-- THRESHOLD DWELLINGS

One dwelling and a community place

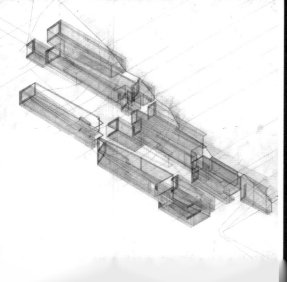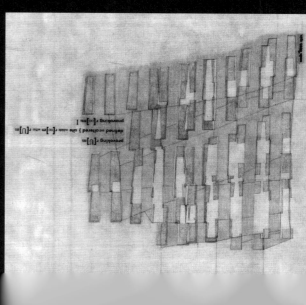

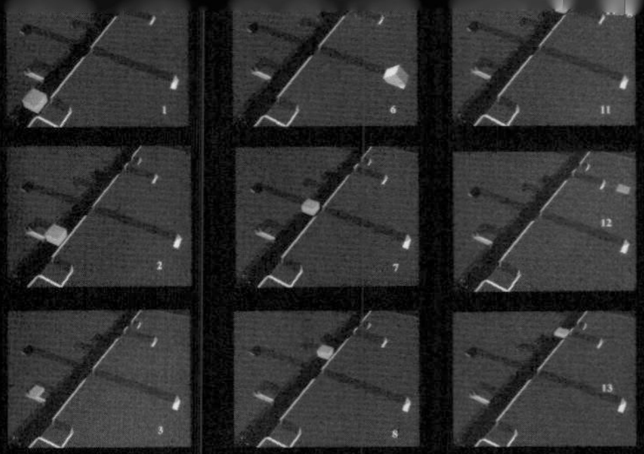

Therese Hegland SEQUENCE OF MOVEMENT STOPPAGES

Andreas Stahre SITES OF INCLUSION/EXCLUSION, EXPLORING MULTIPLE BOUNDA

Nazila Maghzian THE SPACE OF ORANGE-, WHITE-, AND BLUENESS: STRATEGIES OF RELATIONS

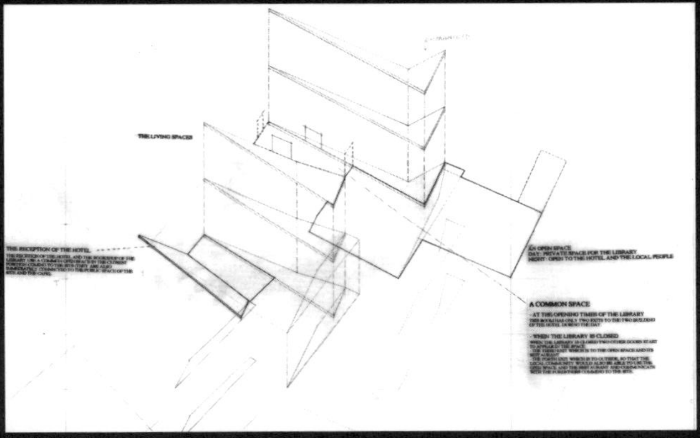

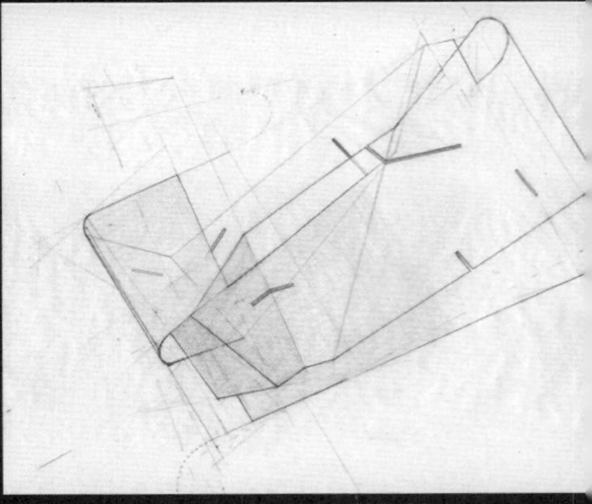

Jin Bok Wee LINES OF INFINITE REFERENCE

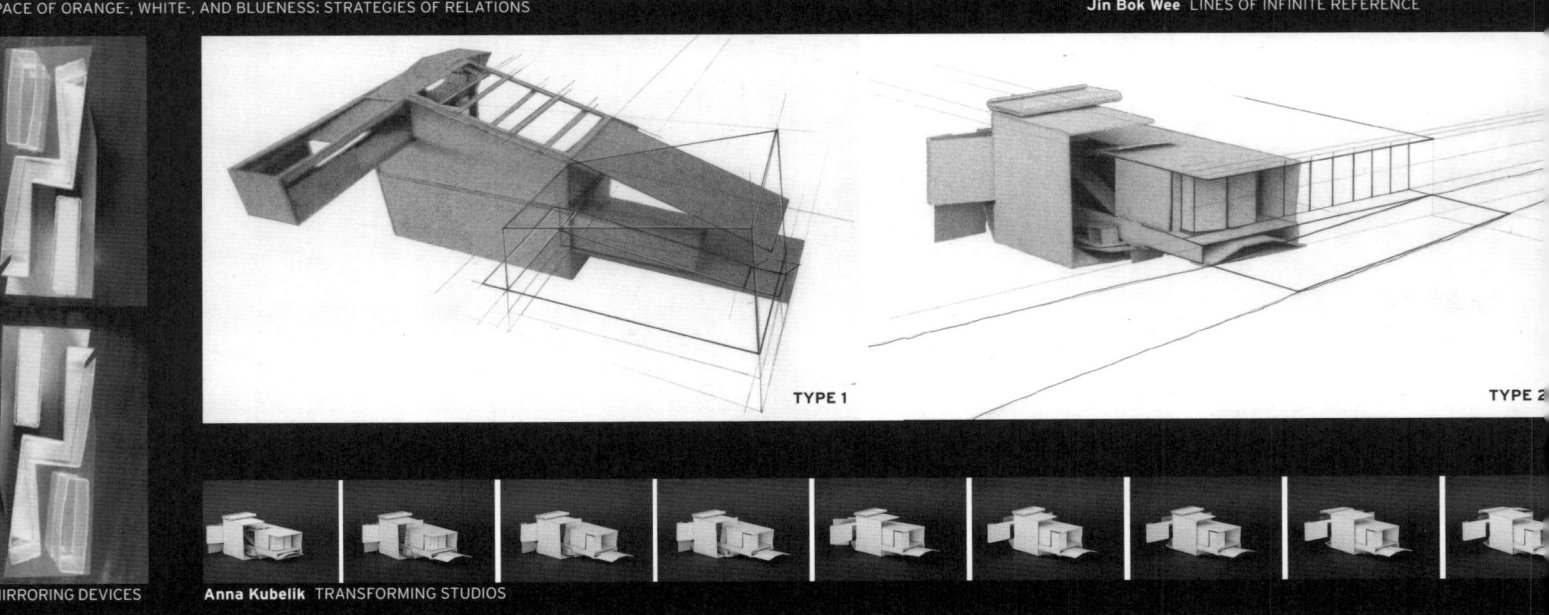

TYPE 1

TYPE 2

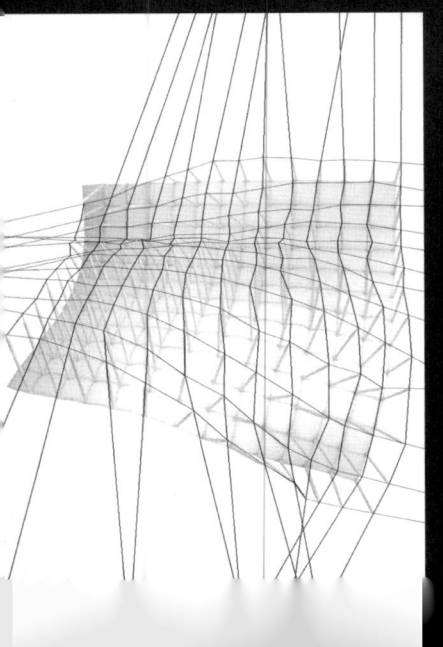

Tiffany Beriro MIRRORING DEVICES

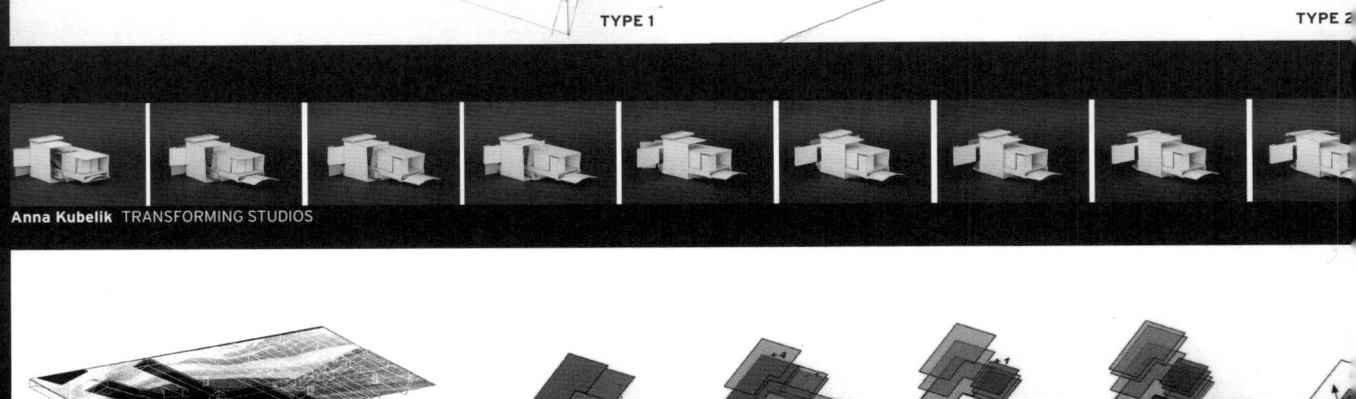

Anna Kubelik TRANSFORMING STUDIOS

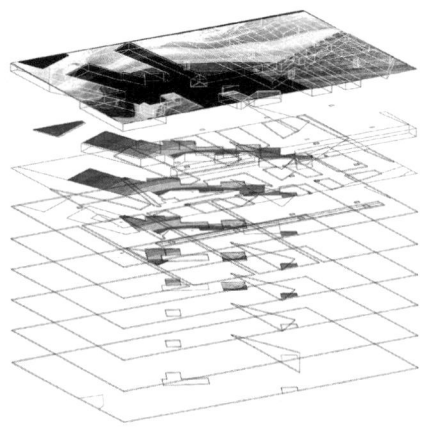

topo fiction panel V

fallow field rotation/phase 1–phase 7

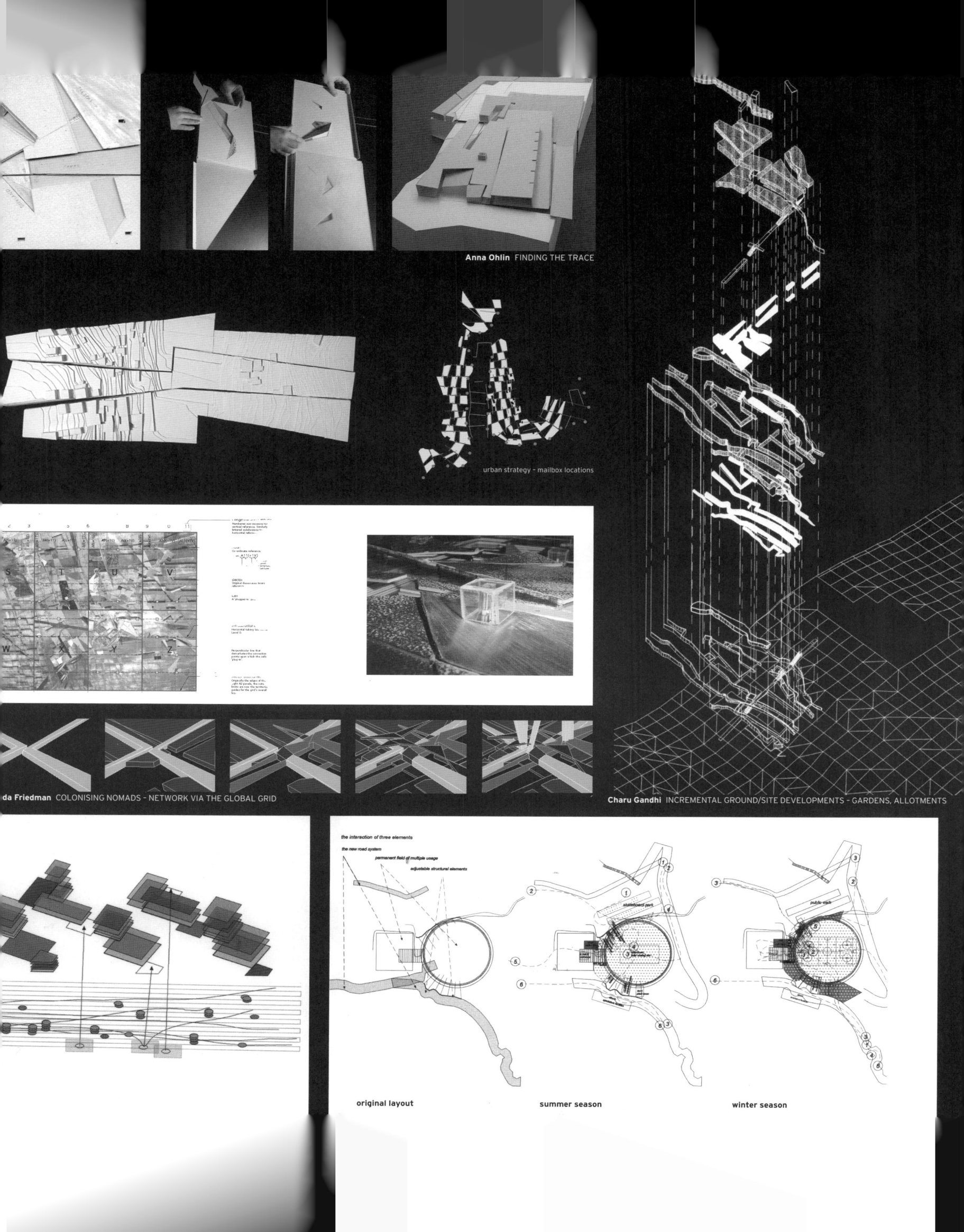

Anna Ohlin FINDING THE TRACE

urban strategy - mailbox locations

Charu Gandhi INCREMENTAL GROUND/SITE DEVELOPMENTS - GARDENS, ALLOTMENTS

da Friedman COLONISING NOMADS - NETWORK VIA THE GLOBAL GRID

the interaction of three elements

the new road system

permanent field of multiple usage

adjustable structural elements

original layout   summer season   winter season

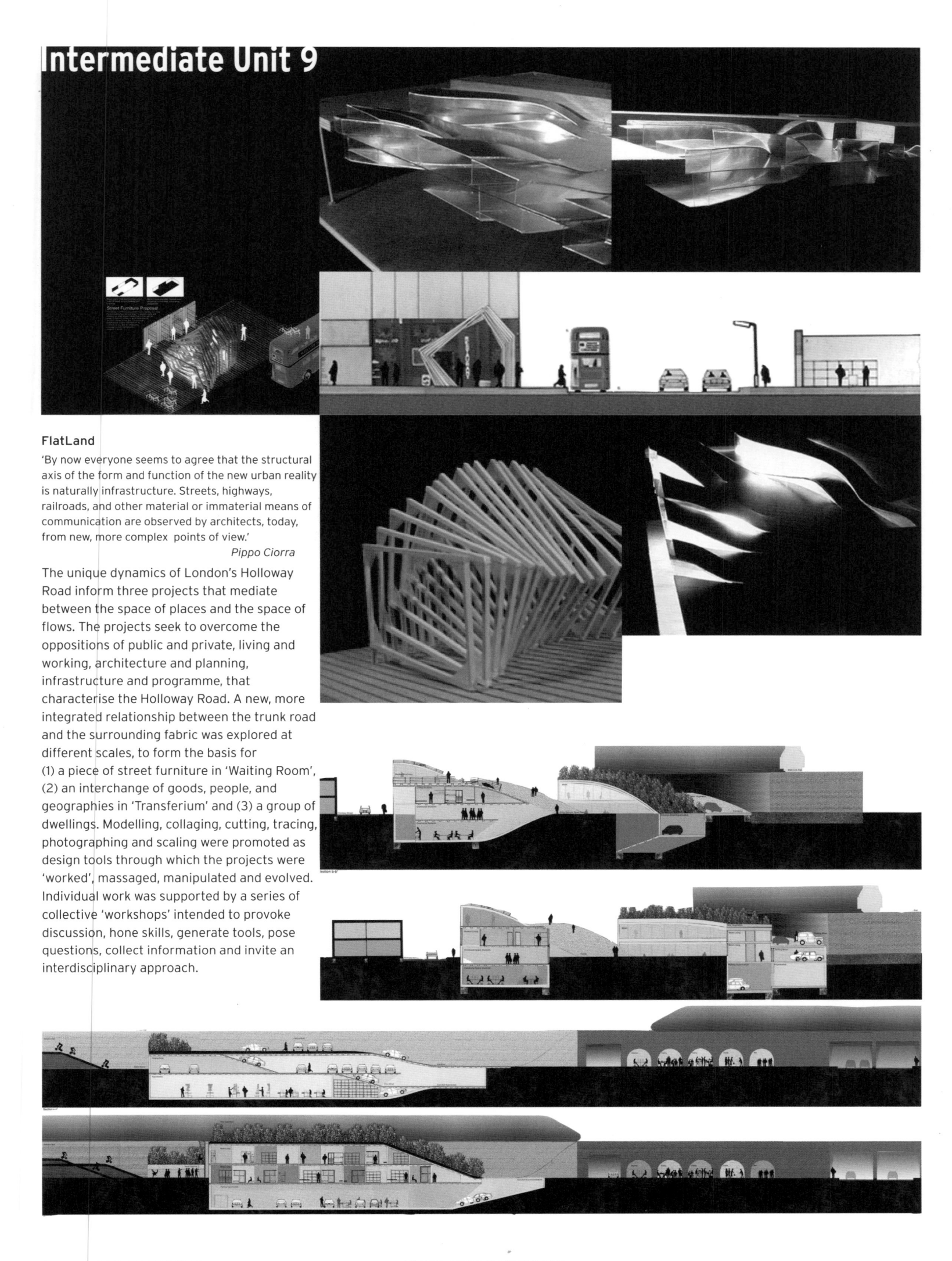

FlatLand

'By now everyone seems to agree that the structural axis of the form and function of the new urban reality is naturally infrastructure. Streets, highways, railroads, and other material or immaterial means of communication are observed by architects, today, from new, more complex points of view.'

Pippo Ciorra

The unique dynamics of London's Holloway Road inform three projects that mediate between the space of places and the space of flows. The projects seek to overcome the oppositions of public and private, living and working, architecture and planning, infrastructure and programme, that characterise the Holloway Road. A new, more integrated relationship between the trunk road and the surrounding fabric was explored at different scales, to form the basis for (1) a piece of street furniture in 'Waiting Room', (2) an interchange of goods, people, and geographies in 'Transferium' and (3) a group of dwellings. Modelling, collaging, cutting, tracing, photographing and scaling were promoted as design tools through which the projects were 'worked', massaged, manipulated and evolved. Individual work was supported by a series of collective 'workshops' intended to provoke discussion, hone skills, generate tools, pose questions, collect information and invite an interdisciplinary approach.

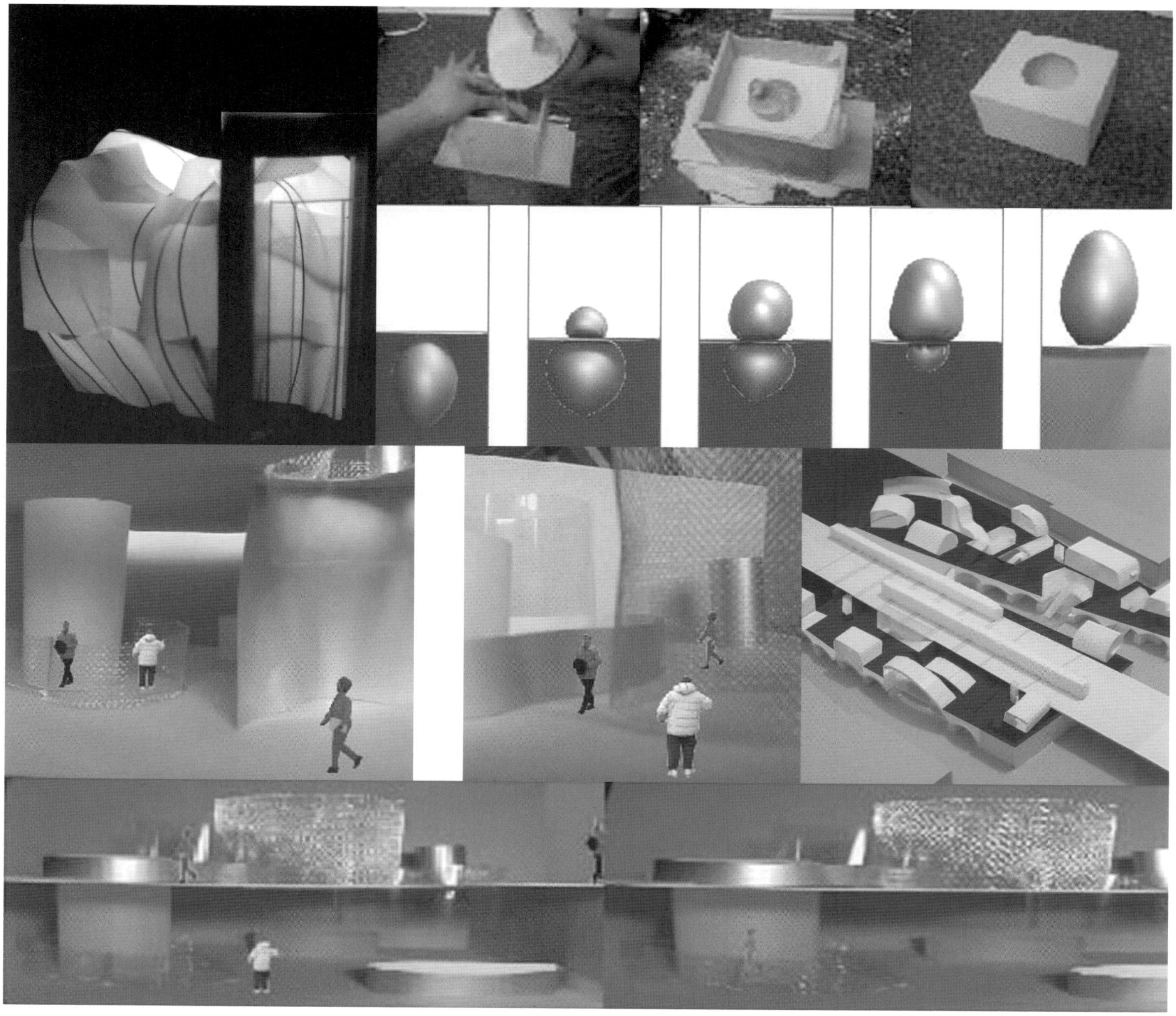

'Incorporate' – Waiting Room

Students chose from a series of selected sites along a fictional bus route. These sites were postcards of the trunk-road experience: Gaps, asphalt, and the still-born remnants of a bright new future. They were encouraged to exploit the location and its infrastructure, inventing a programme, to accompany a bus stop and a conductor's office, that maximised the time-based performance of the project and supported public life. Ultimately the proposal was shaped as a mingling of the conflicting conditions of the Holloway Road and the ambitions of the high street to form a new public space of interchange.

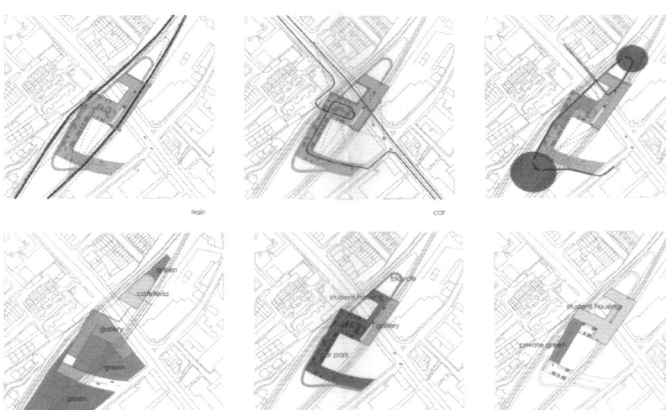

'Insinuate' – Transferium

A site that bridges the mainline rail track and spans a 'thick section' delineated by a nineteenth-century viaduct, a university tower, housing blocks and Holloway Road Tube Station, was selected for the creation of a 'topographical' transferium. Park for a moment, stay a while, stop for a bit, eat a bite, buy a thing, pop in for tea. Sometimes parking, sometimes storage, sometimes programme, this modulating plane becomes the site for the third project, the invention of housing. Internal and external conditions shaped the landscaped proposals, the objective being to examine the transitional properties needed to move between fast and slow, public and private.

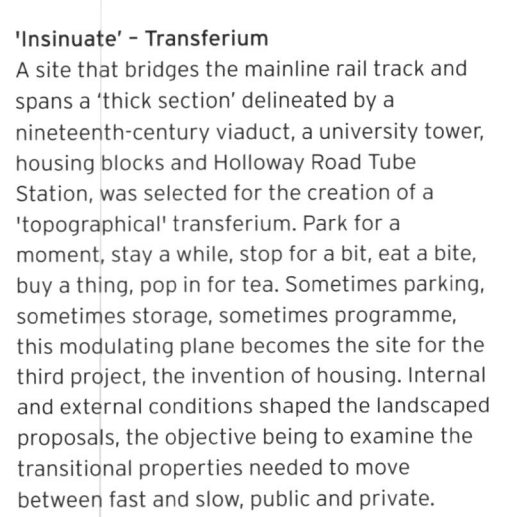

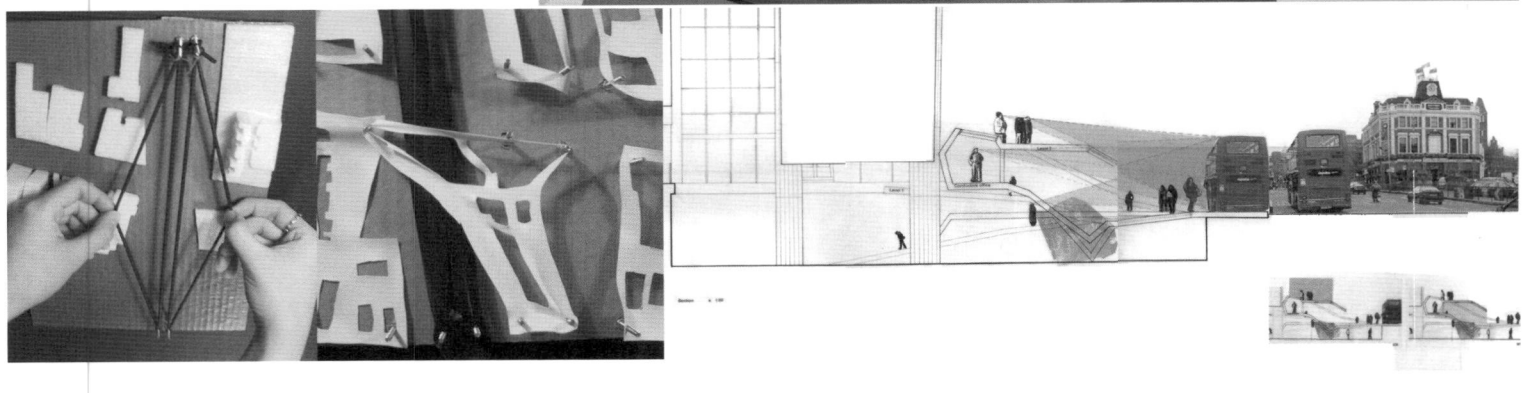

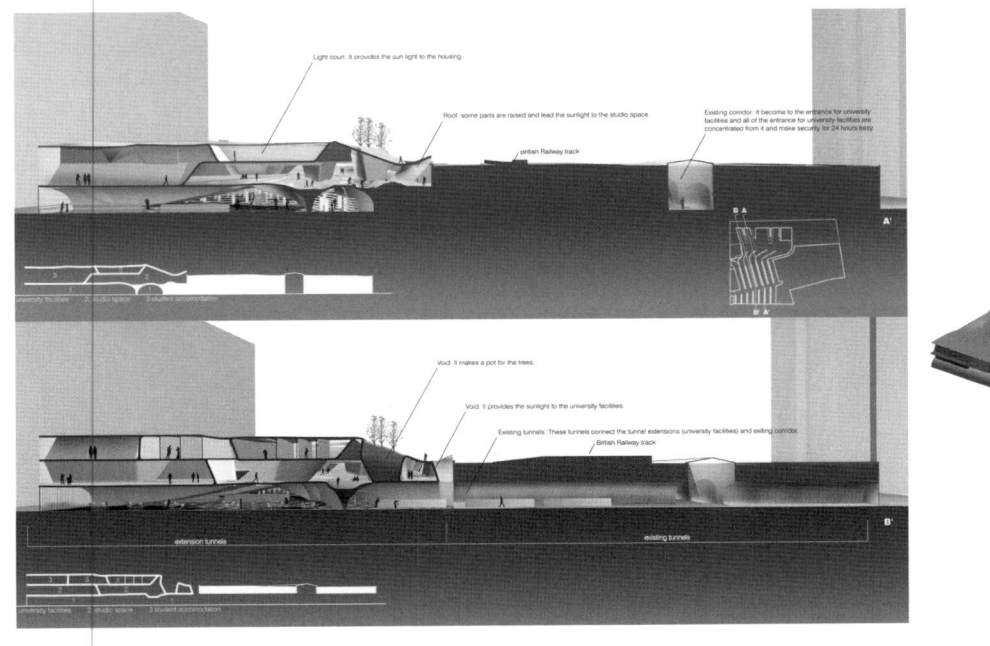

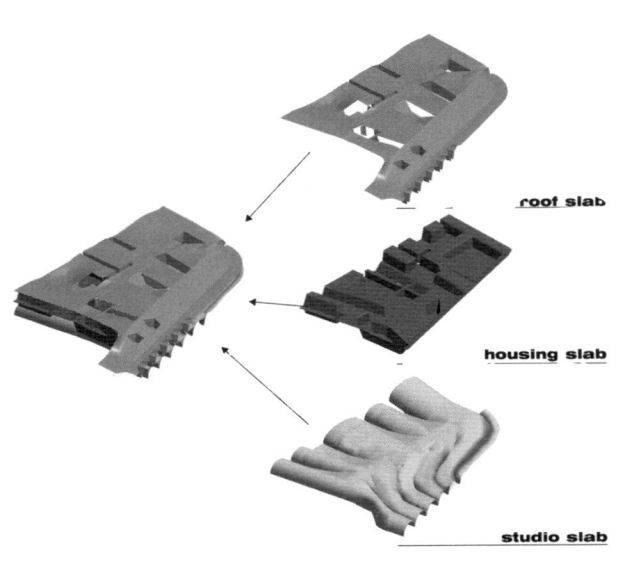

root slab

housing slab

studio slab

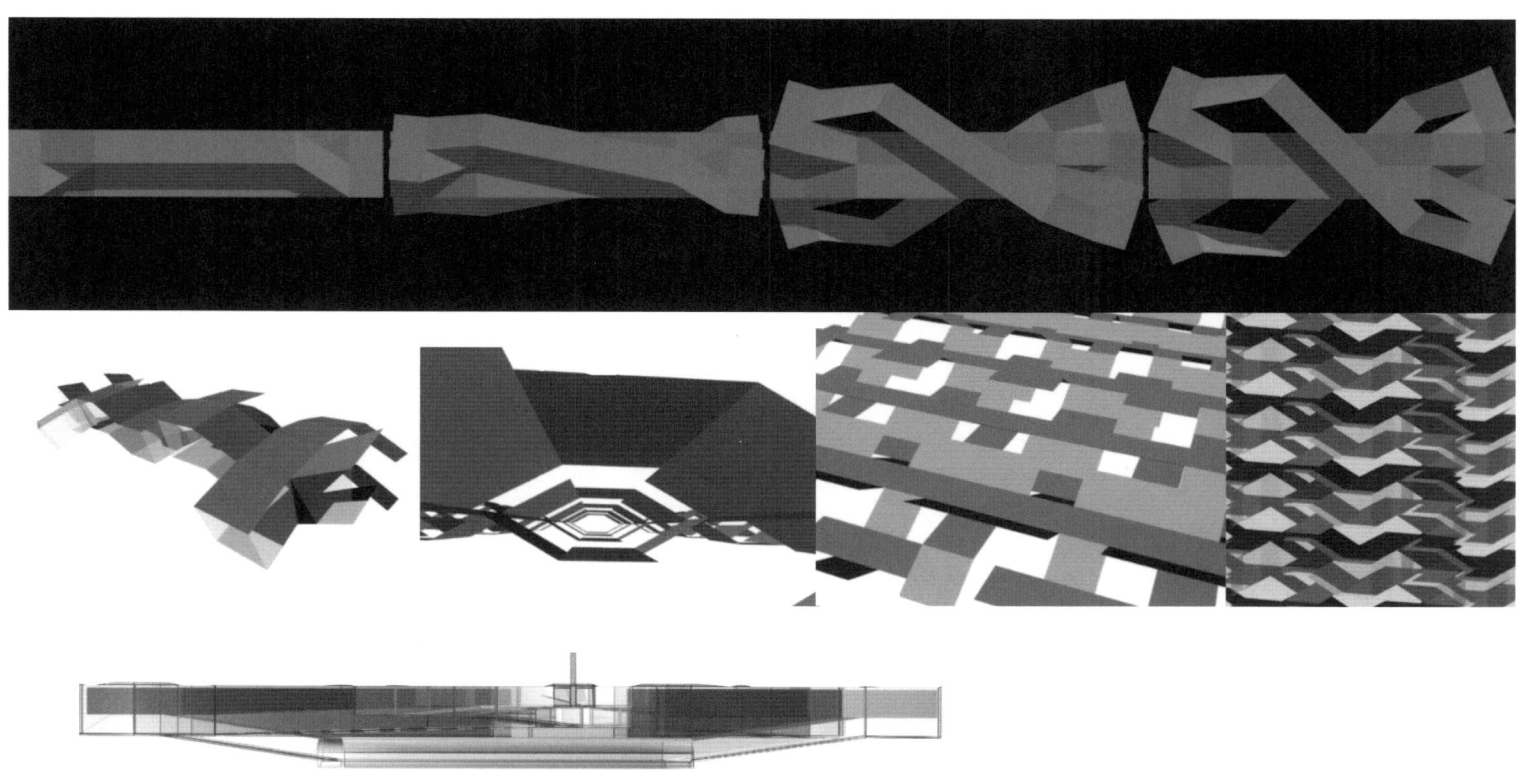

Unit Staff
Dominic Papa and Jonathan Woodroffe

Students
Yoo Ran Hong, Leonidas Lazarakis, Julian
Loffler, Chihiro Nakagawa, Miki Nakayasu,
Michie Shibusawa, Takumi Sugimoto,
Yee Seng Tan, Yeena Yoon.

The unit would like to thank
Larry Barth, Javier Castañon, Rosamund
Diamond, Luke Engleback, Mark Hemel, Hugo
Hinsley, Andrew Houlton, Mohsen Mostafavi,
Alex de Rijke, Charles Tashima, Stephen Taylor

Intermediate Unit 10

on the make

After establishing our path through the making and unmaking of bodysuits we turned towards the valley of Mutten in the Swiss Alps, where we implemented the 'making-tool' to introduce a bridge/guesthouse connecting the villages of Mutten and Solas. We used our toolboxes to determine materials and structure while travelling along conceptual paths.

Intermediate Unit 10 considers making and unmaking to be the driving force towards architectural articulation, tectonic invention and tactile poetics.

Students

Cecilia Ramirez Corzo, Maria Kouloumbrip, Aoi Kume, Marie Langen, Jordi Rafols Lloret, Aya Maeda, Yusuke Miyake, Hayssam Moubayed, Hoi Chi Ng, Wan Sophonpanich, Paul La Tourelle, Juan Pablo Trejo, Naoko Yamada, Assaf Zucker

Special Thanks

Jürg Conzett - Chris Leubkeman, Javier Castañon, Jean Michel Crettaz, Ros Diamond, Antony Gormley, Takuro Hoshino, Anderson Inge, Martha LaGess, Andreas Lang, Urs Meister, Mohsen Mostafavi, David Racz, Goswin Schwendinger, Christian Spencer-Davis, Tony Swannell, Charles Tashima, Silvia Venuti, Mike Weinstock

Unit Staff

Johannes Käferstein, Jamie Fobert

JRL

JRL

Bodysuit Tool

Two materials of your choice will be crafted into a bodysuit. One will be connecting, the other connected. Disrespect everything you think you know. Respect what you discover through observation and experimentation. Think about scale and your new appearance within a room. How do you move? What do you move? How do you want to be perceived? How do you influence your environment? Dressing and undressing will be part of your presentation.

Transformsuit Tool

We will be going on a field trip. Unmake your first 'make' by changing it to a suitable size for transportation. You might have to insert cuts in order to do this. Before cutting think about reassembly. Each single piece has to keep the formal qualities of the whole. Think about concept. Draw the 'unmake' to scale 1:10. Map your transformation lines. Use a pencil or a computer. Format A2.

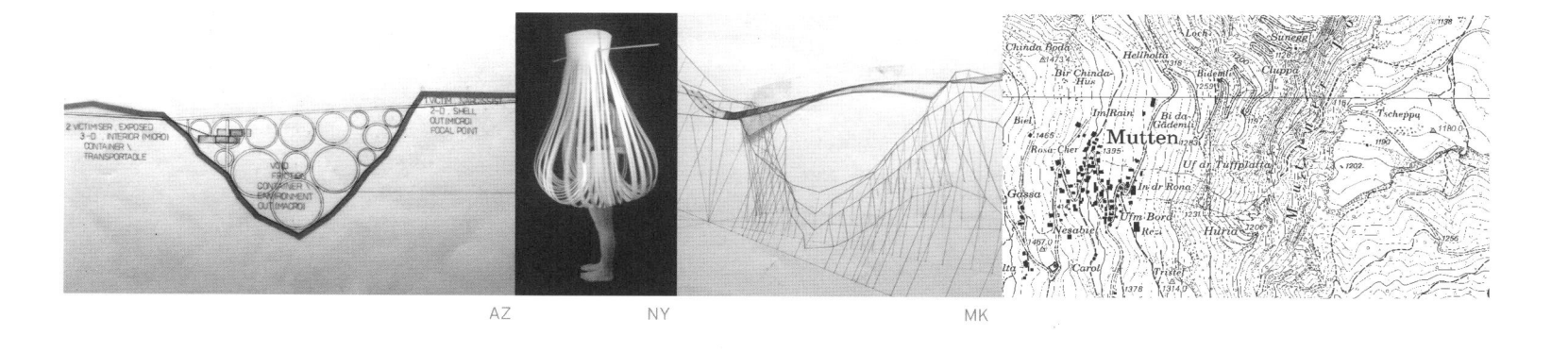

AZ   NY   MK

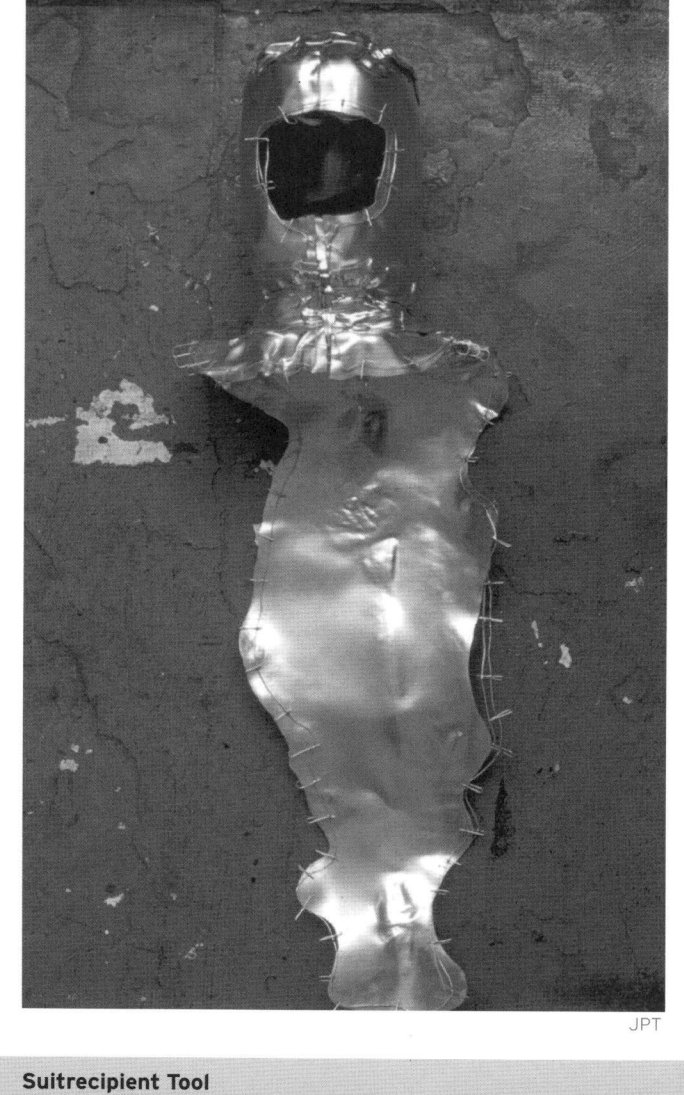

JPT

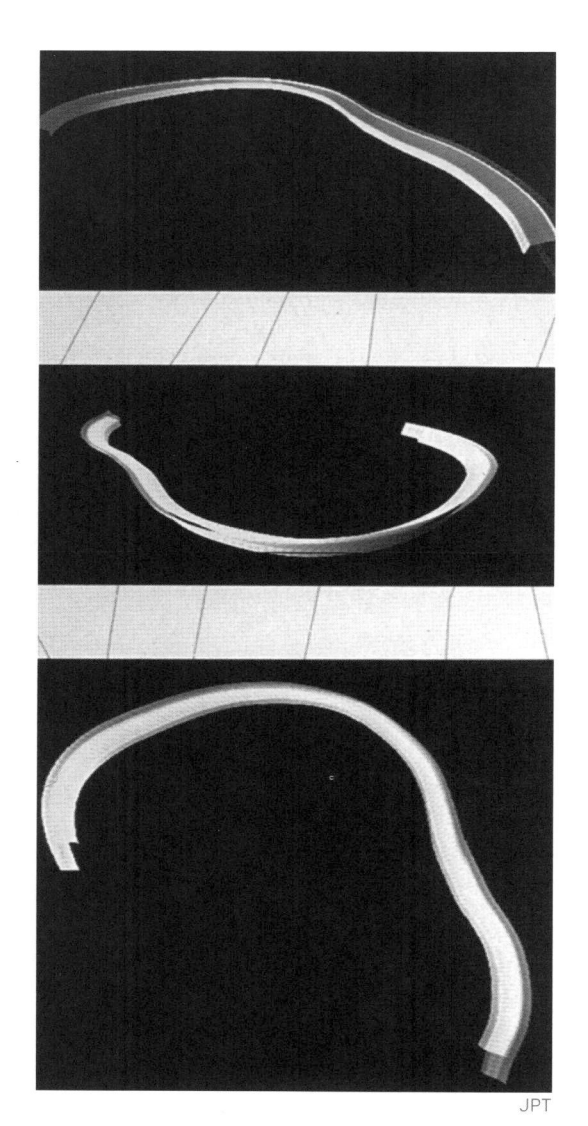

JPT

Suitrecipient Tool

We are working through physical lines of thought by a process of making and unmaking. We are creating tools to produce new tools that will enable us to establish our conceptual path. The conceptual approach is undergoing formal transformation through fabrication, confronting the laws of quality and character that are part of being material.

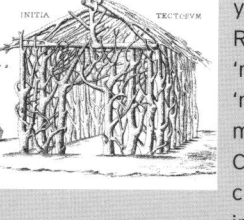

Your third 'make' will be a recipient/container to give room to your previous 'makes'. Use an appropriate material to underline the conceptual criteria of your work. Think about the meaning of a tool.

Use drawing as a research tool for your undertakings. Your presentation should visualise your conceptual path.

Pathperception Tool

Goswin Schwendinger will join us for a one-week photographic workshop. Use photographic methods and tools to represent your three 'makes' and their line of thought. Regard your representations as the fourth 'make', consistent with this series of 'makes'. Think about the contained environment in a photographic representation. Create an environment for your 'makes' including yourself. Bring yourself back as the instigator and victim. Consider the positive and the negative path, the visible and the invisible object/subject. Work with moods.

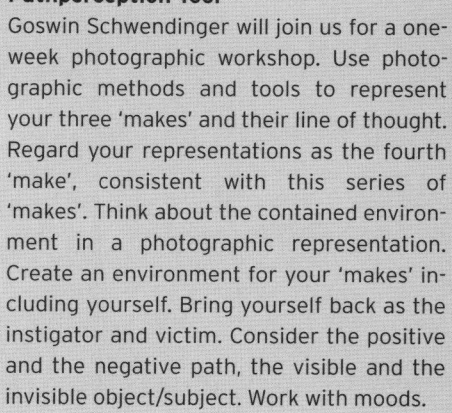

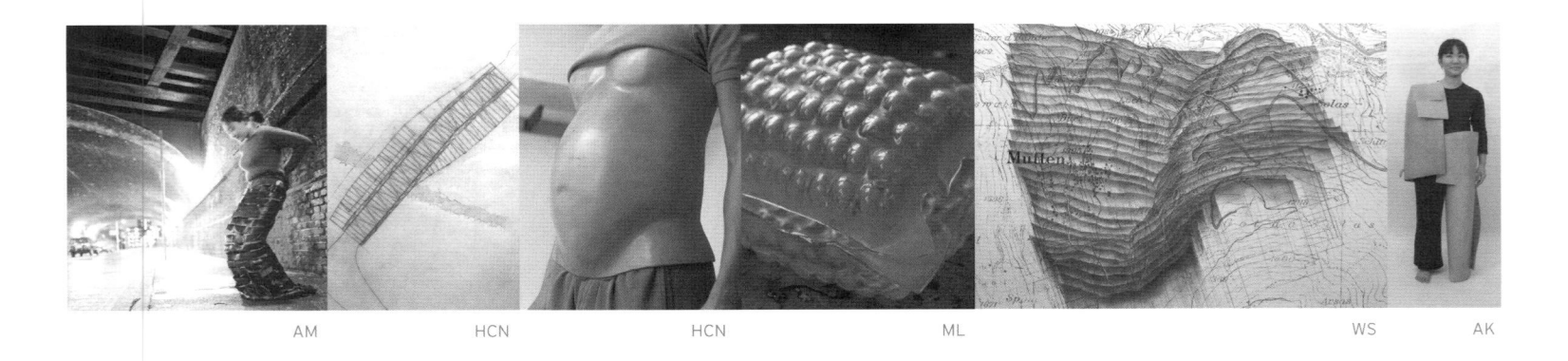

AM   HCN   HCN   ML   WS   AK

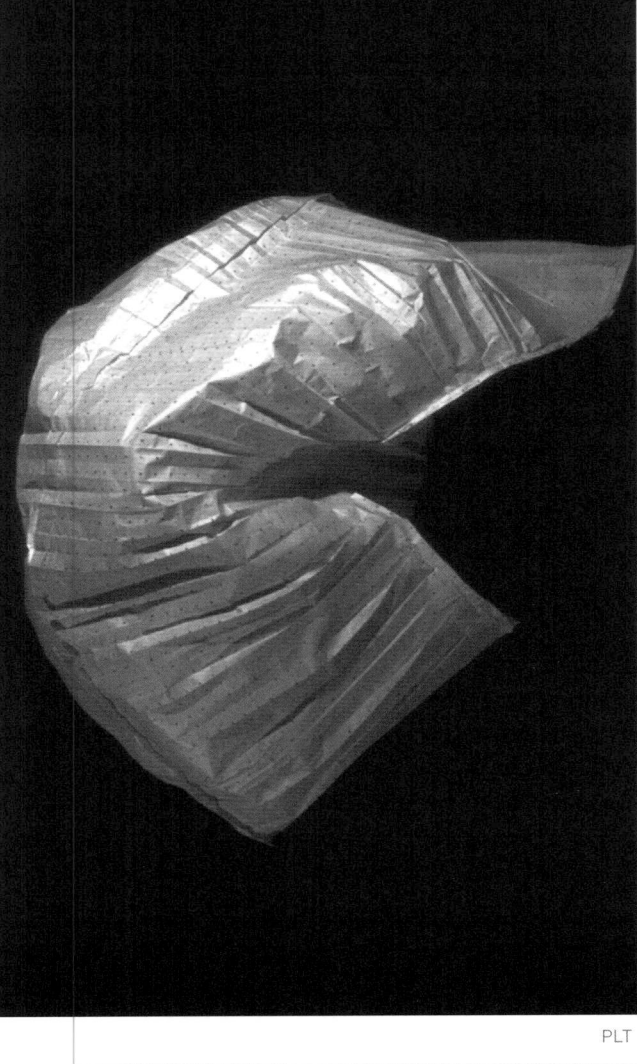

PLT

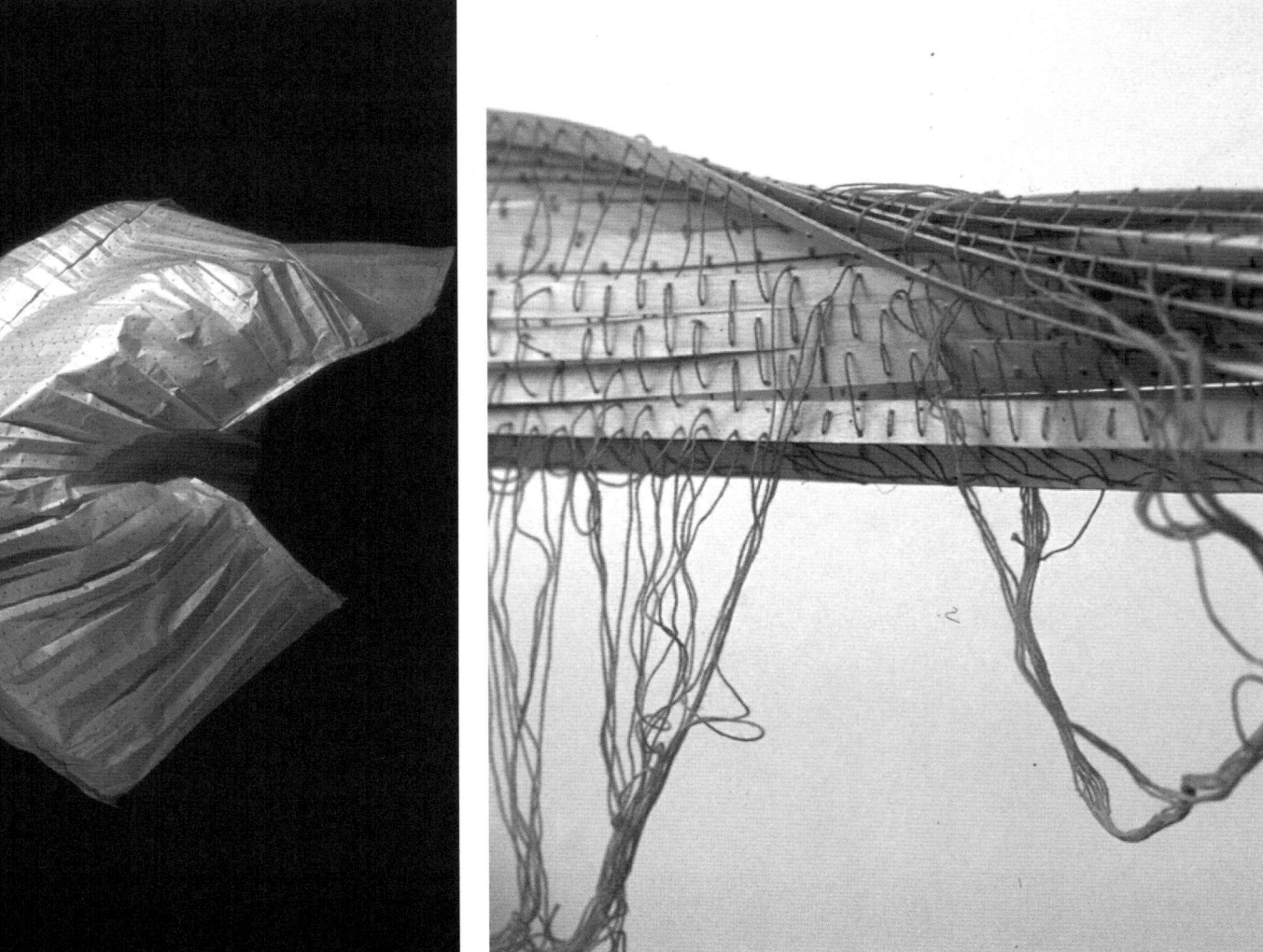

PLT

Implementation Tool

You have been travelling on lines of thought, in some way or other, throughout the first term. You have established a number of tools for confronting an architectural project situated in the Swiss Alps. Describe your conceptual path and the way you gave it a physical body. Articulate the making, the unmaking, the enclosing and the search for a suitable environment in your work. Consider the positive and the negative path, the visible and the invisible object/subject. Redefine the meaning of tool. Type two A4 pages. You will be presenting your essay to the unit. Illustrate with a slide that shows your underlying thoughts.

Tool to Tool

Consider your essay as part of your toolbox. We will set two tables at a distance of one metre apart. Their height is 0.75m. Be aware of the volumetric void between the tables.

Span the gap according to the path you are travelling on.

Reconsider the positive and the negative, the visible and the invisible object/subject.

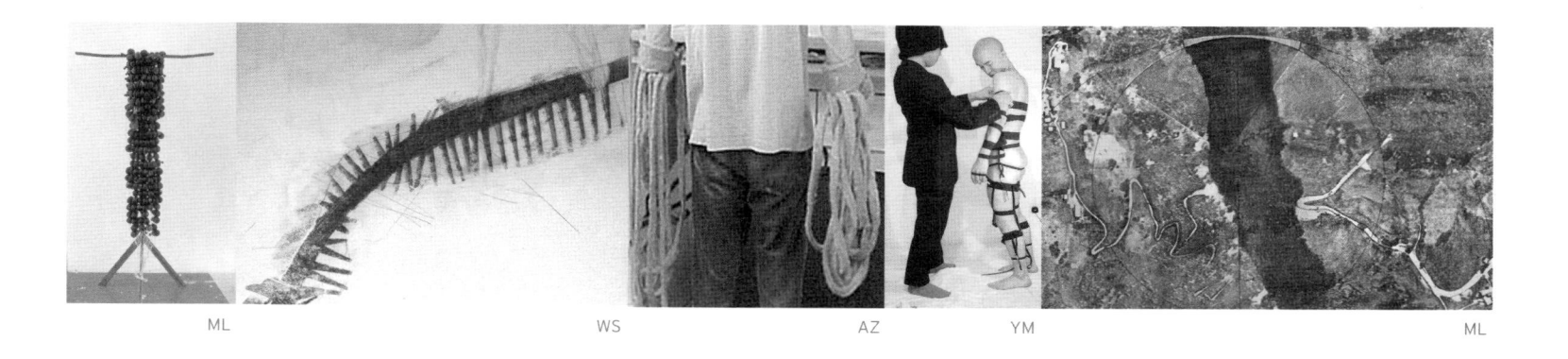

ML   WS   AZ   YM   ML

ML

ML

Bridge

You have seen the gorge of Mutten and the surrounding alpine landscape. You have built a site model at the scale of 1:500.

Introduce a bridge and a small hotel connecting Mutten and Obermutten to the new road descending into the valley of Schin. Choose your site with care. Evaluate the height at which you cross the gorge. How do you access the bridge? Use your toolbox to determine materials and structure, travel along your conceptual path. Programme for the hotel: 16 double bedrooms, baths, showers and toilets along corridors, kitchen, eating room, bar. Present a site plan at 1:1000, plans, sections, elevations, perspectives at 1:500, and a model to be set in the landscape model at 1:500.

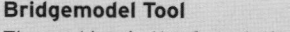

Bridgemodel Tool

The making is the foundation of our course. How far is making informing your bridge project? This week we are working in collaboration with Christian Spencer-Davis of A-Models. You will be building a bridge model at scale 1:100. This 'make' will serve as a basis for your final model at the end of the year. Draw construction sketches at scale 1:100 according to how you imagine building your bridge. Choose materials which conceptually join bridge and bodysuit. Discuss your ideas with Christian Spencer-Davis. Start building immediately. A photo of you and your bridge-make will be taken at the end of the workshop.

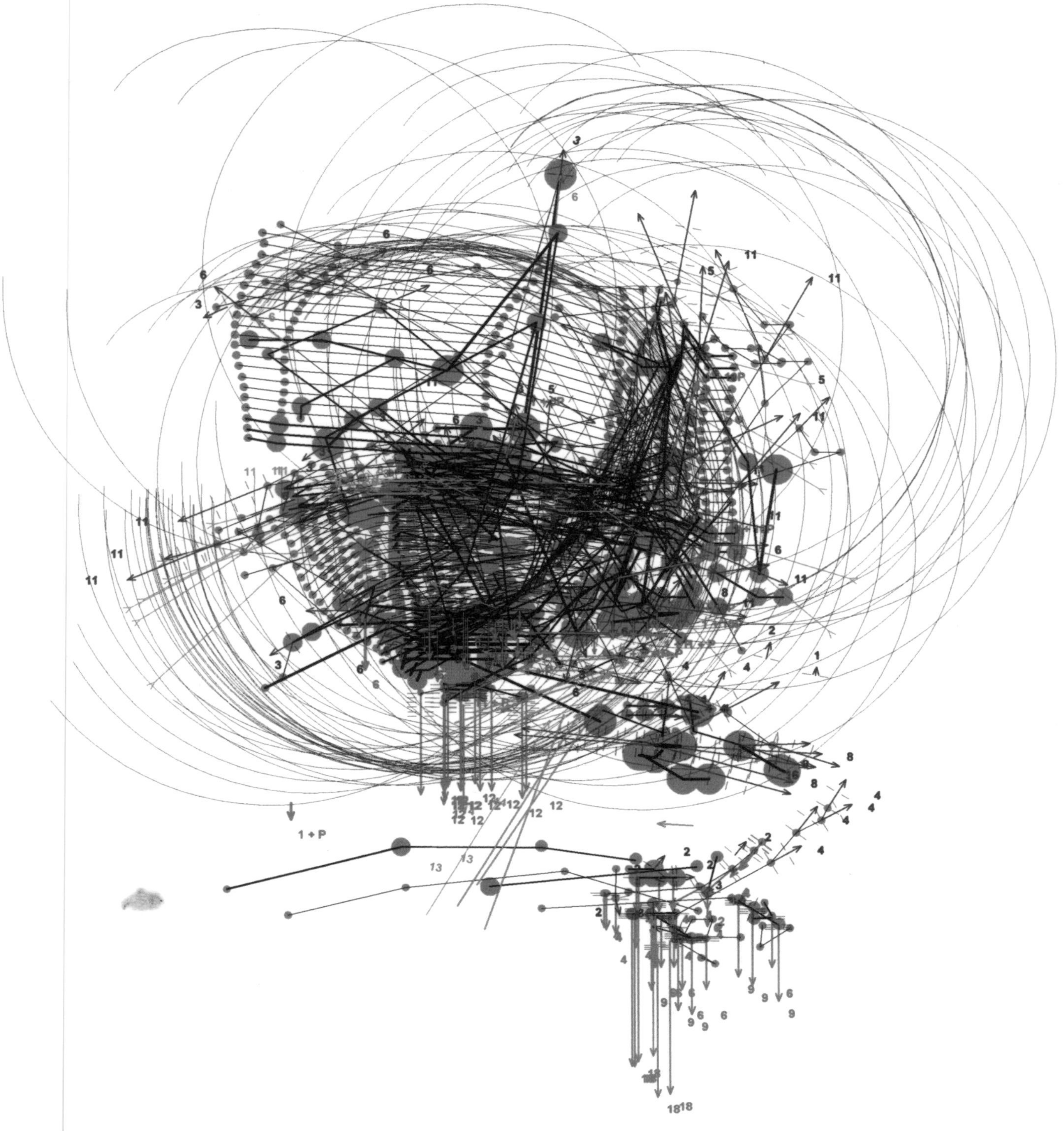
1 + P

DIPLOMA SCHOOL->

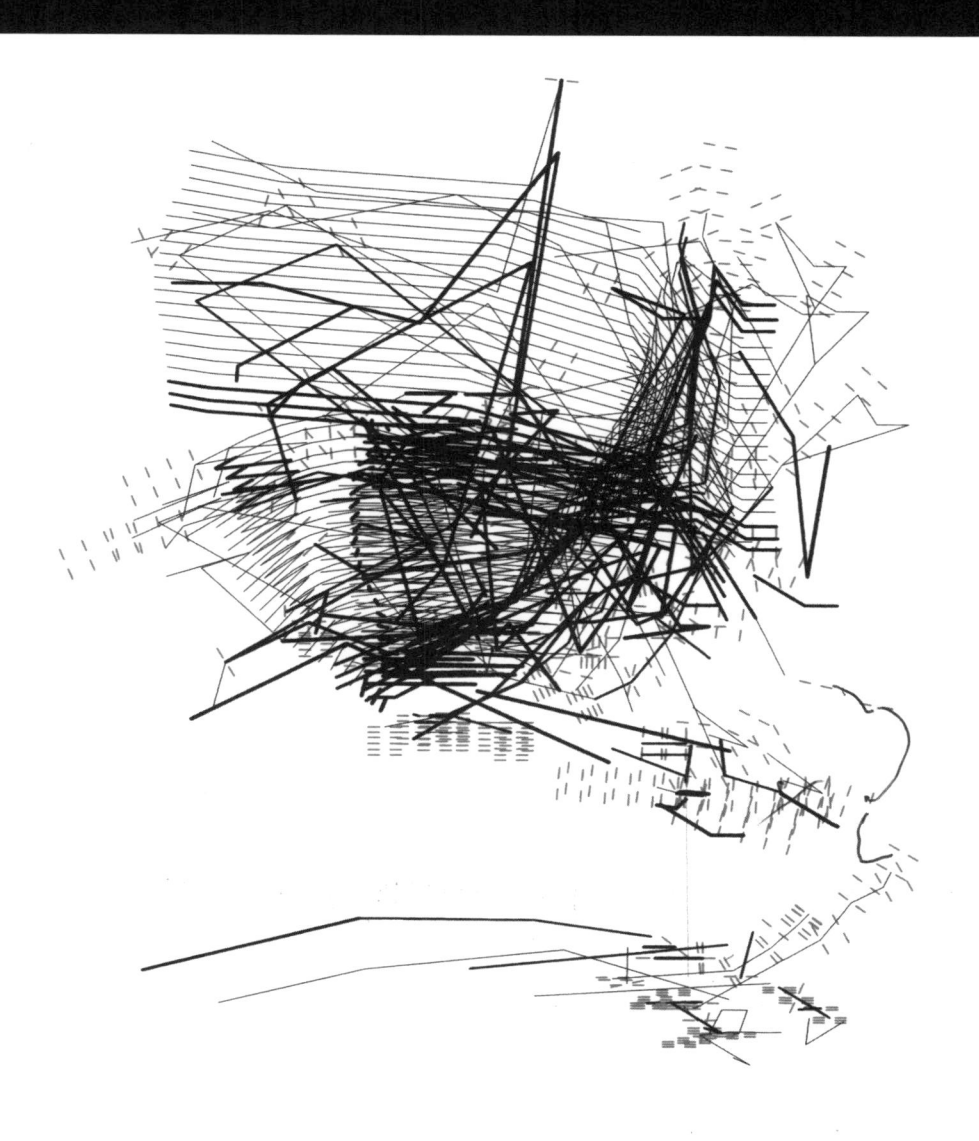

Diploma Unit 1

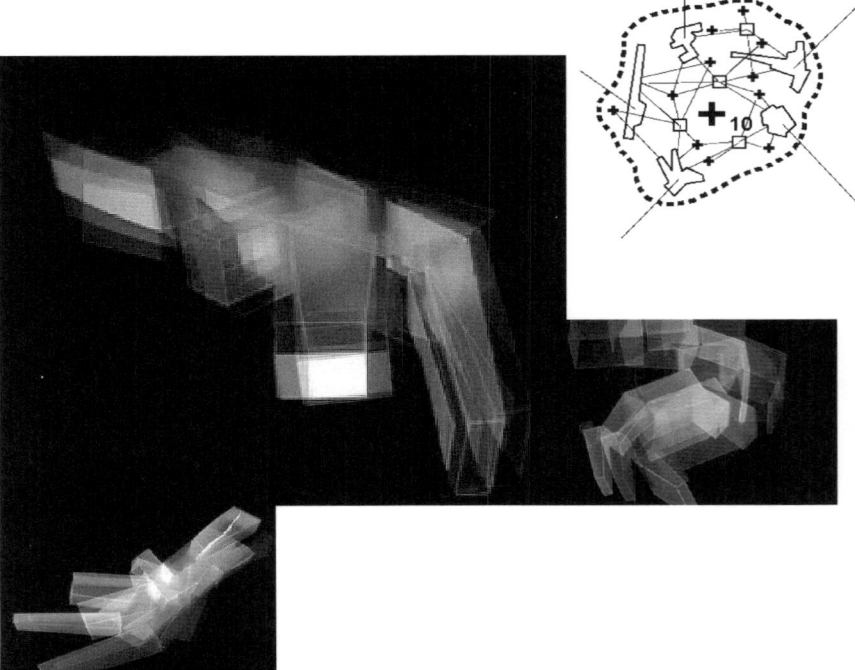

ADAPTABLE ORGANISM - Hiro Nishizawa
topic: poor diversity of small business
life-form: small businesses and self-generated mutual support system
architecture: small adaptable units located in the former docks stimulate
interaction among the existing and new small businesses and instigate
self-organisation

s-world

Current debates over globalisation issues dominate various fields of study, including the discourse in architecture and urbanism. Design policies for the living environment fluctuate between opposing positions. Globalisation is viewed by some as a positive, system-oriented phenomenon; others experience an emotionally driven repulsion against this phenomenon. Depending on the position, our world is painted in different colours. Each approach fails to address the opposing viewpoint as an integral part of the ambivalent nature of the same subject.

topic

Our site, the Isle of Dogs, mirrors the contradictory viewpoints that appear to provoke many of the existing conflicts: social segregation and economic deprivation, ill-coordinated urban planning, unsustainable policies, lack of distinctive urban culture, etc. The two opposing views, both valid in their own right, lack a faculty for dealing with the complex and paradoxical nature of the phenomenon of change. The approach we are proposing is neither global nor local but

ARTIFICIAL WATER LIFE - Nicolo Stassano
topic: value system which operates in two realms; one symbolic, the other physical
life-form: paradoxical entities which operate in both realms
architecture: a series of architectural components, prototypes of water purification
and public platforms thrive on the existing conflicts of the use of the water space in
the Isle of Dogs docks

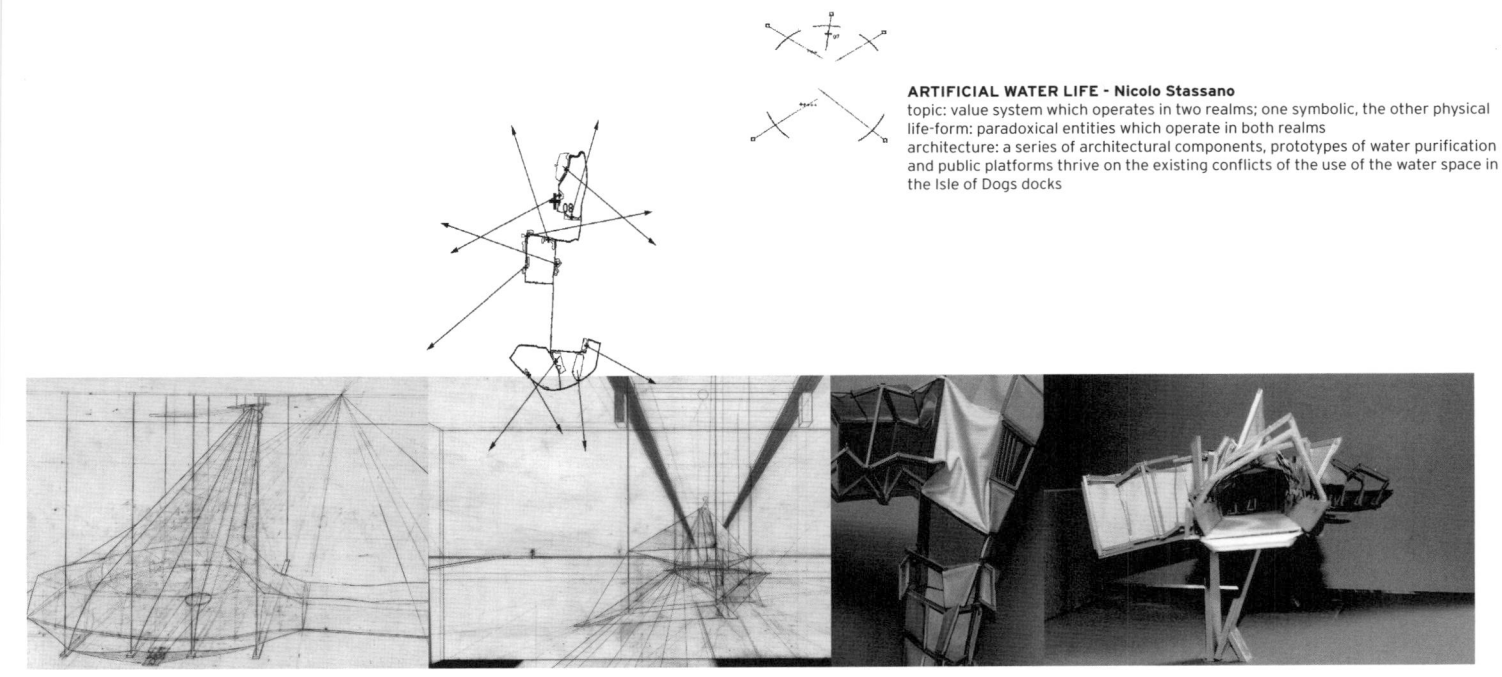

BODY-MIND SPACE - Lyzadie Renault
topic: rigid urban components
life-form: itinerant groups stretch existing social system to its limit
architecture: an elevated walkway for various sports programmes and recreation spaces introduce a new layer into the city, designed to link and transform various unconnected pocket sites

rapid adaptable urban programmes   artificial life-forms and ecosystem

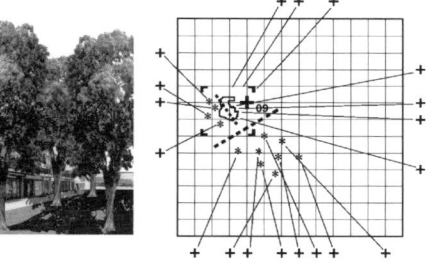

URBAN FOREST - Aud Koht
topic: a mono-cultural industrial woodland
life-form: external agents generate diversity and a fertile ground for skills
architecture: urban forest over open spaces generate a variety of activities
enhancing existing resources

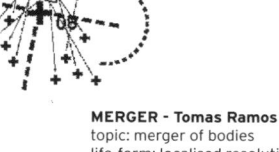

MERGER - Tomas Ramos
topic: merger of bodies
life-form: localised resolution of conflicts between different organisations allows for sporadic association
architecture: the design of an inhabited bridge and whale-like structure facilitates the union of the confronting communities of Canary Wharf and the indigenous
population

ubiquitous – an attribute of the s-world: a multidimensional and smooth continuum defined by something other than a specific scale, such as global or local.
To intensify these conditions we set a rhetorical framework in the form of the hypothetical conjecture: 'The Independent State of the Isle of Dogs'.

We have conducted two comparative field-work studies, starting in the Isle of Dogs, followed by a visit to Havana, Cuba. Cuba is an s-world, a place undergoing radical change following direct exposure to global forces: speculative property investments (accelerated by UNESCO World Heritage involvement), radical economic uncertainty due to the fluctuating US policy towards Cuba, the inability of Castro's ailing regime to respond to changes taking place elsewhere in the world, and the influx of tourists, lured by the cultural diversity exploited by the world media. Despite the negative factors, we saw a much brighter reality: a swarming energy of people that appropriate and 'corrupt' all available resources – either extreme capitalism or socialism – through individual ingenuity and rapid adaptations of the

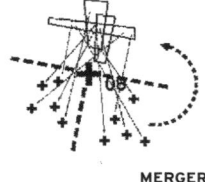

DYNAMIC BORDER - Tamar Jacobs
topic: social and spatial division and the lack of an operational border; a physical entity that can be negotiated
life-form: dynamic interactions across the border of the Isle of Dogs
architecture: establishment on the island of a film industry, together with its related media, culminating in a harbour terminal and a film complex on the river bank

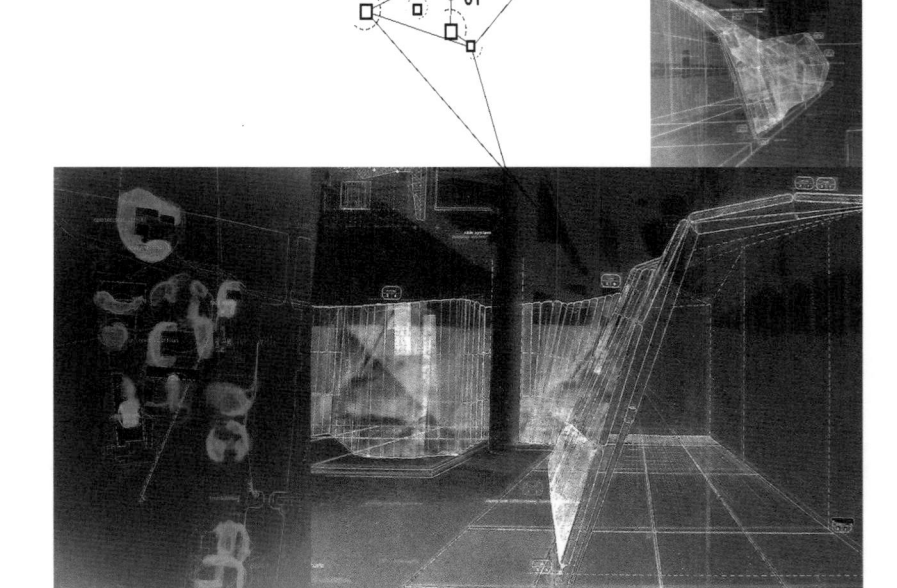

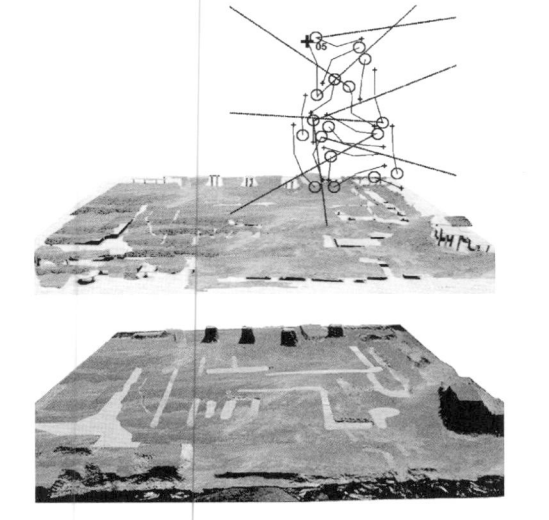

CUBAN CUBE - Asma Zeenni
topic: rigidity of spatial and temporal organisation
life-form: fluid condition of spontaneous interactions and continuous reconfiguration of relations in public spaces
architecture: a programmatic container imported from Havana to the multi-storey car park below Cabot Square

TRANS-SKIN - Jennifer Singer
topic: social segregation of the Isle of Dogs and policy of spatial use
life-form: a holistic view of vacant properties and market mechanism, deep-pocketing as a long-term investment strategy, which utilises derelict and redundant structures
architecture: a series of temporary shelters housing interim programmes are infiltrating the Millennium Quarter masterplan

instinct for survival. The emerging architecture thrives on conflicts created by the direct confrontation of the two worlds, its raw energy evident throughout Havana. These new architectural forms are instrumental in allowing Cubans to exploit and negotiate the forceful systems imposed on their environment.

Our questions are 'what are the new forms of architectural culture emerging from the global conditions undergoing radical change?' and 'can we localise and instigate such transformations with the life-forms on our site, as an instrument of metamorphosis for both global and local fields?' Accordingly, each individual project forms an interactive component. This co-relation leads to the formation of individual prototypes and establishes the basis for a new value-system with which to evaluate them.
The two approaches revolve around the issue of the human, intelligent (including emotional) activities of science and art. These two fields of human knowledge

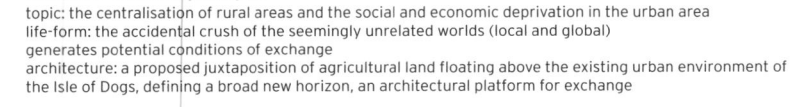

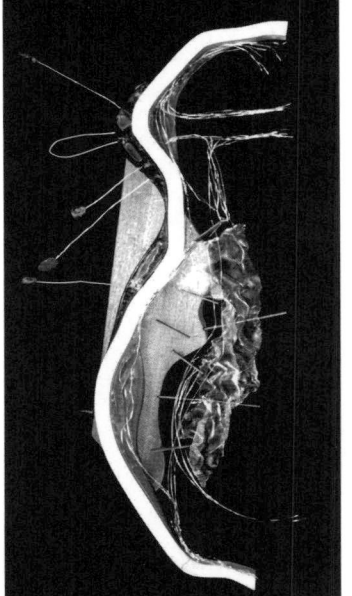

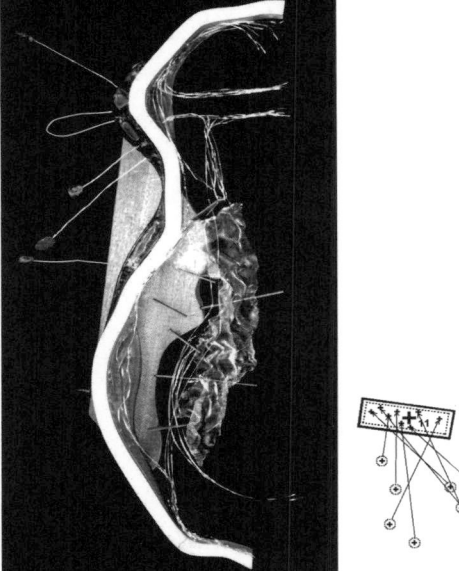

HORIZON - Talar Kouyoumdjian
topic: the centralisation of rural areas and the social and economic deprivation in the urban area
life-form: the accidental crush of the seemingly unrelated worlds (local and global)
generates potential conditions of exchange
architecture: a proposed juxtaposition of agricultural land floating above the existing urban environment of the Isle of Dogs, defining a broad new horizon, an architectural platform for exchange

INHABITING AN IMAGE - Amrit Pal Marway
topic: lack of self image
life-form: icon of place appropriated by people and their identity
architecture: a large tent-like structure spans the open spaces of Canary Wharf

participation into creation of the place

SMOOTH OPERATOR - Martha Giannacopoulou
topic: the employment of social segregation and participation for the creation of place
life-form: through rapid adaptation the smooth operator appropriates available resources
architecture: a horse race event transforms existing private and public spaces along the river bank into a race track

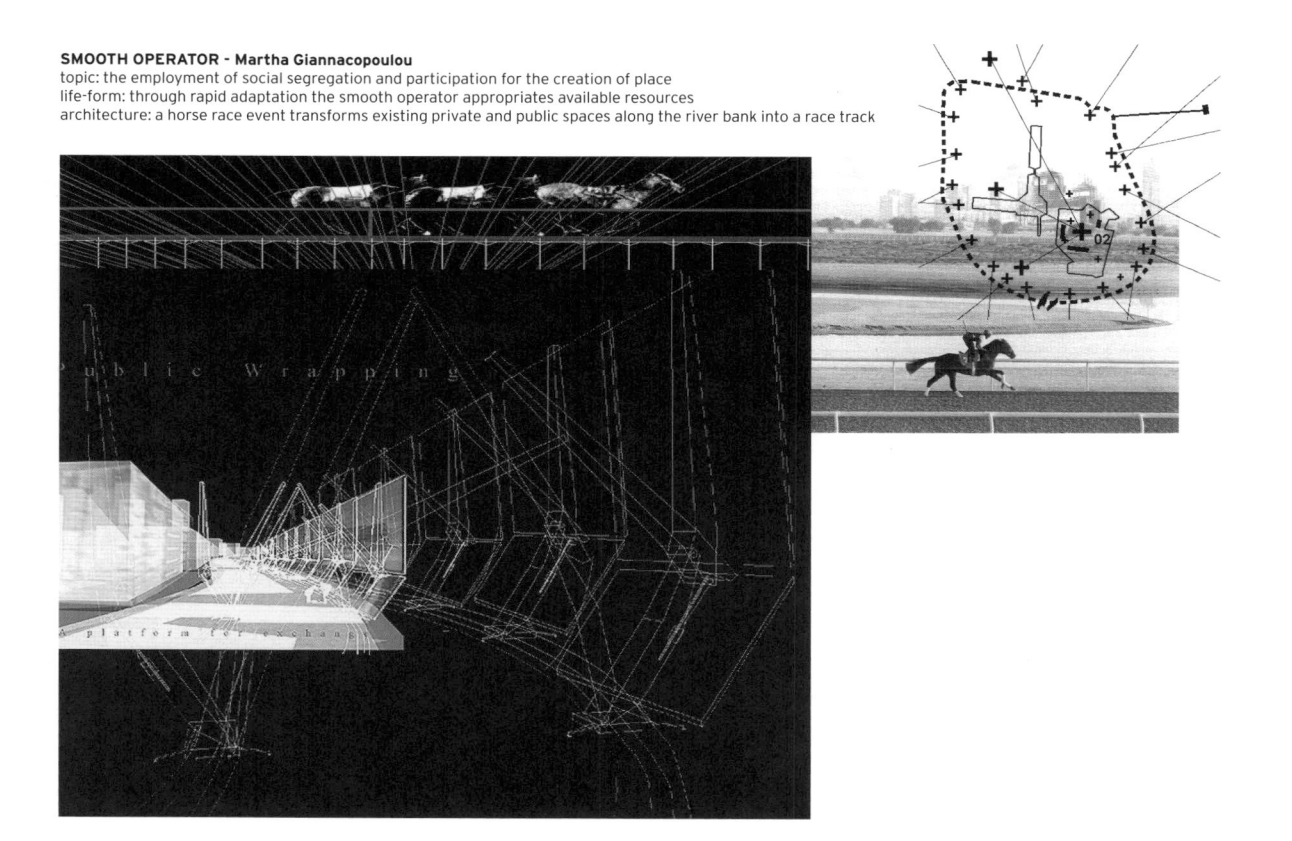

need to be united on the basis of a common ground in order to be able to deal with the emerging entity. The common ground is based on humanity, a complex totality from which all our intellectual activities span. It defines the foundation of our value-system and gives meaning to architectural form.

practice

Complex urban issues are to be dealt with as open-ended generative structures; its components consist of architecture – forms changing over time, as life adapts to its environment – and of instruments for instigating such changes. How can we design such a prototype? Or, in other words, how can we design a life-form? Our work embodies experiments in search of an emergent architecture and provides the ingredients for new forms of practice.

Jean Michel Crettaz and **Takuro Hoshino**

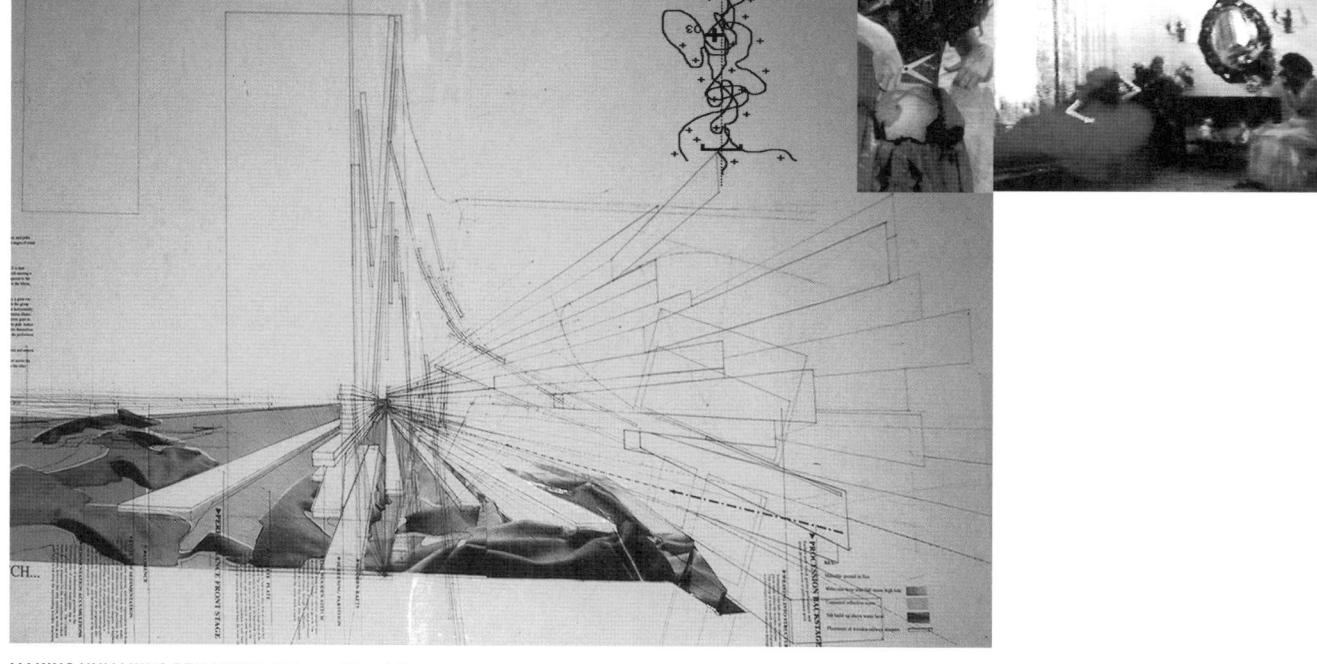

MAKING UNMAKING REMAKING - Rebecca Richwhite
topic: economic and demographic growth, and an appropriate mechanism for social transformation
life-form: use of rituals as space-defining mechanisms
architecture: through an open cut, a new water-land environment is put into place, connecting the existing docks to the river, thus creating spaces for new urban rituals

cultural interaction and social transformation

Diploma Unit 2

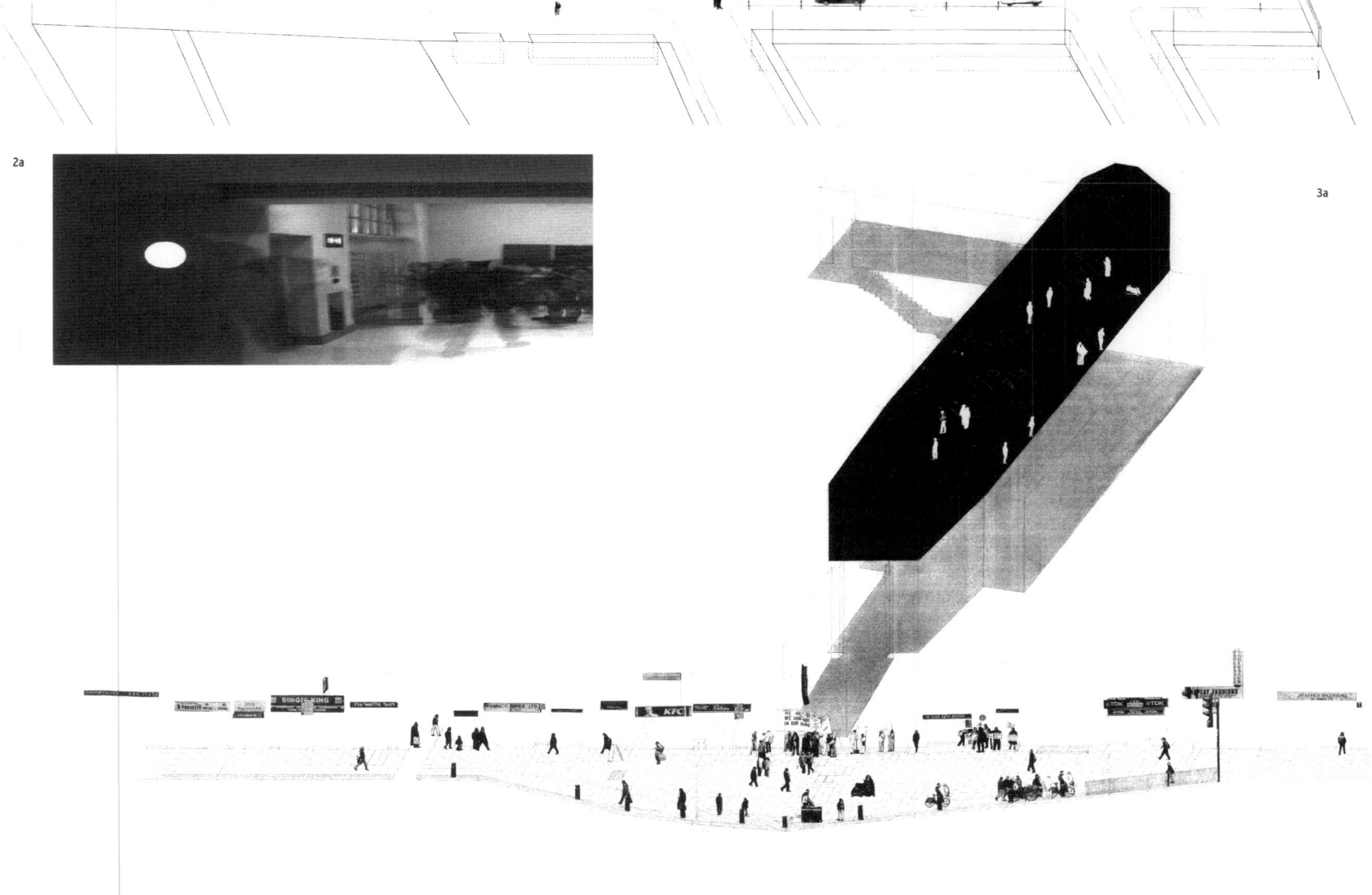

Stasis, Performance
(cultivating light)

The year has centred on the design of a simple gallery and associated performance space on one of two selected sites in Stockholm. The attempt has been to consider new conditions of public space with respect to these two specific and contrasting urban conditions. The first site is a desolate former gasworks, a typical post-industrial landscape whose future development is currently under discussion by the city; the second is a residential suburb lacking any conventional urban centre but nevertheless with a massive daily influx of workers to its high-tech industries and international exhibition centre.

1. A study of the Almeida Theatre in London revealed the street as a foyer. The limited courtyard beside the theatre and the stairs which access the upper galleries open directly onto the street. The threshold between street and interior is collapsed. Drawing the theatre in the context of the street indicates other proximities, in particular the close relationship between house and performance space.

2 a+b. The foyer space of the Whitechapel Gallery was recorded in a series of photographs, five of which were overlayed to create this simultaneous image of distinct moments in the occupation of the space. In this first study, titled 'crowdspace_performance', reference was made to the museum photography of

Thomas Struth, in particular one image published in the book *Strangers and Friends* ('Stanze di Raffaello' II, Rome 1990, p. 16). This image shows a crowd of visitors in the main Raphael Salon. A few faces are discernible but the general sense is of a large mass of people, structured according to particular groups of families or friends. We were drawn to the text by Richard Sennett that accompanies the images: 'And, respecting these boundaries, we come to acknowledge that others are endowed with a life of their own. "Urbanity" means that people guard their separateness even as they present themselves

directly to others.' Richard Sennett 'Recovery, the Photography of Thomas Struth', in Struth's *Strangers and Friends*, MIT Press, 1994.

3 a+b. The display rooms of the Whitechapel are distanced from the high street by a large matted lobby and a cool white terrazzo hall, reworked by Colquhoun and Miller in their alterations dating from the mid 1980s. The gallery was originally founded as an institution dedicated to bringing art to the 'working people' of east London, and it still sees this as its primary role. This drawing seeks to understand the relationship between the street and the upper exhibition gallery – the most rarified space in the building. The drawing describes an occurrence one Saturday afternoon in October during the exhibition 'Protest and Survive'. Disparate groups

The brief, for a 'high art' space, was seen as a kind of provocation, a charged context in which to consider the space of the crowd and public proximity. The intention of taking the hybrid brief of gallery and performance space together was to support the

consideration of a range of contemporary art practices which themselves challenge and construct new conditions of public space.

Work at the beginning of the year involved meetings with staff of the Whitechapel

Gallery in London, and with the performance duo Reich and Szyber in Stockholm.

of demonstrators paraded in front of the building – some were artists intent on staging a protest event as a part of the show, while others were attempting to raise a genuine concern over the local authority's proposed sale of the adjacent public library.

4. One of the recent trends in contemporary art practice is the proliferation of video as a medium of expression. Several of the projects made this year try to address this issue and propose alternatives to either the 'black box' or 'white cube' models of gallery space. This image shows part of a detailed study of screens and meshes which allow partial transmission and reflection of a beamed light source. The project went on to develop a series of unconventional surfaces

of projection – for example, a combined Trombe/video wall orientated with a sensitivity to seasonal dusk conditions.

5. This image shows one of the first experimental models of the year, made before any site visit. It constructs a new room around an articulated ground, considering the specific conditions of scale and illumination. The study established a potential range of filtered ambient light, ranging from relatively sharp conditions in which the shadows of trees might be cast directly against the translucent walls of the space, to a much softer condition where the distinctions of illumination of wall and soffit are damped out, creating an 'ungrounded' space.

6a +b. Two distinct crowds were seen to occupy the same space, one intent on

watching the screening of a chess championship taking place in the adjacent studio, the other interested only in drinking and talking. This drawing shows the two groups recorded at the Riverside Studios in October. The project for Stockholm went on to develop this idea of doubling of spaces: rooms set in other rooms, two sets of occupants in one space, one hardly sensing the other.

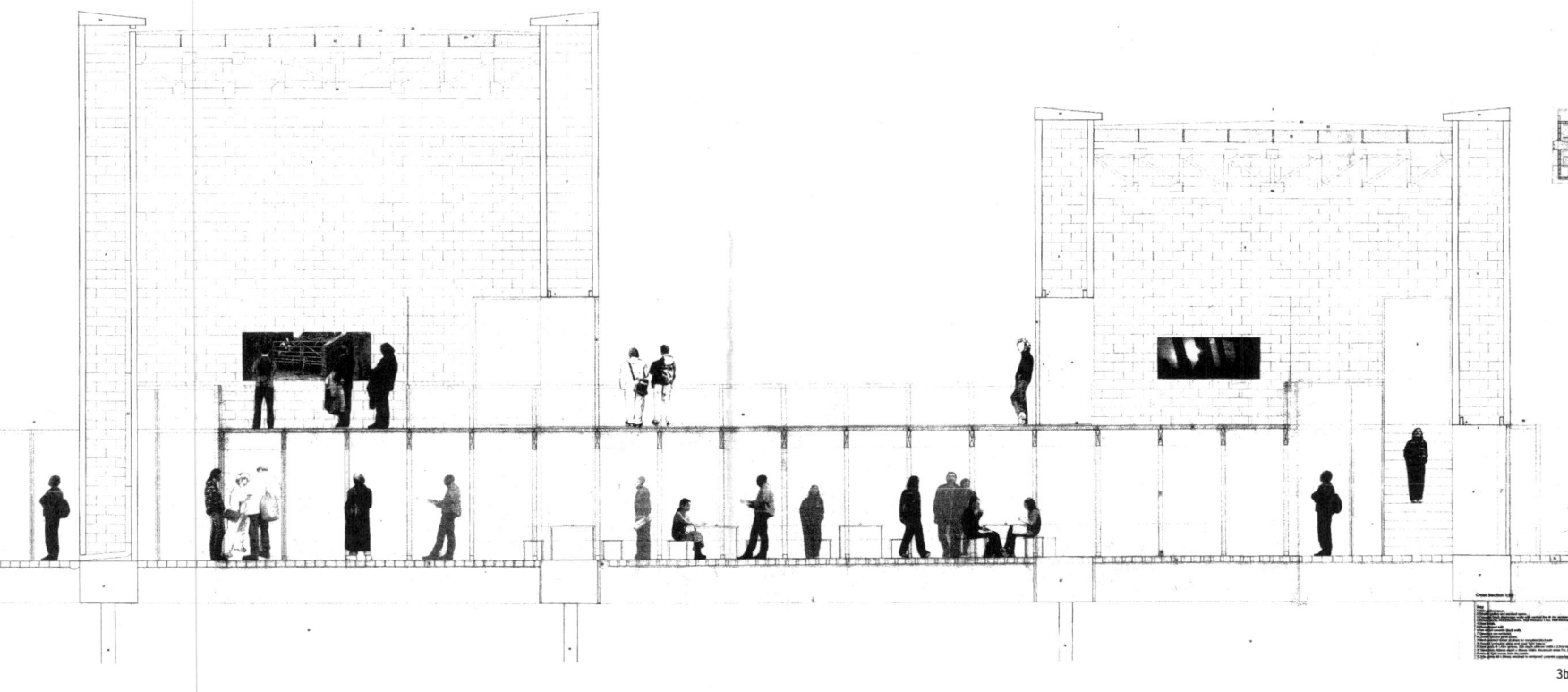

One of our key architectural precedents has been the 'Teatro Oficina', built by Lina Bo Bardi in São Paulo in the 1970s, a highly attenuated, long and narrow room - a naturally lit figure which precludes any conventional understanding of auditorium space and forces its participants out of the preconceived role of a detached spectator.

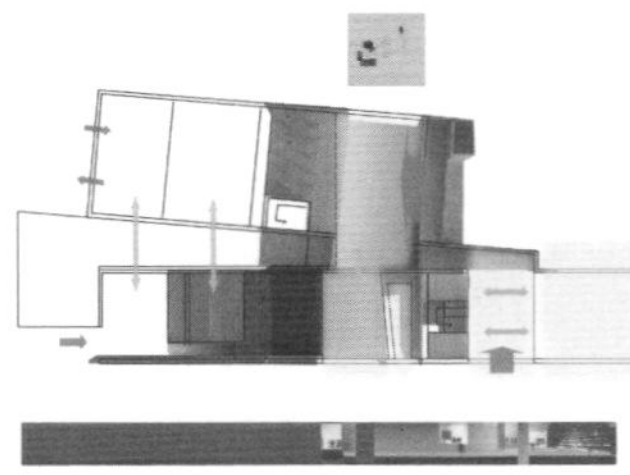

Unit Staff: Peter Beard, Jim McKinney
Students: Iris Argyroupolou (3),
Artur Carulla (4), Michael Daines,
Thomas Goodey (9), Seijiro Hayashi (8),
Aidan Hodgkinson (2), Sandra Kesselring (13),

7 a+b. The work of the artist Maria Neudecker uses tank structures, much like domestic fish tanks, to house models representing archetypal landscape situations – a mountainscape, a forest, or a wreck at sea. The water surrounding these models is treated with chemicals and pigments to render it obscure. Lights within the tanks allow the apprehension of details within an otherwise blurred space. A series of models was made studying parallel spatial themes at the scale of rooms and building objects.

8. As part of a strategic scale proposal for the site at Ropsten, a series of reedbed-lined channels are cut into the polluted ground. Concurrent with these channels runs a sequence of earth rooms and walkways – a collection of complex interrelated performance spaces.

9. Four rooms are raised up above the wasteground of the former gasworks, creating a generous portico space below. The low winter sun penetrates deep into this undercroft. The heavy structure that supports the roofs of these rooms also serves to frame and enclose the space, limiting the picture-window views of the landscape beyond.

10. A series of rooms with varying light qualities are placed in oblique relation to each other both in plan and in section. Their open corners allow an awareness of spaces beyond. High up in the building, beneath a tower containing a hotel and office spaces, is a room in which translucent facades, packed with light fittings, fake the presence of natural light during hours of darkness.

11. A long room captured inside a rusting cor-ten steel box forms a new threshold between polluted ground and the water. In one version of performance, the audience is pushed up against actors, across the short axis of this space, and the landscape beyond becomes a glazed strip of scenery.

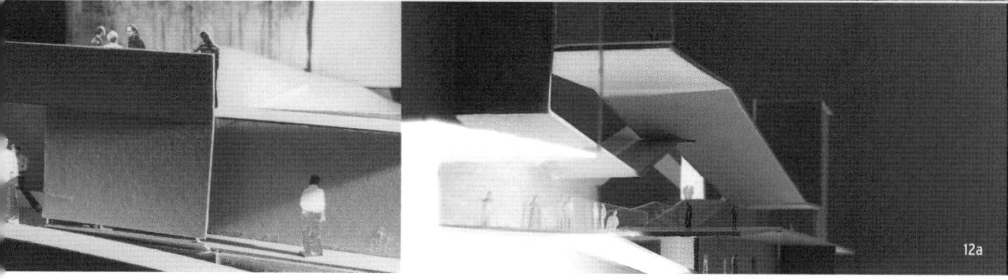

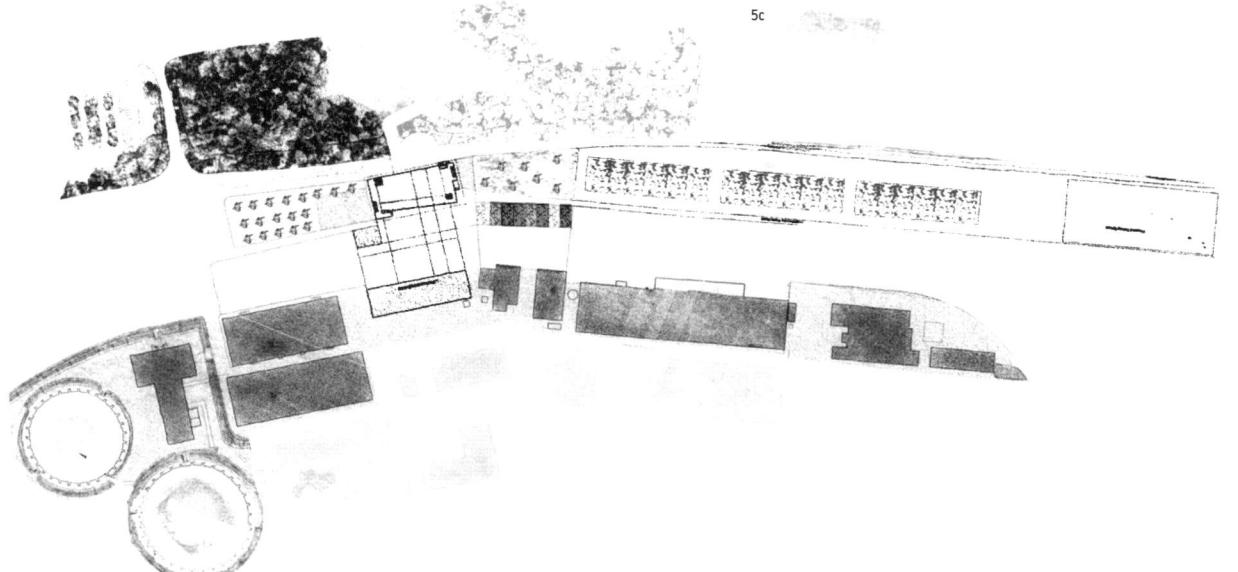

5c

Ayako Kodera (6), Henrik Lønberg (11), Kazuyo Matsuda (1), Young-In Oh (5), Aikari Paing (7), Valeriy Petruschechkin (10), Beng Kiat Phua (15), Ravindren Ponniah (14), Eleni Stika (12)

With thanks to: Diego Ferrari, Rose Fenton, Theresa Wuthenau, Bogdan Szyber, Carina Reich, Shin Egashira, Juliet Bidgood, Irénée Scalbert, Andrew Houlton, John Glew, Anders Johansson, Erik Dahlen at Birkagas,

Charles Tashima, Michael Weinstock, Florence Lam, Wolf Mangelsdorf, Neil Leach, Helene Furján, Nikolaus Hirsch, Simon English, Diana Periton, Michael McNamara, and Chris Jackson at the UCL lighting simulator.

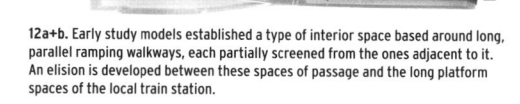

12a+b. Early study models established a type of interior space based around long, parallel ramping walkways, each partially screened from the ones adjacent to it. An elision is developed between these spaces of passage and the long platform spaces of the local train station.

13. Two parallel concrete walls align themselves with the rail-tracks. A sequence of bridge/rooms are constructed between them, forming a patchwork space of uncertain extent. Mesh screen walls complete the sub-division of the space.

14 a+b. The old canteen of the gasworks (still well used) is currently housed in a building at the centre of the now much reduced works site. This project proposes the relocation of the canteen on the former coal grounds, as a partner to the new gallery/performance building.

15. The landscape condition of Stockholm is characterised by clusters of small granite outcrops formed by glacial action, technically known as drumlins. A new public ground is established on the side of one of these drumlins by the grouping of a twelve-metre-high shed, a long earth stage (exterior) built along the line of a former dirt road, and a small 'dressing room' building. The landscape itself becomes the site of performance.

Diploma Unit 3

Drawing the line of thought: à la recherche de l'architecture perdue

Pascal Schöning

As an initial subject we used the Portofino scene from the Antonioni/Wenders film 'Beyond the Clouds' and refilmed it in parts, on location, to get an introduction to the relationship between space/object and process/subject.

The task of designing 'the most beautiful house' – a house which is invisible but filled with visions and events of life – introduces questions that do not have straight answers. This is a tradition of the unit.

Approaching these questions through the *processes* of questioning and of making decisions, leads not to eternal answers but to other provisional questions and other provisional decisions, and then to more questions and more decisions, in a *continuous* *process*. This process *formulates* the *line* of thought, and *draws* it, at the same time *drawing* the mental *architecture*. Each question/decision-making *time-space* *formulates* a part of the mental *construction* – a mental *material*, a mental *detail*. Collected together, they build up an unbearable pressure – until they explode in an event of *imaginative* *formulation*, in a *space* and *shape* which is at that moment, through its *visualisation*, a document of creative *physicality*: a temporary speculative answer of architectonic physicalisation, defined not by physical but by mental *building elements*. One has *drawn* the *line* of thought.

To *draw* processes one cannot use static means, so the *drawing sheet* is replaced by *books* (a storyboard with imaginative stills) and video films (a transitional imaginal row).

Thanks to
Clara Kraft
Andreas Lang
Thomas Durner
Josef Pausch
Ron Kenley
Jean Attali
Michael Hensel
Carlos Villanueva Brandt
Elena Radl
Mark Cousins
Mohsen Mostafavi
Don Bates and more.

Fine misty rain,
gently touching my skin.

The white cotton skin above me
also started noticing the touch,
slowly changing its colour
adding a little transparency.

With the fresh spring air,
this warm rain seems to know
how to bring me and my house
out from the wintery solitude.

Miki Ando

Touched: skin, rain, a disappeared touch

The most beautiful house 'appears' when a touch between you and your surrounding stimuli, both physical and mental, becomes so intense that it naturally disappears into co-existence.
Without consciously ignoring, nor accepting, a touch disappears into the condition of 'being touched'.

I am proposing several settings in London for this 'touched' moment to appear.

This city is full of stimuli, and we ourselves possess extraordinary sensory systems.
My device is a renewed 'epidermis', the outer-most skin surface. Its layers, consisting of various materials, intensify the touch between us and stimuli such as rain and the city itself.

Rubens Azevedo

What I cannot see I imagine.
Trying to create a space of intrigue, a space of announcement. Every time I walk through the city, passing by walls, I imagine stories about other things. The walls hide the landscape and reveal other stories, the ones I imagine. And the city is constructed while I perform it.

In the film 'Beyond the Clouds' the girl is the physicality, she is the building, the wall who conceals and then reveals much more. The story is just the story of a girl up to the moment when she says, 'I killed my father'. At that moment, the girl's presence interrupts the story. It creates a 'hole' in the narrative, a hole that has to be filled with imagination.

I am proposing a house built with missing parts, 'holes' in the narrative, a house constructed while being performed, a house that only exists in the moment of the encounter. When I cannot see and I have to imagine it.

Stefanie Berchtenbreiter Overbeck

Beauty derives from pleasure and disgust, as it can be found in the process leading up to a relieving mental freedom.

This process is provoked by something which reminds us of a past experience. There was a moment in which the absolute relieved state of mind was achieved. The focus of the project is to define a spatial condition in a process of time which could suggest this sense of relieving freedom in relation to the physical world around us. The challenge is to define how the personal experience of smelling a lemon could possibly become a house.

Reem Charif

The space of the perfect gesture (the platform of exchange): on a hot day, a beautiful city melted away, creating a coloured river that wrapped round the half of the city that remained intact. In the river flowed all the inhabitants' possessions, especially those things that were not loved. In the melted city it was easy to share, for there was nothing to sell or steal – when you needed something you would just go to the river and find what you were looking for and exchange it for what you would like to have.

Can the city melt through exchange?
How much space can one share without losing
  one's freedom?
Is there a difference between space and property?
Does it matter who owns an empty space when
  there is a demand for it?

The space of the perfect gesture is the space of the meeting of two dreams that perfectly complement each other (exchange). Two dreams that have been looking for each other for a long time but keep missing each other.

" it tears her
from her safe & quiet place,
And so she looks
but she nolonger sees.
She dreams to return
to her safe & quiet place."

S S O U N D(ing) N D I N G
(a) SENSE OF BELONGING

Tamsin Ford

SOUND(ing) – (a) SENSE OF BELONGING

a cautious investigation:
into the beautiful space between deafness and here-ing.

Re-discovering a memory, of the beautiful moment between deafness and hearing, the mental house is sited in the shell that transports us to a safe and quiet place. Bringing the shell(-ter) to the city, the volume of the house becomes that of the city and the sound of the most intimate space. It invites a dialogue between the internal noise *(fears)* and the sounds of the city *(physicality)*. The shell/house is only inhabited in passing: however the memory may endure.

Ingrid Frydenbo

JUST A MOMENT

A street in the centre of the city. On the way to an everyday destination.

A place rendered invisible by routine. A site for the Most Beautiful House.

A house for escaping the disengaging city. A house where the city has got so close it has disappeared from view. A house built with the memories of other places. Memories overlaid with the physicality of the city, at a moment in time when the city leaves space for projection.

The Most Beautiful House lives in the moment our memories and the physical place come together and create an imaginary reality.

No boundaries,
everything comes close.
The sense of space gets lost.
Where do I know
where I end
and the others begin.

Memory   **Reality**   Projection
├──── "I" ────┤
[Past]   [Present]   [Future]

The pictures start to blur,
appear
unexpectedly
and disappear again.
I loose the sense of myself.
I am in the clouds and yet,
cannot reach beyond.

My horizon is within me.

Dominik Kremerskothen

All you need to build a house is a girl and a gun.

The house is a girl. It creates a dialogue. To sustain the dialogue you need love.

The house is a construction, a place with a name. Presence or absence, existence enables meetings. The house is a gun.

The house is a relationship. It goes through stages:

Solitude
Our Space
In the World together
Being One
Solitude...

The elements assemble in any order. The ephemeral is eternal.

In fear, we pull the trigger. Walls appear – space for new projections.

To love means to build. The house has no image – only beauty!

Quintin Lake

THE FIFTH SEASON – 'Arctic' sublime in the city

Supposing, when people had 'to get out of the city' they went up rather than out, to an ephemeral place, a place of mystery and lightness, a place above the houses where no forms are constraining, a place of the Fifth Season.

The House of the Fifth Season is a point of being in which the substantial and insubstantial fuse. The essence of this fusion is best exemplified by laser light which, through its qualities of coherent scaleless light, assumes the architectural beauty of the sublime.

Sylvia Ng
Encircling emotions

To design the most beautiful house, I borrowed the mental situation from Antonioni's film as a datum to search for similar situations and identified three main influences - chance, changing perspective and sharing an island of thought - which were later used to transport my mental situation into a physical house. Focusing on the island of thought as a mental construction, I further defined the situation in 'Beyond the Clouds' where the two protagonists had a spontaneous moment of connection so intense that their moment seemed to be disconnected with their surroundings, forming the mental space of an island.

The island site was chosen because of its quality of change, connected and disconnected by the tide. The space - a reverse aquarium - has an open-top translucent island that separates the water from within. A place for the public who seek solitude or a meeting.

Tim Sudweeks

The Most Beautiful House
is an Open Prison

The way we construct has always been a paradigm of the way we see ourselves in the world. Trapped in the monotony of my suburban situation I want to transform the place where I live, to create a fixing point from which to go out and explore. A place that houses my memories, holding them inside but allowing them to shine out in order to give me direction, orientation and stability within the world. Created from the story of my experiences, a strategy is born for transforming the typical suburban dwelling.

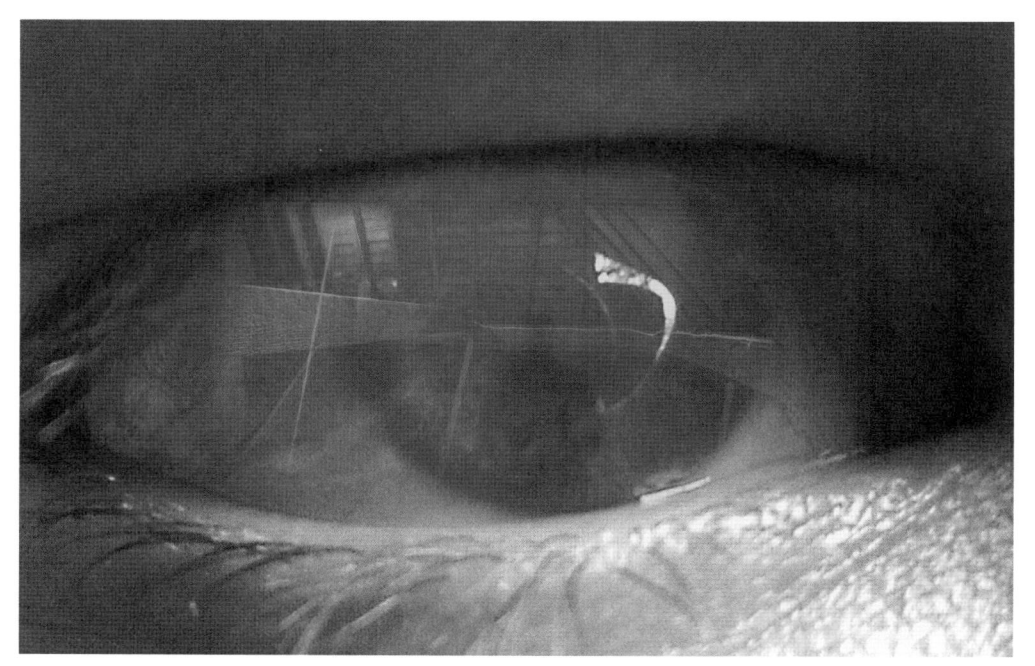

Dip4_Urban Studio

Animation sequence showing proposed re-routability of public transport

ORGANISATIONAL MODELLING

DIP4 Michael Hensel, Ludo Grooteman
Sinobi Achara, Lip-Khoon Chiong, Annie Chung,
Mariano Ciccone, Takashi Fukunaga, Satoshi Isono,
Jelena Jovic, Maija Korpak, Adrian Lai, Benjamin
Toh Onn Ling, Achim Menges, Ted Nordstrom,
Cristobal Palma, Nathalie Rozencwajg, Stefan Rydin,
Borja Santamaria, Ali Seghatoleslahmi, Tahir Tikari,
Gorana Vucic, Oshri Yaniv

Interactive 3D-model of the tectonic layers of the building proposal

PRE-TECTONIC MODELLING

DIP4 Expert Team
Greater London Authority, Strategy Directorate,
Planning Decisions Unit: Richard Linton,
Ove Arup & Partners, London, Consulting Engineers:
Chris Carroll, Michele Janner, David Johnston, Rory
McGowan, Tristan Simmonds, Charles Walker

BUILT ARTICULATION

DIP4 would like to thank
AA H&U (The AA Housing & Urbanism Programme),
PROURB (The Federal University of Rio de Janeiro),
IBA RJ (The Institute of Brazilian Architects), Peter
Beard, Pablo Benetti, Milton Braga, Jose Zeca Brandao,
Angelo Bucci, Eva Castro, Mark Cousins, Max de Rosee,
Shin Egashira, Jorge Fiori, Jane Harrison, Mark Hemel,

URBAN STRATEGIES

Christopher Hight, Hugo Hinsley, Holger Kehne, Nate
Kolbe, Mohsen Mostafavi, Ciro Najle, Joel Newman,
Maria Lúcia Petersen, Veronika Schmid, Pascal
Schöning, Dr. Kristina Shea, Jeff Turko, Carlos
Villanueva Brandt, Michael Weinstock

Animation sequence of pedestrian nodes and connections

*Above all we must remember that nothing exists or comes into being, lasts or passes, can be thought of as entirely isolated, entirely unadulterated.
One thing is always permeated, accompanied, covered, or enveloped by another; it produces effects and endures them. And when so many things work
through one another, where are we to find the insight to discover what governs and what serves, what leads the way and what follows?*

Johann Wolfgang von Goethe

Research Agenda

Since 1995 DIP4 has been committed to ongoing experimental research into a middle scale between the architectures and the urban design of
European cities. It has focused on devising and testing alternative types of urban fabric and organisational structures in order to move towards
satsifying the demand for an increased capacity for programmatic diversification, and intensification. This year's sites included London Bridge
Station, Amsterdam Zuidas and Stockholm Slussen, all of which are characterised by a high demand for programmatic and infrastructural diversity,

AMSTERDAM_ZUIDAS   LONDON_LONDON BRIDGE

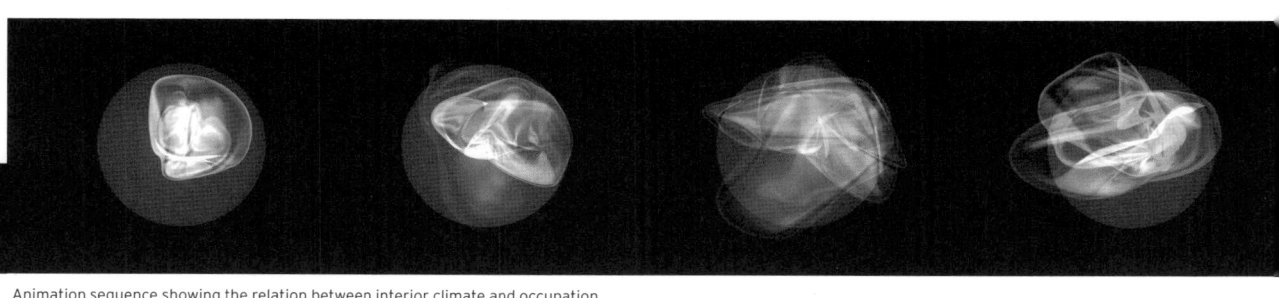

Animation sequence showing the relation between interior climate and occupation

3D-model showing layered tectonic landscape

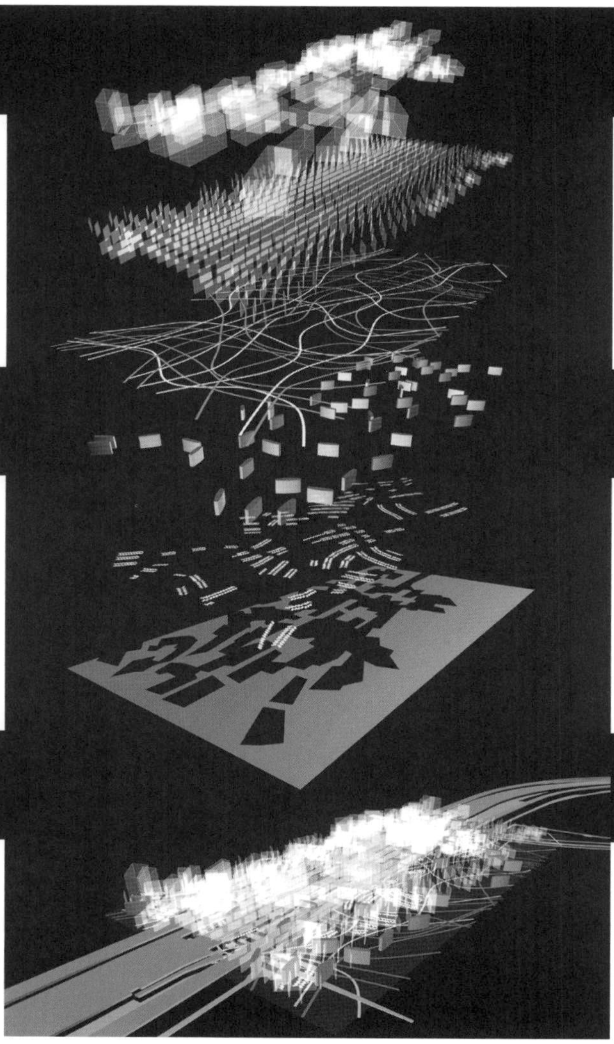

Models showing folded tectonic landscape

Models showing woven tectonic landscape

and adaptability. These sites anticipate major changes: their high demand on dynamic variability cannot be catered for by the exclusive zoning methods and figure-ground organisations of traditional master-planning.

In response to this design problem DIP4 explored time-based modelling methods that aimed at instrumentalising and regulating the relational dynamic between spatial articulation and occupational provision and potential. The task was to create an evolving urban fabric that engenders multiple space use and multiple ground datum structures as both substrate and catalyst for intensified urban growth. Organisational and tectonic models were devised, in the form of pilot projects, as adaptable and expandable multi-purpose structures, and were further examined and developed into urban intensification strategies and schemes. The related structural explorations included a broad spectrum of rational free-form structures ranging from the dynamics of large-scale pneumatic structures, to differential space-frames and modulated surface tectonics, always addressing specific provision for activation and inhabitation.

On an urban scale the investigation focused on the comparison of strategic national and municipal top-down planning structures [Amsterdam,

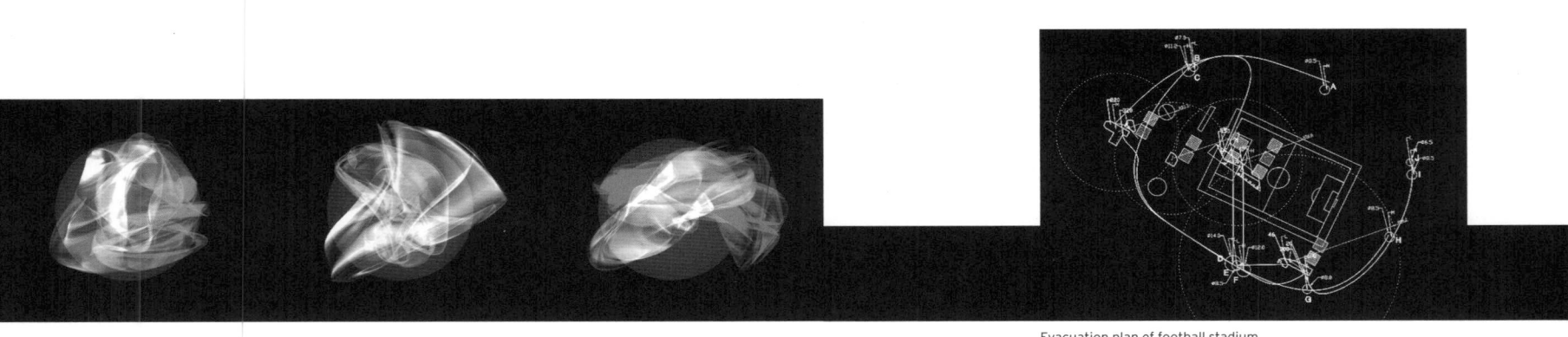
Evacuation plan of football stadium

Model showing programme volumes and connections

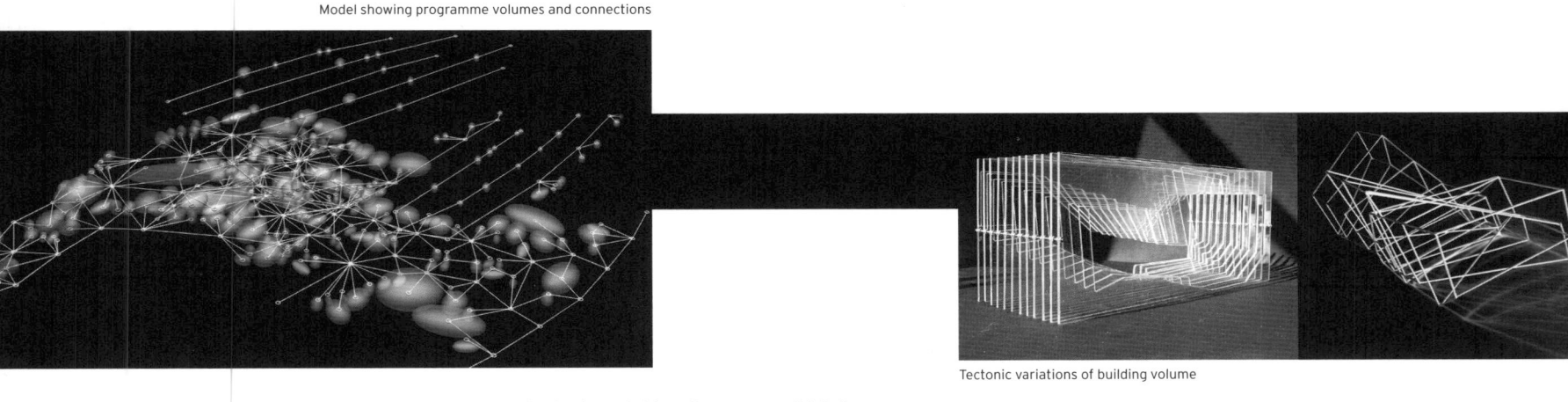
Tectonic variations of building volume

Plan drawing showing pedestrian paths programme distribution

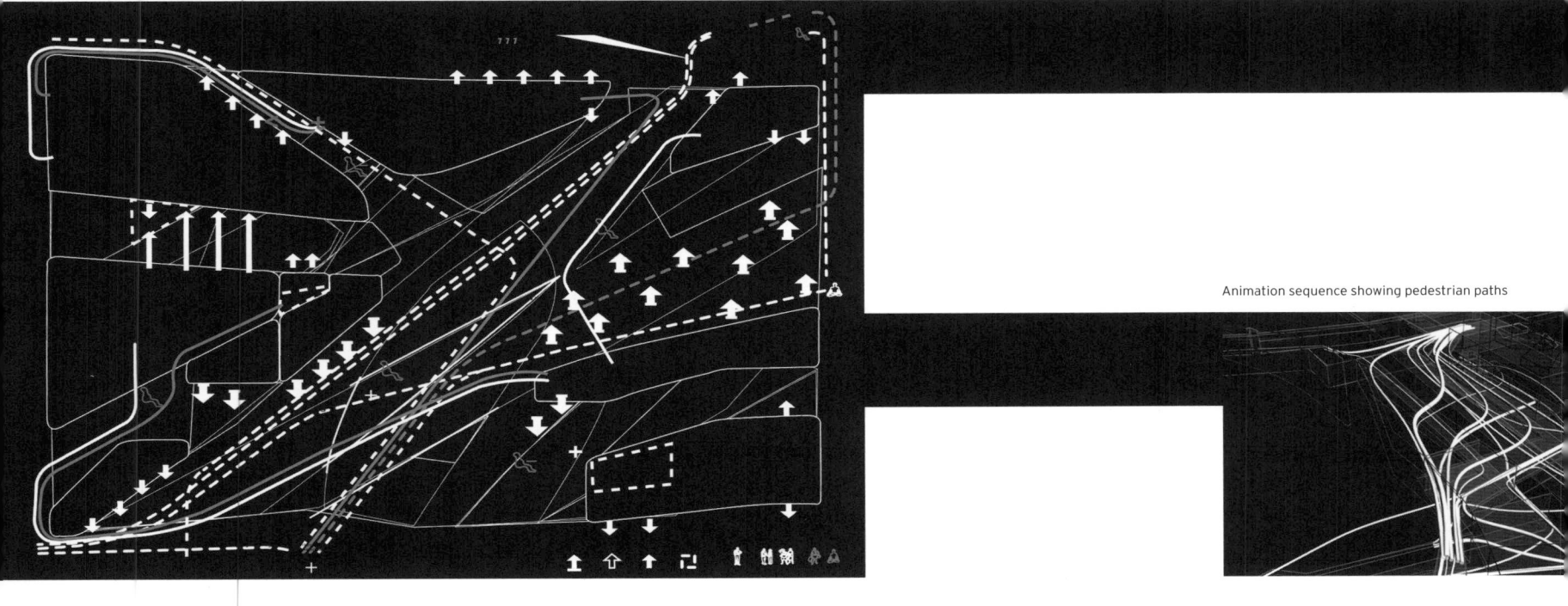
Animation sequence showing pedestrian paths

Stockholm] with tactical bottom-up approaches to urban design [Favela-Bairro Programme of Rio de Janeiro] and the possibility for emergent combined approaches [London]. The government of the Netherlands issues national planning guidelines in the form of Memoranda [Nota] that serve as guidelines for regional and municipal planning. The current 5th Nota outlines the study and implementation of modes of urban densification, and puts forward ideas such as extensive underground and/or multiple ground developments. In comparison, the currently established, centralised institution of the Greater London Authority also promotes urban densification through XL-building schemes and high-rise developments, with the additional difficulty of having to negotiate planning proposals with the largely independent boroughs of London. The careful analysis of the various planning systems serves to devise differential planning methods that allow for decisive urban development approaches [the intentional] that remain at the same time open to incorporate unforeseen conditions and contingencies [the tendential]. In doing so, the projects relinquish notions of finitude and completeness, and shift towards provisional configurations that are facilitated by periodic reassessment and reconfiguration along specifically established performance criteria, throughout various [time] scales.

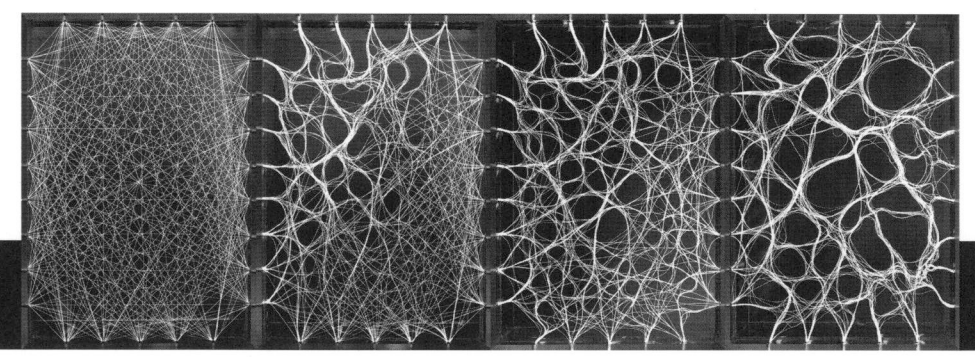

Model of animation sequence showing various path configurations

Interior view

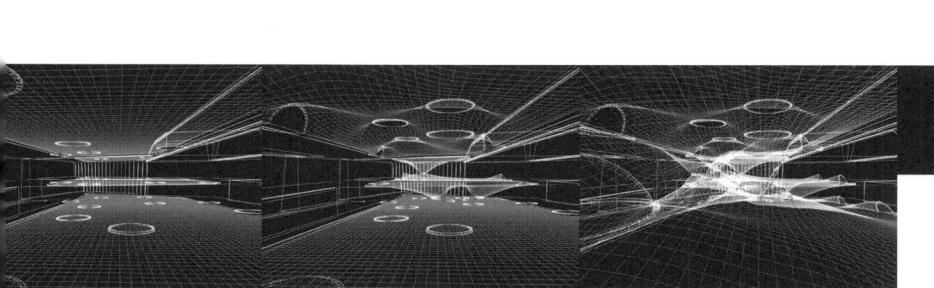

Animation sequence showing reconfiguration of interior space

3D-model showing building structure on railway arches

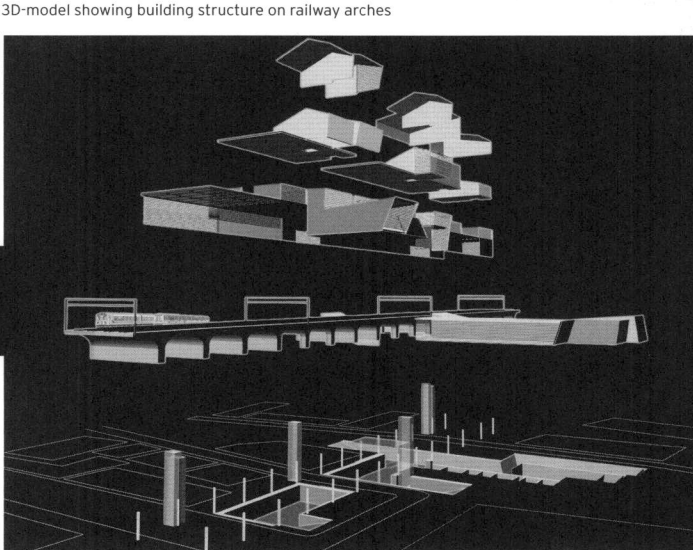

DIP4's experimental research in design progressed through a number of workshop sessions that aimed at developing and testing ideas and instrumental methods. Both the individual participants' inquiries and the collective research of DIP4 was catalysed by the workshop sessions that focused on problems of designed versus emergent conditions, as well as the development and deployment of time-based modelling techniques. The sessions included: Virtual Modelling + Digital Animation, Time-based Modelling + Analytical Methods, Pre-tectonic Modelling + Organisational Structures , 3D Modelling + Free-Form Structures, Spitalfields – Joint Urban Design Workshop 1 *, Port of Rio – Joint Urban Design Workshop 2 * [* in collaboration with the AA Housing & Urbanism Programme and PROURB Federal University of Rio de Janeiro].

Professional feedback was provided by the Planning Decisions Unit of the Greater London Authority Strategy Directorate and Team 2 of Ove Arup & Partners, London, Consulting Engineers, who joined the DIP4 Expert Team to collaborate in the research, with the aim of addressing architectural and urban design problems in an inclusive and synergetic way.

Diploma Unit 6

Unit Masters
Kevin Rhowbotham
Cedric Price

Technical Tutor
Youif Albustani

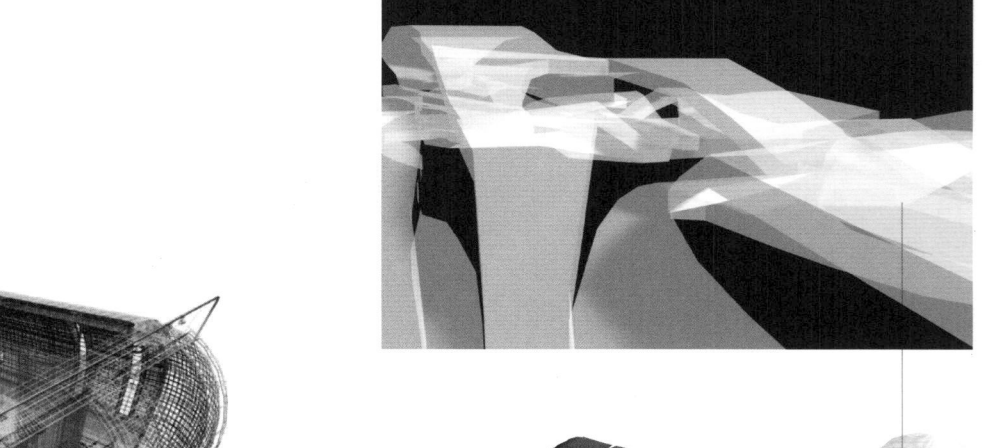

Thanks to
Guido Horn
Michael Hensel
Martha LaGess
Michael McNamara
Clive Sall
Yousif Albustani
John Buck
John Bell
Michael Weinstock
Roger Zogolovitch
Paul Finch
Carlos Villanueva-Brandt
Mohsen Mostafavi

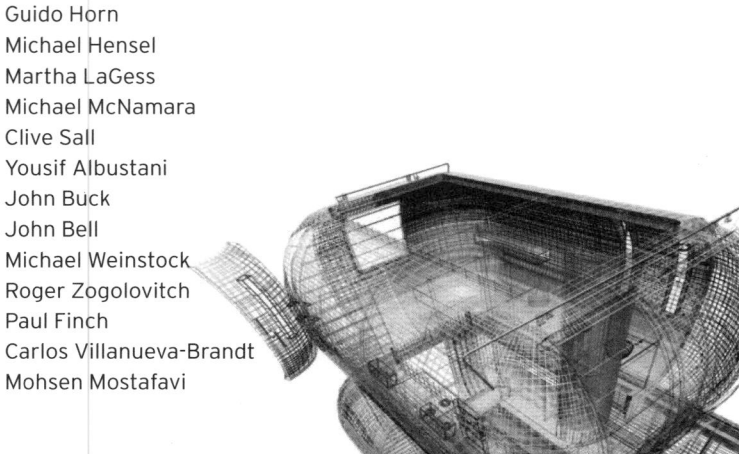

Students
Geoffrey Poon
Nigel Height
John O'Mara
Babette Bischoff
Rodrigo Rada Jarman
Cheng-tat Lee
Jeng Jyh
Mark Tavener
Takako Hasegawa
Keb Gravito
Zachary Carey
Nausicaa Voukalis
Bobby Wong
Anthony Fairhurst

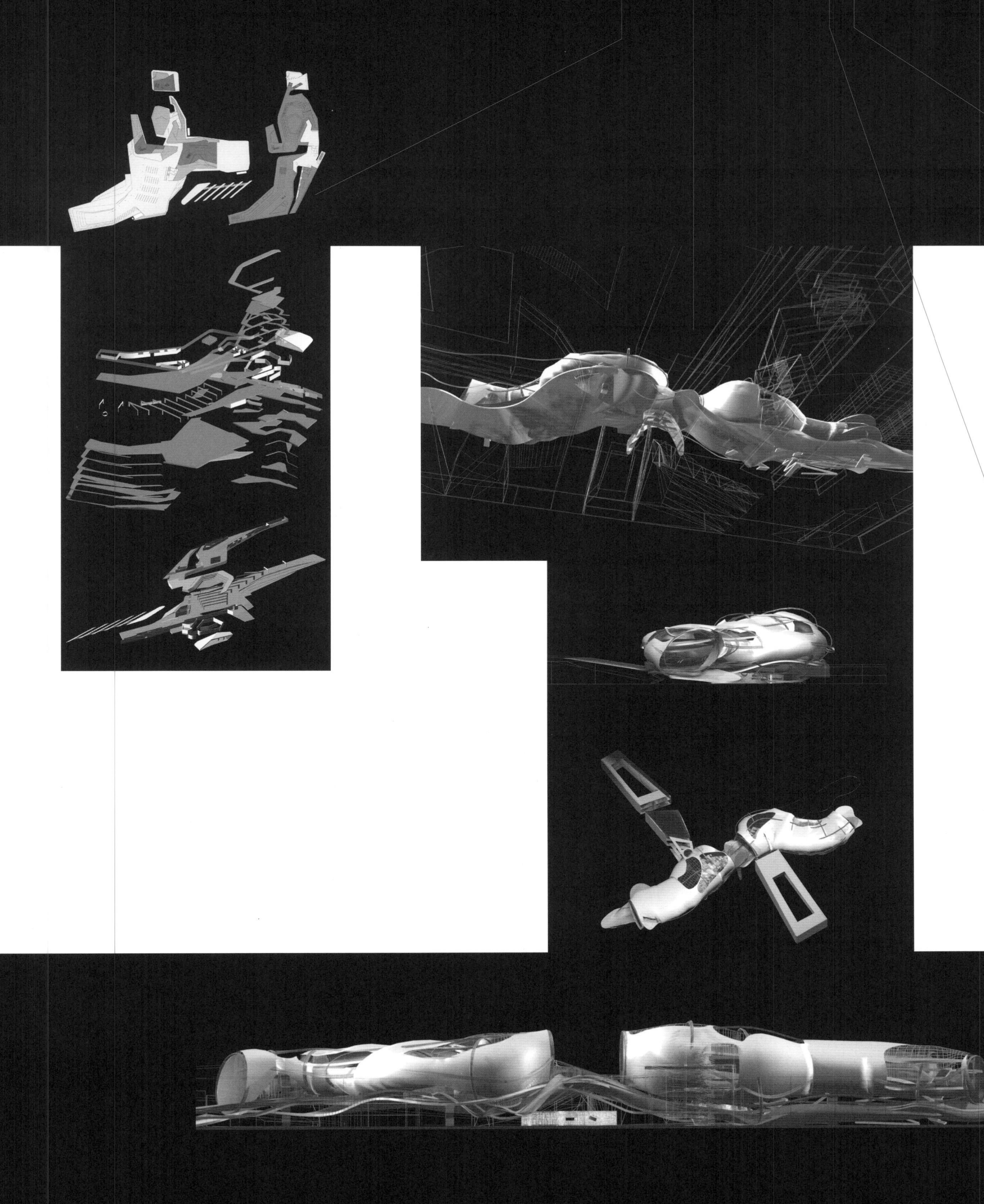

Urban Incubator

'These days the relative speed of the city seems to be increasing.'

'The city is less a collection of static buildings, more a piling up of people's activities and these change quicker than buildings can respond or architects can develop ideas to cope with them.'

'The past, the present, and the future... overlap in a messy configuration and have ceased to be discrete entities in their own right.'

'Architects can never acquire and retain control of all the factors in a city since they are always and already in excess and their dimensions are never geometrical nor predictable but are rather collections, aggregations, accumulations of patched-up, extendable, overlapping and developing forms.'

At a time when difference is being progressively reduced by the indigenous homogenisation of mass culture, and at a time when architecture has ceased to be interested in the nature of diversity in society, as well as in space, it seems altogether pertinent, not to say urgent, that a new and more contemporary view might be taken of the metropolitan context with specific reference to the nature of social space and how it might be constructed.
What are the political restrictions on the occupation of the city?

Who inhabits what?

How can social movement and the elasticity of social groupings be enhanced by contemporary architecture?

Can architecture support rather than restrict social change?

What are the real architectural consequences of contemporary demographic shifts?

Is inhabitable and usable public urban space still achievable?

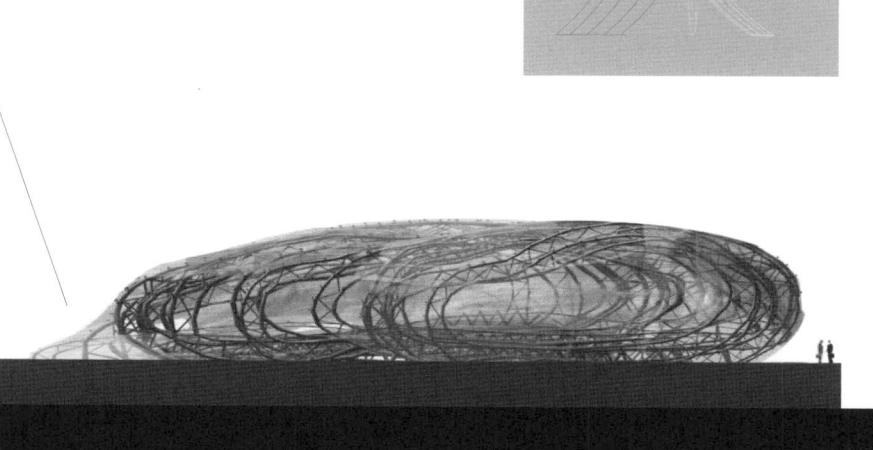

Can we construct an architecture based on the needs of a broadening and more variegated social mix, an architecture which might formulate, from the condition of an unprecedented social mobility, a relevant aesthetic based on inventive economy and practical execution? Diploma Unit 6 confronted these and other associated issues and focused upon the construction of what came to be known, within the unit, as a weak architecture. We defined this as an architecture disinterested in the resistant geometries of the Miesian aesthetic paradigm; an architecture driven by a much more flexible response to programme. Plural, inclusive, complex and formally pliable, such a weakness retained the strength of contemporary pertinence.

Diploma Unit 7

Unit Staff Nikolaus Hirsch Makoto Saito

Students Rasha Abusido Valentina Giacinti Mischa Gorchov Nikolas Heep Kentaro Ishida Spyridon Kaprinis Peter Lee Philipp Misselwitz Silvio Tonolli Britta van Egmond

Guest critics/Experts Frank Barkow Peter Beard Dirk Beusch Katharina Borsi Ludo Grooteman Finn Geipel Hugo Hinsley Neil Leach Wolf Mangelsdorf Florian Migsch Michael Mönninger Ciro Najle Kevin Rhowbotham Irénée Scalbert Nicolaus Schafhausen Stephie Schmidt Brett Steele Teresa Stoppani Charles Tashima Spela Videcnik Carlos Villanueva Brandt Wilfried Wang Mike Weinstock Markus Weisbeck Thilo Wermke

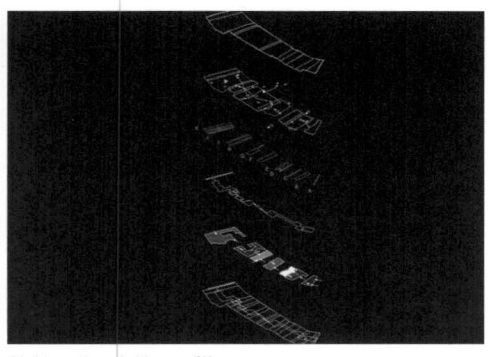

Stable and unstable conditions
Technological and economic change, including globalisation, poses a fundamental challenge to architecture and its pretensions to stability and determination. Whilst architectural research of the past decade has reacted to this situation with time-based concepts for rather generic contexts, the centres of political and cultural identity have remained in a timeless stasis. The aim of Unit 7 was to expand this research and investigate the relation between stability and instability in areas where the ambition of spatial control and fixed identity is traditionally high. The former centre of East Berlin was chosen as research and project field: on one hand it shows prototypically the collapse of a politically overloaded architectural concept, on the other hand it has again become a territory of political and cultural projection.

Centrality
Analysing paradigms of spatial organisation – from classical models such as the Greek *polis* to new spatial organisations such as the internet – the unit investigated the effects of central and centrifugal phenomena on architectural space. Applied to the decontextualised centre of Berlin, the potential of urban strategies was tested by heterogenous, interconnected parameters (visuality, politics, programme).
A series of material interventions question if and how architecture can embody centrality (or its absence).

History and evolution
Thinking of history and the historicity of buildings in evolutionary terms allowed a reinterpretation of architecture as a structure that oscillates between determination and indetermination, beween fixity and change. The interest was focused on stable, architecturally highly determined frameworks that provide space for the unstable, i.e. elements created by unpredictable and situation-related processes. Economic and social changes thus appear as opportunities and bases for further design, rather than as deviations from some previously defined end-state or final condition.

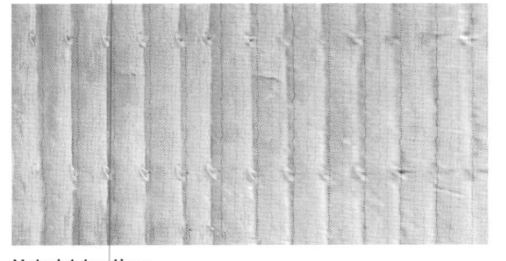

Material durations
Investigating the stable and unstable conditions of material, the unit explored the possibilities and limitations of preserving time in architecture. The material detail is seen as an integral part of the design process, its ideal status would be a detail that reflects a whole concept. In this sense the detail is part of a larger argument: as a basic element it forms architectural coherence; on the other hand it is a component of temporal cycles, structural systems and junctions that concretise the material consequences of change.

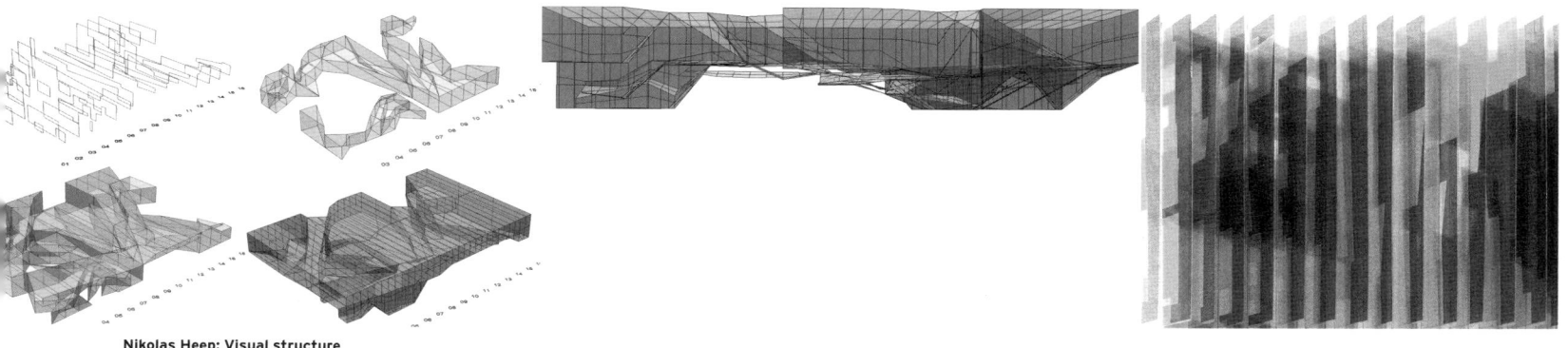

Nikolas Heep: Visual structure
Visual analysis questions and reinforces the notion of centrality of a site which has been the nucleus of urban development in Berlin. The result is a visual architectural object that focuses the city and is in turn focused by it. The visual parameters coincide with structural parameters forming a new museum that separates zones of different densities programmatically and structurally.

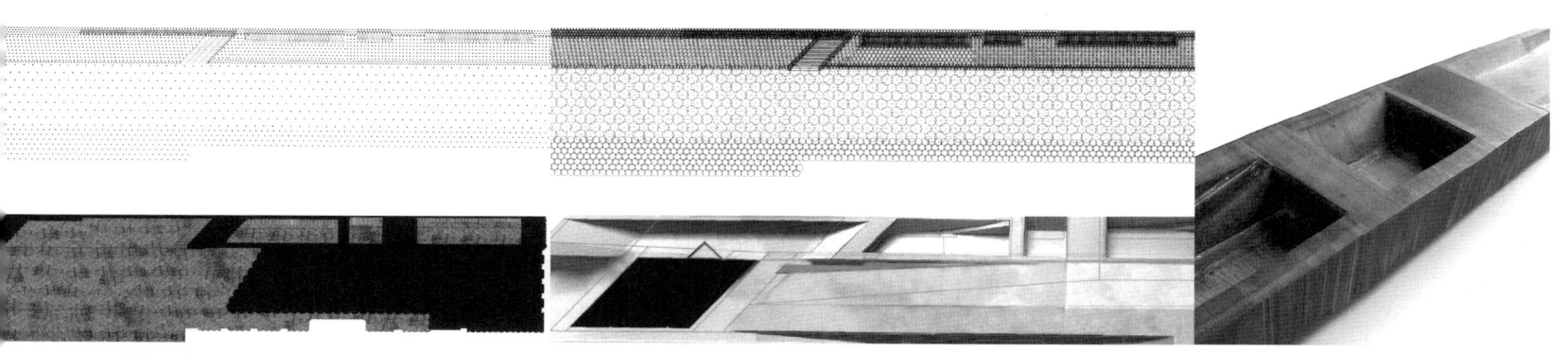

Philipp Misselwitz: Foundations of space
Based on the identification and analysis of symptoms of instability and collapse, the project proposes an urban strategy of gradual consolidation. A series of interventions create new connections between abandoned and decontextualised elements of the former communist axis. Its material is a grouting technique whose concrete structure is manipulated according to the use of the different territories.

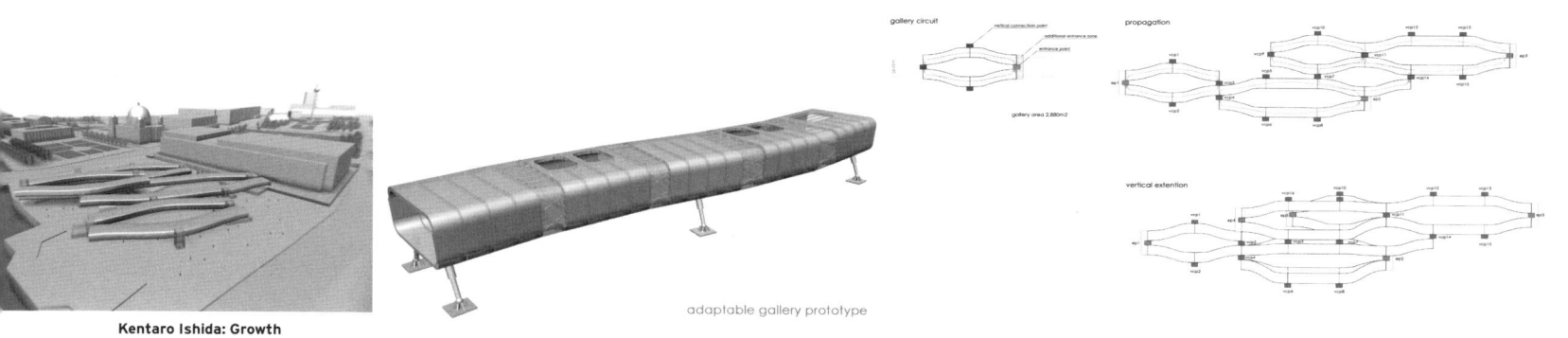

adaptable gallery prototype

Kentaro Ishida: Growth
Extending the museum island, the project explores the possibilities of a growing museum. The process of growth is determined by inherent museal parameters and local conditions of the urban context.

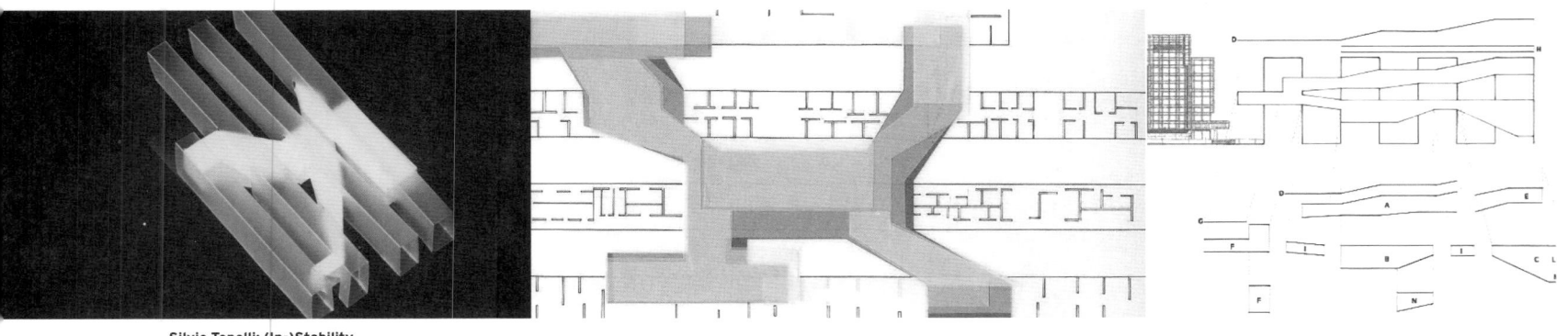

Silvio Tonolli: (In-)Stability
The conflict between stability and instability is addressed in a media museum: on the one hand, strip-like objects that are programmatically stable (i.e. permanent) but structurally unstable; on the other, connecting elements that are programmatically unstable (i.e. non-permanent) but stabilise, in a structural sense, the whole system.

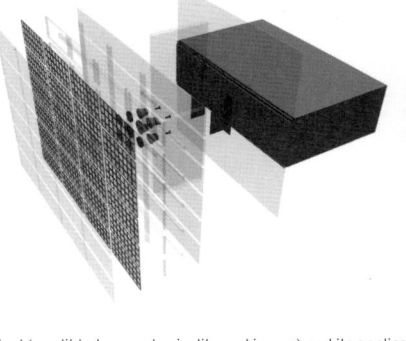

Mischa Gorchov: Conversion
After research on the constitution of architectural 'value' (a split between physicality and image) and its application on the centre of Berlin, the project focused on the abandoned communist Palace of the Republic, transforming it into a mimetic building. A pixelled LED-facade system works both as a changing iconological system of architectural politics and as a new climatical tool for the reuse of a building structure.

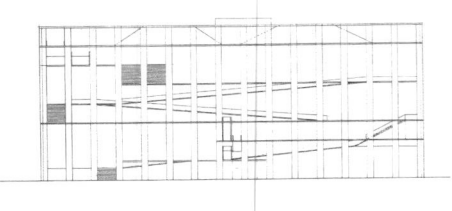
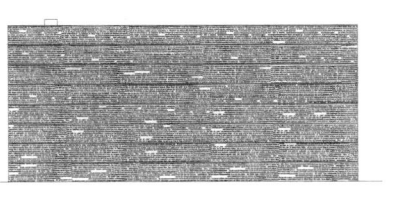

Spyridon Kaprinis: Densities
The work focuses on notions of architectural density. A fusion of structural and programmatic density creates a library as an element of cultural memory and research in the context of the museum island.

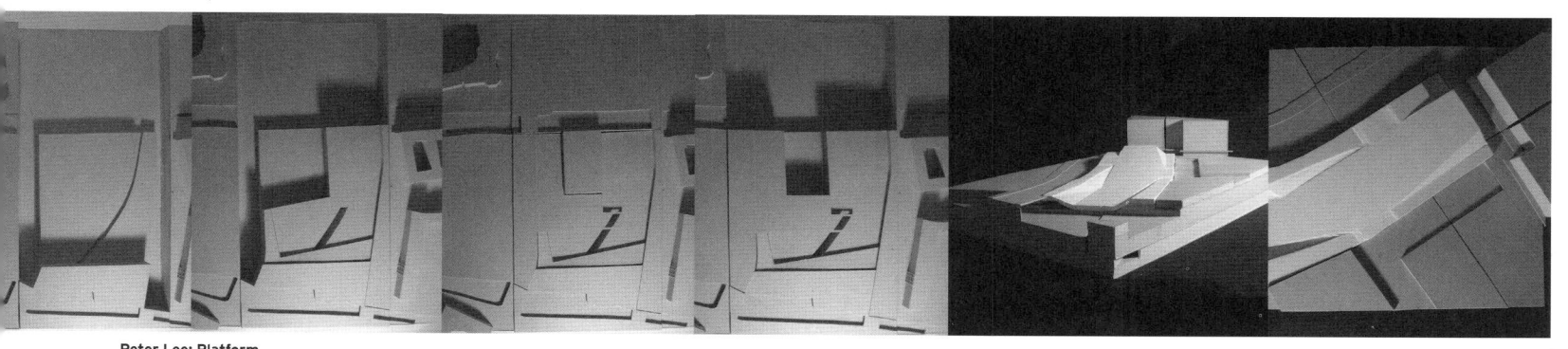

Peter Lee: Platform
A platform connects three different scales on the site: urban scale, local scale, non scale. Determined by precisely identified conditions its architecture works as a historical and geological segmentation. Programmatically an open public platform, it is structurally a floating object whose weight and shape counterbalances the water pressure of a specific ground condition.

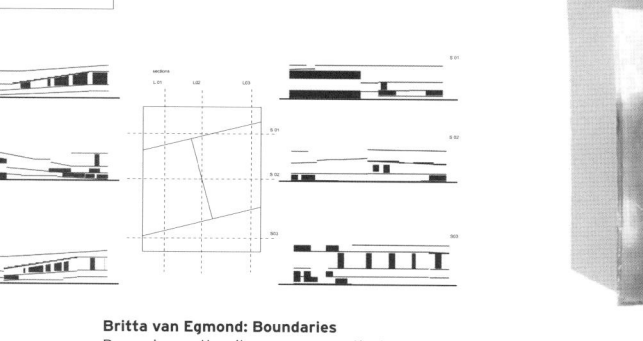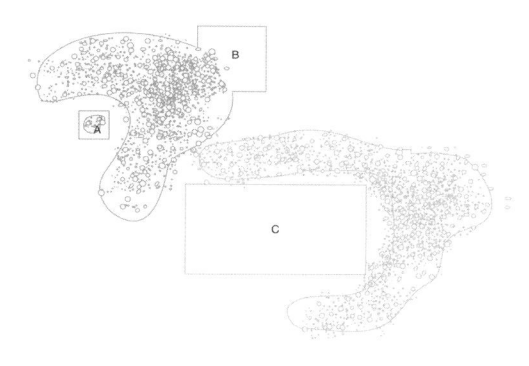

Britta van Egmond: Boundaries
Proposing on the site a programmatical crossover of the centre of Berlin, the project questions monofunctional logic and its impact on public space. The main tool of this approach is the programmatic and technological distinction between specific areas for autonomous functional entities and non-specific areas that are used as a continuous shared space.

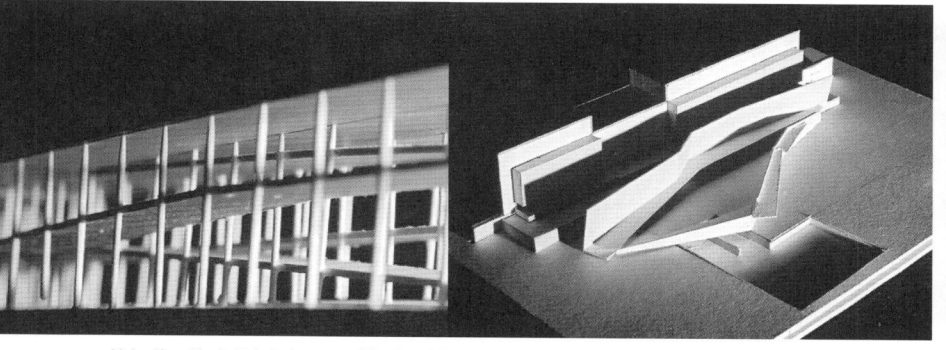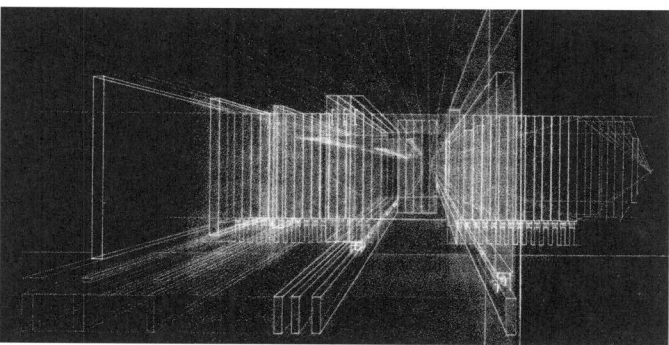

Valentina Giacinti: In between political architecture
The project intervenes in a precisely defined situation: in between the relics of communism and monarchy. The link works in a double sense: metaphorically as a generator of a dialectical image, literally as a possibility of access.

Rasha Abusido: Storing history
A fusion of exhibition and storage questions the role of the museum as cultural hierarchy in a context where the production of culture becomes more and more inflationary. Exploring the mechanism of showing and hiding, the project creates new configurations of exhibitions as an architectural mnemotechnique.

TASK I: implementing the program of the Mobile Factory within the city's existing physical, social and institutional infrastructure.

TASK II: generating an urban strategy for collection of currently randomly distributed waste (scrap tires; scrap metal - predominantly barrels and cars; etc.)

TASK III: defining a spatial layout of 'disposal-collection' stations across the city (gas stations could be used as disposal-collection stations for scrap tires)

TASK IV: developing efficient 'building machines' that could operate within the truck-box environment.

TASK V: producing a catalogue of architectural elements that could be produced in this nomadic manner.

TASK VI: developing scenarios for a building strategy on the site.

urban renewal through the infrastructure of rubbish distribution

materials **free** of charge

Belgrade

Arcadia for all

designs from the european edge: belgrade's new life

A factory on the shores of the Danube acts as an interactive toolbox for refugees to make a house and a new life in a community created from the detritus of the past: Sinisa Rodic

bringing people to the river front

Temporary Housing for the refugees is incorporated into the river scheme so that it 1)revels itself (the issue of the refugees) to the citizens (increases public awareness consequently puts the pressure on government), and 2)provides easier access to jobs refugees (generates a 'platform' for goods exchange near where they live), but also become a subject of interest of the private capital. Now prominent location of the stimulate private entrepreneurs to provide housing for the refugees elsewhere in E their river locati

inserting programs such is green, fish, and second hand MARKETS

connection with the river banks

appropriation of its surroundings

floating structure

causes

and consequently

increase of the flow of people

connection with the river transport

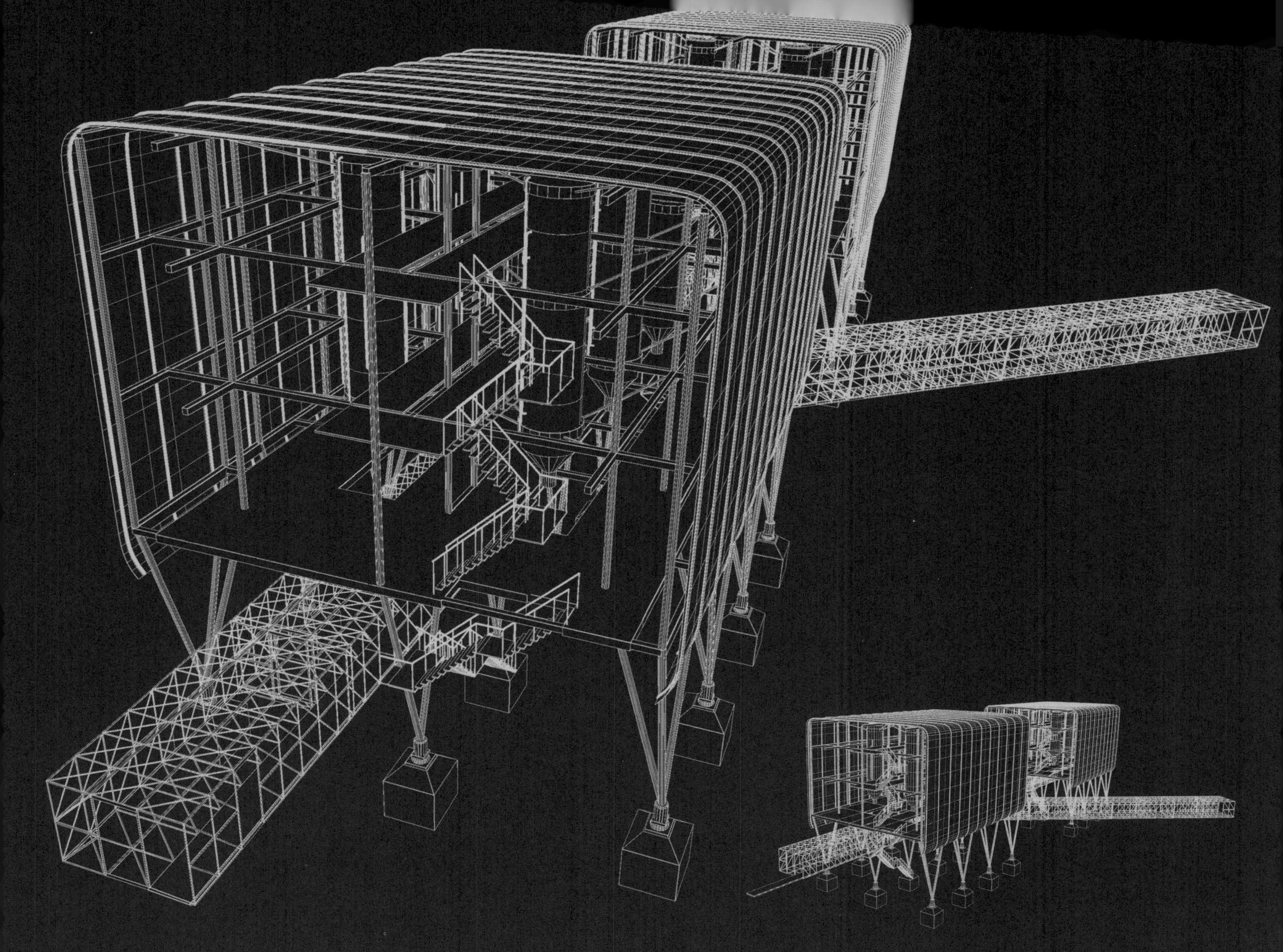

katowice's new minehead industries

A vodka distillery which uses a peculiar technique to surf the waves of mining subsidence and thus maintains employment in a model garden city, with the current visions of the future
being slab blocks and hypermarkets: Sven Steiner

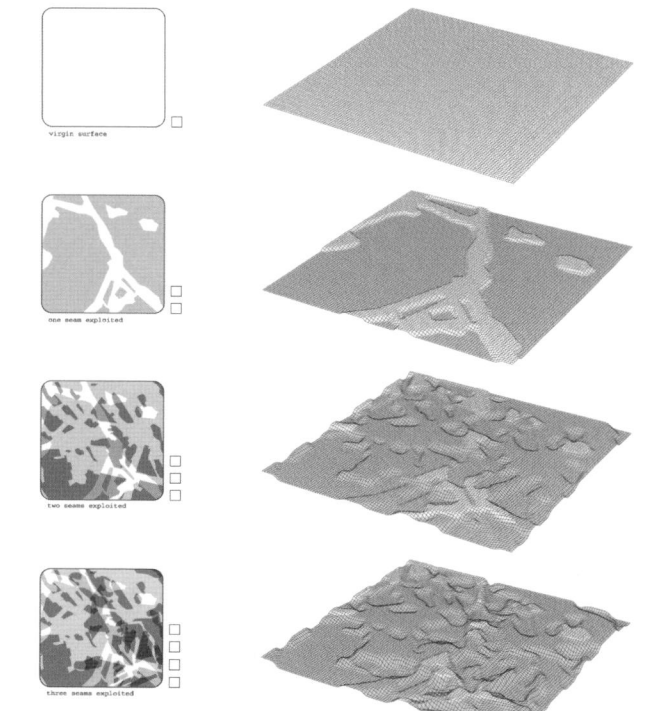

virgin surface

one seam exploited

two seams exploited

three seams exploited

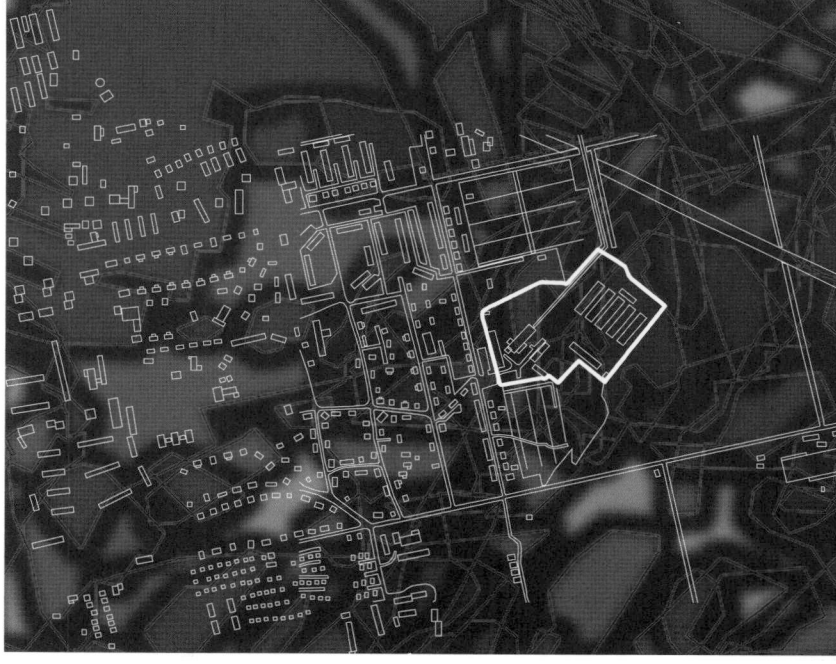

tales from the edge of europe: gdansk's new port

A specialised shipyard in Gdansk that by incorporating a university and a commercial centre capitalises on the city's embodied skills in making high-value products: Ho Yin Ng

A partially temporary structure that puts the Notting Hill Carnival above the Westway and addresses the various cultures of post-imperial England.

Maria Cheung

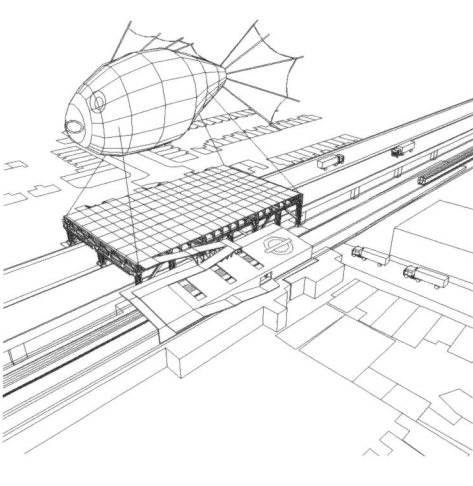

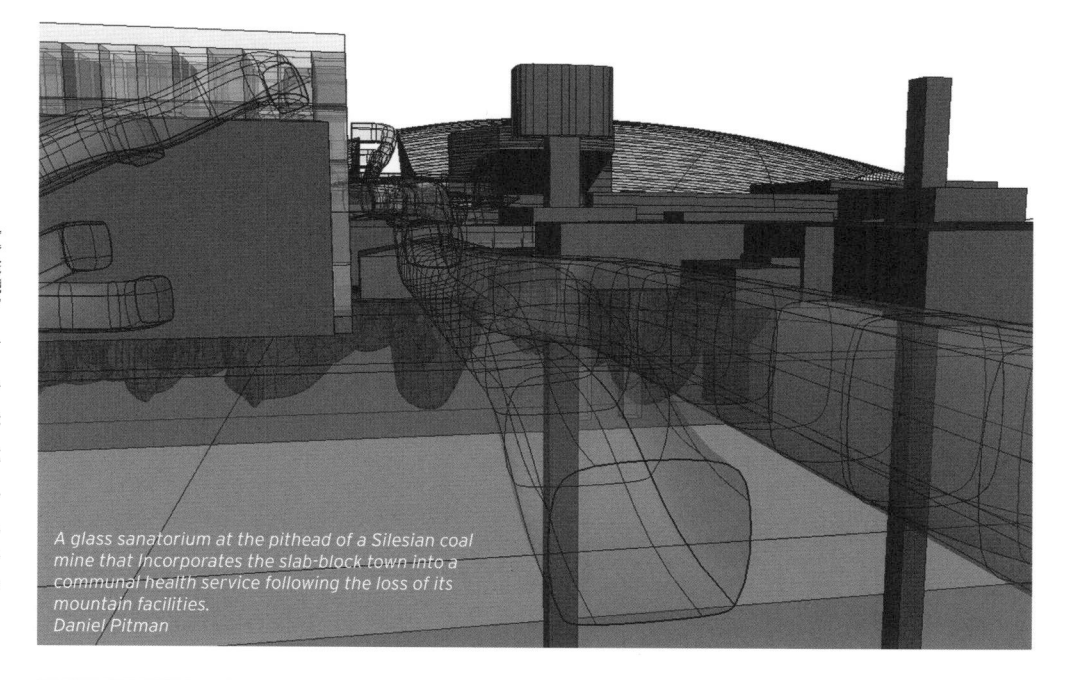

A glass sanatorium at the pithead of a Silesian coal mine that incorporates the slab-block town into a communal health service following the loss of its mountain facilities.
Daniel Pitman

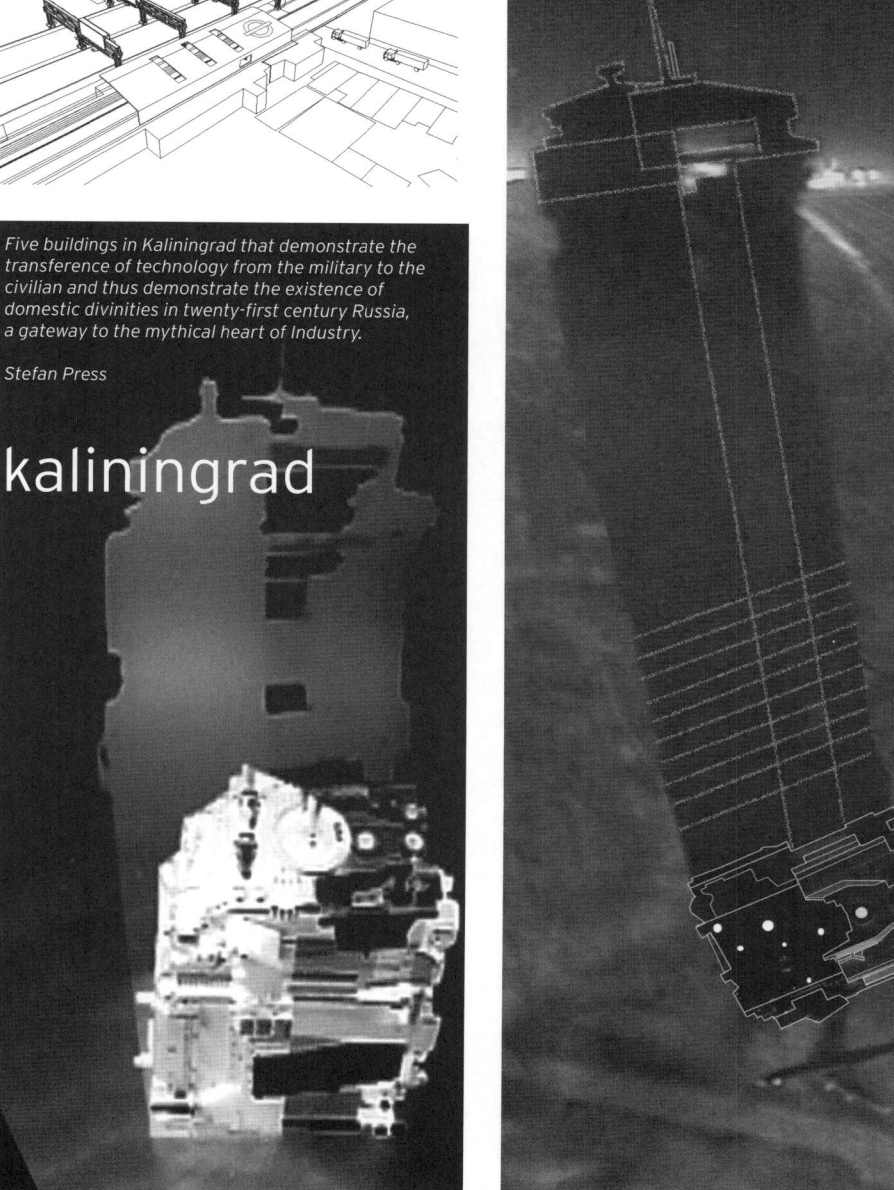

Five buildings in Kaliningrad that demonstrate the transference of technology from the military to the civilian and thus demonstrate the existence of domestic divinities in twenty-first century Russia, a gateway to the mythical heart of Industry.

Stefan Press

kaliningrad

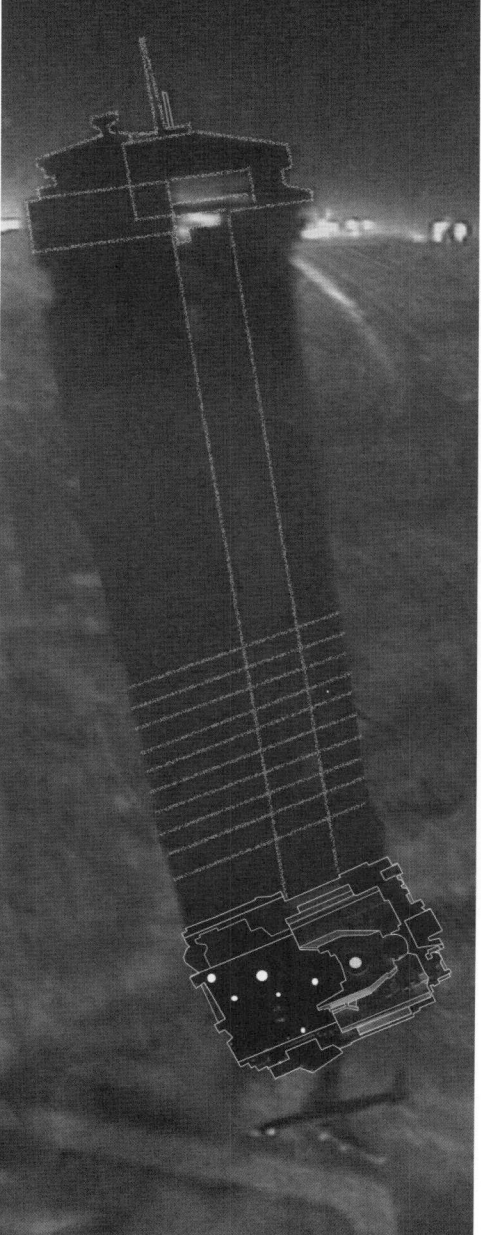

Five factory and service buildings in Berlin which through the medium of sausages make an architectural mirror to the process of rebuilding the new capital of Germany.

Lena Nalbach

Unit Staff
Mark Prizeman
Kevin Shepherd
Peter Thomas

Students
Maria Cheung
Lea Katseli
Matthew John Lynch
Lena Nalbach
Yuko Nanno
Ho Yin Ng
Daniel Pitman
Stefan Press
Sinisa Rodic
Sven Steiner

... who all wish to thank:
Mark Fisher
David Greene
Brian Hatton
Jeffrey James
Marysia Lewandowska
Benny O'Looney
Guy Mannes Abbott
Mike Roberts
Jenny Romyn
Martin Sexton
Mike Weinstock

Diploma Unit 9

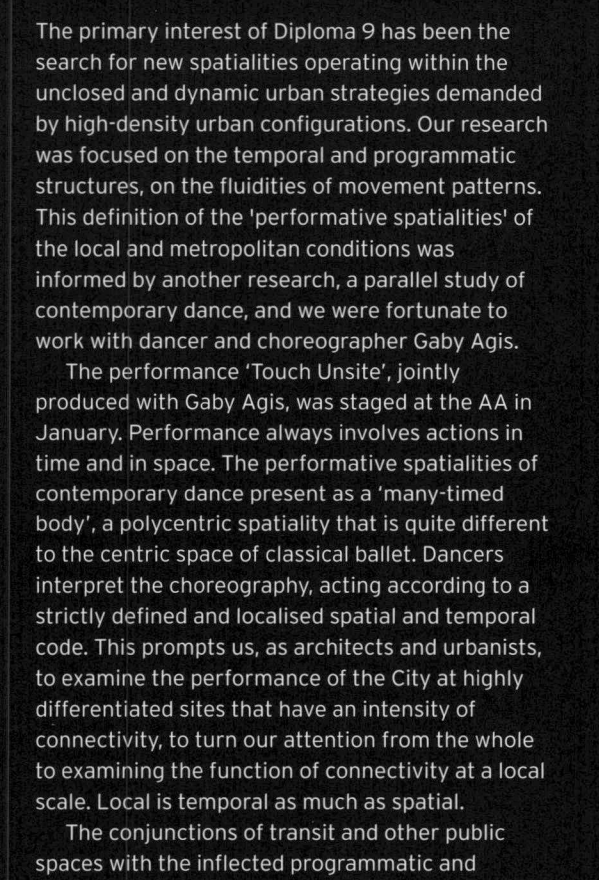

The primary interest of Diploma 9 has been the search for new spatialities operating within the unclosed and dynamic urban strategies demanded by high-density urban configurations. Our research was focused on the temporal and programmatic structures, on the fluidities of movement patterns. This definition of the 'performative spatialities' of the local and metropolitan conditions was informed by another research, a parallel study of contemporary dance, and we were fortunate to work with dancer and choreographer Gaby Agis.

The performance 'Touch Unsite', jointly produced with Gaby Agis, was staged at the AA in January. Performance always involves actions in time and in space. The performative spatialities of contemporary dance present as a 'many-timed body', a polycentric spatiality that is quite different to the centric space of classical ballet. Dancers interpret the choreography, acting according to a strictly defined and localised spatial and temporal code. This prompts us, as architects and urbanists, to examine the performance of the City at highly differentiated sites that have an intensity of connectivity, to turn our attention from the whole to examining the function of connectivity at a local scale. Local is temporal as much as spatial.

The conjunctions of transit and other public spaces with the inflected programmatic and temporal patterns of urban trajectories were the subject of an investigation in Shibuya, Tokyo. The collaborative workshop was hosted by Nobuyuki Nomura and by Tokyo University.

These investigations, in London and Tokyo, included the analysis of flows and movements, of temporal networks and vectors of spatial orientation, of organisational paradigms particular to transit and high rise. They are the base code from which architectures and performative spatialities for the intensification of the South Bank were evolved.

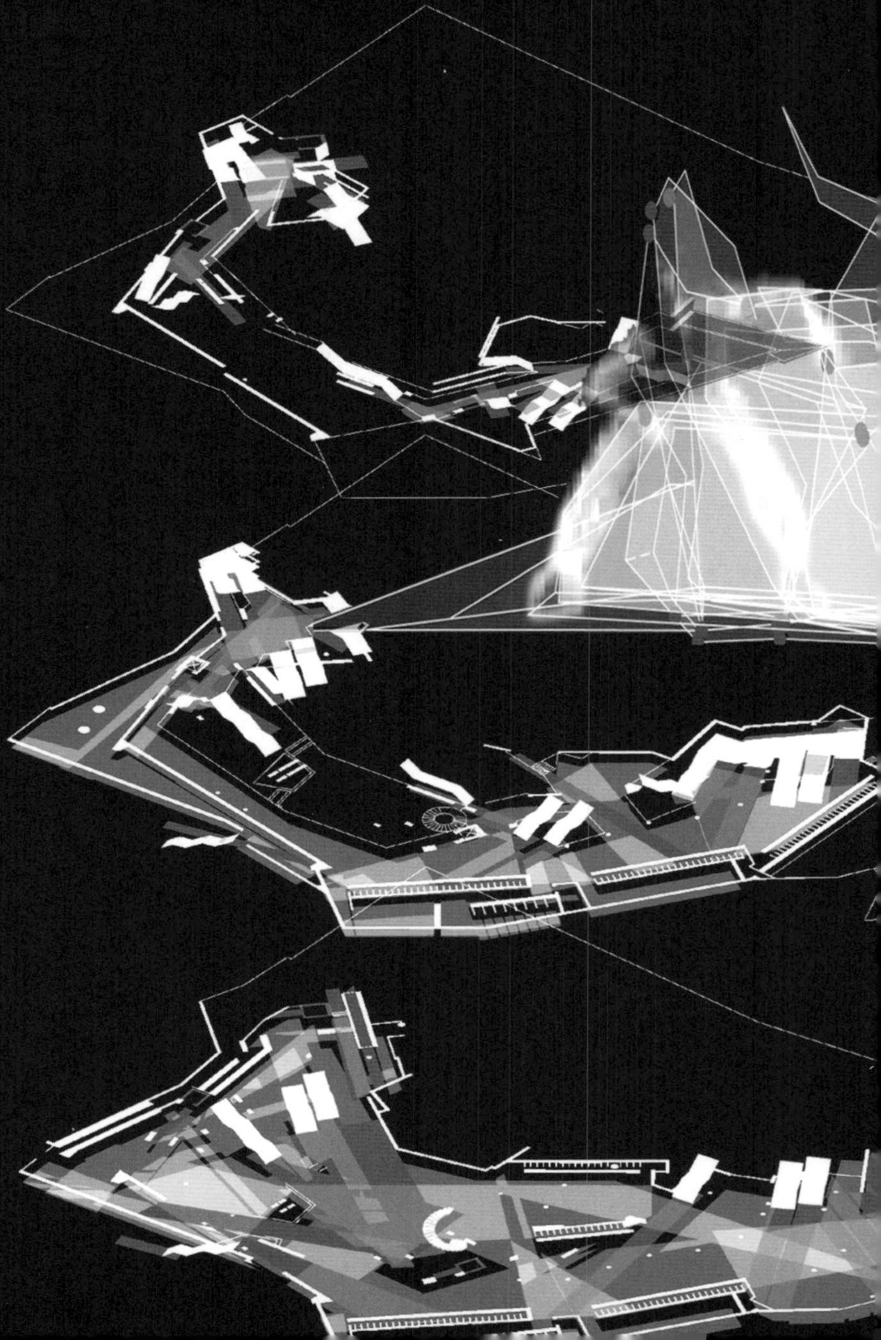

Unit Master
Michael Weinstock

Students
Jite Brume
Jan Clostermann
Rahkee Kantarian
Sarah Mackie
Pasi Makonnen
Kayoko Ohtsuki
Jordi Pagés Ramon
Eva Scheffler
Bibiana Zapf

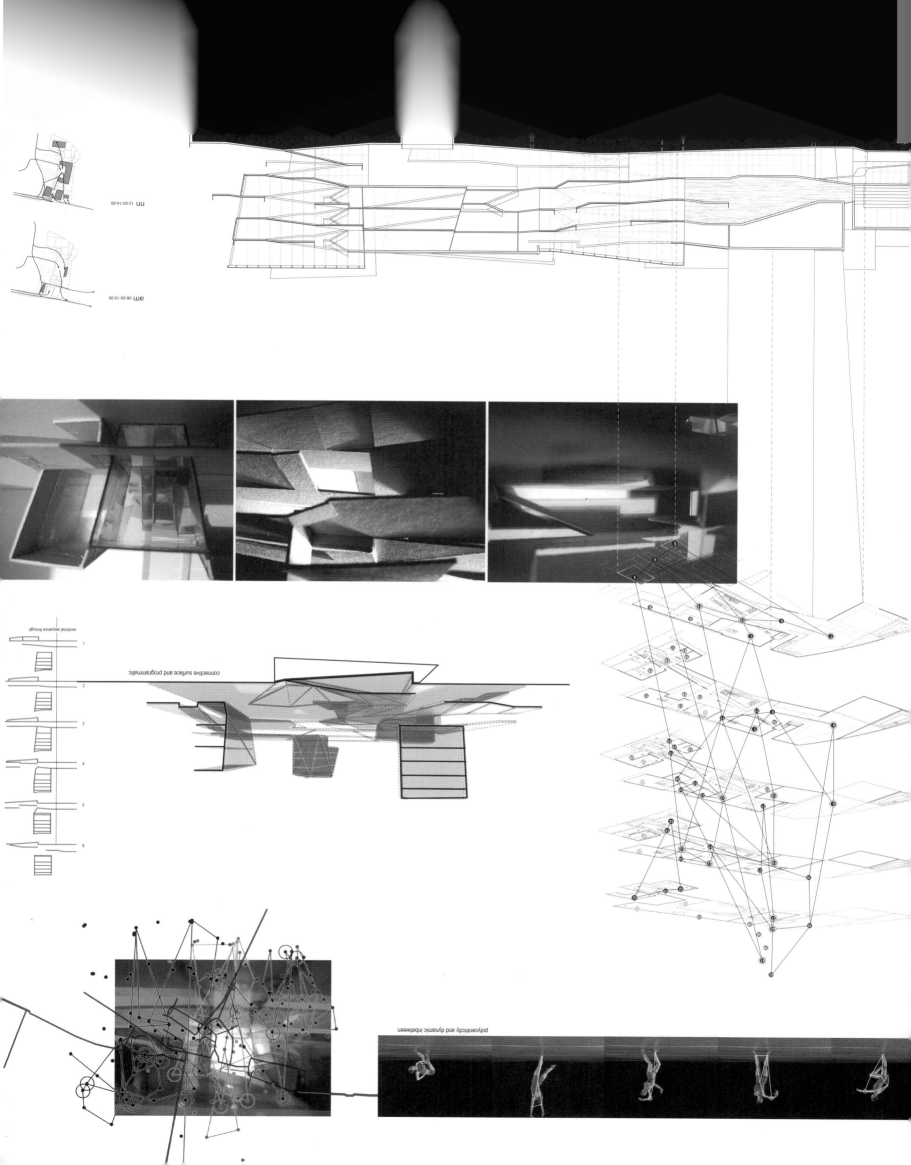

nn 12.00-14.00

am 08.00-10.00

sectional sequence through

connective surface and programmatic

polycentricity and dynamic inbetween

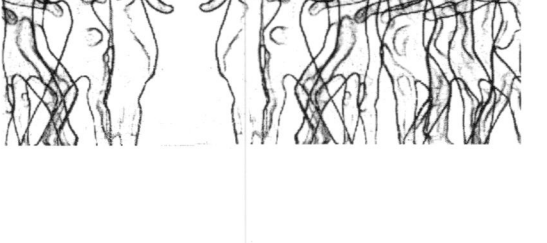

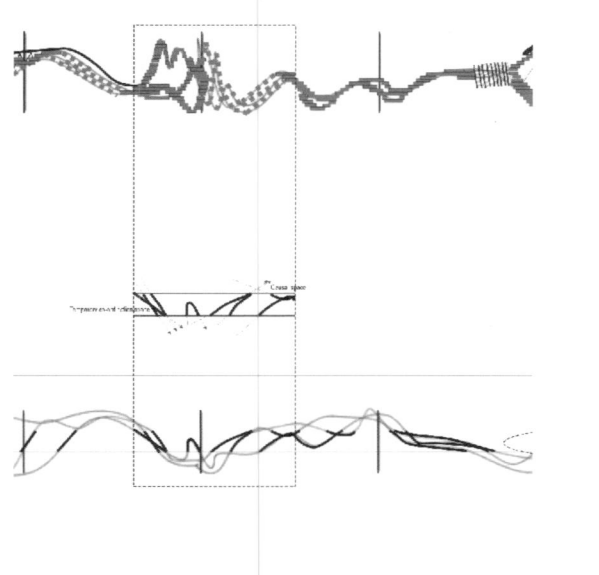

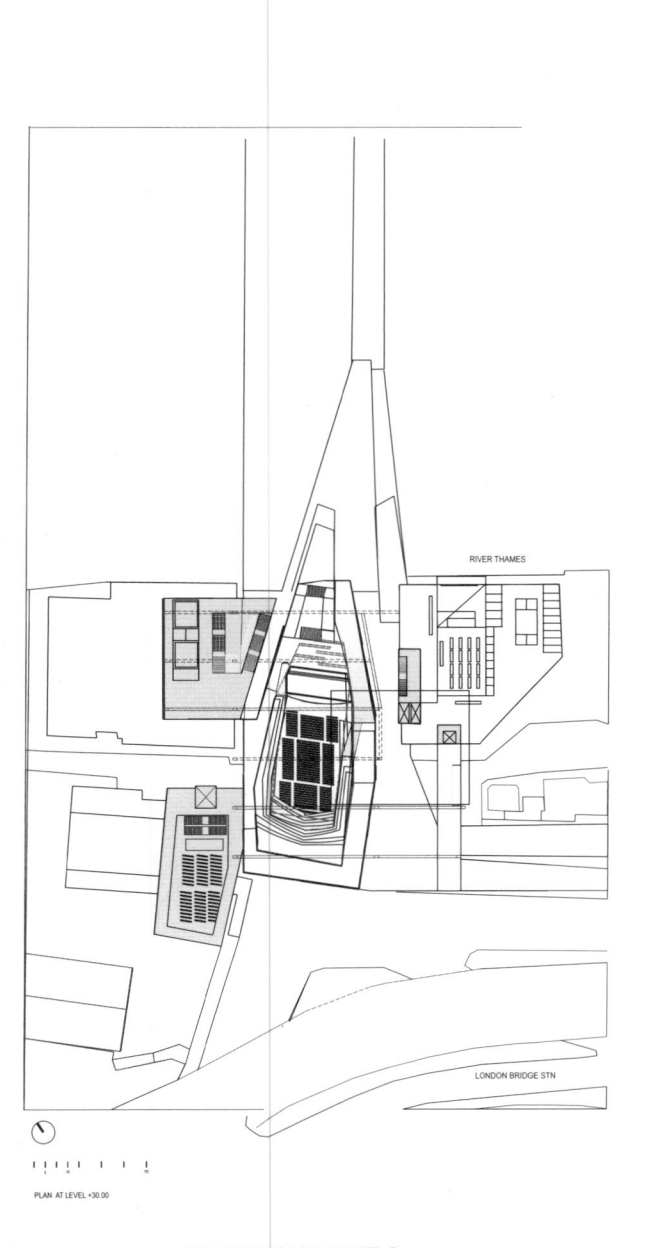

RIVER THAMES

LONDON BRIDGE STN

PLAN AT LEVEL +30.00

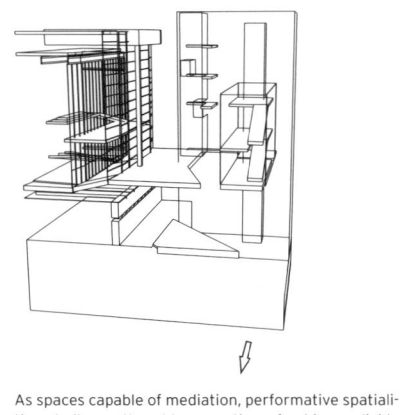

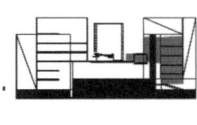
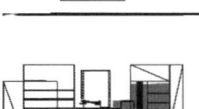
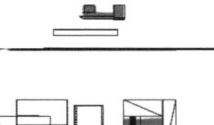
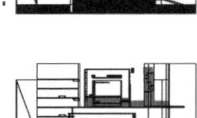
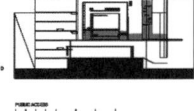

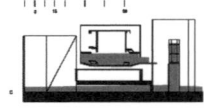
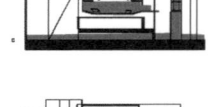
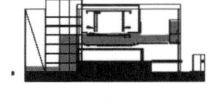

As spaces capable of mediation, performative spatiali-ties challenge the old conception of a binary divide between inside and outside, between physical and programmatic conditions. They promote a shift of conditions, devised in such a way that functions of traditional boundaries and envelopes (such as sec-urity, environmental encapsulations and social con-trol) can be expressed in a more open and inclusive environment. Performative spatialities mediate and expand spatial imagination. They expose the entrails of urbanism and propose a break in the hierarchical design approaches.

Performative spatialities operate best in dense urban environments; they can relax congested conditions and negotiate polarities. Highly interconnective, they can be choreographed into an unfolding sequence that provides a possibility for highly varied social practices to contest.

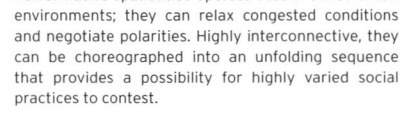

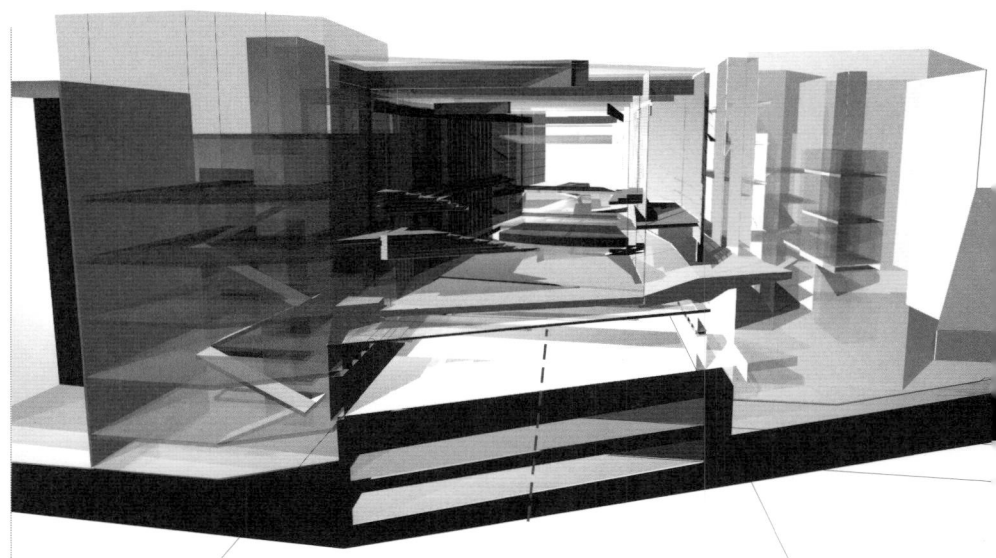

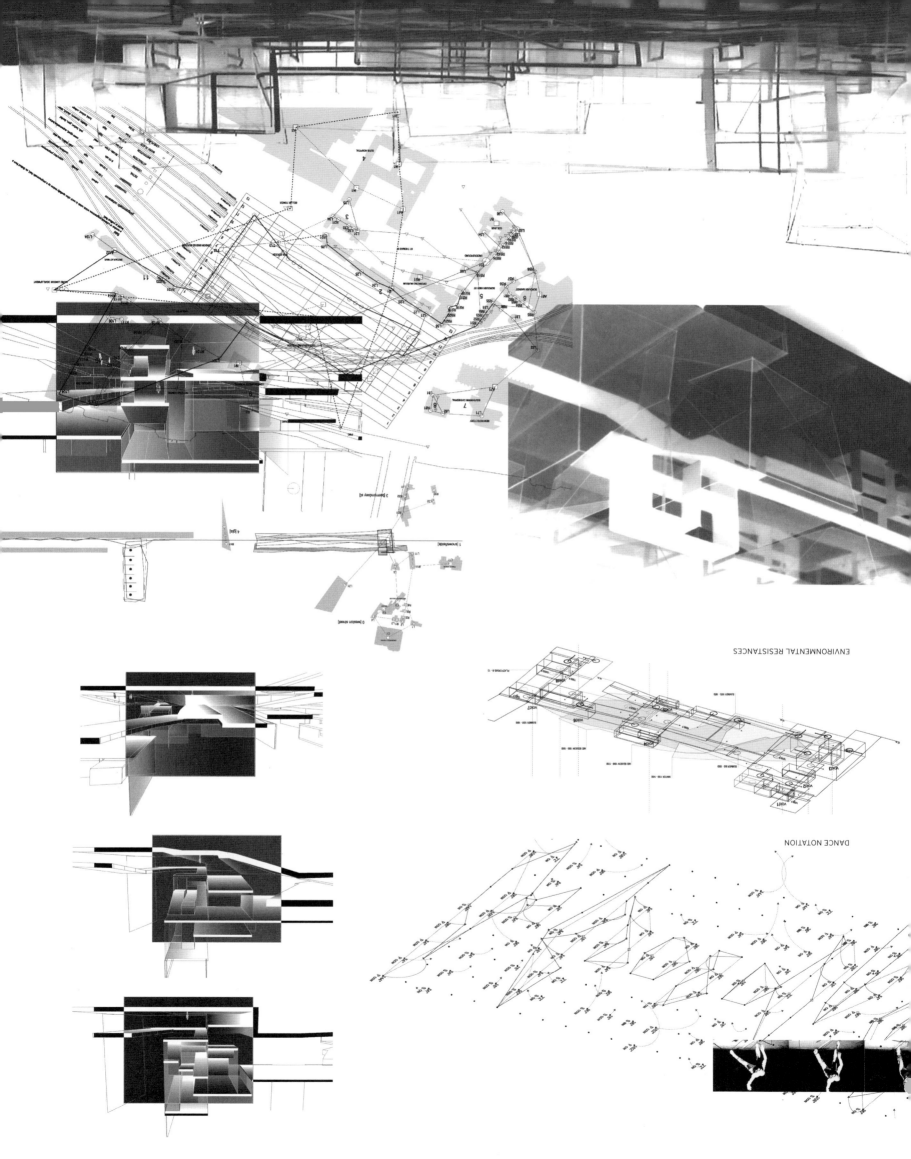

ENVIRONMENTAL RESISTANCES

DANCE NOTATION

Diploma Unit 10

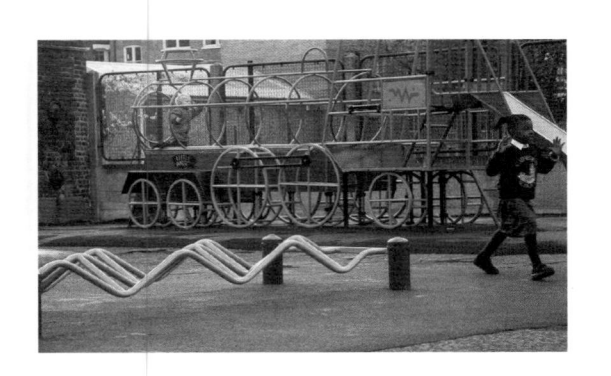

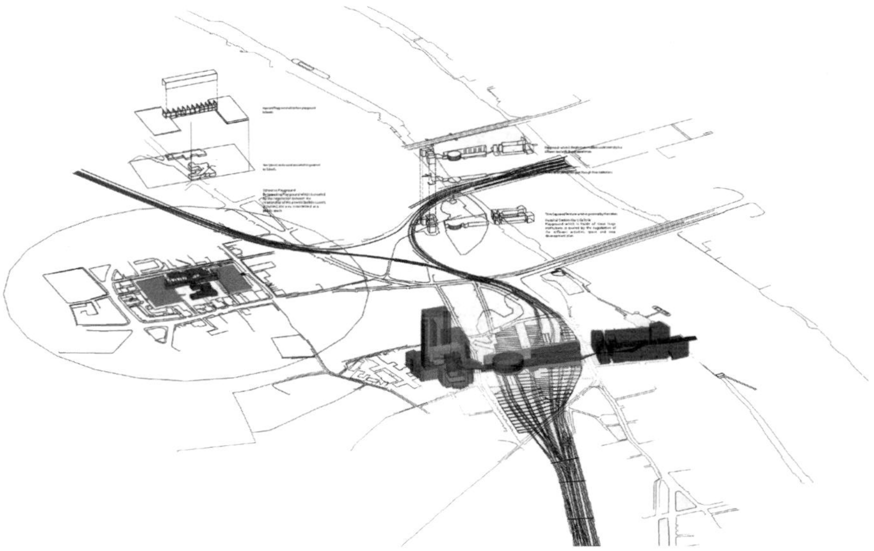

9. PLAYGROUNDS: 1 + 2

Three centres of change in London: the Junction (public), the Infrastructure (social) and the Institution (physical). The Junction reassesses existing boundaries

4. PRISON: PENTONVILLE CORRIDORS

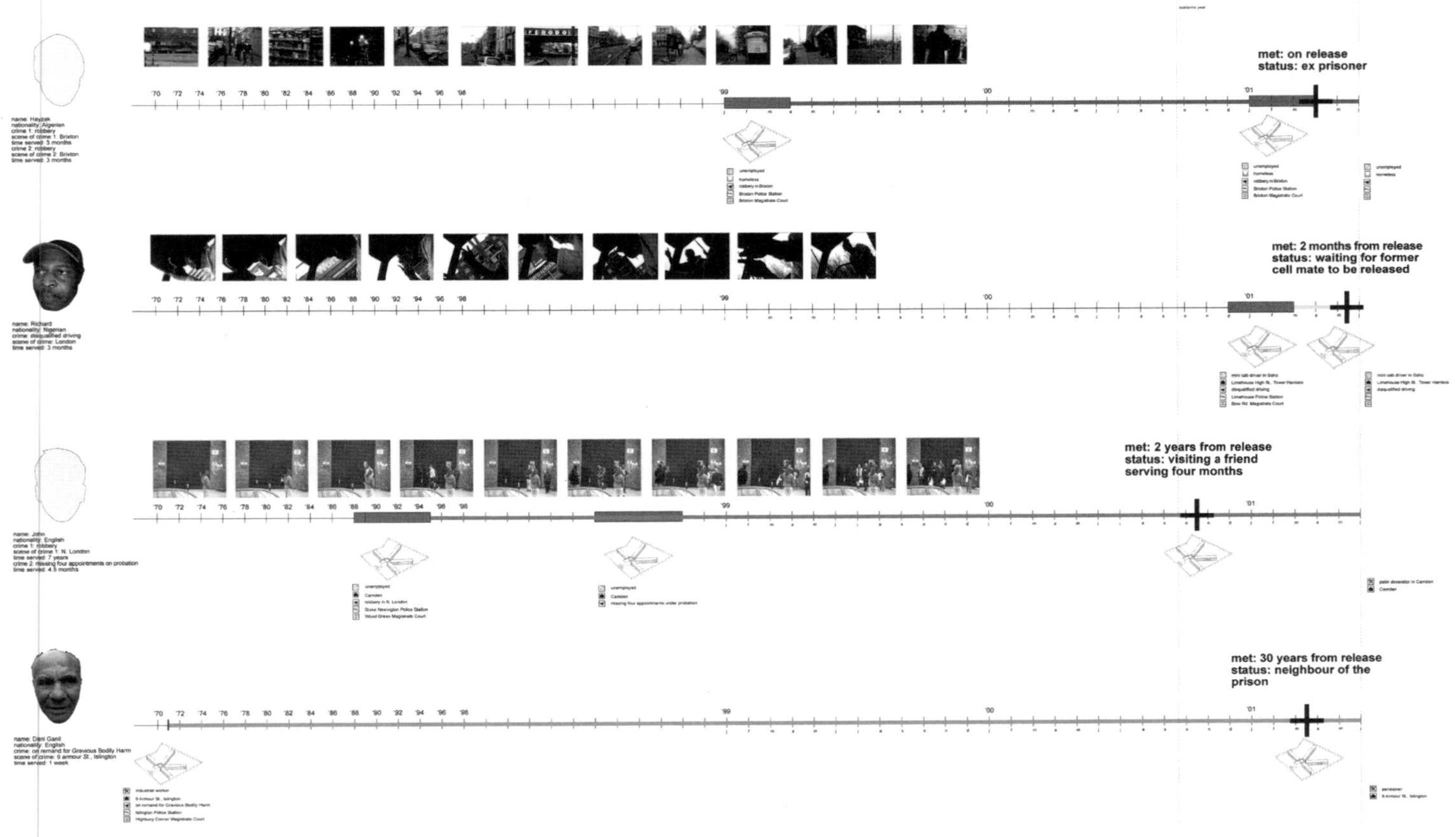
met: on release
status: ex prisoner
met: 2 months from release
status: waiting for former cell mate to be released
met: 2 years from release
status: visiting a friend serving four months
met: 30 years from release
status: neighbour of the prison

3. SCHOOL: 15ZONE

A
B
C
river thames
lt bus stop
more london
city mission
domino
lewis house
tooley st
gla
arches
spendloads
neckinger
warehouse
M
T
W
T
F
S
S

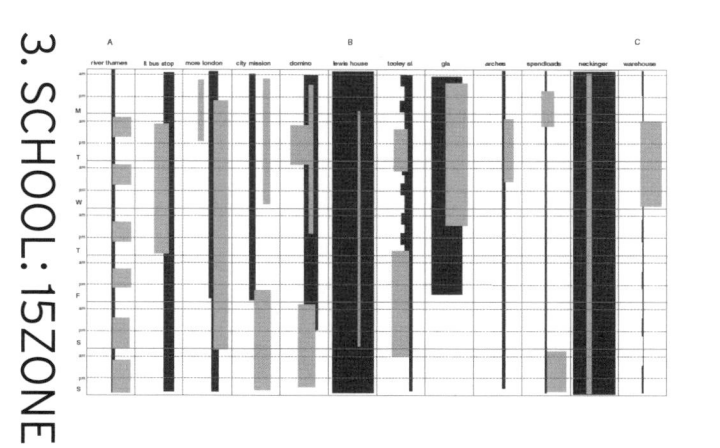

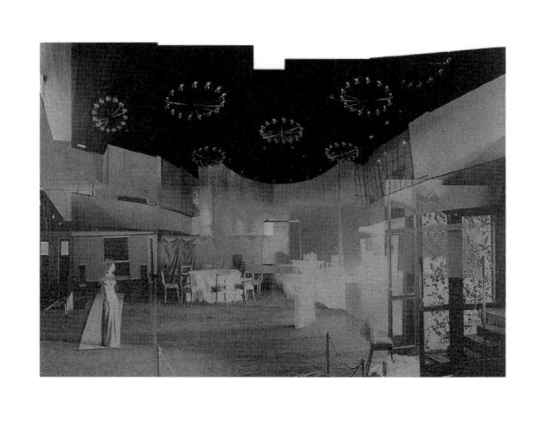

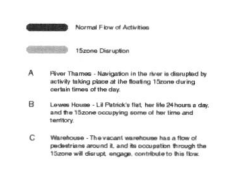

Normal Flow of Activities

15zone Disruption

A River Thames - Navigation in the river is disrupted by activity taking place at the floating 15zone during certain times of the day.

B Lewes House - Lil Patrick's flat, her life 24 hours a day, and the 15zone occupying some of her time and territory.

C Warehouse - The vacant warehouse has a flow of pedestrians around it, and its occupation through the 15zone will disrupt, engage, contribute to this flow.

and existing physical structures. The Infrastructure imposes cultural structures as instruments of change. The Institution combines physical, cultural and

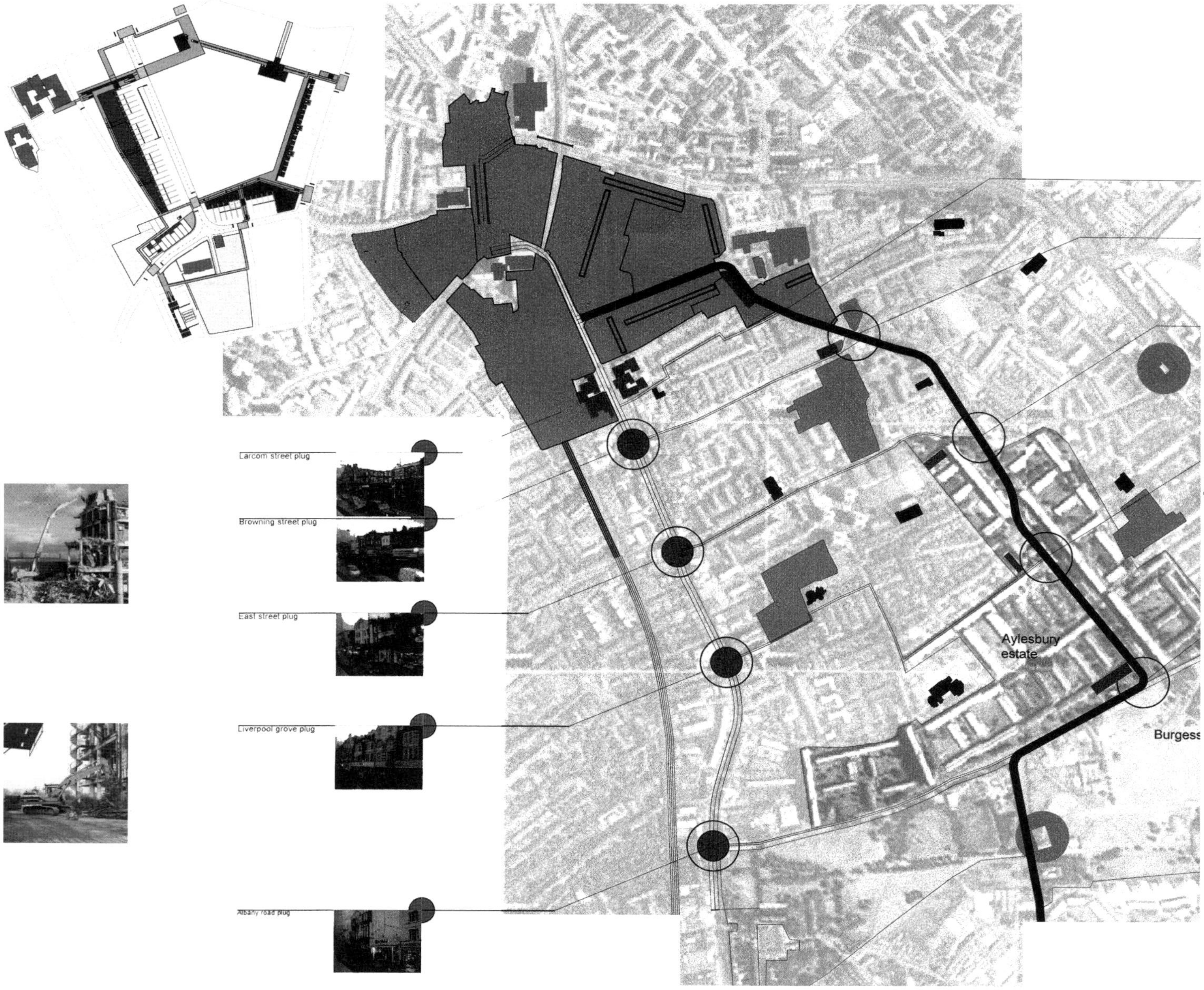

Larcom street plug
Browning street plug
East street plug
Liverpool grove plug
Albany road plug
Aylesbury estate
Burgess

8. LIBRARY: TRANSITIONAL/RESIDUAL

conceptual space. Change acts at three scales: the urban (Junction) manipulates and adds to the existing urban space, the social (Infrastructure)

7. SCHOOL: ORANGE CURRICULUM

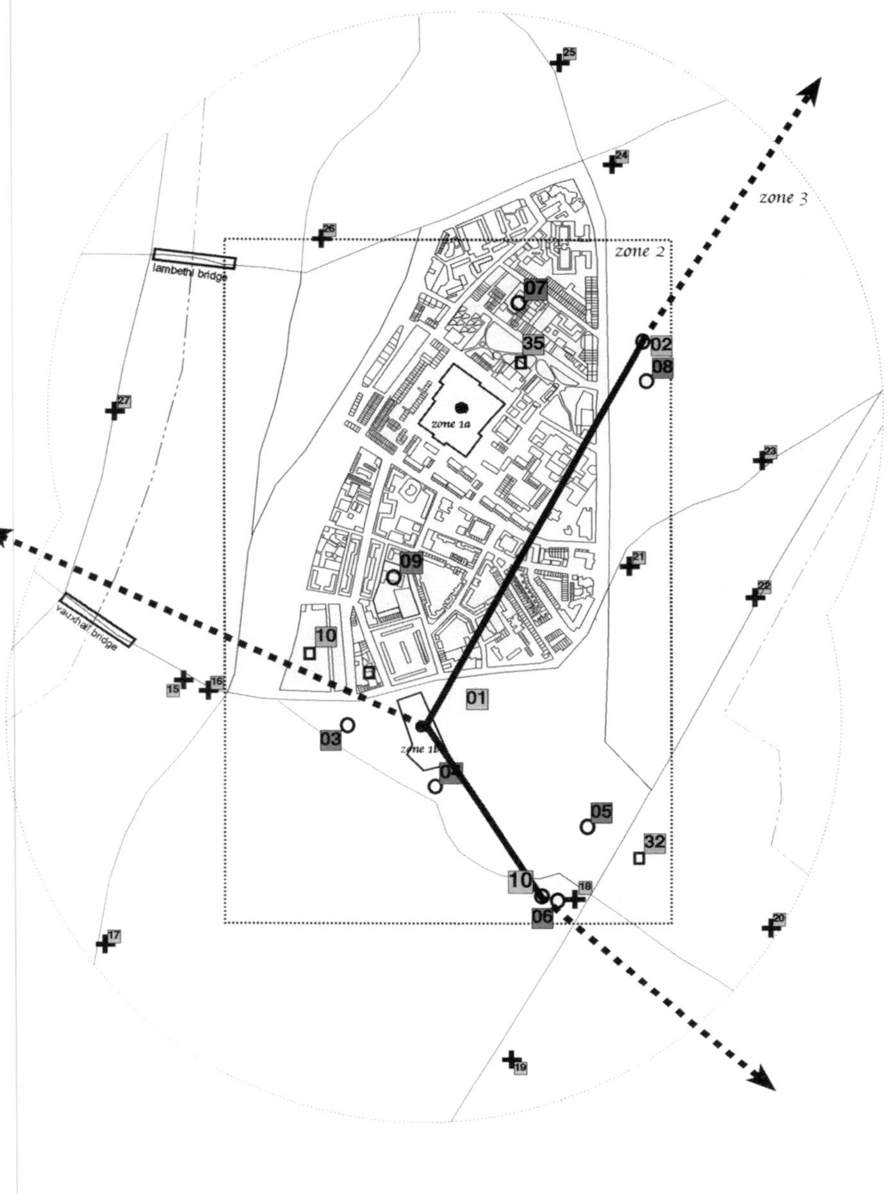

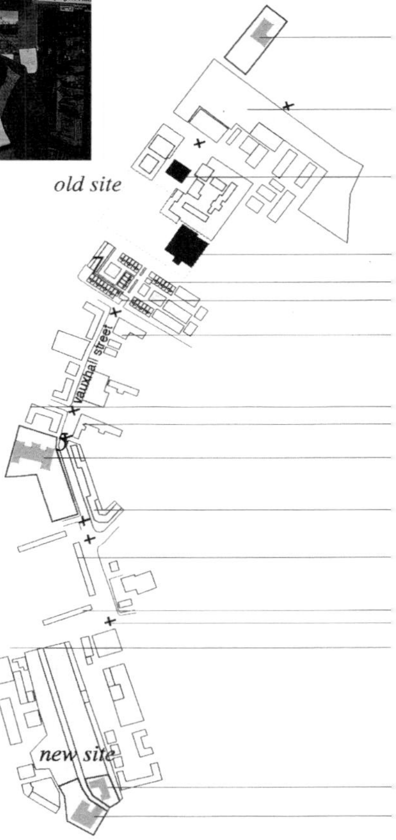

old site

new site

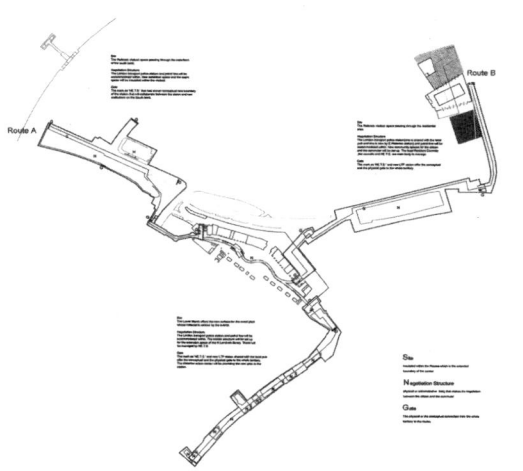

Route A

participates in and influences social space, and the architectural (Institution) designs and generates architectural space.

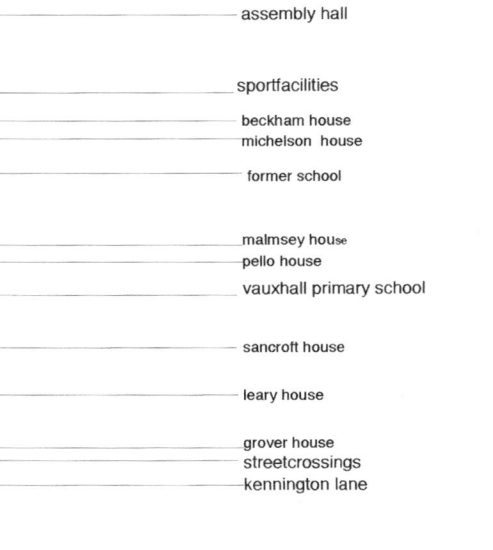

walnuttree primary school

lambeth walk open space

assembly hall

sportfacilities

beckham house
michelson house

former school

malmsey house
pello house

vauxhall primary school

sancroft house

leary house

grover house
streetcrossings
kennington lane

nursery school

st marks primary school

Services Backbone

Strips

Adoptive Strips

Red-route Ring

Students
1. Rita Akermane
2. Sharon Harvey
3. Rumi Kubokawa
4. Gaspar Libedinsky
5. Joseph Macedo
6. Jin-Seok Park
7. Susanne Schmelcher
8. Alexandra Stratou
9. JungHun Whang

Unit Master
Carlos Villanueva Brandt

5. STRIPS: ADOPTED CULTURE

Diploma Unit 11

1

2

Body as textural details of the city

After an initial period of research into materials of industry in London, the unit was joined by Tadashi Kawamata for a collaborative project, 'Lodging London/Tokyo'. The project became not so much a search for comfort, as an opportunity to place the body in a more potent relation to the familiar – to lodge it within a piece of micro-architecture made of materials that had been washed up on the shores of consumption.

Testing ground

Haneda is an old town adjacent to the reclaimed island that includes Tokyo Haneda airport. When the US military took over the island at the end of WW2, it evicted the whole fishing community at 48 hours' notice. Haneda, linked to the island by a small bridge, doubled its population and density at a stroke.

Interior-Landscape

The post-war industrialisation of Tokyo began with intensified communities of cottage industries. In Haneda we found specialised individual families with skills that could bridge the gap between mass-production and prototype-fabrication. Although their methods appear to be very anarchic they are in fact highly organised and flexible.

The entire fabric of Haneda has grown wildly and condensed as a complex of cottage industries. Buried in a small factory within this dense fabric, we found a couple producing the most technically advanced prototype detail for the fastest train in the world.

4

3

5

6

Haneda, Tokyo

7

8

1, 2: Furnishing gaps of Haneda/Peter Tso, Barbara Perez, Yu Iwai. 3, 10: Skins of diary/Greg Sheng, Christina Pappa, Barbara Perez, (drawn by Greg Sheng). 4, 5: Caving on the water for Lodging in Hackney Marsh/Rentaro Nishimura, Carlos Pena Ponte. 6: Glass study, flat milk bottles/Yoko Murakami. 7: Soil study, Earth Puzzles/Rentaro Nishimura, Barbara Perez. 8: Sand-casting factory study, interior landscape/Peter Tso.

9

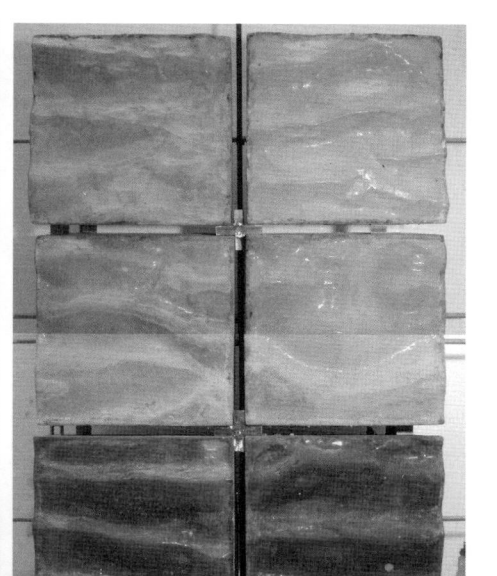

10

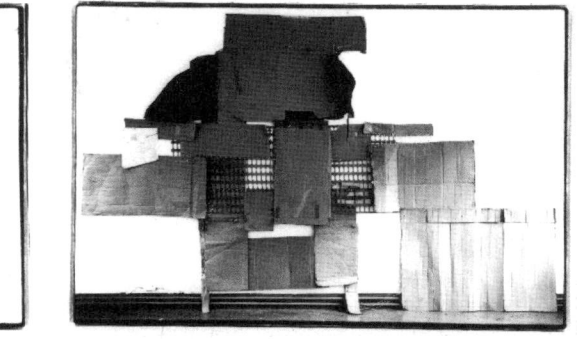

11

14

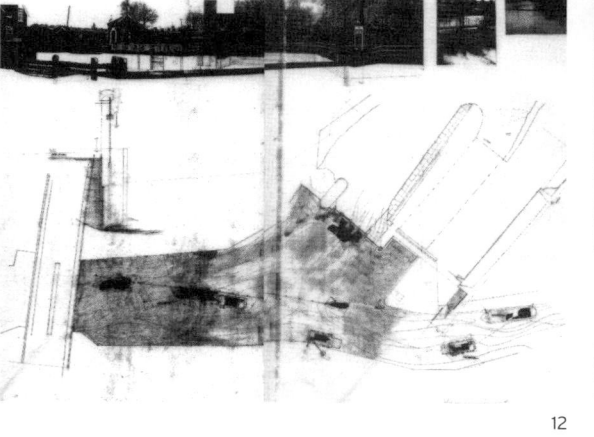

9: Skip rearranged by Lodging in Bedford Square/
Chris Dukes, Maria Haralambidou.
11, 12, 13: Water surface casting/Carlos Pena Ponte.
14, 15: Copper tailoring/Maria Haralambidou.

12

13

15

We read the floor of the factory as a form of topography, mapping the accumulation, density and flow of material and substances as a sort of mirror of the ebbs and flows of the city itself. Students researched this landscape, inserting rearranged industrial residues into the space of the city and following men who catch metal on the street, not fish in the water. We tried to see this simutaneously as a detail of the city and as the city itself, inside outside/ outside inside.

Body of the city

The unit continued to be concerned with the leftover spaces that result from changing industrial conditions within the urban fablic. Our search for mechanisms that link the scale of our body with that of the city was carried further by looking into leftover production systems and materials circulating in London. Each project attempted to exemplify how certain production systems could become condensers of an interior landscape, slowing down and localising the flows of consumption.

Unit Masters Shin Egashira, David Greene

Tadashi Kawamata (Workshop Collaboration)

Students Simone Shu Yeng Chung, Chris Dukes, Maria Haralambidou, Barbara Perez Marina, Yoko Murakami, Rentaro Nishimura, Christina Pappa, Carlos Pena Ponte, Greg Sheng, Peter Tso, Wendy Yeung

16: Cast-off skins from the hidden corners of the city, rearranged into a room of light/ Simone Shu Yeng Chung.
17, 18: Manure, ice and contaminated soil from around Hackney was reconstituted as a room: a new public storehouse/Rentaro Nishimura.
19, 20, 21: Polystyrene-Concrete, casting the movement of the body: body-scale infrastructures/Greg Sheng.

16   17

19

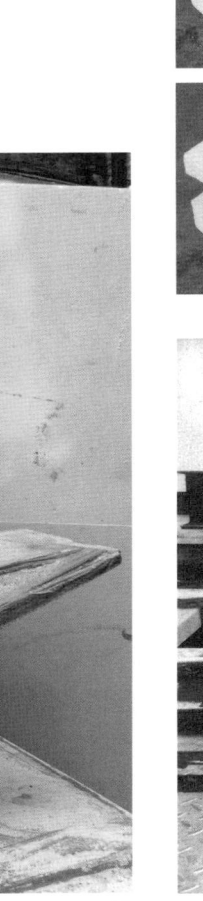

20

21

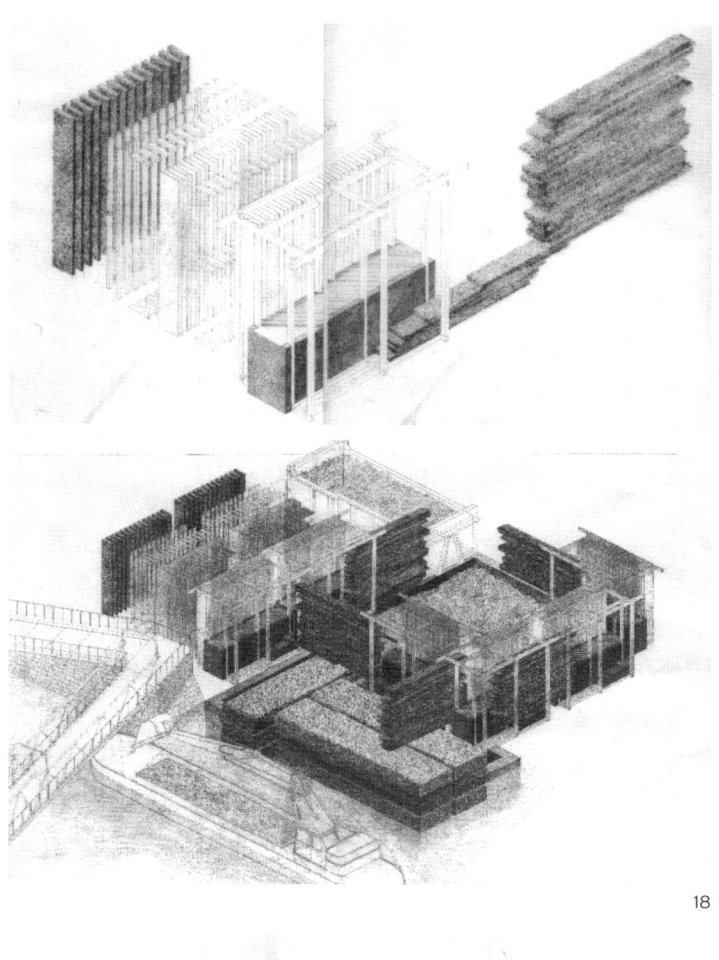

18

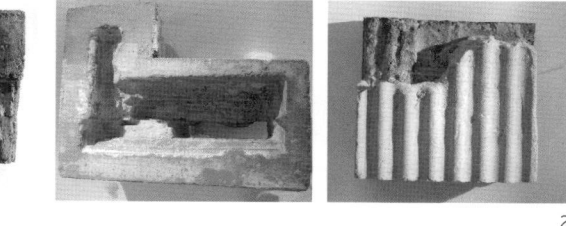

22

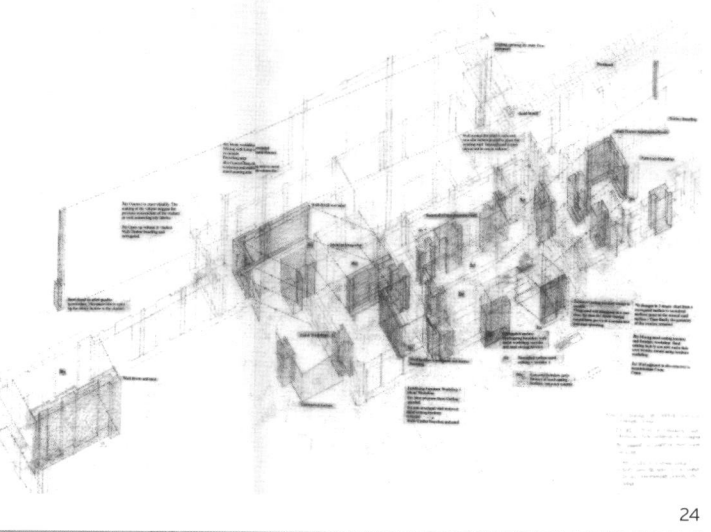

23

24

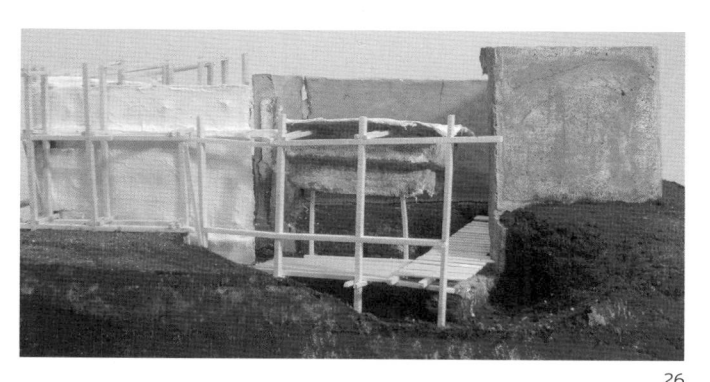

25

26

22: Compost Wall/Barbara Perez. 23, 24: A void between buildings is reclaimed by sand-casting/Peter Tso. 25: Timber store. Light Wall detail/Christ Dukes. 26: Plastering memory wall in progress/Christina Pappa.

Diploma Unit 12

1 [ma]

The Thames Valley

The Thames Valley is one of the key areas currently under development in London. The city is creating a new identity for itself in this space. We have selected a section of this area - London Sector B - and applied to it the planning toolbox of the Urban Gallery.

100,000 Housing Units

The GLA is preparing new development policies for London. These include a plan to increase housing stock by approximately 38,000 units. But is this enough? Does it provide sufficient critical mass for new forms of living to emerge?

To enable the city to reinvent itself in response to a changing society, radically new

planning tools are required. These tools need to be embedded in planning policies, but their effectiveness also depends on the provision of specific operating conditions. We adopted a view that a critical mass of new housing units is required to reach a level where radically new tools and planning constructions can be developed. What if 100,000 new housing units were to be constructed in London Sector B?

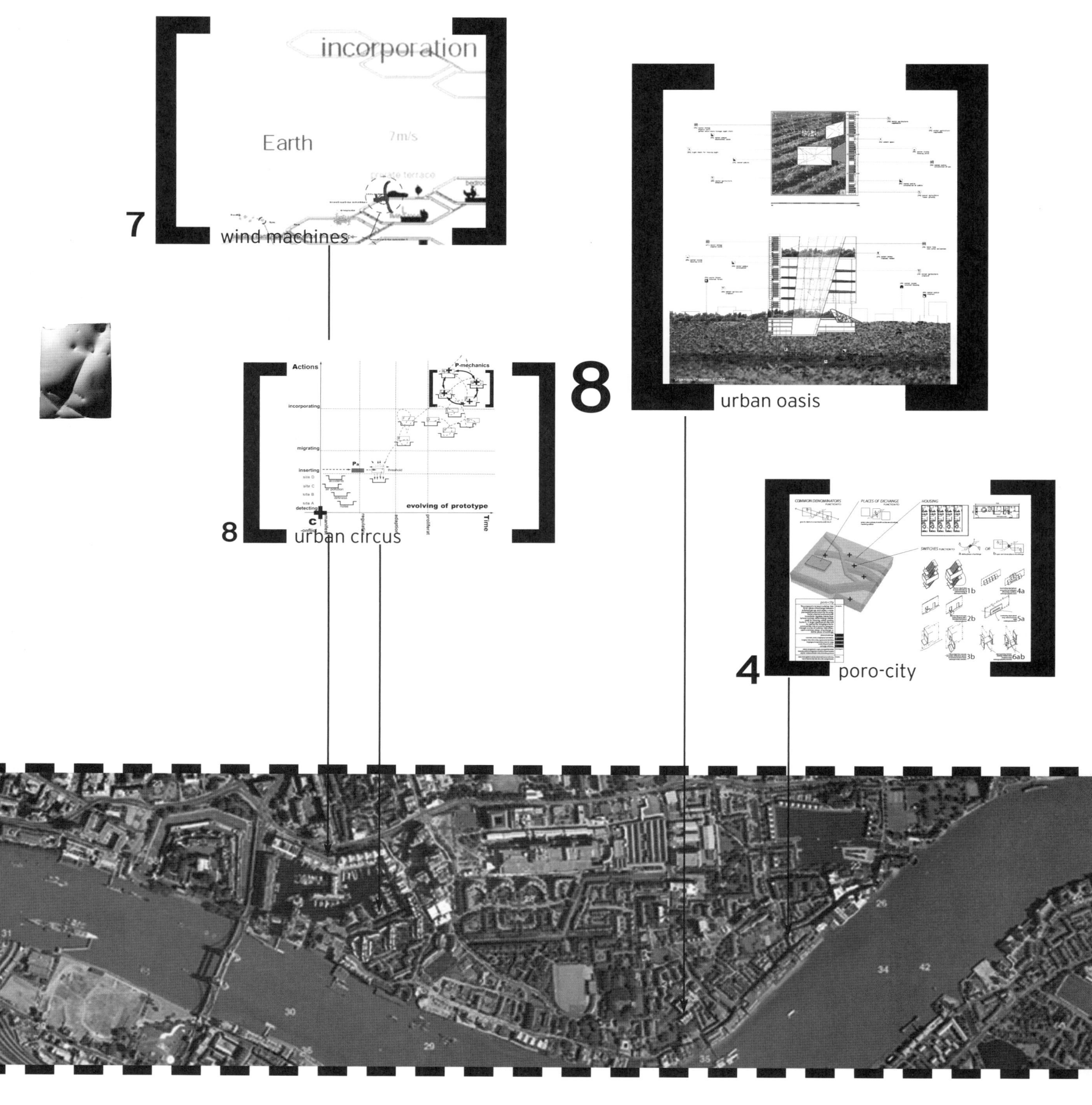

7 wind machines

8 urban oasis

8 urban circus

4 poro-city

What conflicts would arise? What would be the potential for innovative planning and design? How would this affect living and working conditions, or the ecological footprint?

Urban Gallery

The unit used an interactive virtual space to develop and test these critical conditions and to design projects that became possible because of the opportunities offered by the increase in housing units. The projects are in themselves unique, as prototypes, but they evolved in the context of other developments. This interactive space is a Gallery of real phenomena and urban actions, as well as a virtual space in which the phenomena are observed and the actions are negotiated.

The Urban Gallery is a support system that enables comparison between individual projects and simulates the space in which they interact. The Urban Gallery has four parts:
1. A database of miniscenarios registering emergent phenomena, each constructed in a sampling site. Miniscenarios are sources for actors and agents and operational fields.
2. Prototypes: these are individual projects

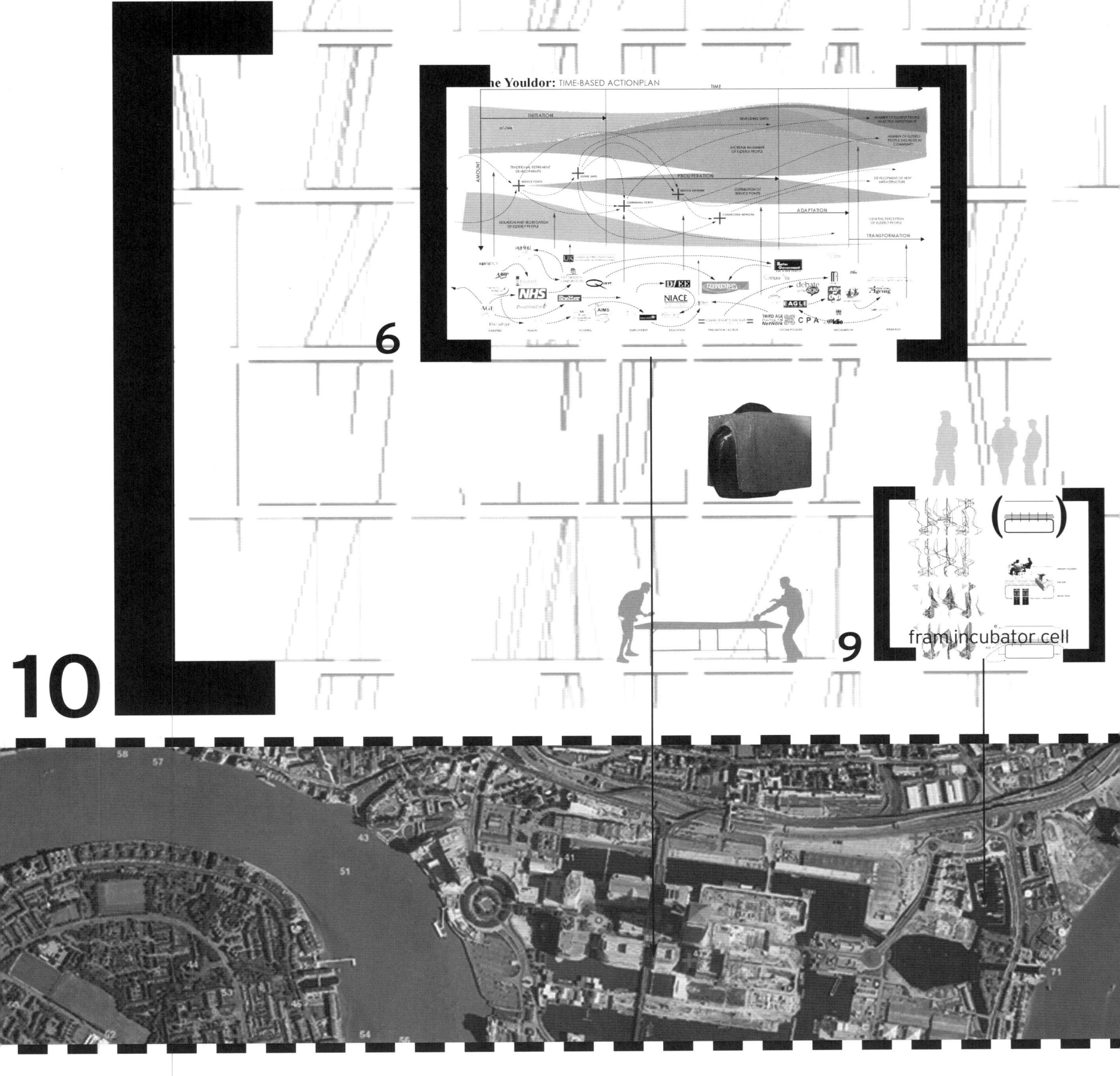

The Youldor: TIME-BASED ACTIONPLAN

10

6

9 fram incubator cell

that create new urban potential.
3. Scenario games: linking the development of individual prototypes and creating the conditions under which they can proliferate and adapt.
4. Action plans: time-based plans for proliferation to other sites and precise rules for this adaptation.

Urban Prototypes

Urban Prototypes are organisational structures that regulate the intertwining of the dynamics of specific operational fields – or programmes – in the city. They combine different forces to create new urban potential.

Unit Book

Each student has developed at least one urban prototype or a situation in which several prototypes act simultaneously. They have carried out team fieldwork on over a hundred sampling sites, created miniscenarios, worked with casting techniques on the plastic expression of these small dynamic models, and

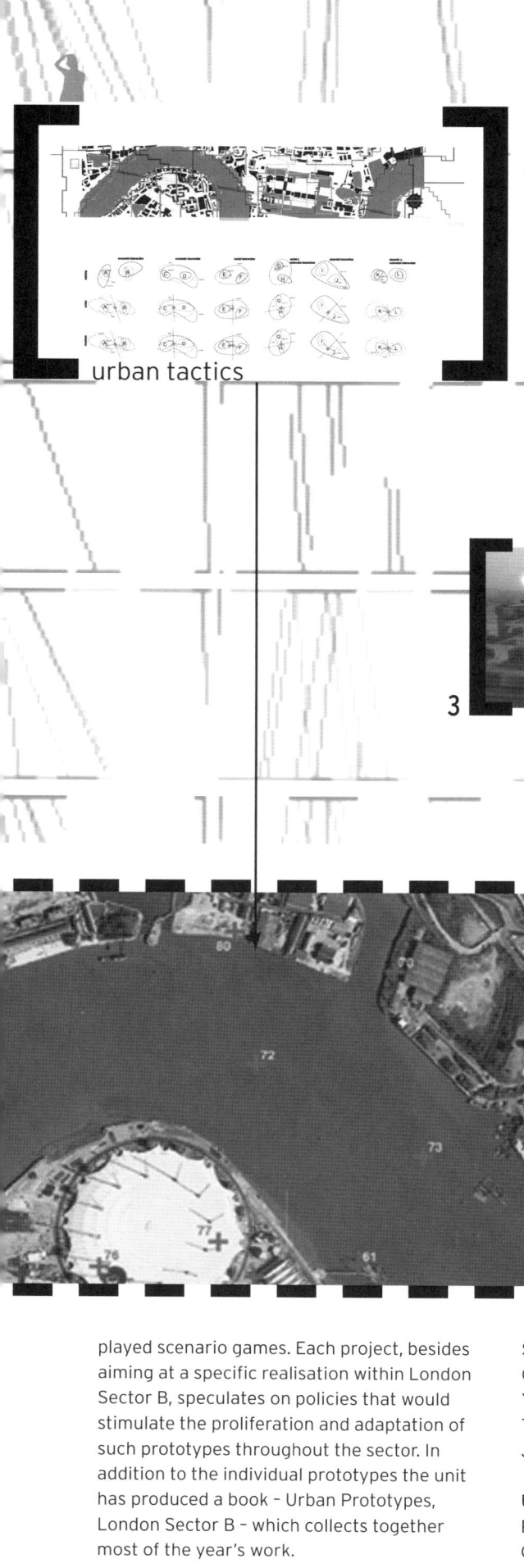

urban tactics

8

3

played scenario games. Each project, besides aiming at a specific realisation within London Sector B, speculates on policies that would stimulate the proliferation and adaptation of such prototypes throughout the sector. In addition to the individual prototypes the unit has produced a book – Urban Prototypes, London Sector B – which collects together most of the year's work.

Students
Gilles Chan, Annette Chu, Tania Combos, Yoav Hashimshony, Dion Ho, Jeong-Der Ho, Thomas Katsibas, Harald Keijer, Peng Ghee Tan, Jonas Upton-Hansen, Cheung-On Yip

Unit Staff
Raoul Bunschoten, Petra Marguc Christian Rogner

Diploma Unit 13

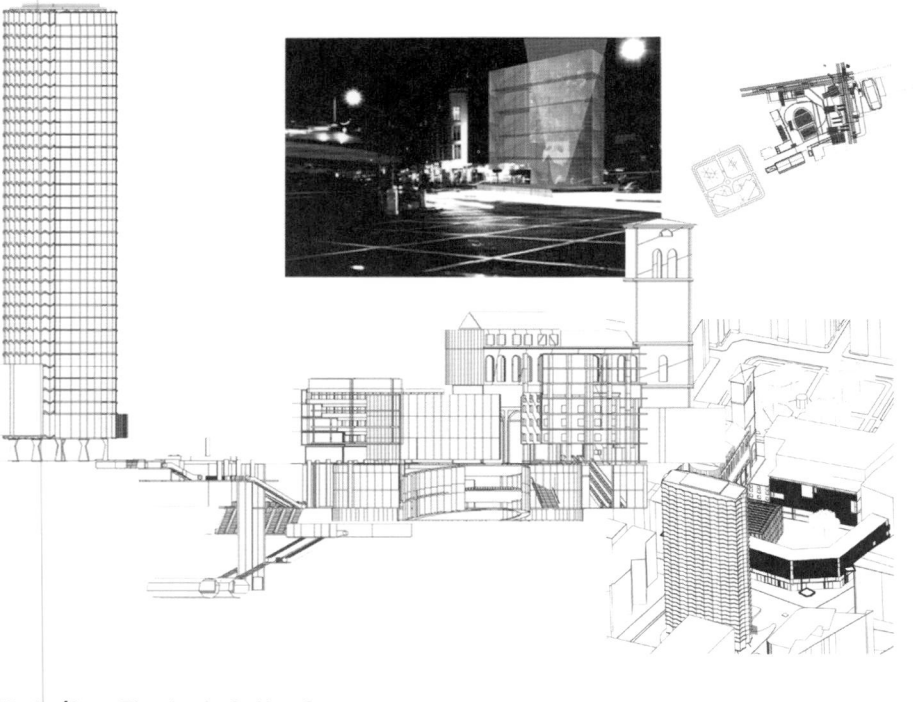

The Under/Over Theatre in Sutton Square

Extra-large street furniture

THE SHOW MUST GO ON

This year the unit took as its generator the site where Oxford Street (the busiest pedestrian street in Europe, with 200 million passers-by a year) intersects with Tottenham Court Road and the underground station. The station is to be improved, in terms of safety and circulation, with a new link to Crossrail and the express train to Heathrow airport. The unit explored vast volumes of subterranean space as well as the area above ground. It concerned itself with buildings, streets, taxis, buses, cars, bikes, businesses, fast locals, slow tourists, crowds...

Centrepoint's new garden

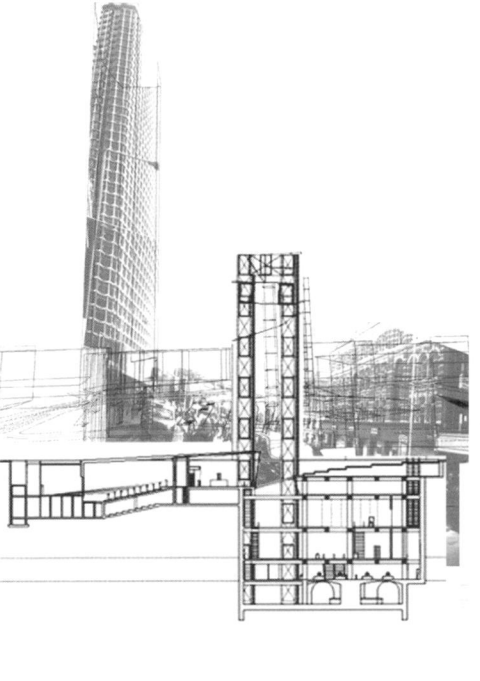

The Pater Noster goes underground

The horizon under the skyscraper

The task was to consider the installation of a theatre into the design for the station complex, taking into account the potential of the station as a commercial booster and a social funnel. For some, the question related to the proximity of the theatre to the station, the street, the shops and daily life; for others, the site became another London square; and for others, the transition from underground to overground was the main focus.

The unit was asked to address the rhythm of everyday life as much as the idea of a performance on stage. Where is the stage? Can the train platform act as the stage, or the shop window? Is the passenger the spectator or the actor? What have commerce and marketing to do with theatre?

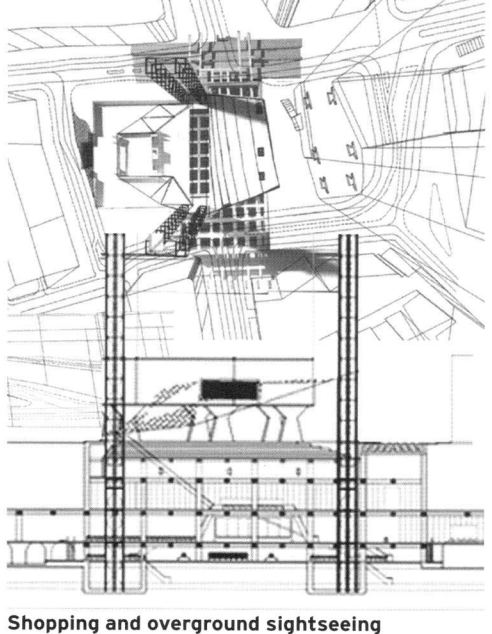

Shopping and overground sightseeing

Shopping fitness and landscapes

The Raking Metropolitan Club

The New London Theatre

The project allows for explorations into the many aspects of commercial desire. At the same time the design of the station's circulation routes and its connections to the street trigger opportunities for underground experiences that can enlighten, delight and stimulate commuter and tourist alike.

The unit continues its agenda of giving technical integrity to the total design process; so safety aspects including fire escapes and people flow were addressed in the design proposals and contributed to the development of the idea.

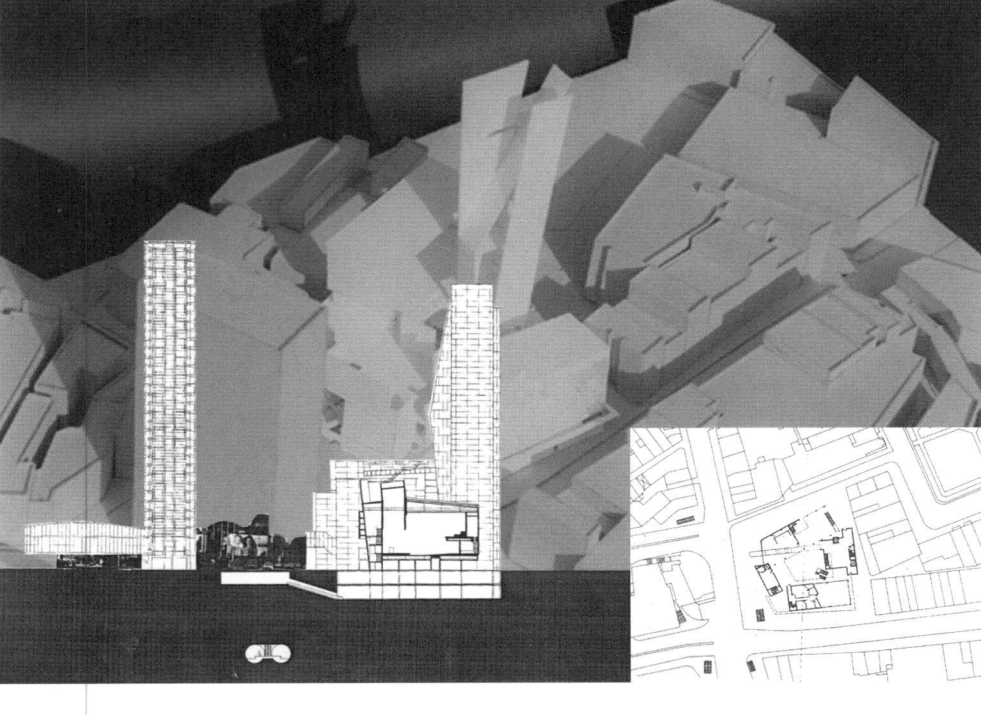

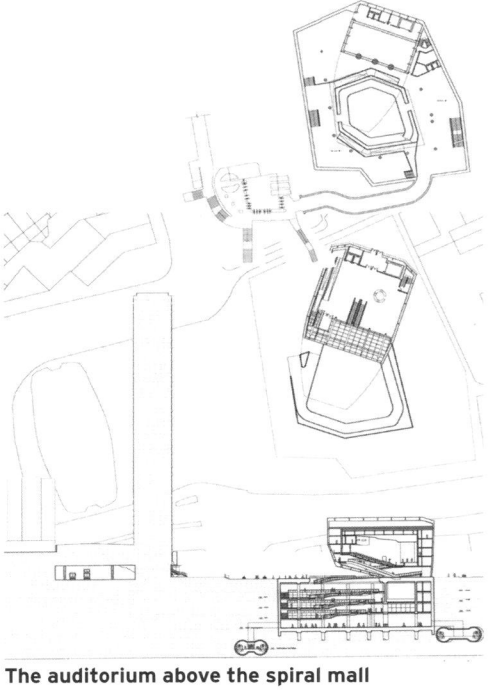

The auditorium above the spiral mall

Thanks to: Larry Barth, Jonnie Bell, Sean Billings, Eric Budzisz, Hugh Collis, Timothy Crum, David Grey, Roger Hawkins, Juwon Kim, Martha LaGess and Michael McNamara (We will miss you both. Farewell and Good Luck!), Anne Minors, Sheila O'Donnell, Cedric Price, John Randle, Joe Solway, David Staples, A&D Wejchert Architects, Richard White, Mohsen Zikri, The Irish Architectural Association

Tutors: Goetz Stoeckmann & Jane Wernick
Students: Ivan Ascanio, Irineos Charitou, Tomonobu Hirayu, I-Ching Huang, Essicka Kimberly, Rita Lambert, Tim Page, Irenie Sheehan, Varudh Varavarn, Simon Yiu, Chul-Hee Yoon

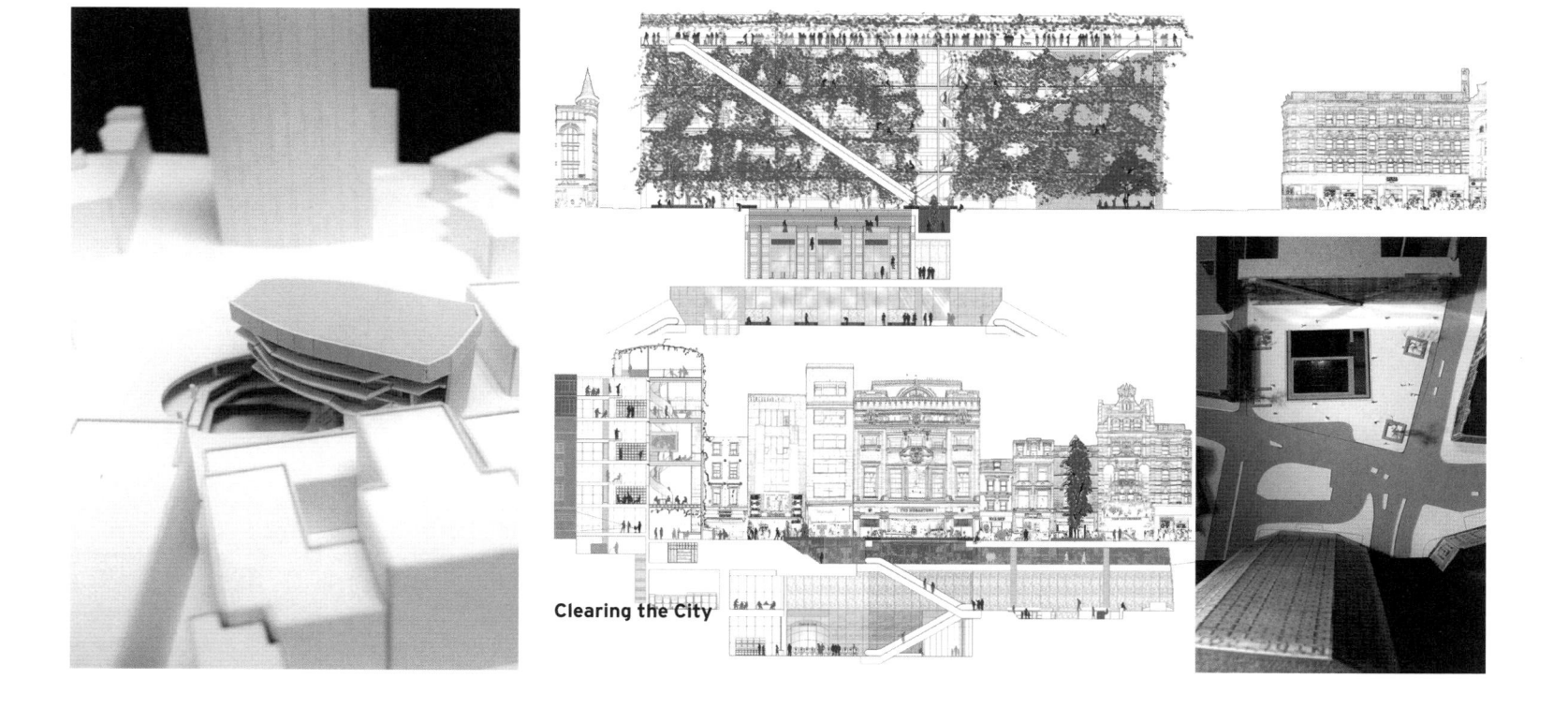

Clearing the City

Diploma Unit 14

Unit Staff
Ciro Najle
Hanif Kara

Workshops
Veronika Schmid
Christian Spencer-Davis
Spela Videcnik

Students
Leire Asensio, Bhupinder Chawla, Hon Kong Chee, Tae-Seok Hah, Taco Hylkema, David Lebenthal, Jieun Lee, Friedrich Ludewig, Sergio Olabegogeaskoetxea, Asako Uchiyama

The unit would like to thank Peter Beard, Eva Castro, Mark Cousins, Ariel Dunkel, Sergio Forster, Alistair Gimm, Michael Hensel, Nikolaus Hirsch, Sebastian Khourian, JR Kim, Mohsen Mostafavi, Teresa Stoppani, Daniel Valle, Tom Verebes, Lluis Viu, Mike Weinstock and Hugh Whitehead for their participation, and Reuben Brambelby, Jessica Brew, Emmanuel Bringer, Peter Evans and Paul Scott from Adams-Kara-Taylor for their collaboration. We would particularly like to thank Neil Leach for his continuous support.

LIFE ENGINEERING

Overdeterminacy engenders indeterminacy. Technological evolutions across fields subject to rapid change and intense contraints (vehicles, weapons, packaging, clothes) have turned deterministic models (and the criticisms of them) upside down: they neither produce ideal conditions (homogeneous, universal, eternal) nor do they become sterile and die. Rather, they have a life of their own, built-in behaviours that define their modes of response to changes in environments that are artificially constructed (war, fashion, technological races). These lives are neither autonomous nor heteronomous, but enact a process of 'becoming' by transforming material potentials, running parallel to yet enfolding what we know as history. Diploma 14 has attempted to engage with these modes of operation and to render them architectonic.

The unit has developed ways to engineer and direct the potentialities emerging from the passages between energy and matter. Instead of machines à habiter, we have constructed living machines: synthetic environments with regimes of sensitivity (parameters, intensities and ranges of performance), able to integrate energy exchanges and structural weakness into organised matter. Four kinds of work have been developed:
1. The disciplinary absorption of techniques able to mediate creatively between dynamic fields of information and modes of material organisation.
2. The constitution of operative systems (systematic relationships between segregated levels of organisation) able to adapt to contingencies in the making.
3. The construction of novel architectonic materials through the invention of new kinds of assemblage of material relationships.

4. The simulation of interference and collaboration between human and material behaviours.

We have explored material potentials. Materials were understood as non-figurative series of organisational relationships. These relationships happen at varying scales, but we focused on engineering particularly tiny ones. As such, materials were treated not as ready-mades but rather as coherent systems of attributes and performances. Here the role of the architect is continuous with that of the engineer, in that both are interested in working on the performance of systems of relations. However, an artificiality of this kind has required the simultaneous construction of attitude able to avoid both the efficiency-based model of the traditional western engineer and the ideology-based model of the traditional western architect. In the dynamics studied, other systemic levels – social, economic or cultural – intervened, leaving sediments of their movements rather than crystallising positions.

The unit has worked on the invention of new Technologies of Habitation. We have aimed at developing a series of prototypical organisations able to construct and distribute house components and complexes throughout London. We have studied several spatial models in organisational terms and at various scales in order to provide impulses for the works: from Y2K to the Kaufmann House, from Falling Water to Villa Savoye, Muller and Moller, the Cushicle, Villa Mairea, Fukuoka... Reverberations and correspondences, typological adjustments and constraints have come from this arena. Along a similar line, technical constraints such as excavation and decontamination methods were explored and transformed into operative tools. Conversely, several kinds of users were scanned in order to constitute non-idealised quantifiable performances: a kind of Virgin Atlantic Dynamic Modulor, tribes of stereotyped tourists, single young professionals expanding their budgets, family organization, constitution, degeneration and regeneration, or people earning money by exposing their routines on the web. These non-idealised users provided frames, ranges and limits of behaviour. And the two simulated performances (material and user) were mediated by diagramming techniques that transferred information between them and mutually transformed their logics. In this process, diverse abstract models were introduced into the systems: these included the system of movements of a snake or the performance of its skin; the different genera in the construction of surface-envelopes, from the Sphere to theTorus to the Klein Bottle; the dynamics of salt and various techniques of spatial triangulation. Finally, several material organisations were investigated in their capacity to describe complicated systems of relationships in extremely simple terms, thanks to the simplicity of their regulation: twisted surfaces, folded plates, surface stretching, weaving techniques, burnt material fields.

Diploma 14 has attempted to construct ways of producing architecture by mediating these fields into a systematic set of rules and operations in order to control, direct or make use of the extremely differentiated. The modes of differentiation coming out of these artificial evolutions are what we have called prototypes: consistent series of by-products emergent from operative systems that organise material behaviours and relationships, integrate divergent temporalities, and coordinate a limited yet open range of programmatic performances.

Exposure and privacy are diversified and controlled along lines of spatial differential continuity. Topological models integrate these differentials into a House, which oscillates between a continuous fold of absolute public and a domestic interiority without interior.

AT HOME*
FRIEDRICH LUDEWIG

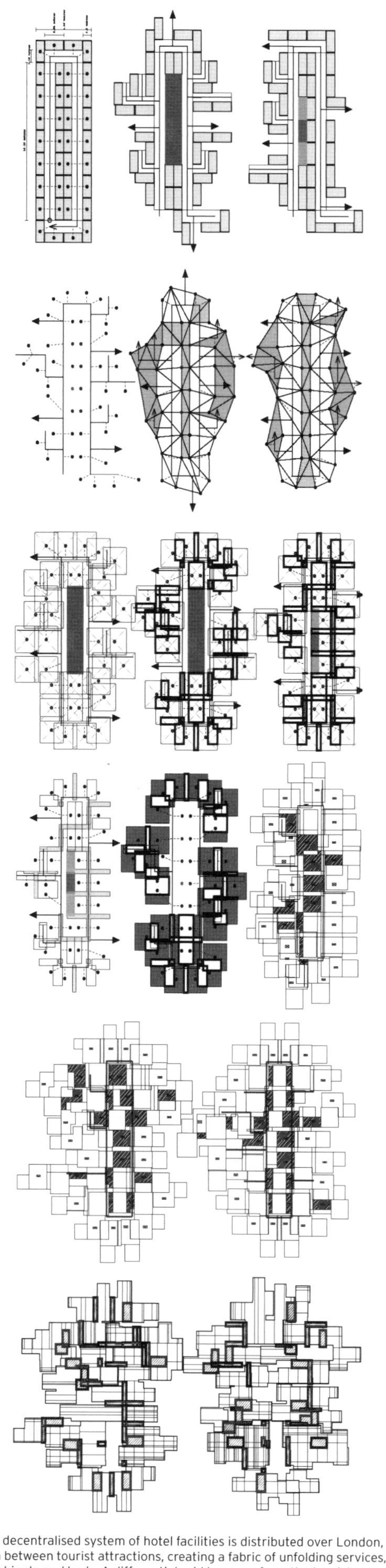

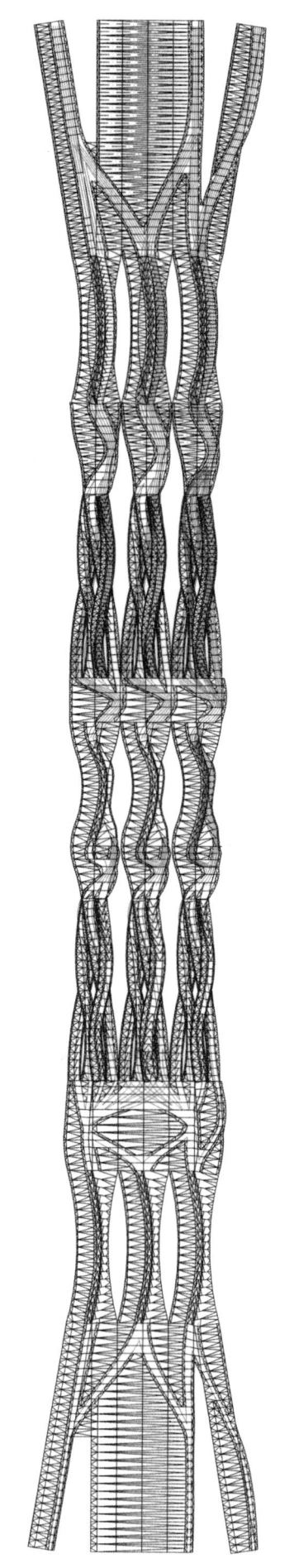

A decentralised system of hotel facilities is distributed over London, in between tourist attractions, creating a fabric of unfolding services, cabinets and beds. A differential grid loops up from the tourist itineraries and integrates diverse services into singular structures.

SWITCH HOTEL
HON KONG CHEE

Following a muscular behaviour, bundles of fibres cushion the movements of a traveller with a range of variations of friction. Systems of support, access, multiple envelopes, image and sound provision and storage are accommodated.

NEWORLD ENVIRONMENT
SERGIO OLABEGOGEASKOETXEA

A folded structural plate prototype grounds tribes of tourists into a system of woven piers. A deep and porous artificial beach absorbs huge variations in the density and composition of population through the year, constructing the new performative image of Torrevieja, Spain.

FLOATING BEACH
LEIRE ASENSIO

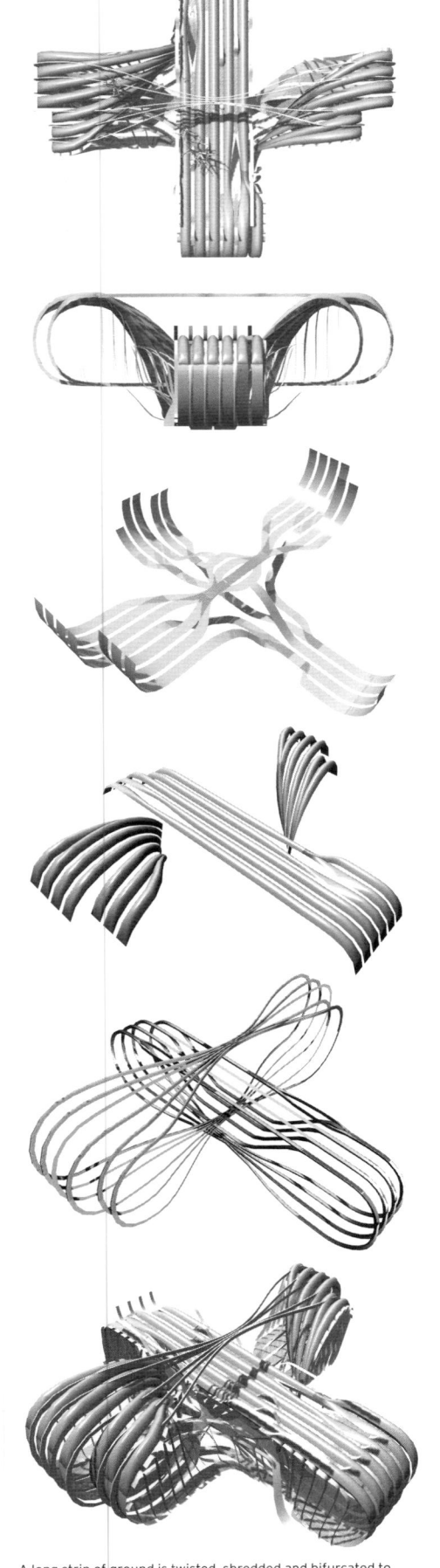

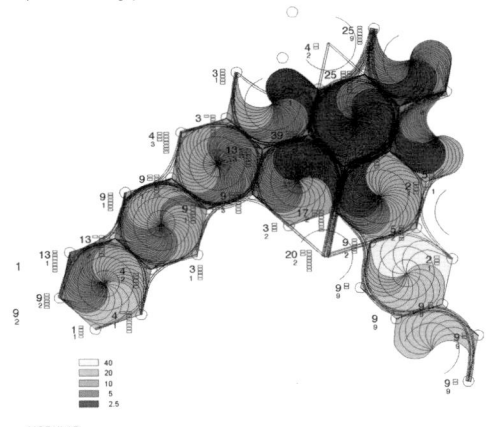

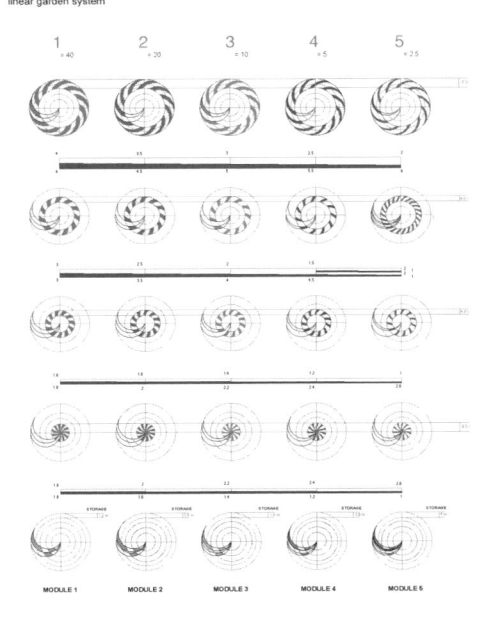

MODULAR
linear garden system

1   2   3   4   5
× 40   × 20   × 10   × 5   × 2.5

MODULE 1   MODULE 2   MODULE 3   MODULE 4   MODULE 5

SECTION MODULE

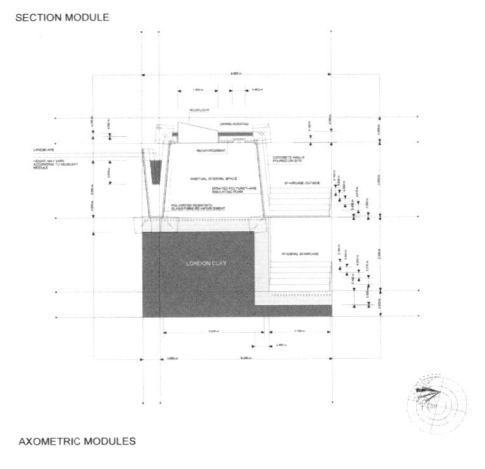

AXOMETRIC MODULES

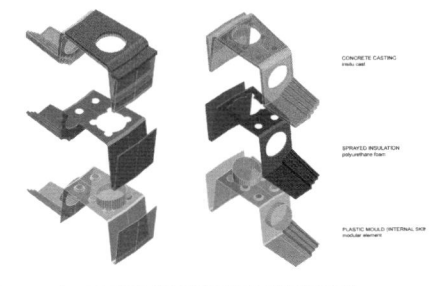

Albums
Bath
Bed
Books
Boiler
Bucket
Camera
Cd's
Chair
Chest
Clock
Clothes
Coats
Computer
Cooker
Couch
Cups
Curtains
Cutlery
Dishwasher
Drafting Table
Drawer
Fridge
Glasses
Hangers
Heater
Hoover
Iron
Ironing Board
Jackets
Jeans
Kitchen Table
Kitchen Sink
Lamp
Laundry Bin
Linens
Luggage
Magazines
Mirror
Mobile
Monitor
Mop
MP3 player
Oven
Pans
Pants
People
Phone
Plants
Plates
Playstation
Portfoilio
Pots
Printer
Projector
Rack
Scanner
Shirts
Shower
Sink
Shoes
Shorts
Socks
Speakers
Sterio
Supplies
Sweaters
Table
Ties
Toilet
Toiletries
Towels
Toys
Trainers
Trash
T–shirts
TV
VCR
Washing Machine

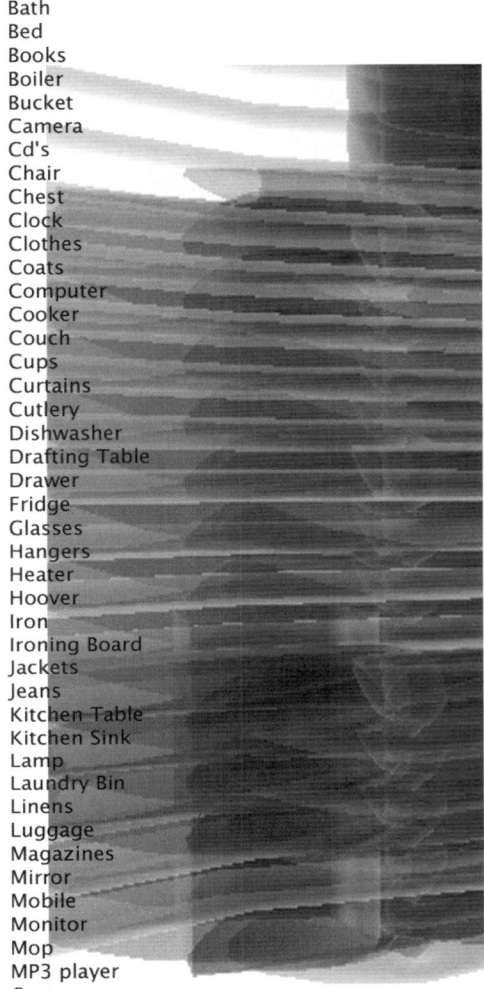

A long strip of ground is twisted, shredded and bifurcated to construct a programmatically driven circulatory system. The structure stiffens as the system proliferates into shadings, secondary grounds and partitions.

REVERSIBLE GROUND
TAE-SEOK HAH

A double-ground receives public and private surfaces and integrates social diversity in-between, into a series of pockets arranged in rings of varying size. Diverse housing combinations of a range of densities can be mapped onto it.

PLASTIC-DOUBLE
TACO HYLKEMA

The prototype addresses the problem of storage through the differentiation of multiple storage typologies over time. Growth patterns feed the prototype by dictating its level of tolerance and range of adaptability.

MIGRANTS' STORAGE SYSTEM
DAVID LEBENTHAL

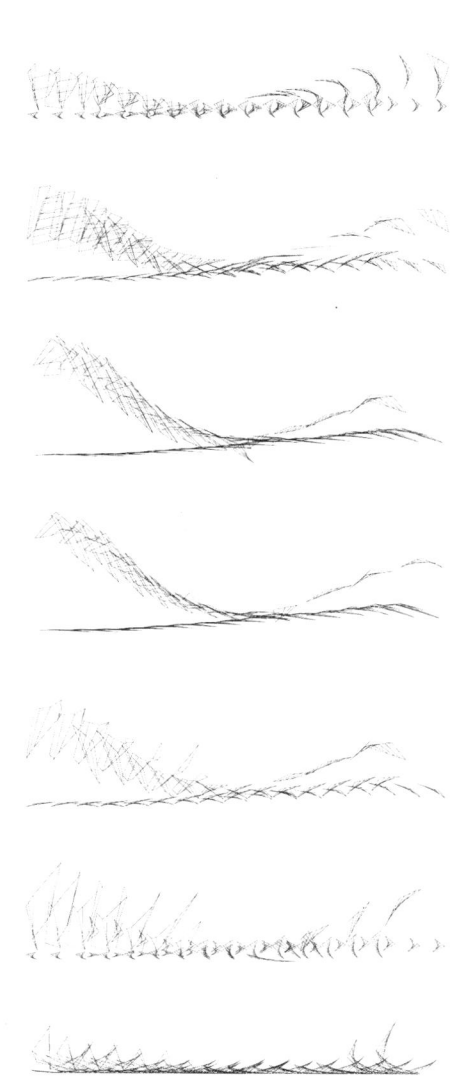

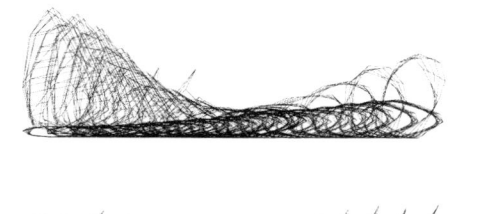

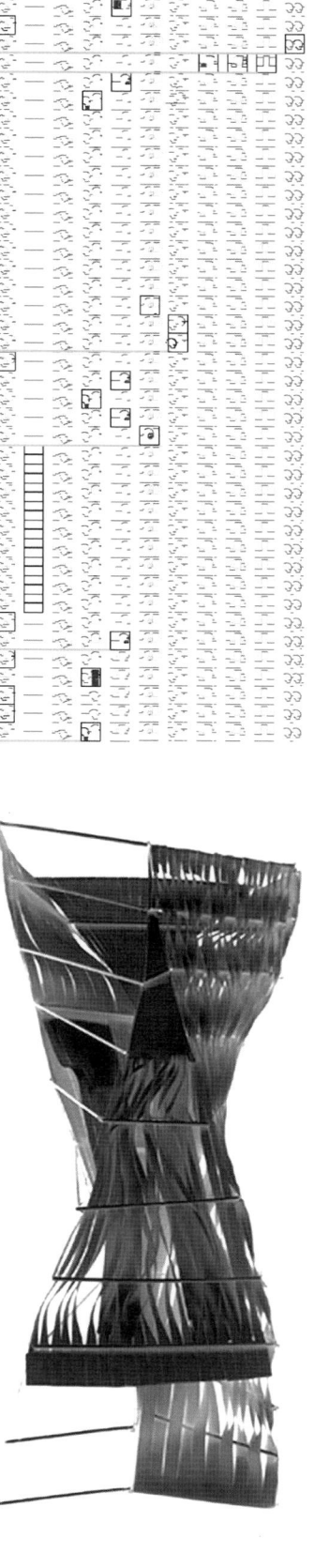

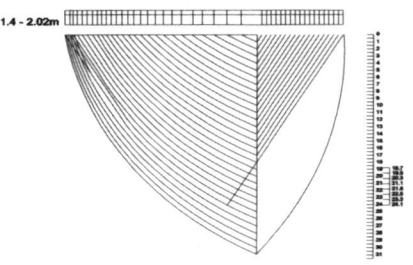

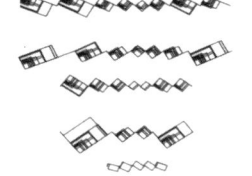

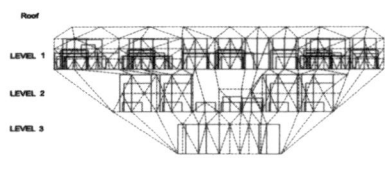

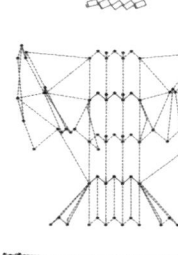

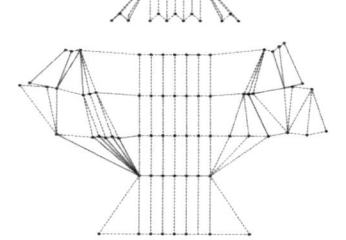

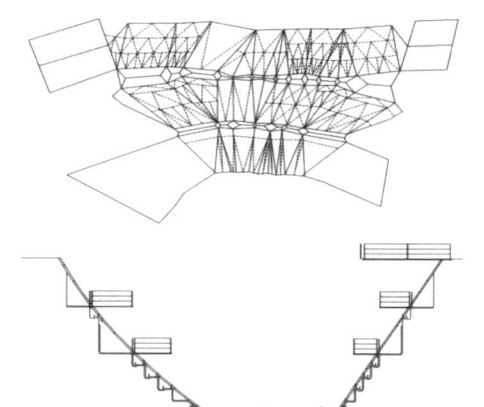

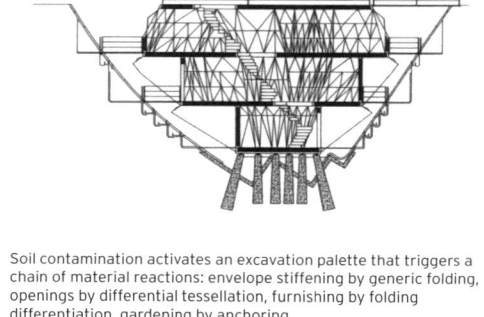

The sidewalk, understood as a territory of habitation and accommodation of flows, is qualitatively reconfigured as it is opened sectionally through the proliferation of variations in a pattern of woven bands.

INHABITABLE SIDEWALK
JIEUN LEE

A massive structural collaboration between hanging twisted surfaces generates an integrated system of two-layered rooms. Twists allow for diversifying stiffness and transparency to light. Secondary bands customise and furnish the system.

SPATIAL TRANSITIONS
ASAKO UCHIYAMA

Soil contamination activates an excavation palette that triggers a chain of material reactions: envelope stiffening by generic folding, openings by differential tessellation, furnishing by folding differentiation, gardening by anchoring.

DECONTAMINATING CRYSTALS
BHUPINDER CHAWLA

Diploma Unit 15

As the modern city continues to be characterised as a site of expansions, tactical and strategic interventions, confrontations between constructed space (architectonic and urbanistic) and special effects, flows, networks, transfers, transits (the immaterial images, messages, and vectors of communications and transportations), it is increasingly difficult to imagine how we still manage to carve out a space of habitation. As we are theorising our cities as spaces of atomisation or estrangement, it is equally difficult to imagine how we are to 'dwell' in them. This unit addresses the question of how we are to bring the concept of home into confrontation with the city (not just as a refuge outside it), and how to bring a practice and a history of architectonic urbanism into confrontation with the flows and networks of the modern city. The project aims to develop research and design methods that will allow the students to generate a proposal through an examination of the existing conditions (site conditions; local economic, political, and social conditions; cultural or ideological issues; a history or tradition of building, construction methods, techniques, etc.), and the contemporary context (development of new materials, techniques, or programme typologies, theoretical or conceptual interventions, evolution of alternative urban fabrics).

Term 1
'Haus/house' uses the German Haus as a means to formally, theoretically, and culturally explore a wide range of (urban) building types encompassed under the term (warehouse, art house, schoolhouse, house, housing, production house, etc.) so that the idea of 'house' can be questioned beyond the notion of 'home,' challenging preconceptions.

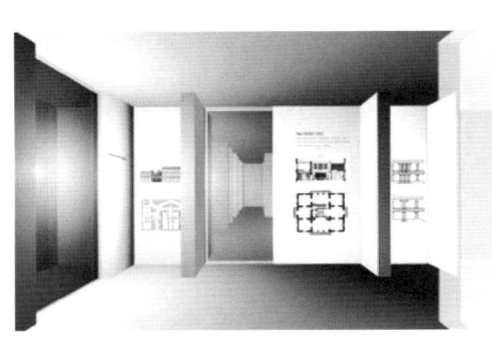

Carolina Theodorakis

Study of Ungers Summer residence, Köln

Proposal for a Schinkel Exhibition Pavilion Charlottenburg, Berlin

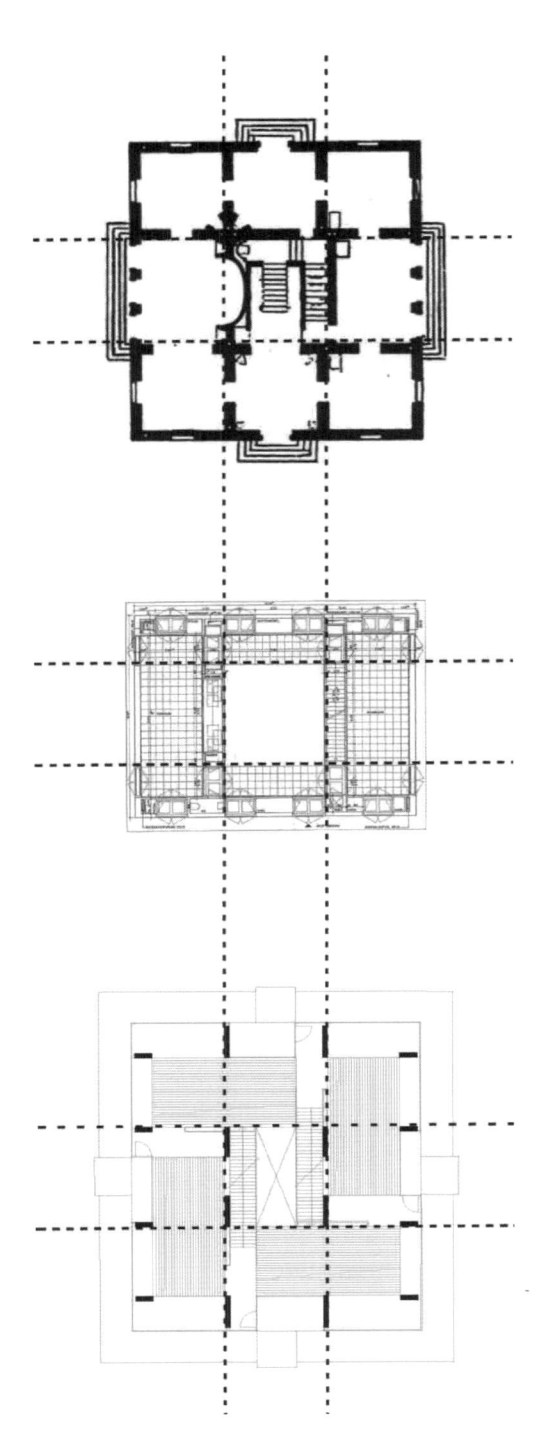

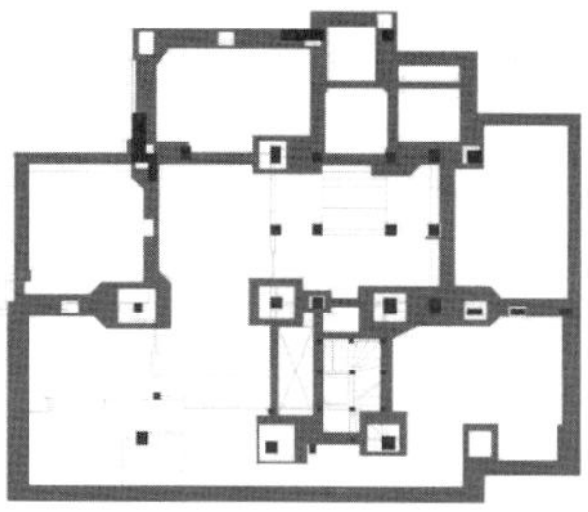

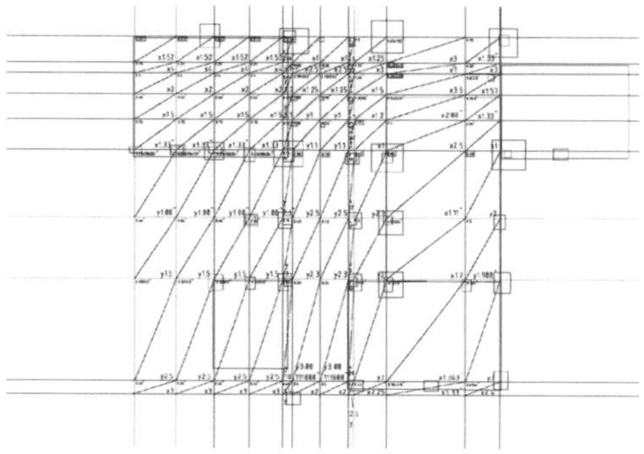

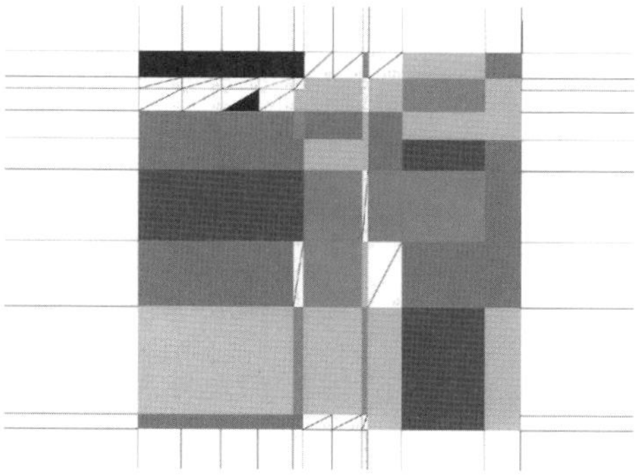

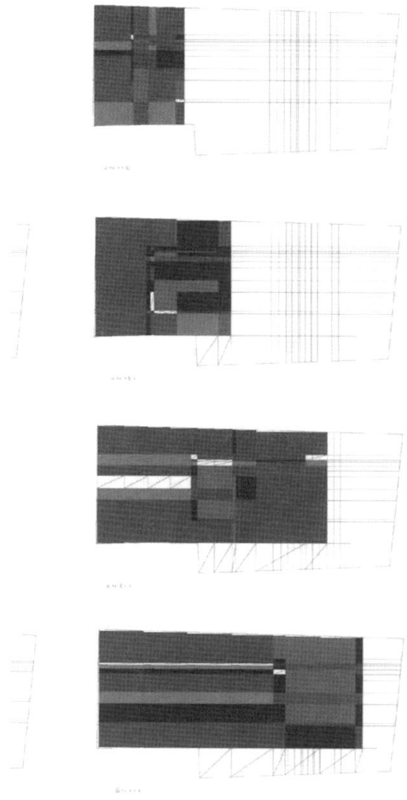

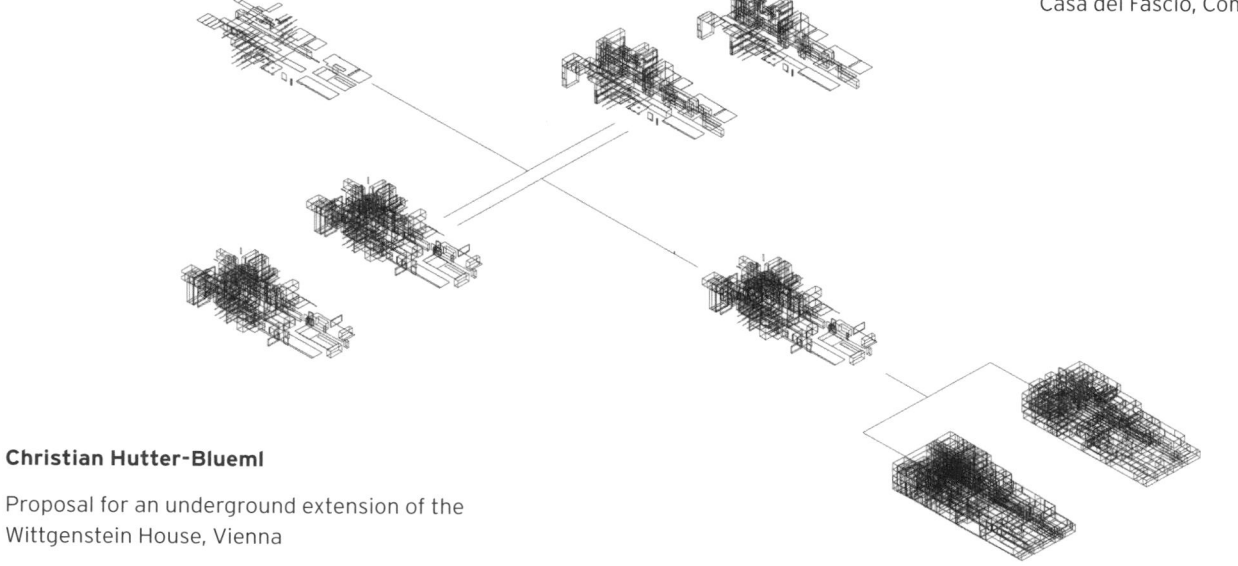

Naoko Shinoyama

Proposal for a temporary stage design at the Casa del Fascio, Como

Christian Hutter-Blueml

Proposal for an underground extension of the Wittgenstein House, Vienna

Terms 2 & 3

'Housing' involves the densification of an urban Haus for an industrial re-use scheme in Basel. It forms an inter-connection between the different flows and speeds of transportation networks and hubs, and the deceleration/stasis of 'house'. In doing so, it negotiates confrontations between residential, commercial and industrial fabrics (including a recent history of temporary immigrant housing, and the transformation of nineteenth-century industries into powerful multi-national pharmaceutical companies). The project questions what it is to dwell in an urban context (housing as city, rather than in the city); and asks, critically, how one is to build in an existing urban fabric that is dense with history, culture, representation, and politics.

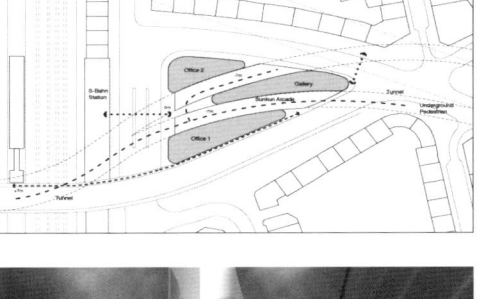

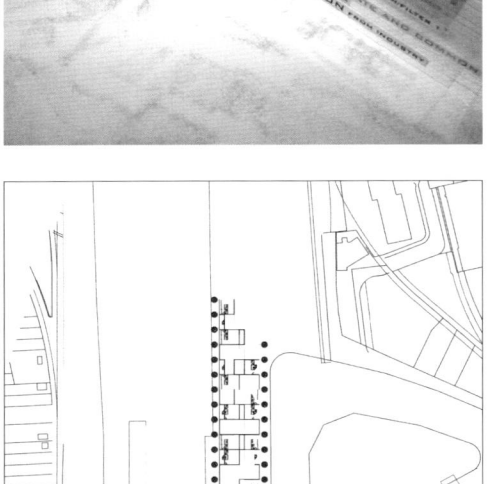

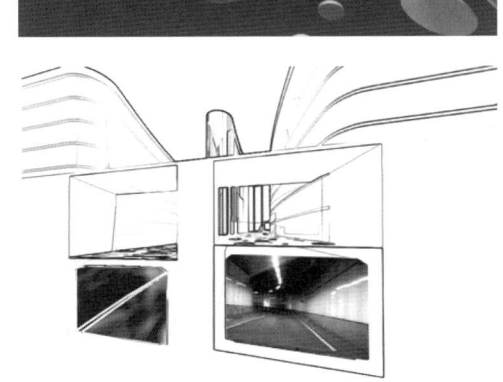

Namju Kim

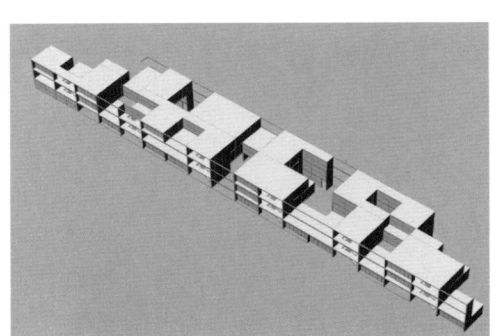

Naoko Shinoyama

Train station / train traffic

Digital image
Sound barrier
Flat entrances / inner courtyards / sleeping

Entrance to station / living / working / shops

Static image

Piazza / tram stop / parking

Static image
Shops / offices
Digital image

Main cross road / city

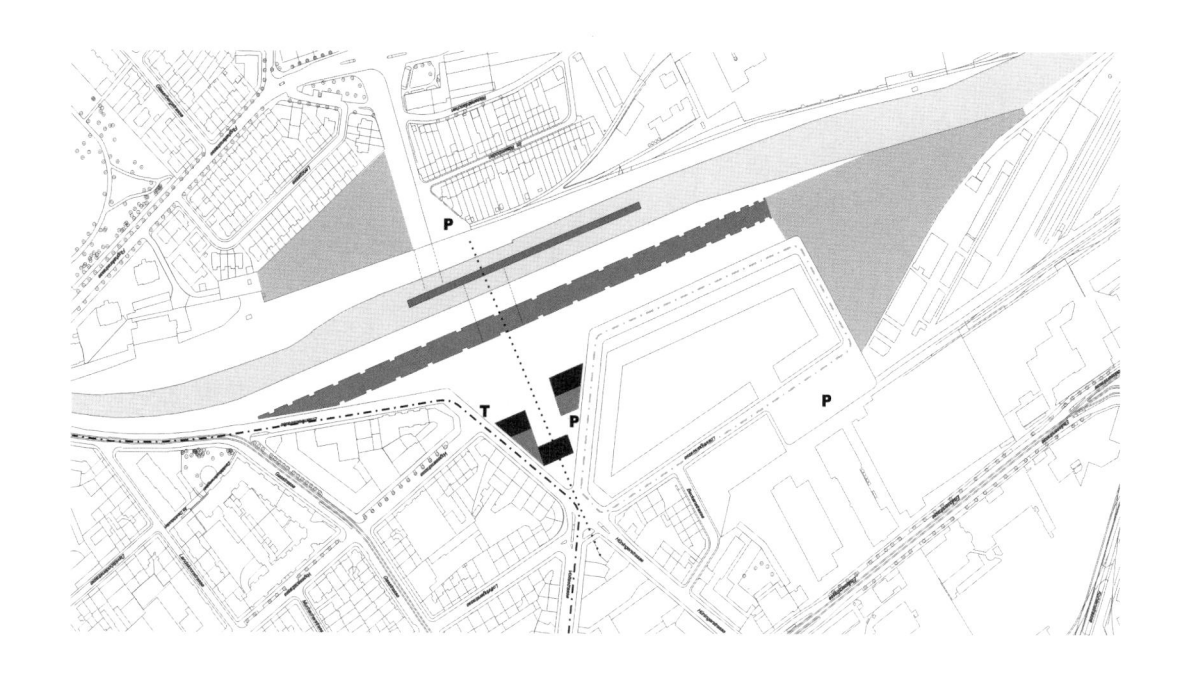

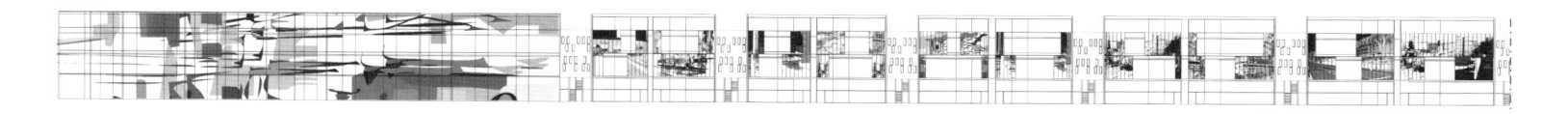

Carolina Theodorakis

Unit Staff
Christian Kieckens, Helene Furján

Students
Christian Hutter-Blueml, Namju Kim,
Amanda Ku, Naoko Shinoyama,
Danni Sutresna, Carolina Theodorakis

Thanks to:
Peter Beard, Jürg Conzett, Mark Cousins,
Anthony Hoete, Mohsen Mostafavi, Rik Nijs,
Caroline Voet, Roland Zaug

External Students

STUDENTS ON EXTENSION

Ziyad Mahmoud

The space of the car, and its impact on the landscape.

'Driving to a supermarket car park and spending Sunday with the car door open, listening to the radio while the children play in the car park – a highly respectable custom where the users surround themselves with the objects most dear to them: the car, the children, the radio.' Eduard Bru, *Vall d'Hebron*

Located on a motorway junction 10km from Florence this building is gently inserted between the motorway and the agricultural fields. An exhibition/events space, it is designed as a platform onto which the users of the motorway are raised. It provides an alternative landscape, a garden, a place of rest from where its users can observe the surrounding landscape and the impact of their movements upon it.

Martand Khosla

This project considers the conditions necessary to achieve parity between 'macro-economic nation-state infrastructure' and 'micro-economic local communities', using the area north of Florence as an example. A wall established to act as a sound barrier between the motorway and the village of Limite completely insulates the two socio-economic scales in both physical and visual terms. The proposal establishes strategic openings along this divide that facilitate cultural and socio-economic cross movement, initiating a dialogue between the two systems. Permeability between the two systems is achieved by the introduction of programmatic interventions in the form of markets, exhibitions and spaces, for travellers to disengage from the uniformity of their existing trajectories.

Miho Hirabayashi

Site: A submarine base in Lorient, Brittany, built by Germans during the Second World War. The local people view the site negatively (association with the war, indestructible nature, pollution, disuse).

Project: The design proposal (a park) unfolds in staged processes detoxifying the highly polluted site.

The land will heal and grow over time.

The entire site, including the buildings, is conceived as a continuous landscape.

Three thematic gardens on the rooftops cultivate the tension between war and respite, garden and cemetery, the damaged and the Utopian.

YEAR OUT STUDENTS

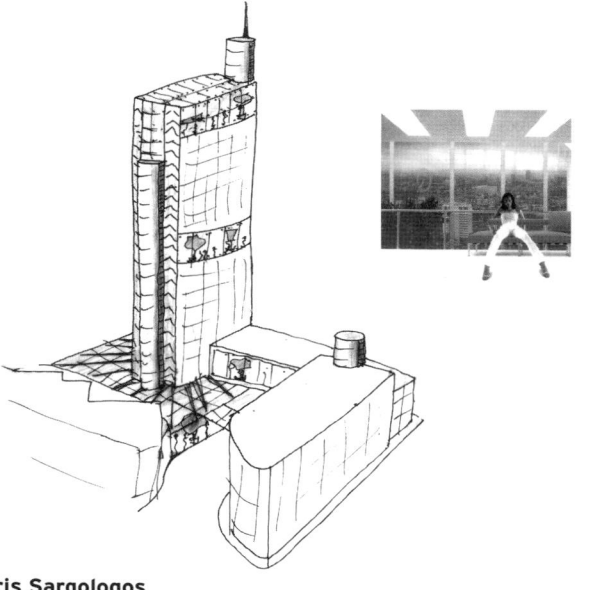

Chie Shimizu

The brand image has an enormous psychological hold over people, but it is also the source of a physical power that occupies vast spaces.

In the Nike extension bridge I have tried to develop the idea of a dialogue between soft architecture and hard architecture – a dialogue between the softness of fabrics of varying degrees of transparency and the hardness of fibreglass and reinforced plastics.

Paris Sargologos

The aim of the project is to incorporate branding into architecture. This is manifest through the transformation of Centrepoint from an outdated office block into the headquarters of easyJet. The newly branded easyTower includes a hotel, offices accommodation, easyShopping, bars and various other programs. The easyTower places the emphasis on branding and corporate identity as the basis for design.

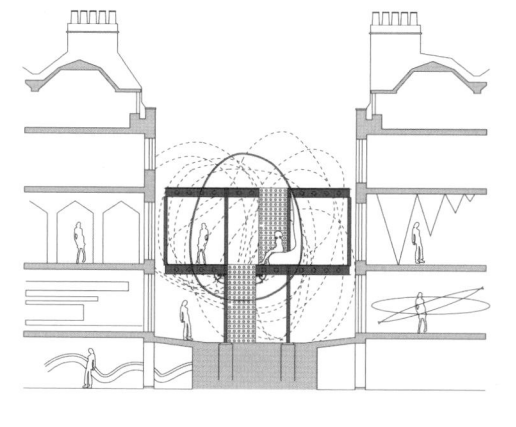

Hyun Jung Jung, Communications: Drawing II – Figure + Site

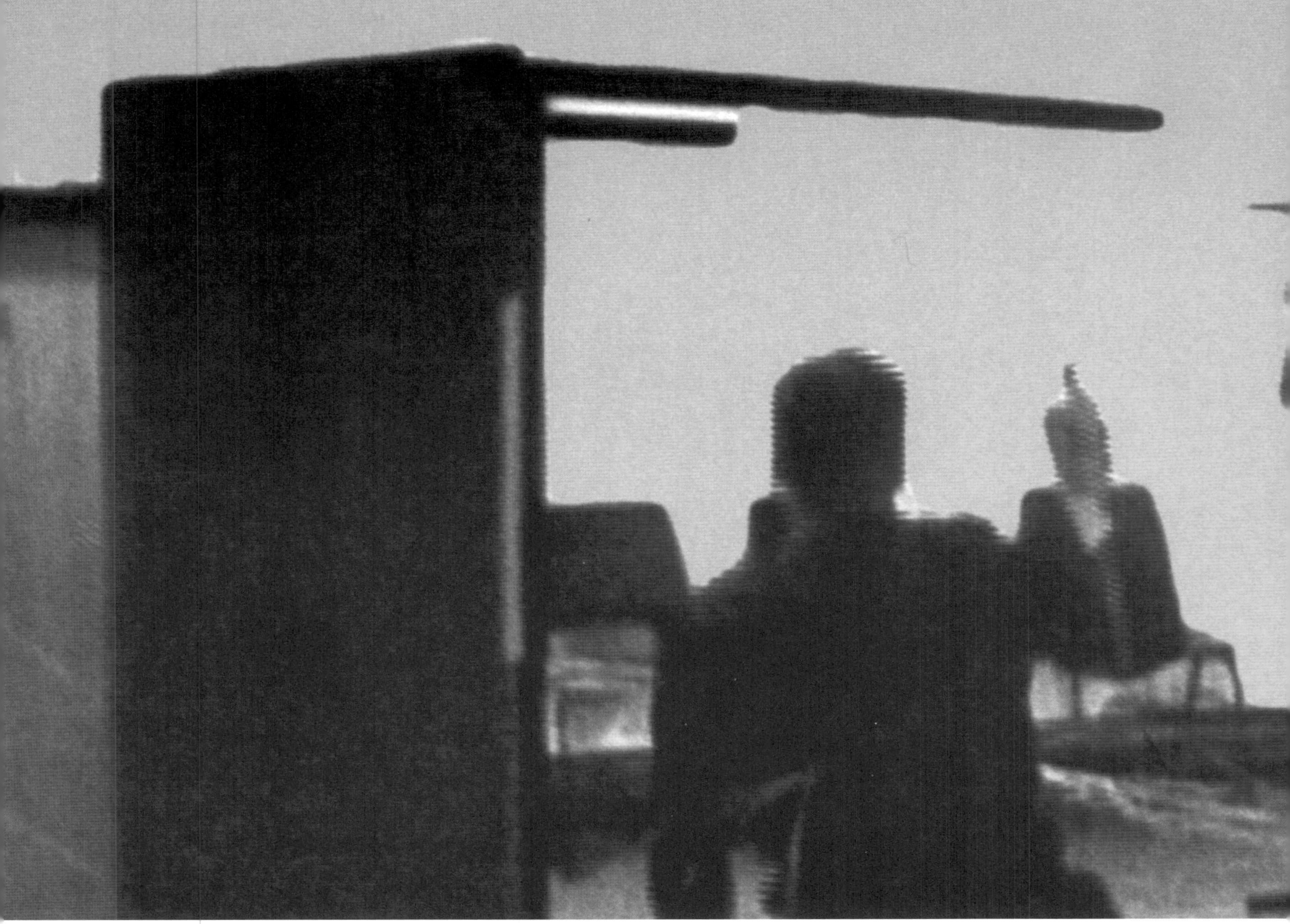

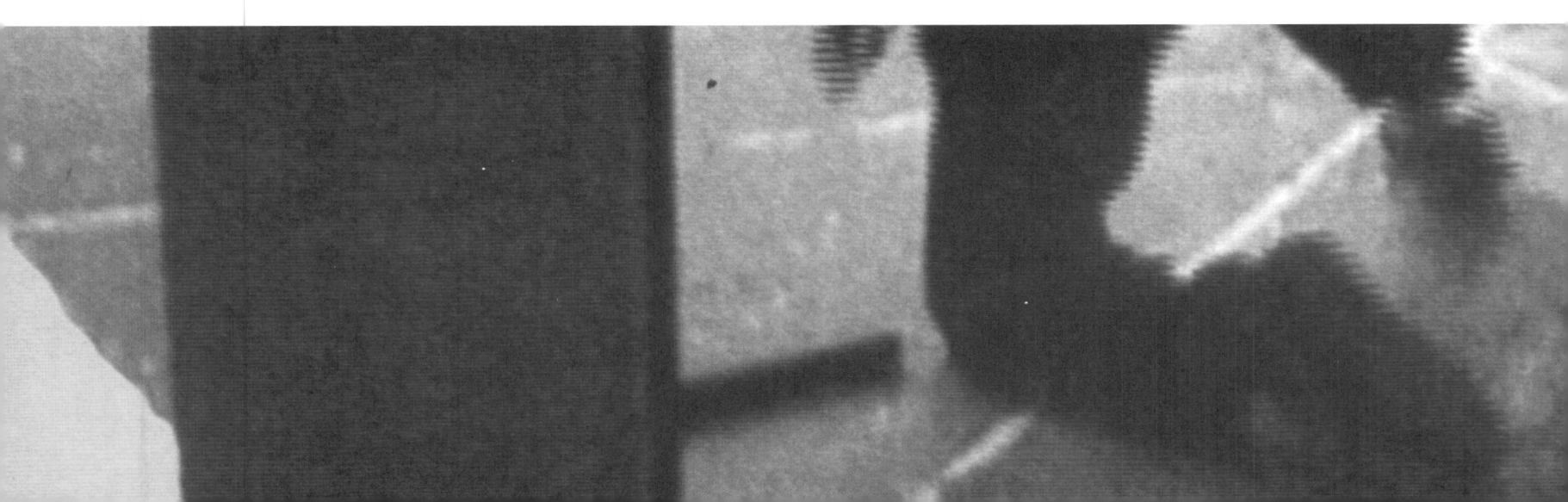

REQUIRED COURSES >

General Studies

After several years of continuous transformation the programme has finally settled into what seems a reasonably permanent framework. Its objectives are to provide students with a series of syllabuses which should help them to enter into the general field of architectural debate and criticism. This involves an entry into architectural theory, architectural history, and debates and analysis of the city. Naturally the staff are aware of the need to continuously respond to changes of interest, but the framework itself now seems a valuable part of the School. It is perhaps relevant to reflect back on the situation only a few years ago, when General Studies appeared to many students to be a quasi-voluntary activity, and the submissions a quasi-punitive act. It is now fair to say that General Studies as a whole is part of the students' normal week. As a consequence the programme has become much more ambitious in its scope and more detailed in its content. Far more demands are placed on the staff in terms of organising and presenting the courses and this has resulted in a far higher degree of co-operation and collective work between the teachers. The First Year is organised by Irénée Scalbert together with Sarah Jackson and Vittoria di Palma. It consists of two courses, one of which, **READING AND WRITING**, introduces them to the written culture of architecture. The second, **EXPERIENCE AND DESCRIPTION**, stresses the disciplined character of looking at architecture and learning how to put this experience into words.

The Intermediate School General Studies programme is now designed and organised by Diana Periton and Irénée Scalbert. In their words: 'The courses in Second Year General Studies are intended to provide an archaeology of contemporary architectural thought. By focusing on the historical exploration of a series of themes, students are encouraged to relate their own understanding to the practices and assumptions on which much current architectural practice, whether explicitly, obscurely or unwittingly, is based. The themes might be described as a selection of critical lenses with which we can question our own architectural preconceptions and perspectives.'

In course terms this means that there is a general course for the whole year, entitled **SCALE AND SURFACE**: 'The themes or topics which structure this course are chosen in order to investigate the experience of architecture, from the city to the individual detail. They explore the value which we give to that experience, and the extent to which assumptions are made about whether it can or indeed should be conceptualised and manipulated.'

The second term divides the course in two: **REPRESENTATION** and **CONSTRUCTION**. The first part: 'How a building is seen, experienced, and understood is as important as how it is constructed. Looking is not a neutral activity; translating what we see into an image or design involves an even greater degree of intellectual intervention. This course situates the act of looking across different cultural

contexts by examining the changing ways that space and light have been thought about in different periods. By considering changing attitudes to techniques that influence the architectural shaping of space (such as perspective and framing), and ideas about visual phenomena (such as light, shadow and colour), this course hopes to develop an awareness of the relativity of design choices, provide a critical perspective for looking at buildings past and present, and challenge fundamental assumptions about how we see.' The second part: 'The making of a building requires construction, the putting together of parts. Yet the way in which decisions are made concerning materials and their assembly is often obscure and always variable. Throughout history architects have understood the meaning of making in radically different terms, from being a divine revelation to a matter of efficient problem-solving (and consequently a question of technology). Through weekly lectures and seminars, this course discusses the changing understanding of materiality and construction, in order to elucidate and explore the themes which influence our own architectural making.'

A third course is open to all students: **SPACE, OR THE BATHROOM VERSUS MODERNITY**: 'This course attempts to present a new way of studying the development of nineteenth- and early-twentieth-century urban culture and its intersection with architecture and spatial organisation. It concentrates on the reaction to the development of city life in terms of a continuous attempt to reform it. This covers a range of issues which are apparently distinct, but which, as we shall try to show, are all woven into a single broad strategy of reform – the emergence of specialised functional institutions, such as prisons, hospitals, asylums, schools and aspects of the factory; the bureaucratic dimension of citizenship and its relation to a statistical knowledge of the population; the rise of urban planning as a distinct discipline; the production of public morality and domestic health – all these are seen as part of the strategy to render the urban subject as a "normal" subject, and the attempt to produce a normalising physical environment.'

In the second term this course also divides. Students may take **THEORY**, taught by Marina Lathouri and Diana Periton: '*Theory* can be a method, an explanation, a poetic suggestion, an elucidation; it might provide answers to definable problems, or make connections which enrich our understanding of the background from which architecture draws. This course asks students to investigate the way in which architectural theory has been instituted and defined, in order to question its current status and to explore the possibilities of its strategic role.'. Or students may choose **PRACTICE, OR 'THE REAL WORLD'**, taught by Irénée Scalbert: 'The inherent tension between artistic and professional matters is a *leitmotif* in architecture. It is arguably more acute presently than it has been in the past, and it is firmly entrenched in the division

between education and practice. Rather than a history of the architectural profession, the course addresses ideas and assumptions held by architects concerning "the real world" – a banal expression which is often used by architects and which for this reason is charged with signification.'

The General Studies programme in the Diploma School takes a different form. Fifteen free-standing courses are offered to students in the Autumn and Spring terms. A full list of them and their syllabuses is to be found in the General Studies course booklet, but reasons of space mean that we cannot elaborate them all here. None the less, it is noteworthy that over the past few years we have been able to put together an outstanding range of courses, working with many external teachers.

Students are expected to take three of these courses over two years or to take one of them combined with a General Studies thesis of around 7,500 words. The thesis, which used to be compulsory in name, though somewhat voluntary in practice, has thus become an optional choice for the student. This seems to have markedly improved the quality of the thesis. This year Neil Leach, Professor of Architecture at Bath, has joined General Studies to stimulate the work of students between the thesis and the units. This has assisted in a situation which has been emerging: students wish to do a thesis because it can support their design work.

Overall, we have a completely renovated

programme which seeks to provide students with a general intellectual framework for their development as architects. It is also interesting that not all the objectives have yet been reached. It is fair to say that the vexed question of architectural history has yet to be resolved. Teachers now covertly wish that students had a greater historical knowledge of architecture, including a historical knowledge of modernism, but it proves, in practice, a very difficult problem to translate that wish into the syllabus. Another contagious area is the field of 'practice'. Clearly a number of external bodies, including RIBA, recommend the incorporation of 'professional' topics into the syllabus, but this seems problematic at the AA for a number of reasons. Firstly, the reference point for students is not necessarily an English one; secondly, many of our students do not end up as practising architects in the traditional sense; thirdly, many of these professional issues seem destined to be radically transformed. These and other issues will continue to provide the construction of the General Studies syllabuses with more than enough controversy to fuel continuing debates.

It can easily be seen that the renovation of the programme has imposed a great deal of additional work upon teachers, but the person who has had most additional work put upon her is the General Studies co-ordinator Belinda Flaherty. She has coped with unfailing and miraculous efficiency, with good humour and with a generosity well beyond the call of duty.

Communications

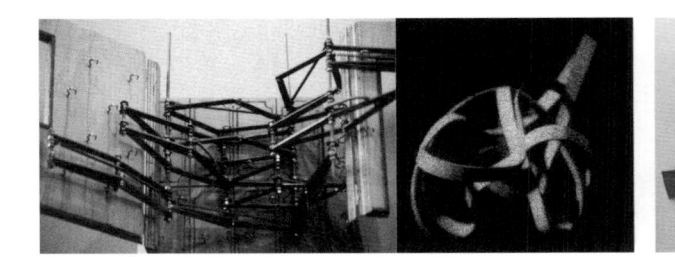

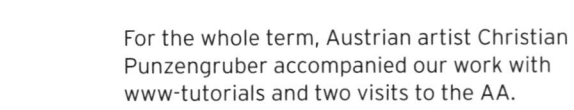

This year's Communications Studies programme evolved from questions that arise with the increasing use of digital media as a tool for architectural research and design, and the necessity for the reinvention and repositioning of established but changing forms and methods of communication. Three main areas of communication have developed independently alongside each other and were investigated collaboratively during the second term:

1: The agenda to creatively investigate and critically assess new media and digital forms of communication, incorporating animated and dynamic processes.

2: The moving image as a model of interrelated exchange set within a cultural framework and in relation to the subject.

3: The human emotional relationship to space and materiality, a dimension keyed in the complex totality of intellectual activities, producing works which reincorporate colour and the use of tangible materiality such as in print object fabrication and photography.

Other than in scientific exercises, communications cannot be dealt with in isolation. The generation, flow and positioning of information are not fixed or linear processes but depend on the fluent and continuous redefinition of the interacting parties and technologies involved. Joint courses furthering cross-media work introduced the re-evaluation and definition of criteria towards a process of selection, appropriation and economy of media. The work, exhibited during the year documented the versatility of Communications activities, ranging from basic acquaintance with technical skills to the experimentation and critical reflection of the employed media.

Course Master Jean Michel Crettaz
Co-ordinator Joanna Maggs

Colour Photography
Goswin Schwendinger
Term 1

Do we care for anything but mystery? And does anything matter more than its apprehension?
Bruce Wagner in 21/4, William Egglestone

In order to use photography, less as a means of recording and reproducing reality, and much more as an instrument to express our unique personal perception of our surroundings, we started to record our daily life as a photographic diary. Analysing this, we became concerned with very individual interests that emerged from the investigation and recording of our everyday lives. Exploring intimate private interests enabled us to use the camera as a 'partner in crime' rather than a 'neutral' instrument.

Asako Mogi looked at the rather magical-appearing motion of objects in her home, whereas Hoi Chi Ng explored the extreme fragility of a new and growing friendship. Beatriz Minguez de Molina's investigations led her to the observation of herself at home. To understand more about the correlations of a 'home' and oneself she chose the extremes of the surreal to act out rather unusual scenarios. Elvira Softic started with a huge collection of photographs of her life. Having understood her life as a constant journey of 'ups and downs' she stopped the documentation at a 'down' and staged the subsequent emotional evolution during the 'up'.

It was then part of the brief to find a coherent and suitable display installation (lightbox) to (re)present the photographic slides, the actual witnesses rather than the reproductions such as prints or projections.

For the whole term, Austrian artist Christian Punzengruber accompanied our work with www-tutorials and two visits to the AA.

Students: Asako Mogi, Asaf Zuker, Teresa Cheung, Ema Bonifacic, Maria Martin, Kristine Bisgaard, Isabel Pietri Medina, Tiffany Beriro, Beatriz Minguez de Molina, Elvira Softic, Hoi Chi Ng, Julia Mauser

Object Fabrication
Katrin Lahusen and Chris Pauling
Terms 1 & 2 - Materials + Tools

'To investigate the formal and spatial potential of a material in relation to its expressiveness, its tactile and structural qualities', has been the starting point for the course.

Through a series of experiments with one chosen material and one tool, a specific way of working was established and a detail invented. This way of processing-shaping-assembling the material became one of the main factors within the form-generating process.

Students: Ran Ankory, Aoi Kume, Takashi Nishibori, Chun Tsai Lin, Yeo Joong Yang, Nazila Maghzian, Yoichiro Akiba, Therese Hegland, Tania Rodriguez, Marie Langen

Drawing
Antoni Malinowski
Term 1 - From 4D to 2D and Back Again

This course focused on drawing as the simplest way of translating four dimensions into two. Drawing with pencil, charcoal or brush is the most direct medium for materialising an idea. Drawing exercises the connection between the mind and the hand. Drawing is about scrutiny and economy. Each line drawn by hand is different.

Architects concern themselves with large-scale projects but most of the time draw at

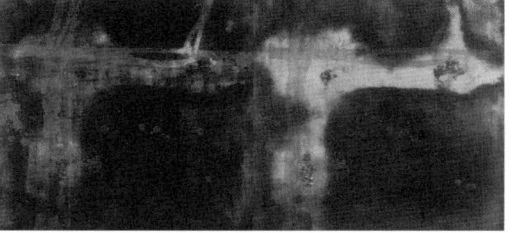
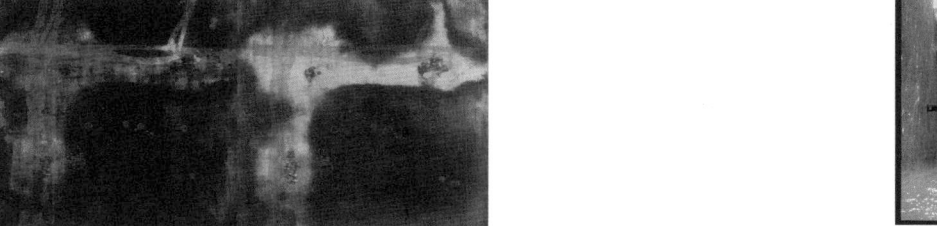

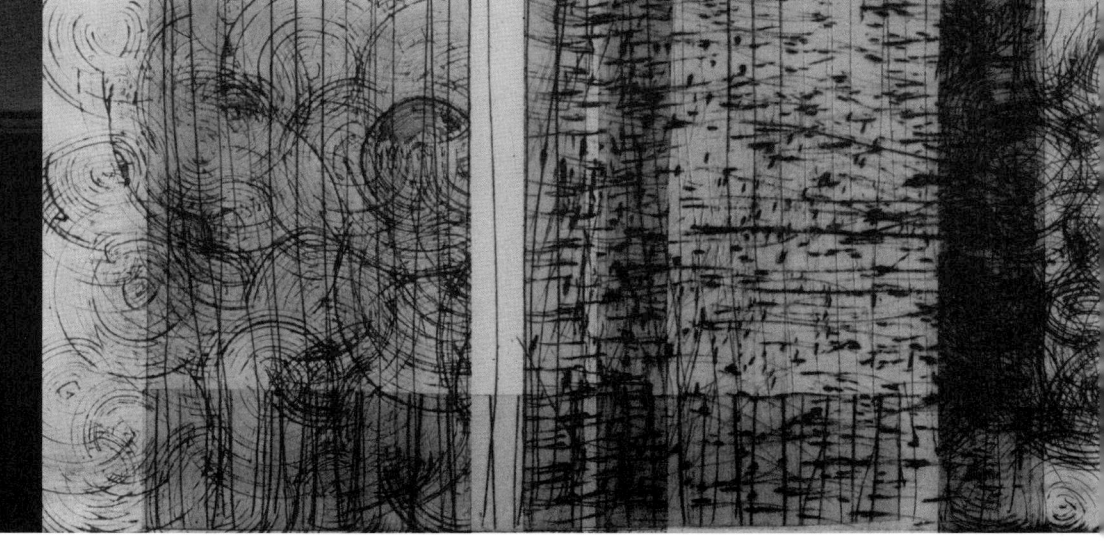
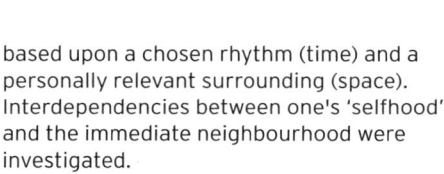

small scale. Yet there are differences in the perception of the work at different scales. Towards the end of the course the students began developing a final piece – a wall-size drawing. The aim was to encourage individual working methods within the medium of drawing using the simplest means; to strengthen personal vision through the development of the poetics of drawing, and to translate a visual concept into a large scale in order to encourage pictorial questioning. Emphasis was on the movement between two and four dimensions – between pictorial space and the timespace of everyday reality.

Students: Philippa Jelfs, Adrian Priestman, Cecilia Ramirez Corzo, Amanda Friedman, Oriel Zinaburg, Maria Kouloumbri, Lucienne Leung, Marie Langen, Aya Maeda, Spyridon Kaprinis

Drawing and Colour Photography
Antoni Malinowski and Goswin Schwendinger
Term 2

I invented the colour of vowels! – A black, E white, I red, O blue, U green, I regulated the form and movement of each consonant and with instinctive rhythms, I prided myself on inventing a poetic language accessible some day to all the senses. I reserve translation rights. Rimbaud

The aim of the course was to make the students aware of different possibilities of the use of colour, ranging from a pigmented surface to translucent and printed photographic images. Students were introduced to the sensibility and materiality of pure pigments. The focus was on 'colour as a matter'. In succession the spatial relations of colour were explored both in 2D and 3D arrangements. Simultaneously students started a photographic series of self-portraits

based upon a chosen rhythm (time) and a personally relevant surrounding (space). Interdependencies between one's 'selfhood' and the immediate neighbourhood were investigated.

To look at the use of colour in architecture the group went to Venice, which has a unique tradition ranging from Byzantine buildings to the modern projects of Carlo Scarpa. This experience served as an impetus to produce the final piece incorporating different spatial and chromatic, analytical and self-representational aspects of the course.

Students: Beatriz Minguez de Molina, Antonia Josten, Isabel Pietri Medina, Maria Martin, Max von Werz, Asako Mogi, Natalie Waters, Lucienne Leung, Spencer Owen, Ana Kubelik, Andrew Heid

Print
Denise Hawrysio
Term 1 – Site-Specific Print

Print I – The Site-Specific Print examined how experimental and conceptual methodologies can be employed in the generating of a print, to reshape traditional notions of representation and to investigate the ways in which the printing process can explore the topography of space and concepts of transformation. The project involved creating a print that is site – and situation – specific, i.e., which is made in direct response to a particular site, re-presented in the studio through an experimental printing technique. The site was St Thomas's Hospital, London.

The aim of this course was to reinvest the print with a human presence: not abandoning it to expressionistic gestures but keeping a clear conceptual structure. Through the intaglio process students explored the topography of space and experimented with situational mark-

making and the distinct procedural qualities of printmaking that could be turned to their advantage. The emphasis was on using printmaking's tactile techniques to transmute material and to use the potentially ephemeral nature of the creative process to reorganise thought and find a spirit of adventure and individuality.

Students: Marina Antsaklis, Junko Yanagisawa, Hiromasa Makino, Alastair Townsend, Hikaru Hattori, Anna Ohlin, Alexia Petridis, Yena Song, Natalia Kokotos

Print and Photography
Denise Hawrysio and Sue Barr
Term 2 – Digital Print

This project was based on East India Dock Basin. The aim was to counter the authoritarianism of technology by reinvesting the printwork with a human presence and by infusing this traditional practice with contemporary concerns and aesthetics. A clear conceptual structure is provided by the exploration of the topography of space through situational mark-making and the intaglio process.

Students: Bregit Jansen, Ho Min Kim, Jinbok Wee, Juan Pablo Trejo, Aoi Kume, Naoko Yamada, Anna Ohlin, Jordi Rafols Lloret
Student Assistant: Jordi Rafols Lloret

Interactive Multimedia
Enrico Benco

An introduction to interactive multimedia authoring. Using Macromedia Director the students went through all the steps of a multimedia production, learning concepts of non-linear navigation, interface design, assets production and the basics of Lingo programming.

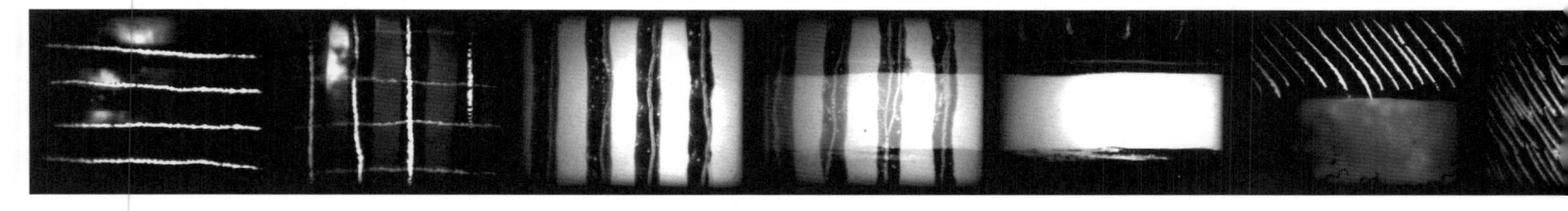

The course involved planning a small project, storyboarding the navigation and the interactivity, prototyping and programming the interface, producing the necessary digital assets and embedding audio and video.

Each student produced a fully functional interactive piece during the course.

Students: Omar Al-Omari, Alan Tam, Athanassios Economou, Hideyuke Kishimoto, Igor Gottschalk, Yee Seng Tan, Yoo Ran Hong, Kelvin Chu, Leonidas Lazarakis, Amilia Zainudin, Rita Lee, Paula Nascimento, Justin Lau

Figure and Site
Simon English
Term 1 - In-Site-Tations

This course examines the interface between the language of drawing and the construction of performance within the context of body/architecture.

'In-Site-Tations' set about lifting line from the drawn surface to find its counterpart in physical performance, which in turn translated itself back into a mixed-media installation at the end of term. The course went through a number of convoluted stages, focusing on a multiplicity of mental and physical interactions within space, examining mixed viewpoints, personal perspectives and the involvement of the spectator.

Through meticulous planning that incorporated improvisational drawing, groundplans, texts, instruction kits, visual storyboards, performer rehearsals and prop and object interventions, each student made a five-minute video performance. The work was diverse in its range with influences from Angela Bulloch to Mike Kelley. One work traced a map of object manoeuvres on a dining table made by two dysfunctional actors, another

transferred the traces of looking at gallery art to elevate a series of complex structures that formed a bridge between memory and desire, unit work and communications.

Much emphasis was placed on the presentation of ideas and the final installation used drawing, text, photography, video and object assemblage to assess, alter and archive the history of the performance as well as construct an imminently new position.

Special thanks to performance artist Anthony Howell and performance installation artist Simon Moretti.

Students: Therese Hegland, Yusuke Miyake, Hyun Jung Jung, Chihiro Nakagawa, Thomas Dulake, Ayako Mizuma, Miki Nakayasu, Yena Song, Oriel Zinaburg

Figure & Site & Photography
Simon English and Etienne Clement
Term 2 - Opening the Shutter

The theme of the course used the familiarity of the photographic image to locate, reveal or conceal private/personal machinations of memory and desire, and aimed to examine both the photographic technique and the psychological impact of the construct/image and *tableau vivant*.

Drawing was used as a means to instigate and project ideas. Students were encouraged to operate with directorial books and small-scale model boxes and to use texts, storyboards and Polaroids to approach the final image.
We were fortunate to have a wealth of photographic exhibitions in town at the time, including 'I am a camera' at the Saatchi Gallery. Students were given an interactive questionnaire to set their own agendas,

picking and mixing from the abstract, social, sexual, psychological and political trays. Time was spent in either group workshops, tableau methodologies or tutorial discussions, with students manipulating their own self-appointed tasks, working with texts or specific images. One student made a meticulous reconstruction of an airport shoot-out, reversing the image and delivering a generic monochrome, raising aesthetic and cultural questions on death in art. Each student fulfilled their remit culminating in an exhibition at the end of term accompanied by a series of instruction books that would allow the image to be reconstructed in any given place.

Special thanks to visiting artist Jemima Stehli and standby attaché, curator Kathy Battista.

Students: Bart Schoonderbeek, Ana Saboia, Joana Pacheco, Tiffany Beriro, Thomas Dulake, Diego Garcia Scaro, Kazuhiro Murayama, Moritz Klatten.

Film
Peter Lewis
Term 1 - Southbank

In the Southbank film project the viewer is persuaded to make a conscious engagement with the forms and materiality of film. The jagged energy of jump-cut and single frame photography creates a rugged poetry of drift, digression and image displacement, which triggers the sensors into a think-see-feel triptych: 1. Think with a loose scepticism towards narrative conceptions of time and space. 2. Space hosts an unlimited number of possible configurations that work just as easily within the principles of mirroring, repetition and rhythm. 3. Feel the highly manipulative, non-organic sensations that filmic space

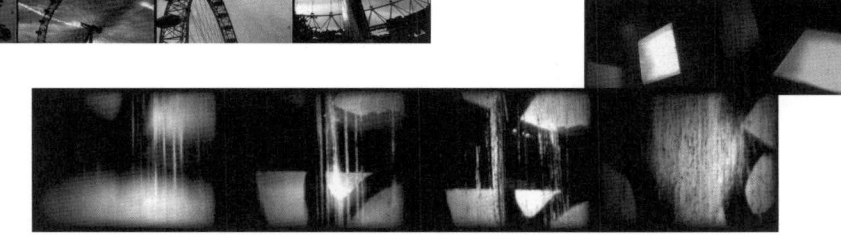

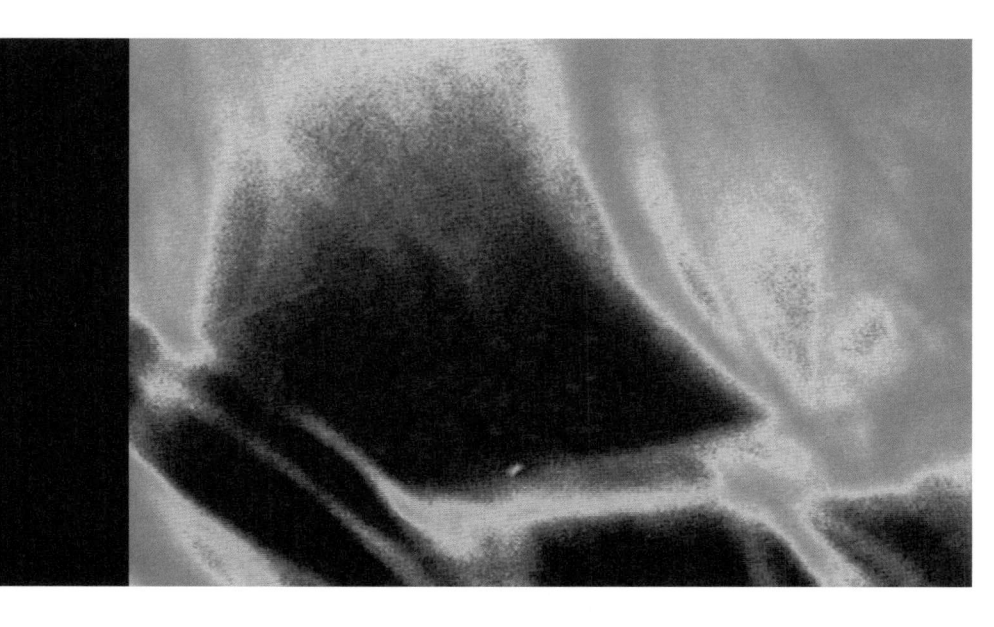

creates within a visual maze. Emphasis was placed on the artificiality of the space shapes created on film and students were encouraged to be playful in attitude and radical in technique when filming and editing their subject.

Students: Ashley Littlewood, Adam Cossey, Edouard Cabay, Nicolas Durr, Ana Saboia, Alex Papadakis, Andrea Di Stefano, Juan Pablo Trejo, Joana Pacheco, Nazaneen Shafaie

Film
Peter Lewis
in collaboration with Pete Gomes
Term 2 – Light

What is light? What is light on film? We set out to chart the extremes of filmic space; in one sense to try and poke a hole in the fabric of the realities that surround us. Students were asked to film the light variations that they observed in both a public and a private space. They were also required to keep a detailed journal of their observations – the approach to these tasks was left open but carefully monitored and discussed in tutorials.

Once filming was completed they were asked to create a third timeline. This was to be a dream-memory space reconstructed from their journals and transformed onto the surface of their films through scratching, painting and bleaching. These three spaces formed the final product of filmic space.

The elusive nature of light forces the filmmaker to find meaning in small fragments of the original objects and to rely on his or her imaginative powers. Watching these films is like watching a mirrored ball or cube spinning in the soft light of personal spaces of memory, with the filmic scene abandoned or handed over to the power of the abstract and sensuous sign.

Students: Hoi Chi Ng, Maija Korpak, Alexia Petridis, Juan Pablo Trejo, Ema Bonifacic, Charu Gandhi, Ashley Littlewood, Joo Eun Sung, Teresa Cheung, Yeo Joong Yang, Raymond Lau

Digital Film
Pete Gomes
Term 1 – Portraits of a City

Digital Film aims to integrate film practice and discipline within a digital work context. This year's course explored two film forms: Internet documentary and abstract film.

The first term project 'Portraits of a City' explored Soho, London, focusing on 18 'zones' within the area. Each student made a short documentary film looking at history, architecture and people in the area, with particular attention to the social, business, and culturally diverse aspects of the area. Subjects included: a primary school surrounded by sex shops, an off-licence owner in Soho's gay village, smokers outside an office block, homeless people near an expensive restaurant, clubbing and the music industry.
The aim was to make a film that straddled tourism, promotion and social documentary, combining them to form a physical and virtual information zone. check:
http:// www.aaschool.ac.uk/digitalfilm/soho

Students: Ho Min Kim, Michael Shevel, Itay Gershi, Ifeanyi Oganwu, Alicia Tan, Peter Staub, JinBok Wee, Stephanie Talbot, Bosmat Brants, Alex Catterall, Ken Hin Teo, Julian Loffler, Paul La Tourelle, Thavanan Tanesdech Sundhara, Isabel Pietri Medina, Antonia Josten

Digital Film
Pete Gomes
in collaboration with Peter Lewis
Term 2

In the second term, stemming from a practice of abstract filmmaking, students set out to explore and observe the condition of light. All images were generated using digital cameras but integrated 'analogue' source material using black and white drawing and collage as a starting point, edited, coloured, and processed on computer. Soundtracks were made by recording live in front of silent projections of the edited films, with the newly created sounds guided by rhythm and changes in density of colour and light in the image. All soundtracks were created using voice, clapping, whistling and tabletop percussion and all were subsequently processed with effects on computer. Particular attention was given to correlation of sound and image, rhythm and colour, making tangential connections to the experiential qualities of architecture, and the resonance and memory of architectural space. Historical and reference material for the project ranged from Jordan Belson to Stockhausen.

Students: Hoi Chi Ng, Maija Korpak, Alexia Petridis, Juan Pablo Trejo, Ema Bonifacic, Charu Gandhi, Ashley Littlewood, Joo Eun Sung, Teresa Cheung, Yeo Joong Yang, Raymond Lau

one example frame showing the anchor points and connections

Intermedia
Pete Gomes
Term 2 - WAP

This project set out to explore the technology of WAP (Wireless Application Protocol) and future mobile devices. The next phase of the internet is about portability and the network's relation to physical location. Portable and wireless devices combine with the real geographies of physical space and the changing dynamics of cities, fusing the network with physical locations that spawn 'terraportals' - combined physical and virtual information cells. People, buildings, information across the world - but they're only relevant if you happen to be standing in the right place. Walk a few paces and the information changes with you - location specific.

A new form of architectural practice: the design of info zones that lock you in, rest over you, guide you through, weave in and out, subvert the real world. What you see is not what you get. Augmented realities.

Brief: Insert an artwork that rests inside Tate Modern but is only accessible by mobile phone - a 'tour' within Tate Modern that begins at the Turbine Hall entrance. This will be a series of interlinking and guiding screens using a conceptual thread. Use physical markers in the building and images on screen to verify location.

The insertion of an artwork tour inside the Tate questions the concepts of boundary, geographies, navigation and the role of the user in relation to technology, as well as the role of the physical in art works.

Q: Did you ask someone if you could do this?

Q: Do they know?
Q: Is it allowed?
A: No. But it is still there.
check: http://www.aaschool.ac.uk/intermedia/wap/

Invited guests: Sheep Dalton, Mark Wayman, Joel Wilkinson, Nokia Senior Mobile Solution Consultant
Students: Takumi Sugimoto, Yee Seng Tan, Leonidas Lazarakis, Alastair Townsend

Photography
Etienne Clement
Term 1 - 'Interiored' Portrait

This course was about exploring the idea of interiority and intimacy. We decided to investigate each separately.

After studying Italian Renaissance painting composition, students were asked to photograph their bedroom in a similar manner using 5x4 cameras. This task enabled them to understand the medium and to become familiarised with the more specific technical aspects of the large-format camera.

For the second task the students were asked to photograph their own body with a 35mm camera. They were asked to explore the given theme more intimately and were able to do so because they understood the camera better and saw in it an outlet for creativity.

Students: Niccolo Montesi, Tania Rodriguez, Paula Nascimento, Rita Lee, Natalie Waters, Dan Narita, Spencer Owen

Cross-Media
Max de Rosee
Terms 1 & 2

The course attempted to complement the traditionally static architectural language of representation (drawing, modelling, etc.) by

providing a tool to convey dynamic information. Students investigated selected video clips, extrapolating certain aspects, and then developed an animation technique for conveying the abstracted and constantly changing piece of information.

Students: Henry Leung, Suk Kyu Hong, Francesco Brenta, Julia Mauser, Anna Kubelik, Alex Papadakis, Andy Meira, Michelangelo Spinelli, Kelvin Chu, Roman Wittmer

Drawing I - First Year
Katrin Lahusen
Terms 1 & 2

Subject: Soane, or a view relating at least two spaces.

First the Soane house was visited and each student chose a specific view. This view became the starting point for a visual/spatial investigation into the labyrinthine space of mirrors/reflections, light/shadow distortions. Through a personal imaginative process of photographing, drawing and construction, the view, or that which was seen, was transformed into something different.

Students: Vanessa Poon, Phoivos Skroumbelos, Angela Cheung, Nausica Gabrielides, Panos Hadjichristofi, Katrin Eliasdottir, Mark Tynan, Ami Giorgi, Ruth Kedar, Esi Carboo, Daniel Castella, Diego Garcia Scaro, Charles Hui, Alex Chalmers, Gabriel Sanchiz Garin

Drawing II - First Year
Denise Hawrysio
Terms 1 & 2 - Image Making

Indeed, today's society is so image-oriented that, to make your mark, you must yourself generate images. Gerhard Mack, from AA publication, Eberswalde Library: Herzog & de Meuron

This workshop used a technique called three-colour mono-printing to transcribe

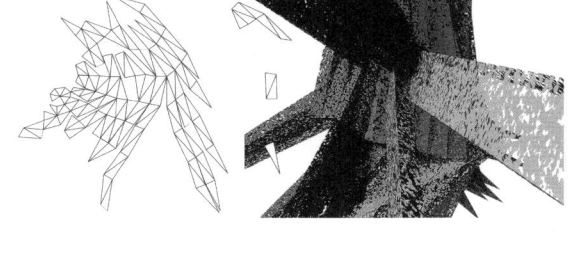

a photograph into a printed image.
The technique is a direct method of layering three colours on top of each other. This type of printing results in very rich and sensuous colour that can be explored in a similar manner to painting. It also emphasises notions of chance and the indeterminate mark, but most importantly reflects an awareness of colour, texture and the strange way images can occur within a limited level of control.
For post-modernity, according to Fredric Jamesonian logic, is axiomatically incompatible with maturity, permanence and any aspiration towards monumentality.

Students: Fumiko Sakata, Tiffany Ogden, Ioanna Ioannidi, William Hai Liang Chen, Serafina Sama, Baco Beaujolin, Jimmy Wan, Tengku Amir Hamzah, Antonis Karides, Akiko Kurayama

Drawing III - First Year
Simon English
Term 1 & 2 - Modern Medicine

Drawing III looked at line as an art form in itself and as an ally to an extended practice.
The course studied drawing as a means of observation and record, research, improvisation and concept projection.
Drawing III operated as a forum in which to raise fundamental issues relating to the use of material, meaning and metaphor. 'Modern Medicine' took the premise that an artist/architect has the power to make metaphor reality - and, as a 'shaman', can transform the meaning and matter of a material object into a metamorphosis of themselves or an acknowledgement of a precise state of being.
Students were asked to transform a found object - through a process of drawing, object and computer manipulation, photography and

in some cases film - to become the manifestation of either: death, a vehicle with which to contemplate notions pertaining to loss or memory, or: sex, a vehicle with which to explore the erotic senses and contemplate notions pertaining to volition and desire. In some cases, as with Keats' Grecian Urn, the object became a culmination of the two.
At the end of the term students presented a mixed-media installation that both conveyed an analogous logic and presented the idea. The emotive actions inflicted on the object, formed the base of an instruction kit allowing a repeat performance to take place anywhere in the world at any given time.

Students: Thomas Smith, Kazuhiro Murayama, Eriko Soga, Hoi Ying Leung, Moritz Klatten, Elizabeth Apostolopoulou, Stefania Batoeva, Eduardo Ardiles, Federico Ferrari, Soon Tak Joo, Daniel Coll I Capdevila, Kuniaki Mogami, Charles Perronin, Nobuyuki Tabata, Krasimir Kotsinov, Edward Wells

Drawing IV - First Year
Mark Hemel
Terms 1 & 2

Some things are topologically defined as being in between 2D and 3D. The principle of a fractal, for instance, is that it is not based on an integer dimension, but takes a position in between two dimensions: a surface-fractal is a line that always incorporates surface, however small a piece you consider. A spatial fractal is a surface that is never flat. We looked at the relationship between a space and the pattern that would be generated when you unfolded the space onto a flat surface. Computer-modelling and non-modelling techniques were used to investigate the relationship between these flat and spatial versions of an object. Several techniques were part of the process of modelling and non-modelling.

1. Sections were used to reproduce a version of a physical object in virtual space.
2. Triangulation was used to influence the resolution and the scale of surface-planes.
3. Virtual unfolding was used to make spatial objects flat.
4. Material refolding in paper was used to physically relate to the virtual processes.
5. Deformations in spatial objects were eventually tested to see their effect on the unfolded versions of the objects.

Students: Chloe Kobayashi, Robert Gluckman, Hadiza Gwadabe, Marija Gonopolskaja, Jun Kawamata, Christos Malecos, Sara Castilho, Anuk Chanyapak, Max Von Werz

Communications Special Projects

Special projects outlines a series of open Communications events designed to respond to specific topics and questions emerging from within the cultural context of the AA.

The film programme, Rare Screenings, is a response to the necessity for a discourse around the burgeoning use of motion and animation technology in architectural communication. In this context, prototypical film work was selected for review and discussion in relation to architectural space, narrative structures and the continuum of psycho-perceptional properties of the moving 'point of view'. All of these areas provided specific insights and revealed techniques to conceive, think and experience space as part of a process of continuous change and redefinition.

Course Master Jean Michel Crettaz
Co-ordinator Joanna Maggs

Rare Screenings
Peter Lewis and David Ward

Rare Screenings is an extended programme of film screenings intended to provide a forum within the School for viewing artists' works. The programme includes highly acclaimed and critically influential film works, which are nevertheless rarely given public screenings. The series does not look to the narrative traditions of cinema production but instead focuses on the innovative work of independent artist filmmakers whose inventive responses to the medium of film continue to affect new generations of artists working with the moving image.

At a time when considerable attention is directed to the potential of digital images, and as video now sits within the mainstream of visual arts media, Rare Screenings draws attention to the material and aesthetic qualities of film. This contributes to the creation of a context within which new work can be seen. The programme to date has therefore ranged from the classic modernism of Jean Vigo, to the sculptural minimalism of the 1970s film work of Richard Serra and Michael Snow, to the poetic lyricism of the most recent films by Jayne Parker made in 2000.
Films by Carolee Schneemann (who toured the UK earlier this year) and Robert Smithson (whose work appeared as a subject in Tacita Dean's recent exhibition at Tate Britain) were included in the series. These screenings reflect wider processes of critical re-evaluation and the current surge of interest in the work of artists who first achieved prominence in the 1970s.

The series ranges across a wide field of film work, involving structural, sculptural and performance-related approaches to the medium. In this way Rare Screenings points to a number of discourses that overlap with the visual arts and architecture. The screenings are followed by informal discussions and are occasionally introduced by visiting artists who have included Tina Keane and Jayne Parker. The series also provides a platform for showing the work of film and video makers teaching at the School, including Joel Newman and Pete Gomes.

To compile the programme Rare Screenings has drawn on the film archives and collections of individual artists, the Lux Cinema, the Arts Council of England and the British Film Institute.

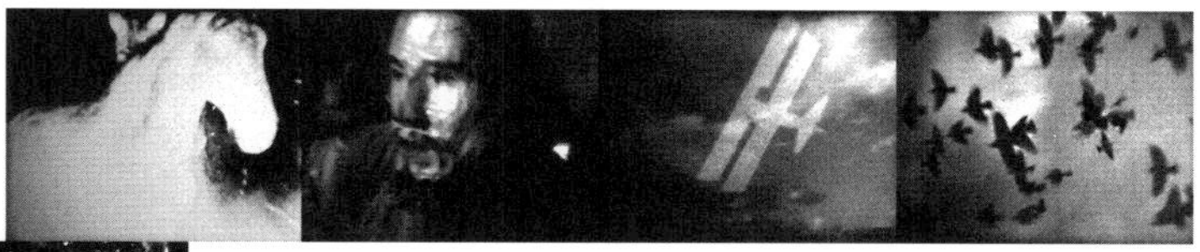

A propos de Nice - Jean Vigo, 1930, 20mins, 35mm, France
Rain - Joris Ivens, 1929, 15mins, 35mm, Holland
Film - Samuel Beckett, 1963, 20mins, 16mm, USA

Autumn Spectrum - Hy Hirsch, 1940, 8 mins, 16mm, France.
Défense d'afficher - Hy Hirsch, 1941, 7mins, 16mm, France.
Come Closer - Hy Hirsch, 1940, 5 mins, 16mm, France

Spiral Jetty - Robert Smithson, 1972, 30mins, 16mm, USA

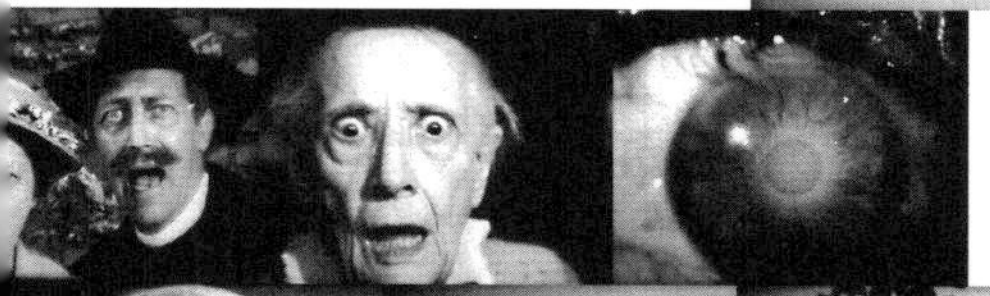

Faded Wallpaper - Tina Keane, 1989, 20mins, 16mm, UK
Shadow of a Journey - Tina Keane, 1984, 10mins, 16mm, UK

Ritual in Transfigured Time - Maya Deren, 1945-6, 16mins, 16mm, USA

Kulu se Mama - Chick Strand, 1967, 4mins, 16mm, USA
Waterfall - Chick Strand, 1968, 3mins, 16mm, USA
Anselo - Chick Strand, 1966, 4mins, 16mm, USA
Blue Angel - Chick Strand, 1967, 4mins, 16mm, USA

Castro Street - Bruce Bailey, 1966, 10mins, 16mm, USA

Artificial Light - Holis Frampton, 1969, 25mins, 16mm, USA

Handpainted Film 1 + 2 - Stan Brakage, 1986-88, 4mins, 16mm, USA
The Wonder Ring - Stan Brakage1955, 6mins, 16mm, USA

Petit Mal - Betzy Bromberg, 1977, 18mins, 16mm, USA
Ciao Bella - Betzy Bromberg, 1978, 13mins, 16mm, USA

Migration - Bill Viola, 1976, 7mins, video, USA
The Reflecting Pool - Bill Viola, 1977-79, 7mins, video, USA

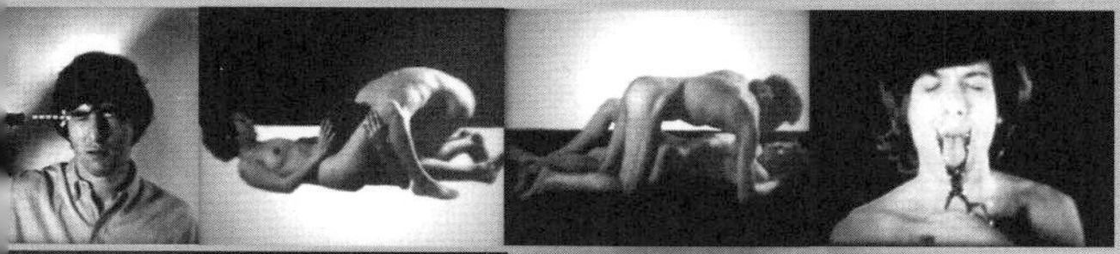

Wavelength - Michael Snow, 1966, 45mins, 16mm, USA

Chain Reaction - Fishli and Weiss, 1987, 30mins, 16mm, Switzerland

There Again - Nicky Hamlyn, 1988-91, 16mins, 16mm, UK

Bird Xerox - Nicky Gordon-Smith, 1983, 8mins, 16mm, UK

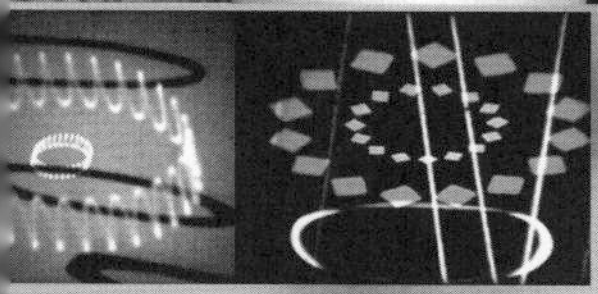

Railroad Turnbridge - Richard Serra, 1976, 19mins, 16mm, USA

Raygun Virus - Paul Sharits, 1966, 14mins, 16mm, USA
T,O,U,C,H,I,N,G - Paul Sharits, 1968, 12mins, 16mm, USA
Piece Mandala/ End War - Paul Sharits, 1966, 5mins, 16mm, USA

Mirror - Robert Morris, 1975, 10mins, 16mm, USA

Filter Bed - Guy Sherwin, 1988, 10mins, Super8, UK

Jaunt - Andrew Kötting
Kipperty Klop - Andrew Kötting, 1984, 12mins, Super8, UK

Girl Chewing Gum - John Smith, 1976, 12mins, 16mm, UK

Plumb Line - Carolee Schneemann, 1968 - 72, 15mins, Super8/16mm, USA
Fuses - Carolee Schneemann, 1964-7, 25mins, 16mm, USA

Crystal Aquarium, Jayne Parker, 1995, 15mins, 16mm, UK
Thinking Twice, Jayne Parker, 1997, 10mins, 16mm, UK
Foxfire Eins, Jayne Parker, 2000, 10mins, 16mm, UK
Blues in B-flat, Jayne Parker, 2000, 8mins, 16mm, UK
Projection 1, Jayne Parker, 2000, 6mins, 16mm, UK
59 _ seconds, Jayne Parker, 2000, 59 seconds, 16mm, UK

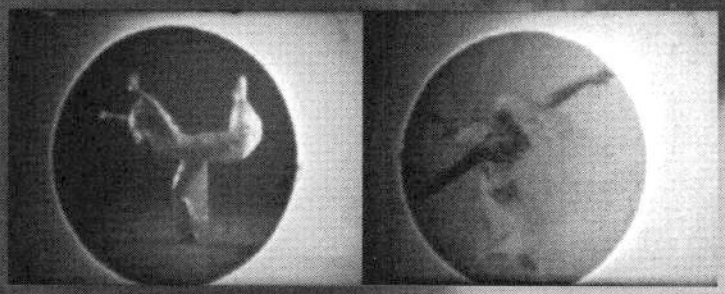

Discs - Marchel Duchamp/John Cage

Berlin Horse - Malcolm LeGrice/Brian Eno, 1970, 8mins, 16mm, UK

Mommy, Mommy, Where's my Brain? - Jon Moritsugu, 1986, 9mins, video, USA

Lapis - James Whitney, 1963-66, 10mins, 35mm, USA

Hat Gamer - Hans Richter, 1929, 10mins, 35mm, Germany

Moon - Scott Bartlett, 1969, 8mins, 16mm, USA

Re-Entry - Jordan Belson, 1964, 6mins, 35mm, USA

Cybernetik 5.3 - John Stehura, 1965-69, 8mins, 35mm, USA

As an appendage to the Rare Screenings events, we showed a number of pieces
by in-house Multimedia artists Joel Newman and Pete Gomes:

Drop, Pete Gomes, 1996, 3 mins, super8, UK
Artificial Sentience, Pete Gomes, 1997, 3mins, Digital Video, UK
Anything is Possible, Pete Gomes, 2000, 2 mins, Digital Video, UK
I Shadow, Pete Gomes, 2001, 3mins, Digital Video, UK
Sensory, Pete Gomes/Marvin Ayres, 1999, 10mins, DVD + surround sound, UK
Cycle, Pete Gomes, 1999, 10mins, Digital Video, UK
End Beginning, Pete Gomes, 2000, 4mins, Digital Video, UK
Chuck Berry vs IBM (Film for Venus Ray), Pete Gomes, 2001,
4mins, Digital Video, UK
Wake, Pete Gomes, 1991-2001, 6mins, 16mm, UK

The Drummer, Joel Newman, 1998, 3mins, Digital Video, UK
Animali 1, Joel Newman, 1998, 3mins, Digital Video, UK
The 60's, Joel Newman, 1998, 4mins, Digital Video, UK
The F Movies, Joel Newman, 2000, 5mins, Digital Video, UK
Fine and Dandy, Joel Newman, 2000, 3mins, Digital Video, UK
New Cons Video, Joel Newman, 2000, 3.5mins, Digital Video, UK
The Gas, Joel Newman, 2000, 3mins, Digital Video, UK
Me, Picachu and Gloria, Joel Newman, 2000, 5mins, Digital Video, UK
Raptor, Joel Newman, 2000, 5mins, Digital Video, UK
London Horse, Joel Newman, 2001, 4.5mins, Digital Video, UK

Technical Studies
First Year

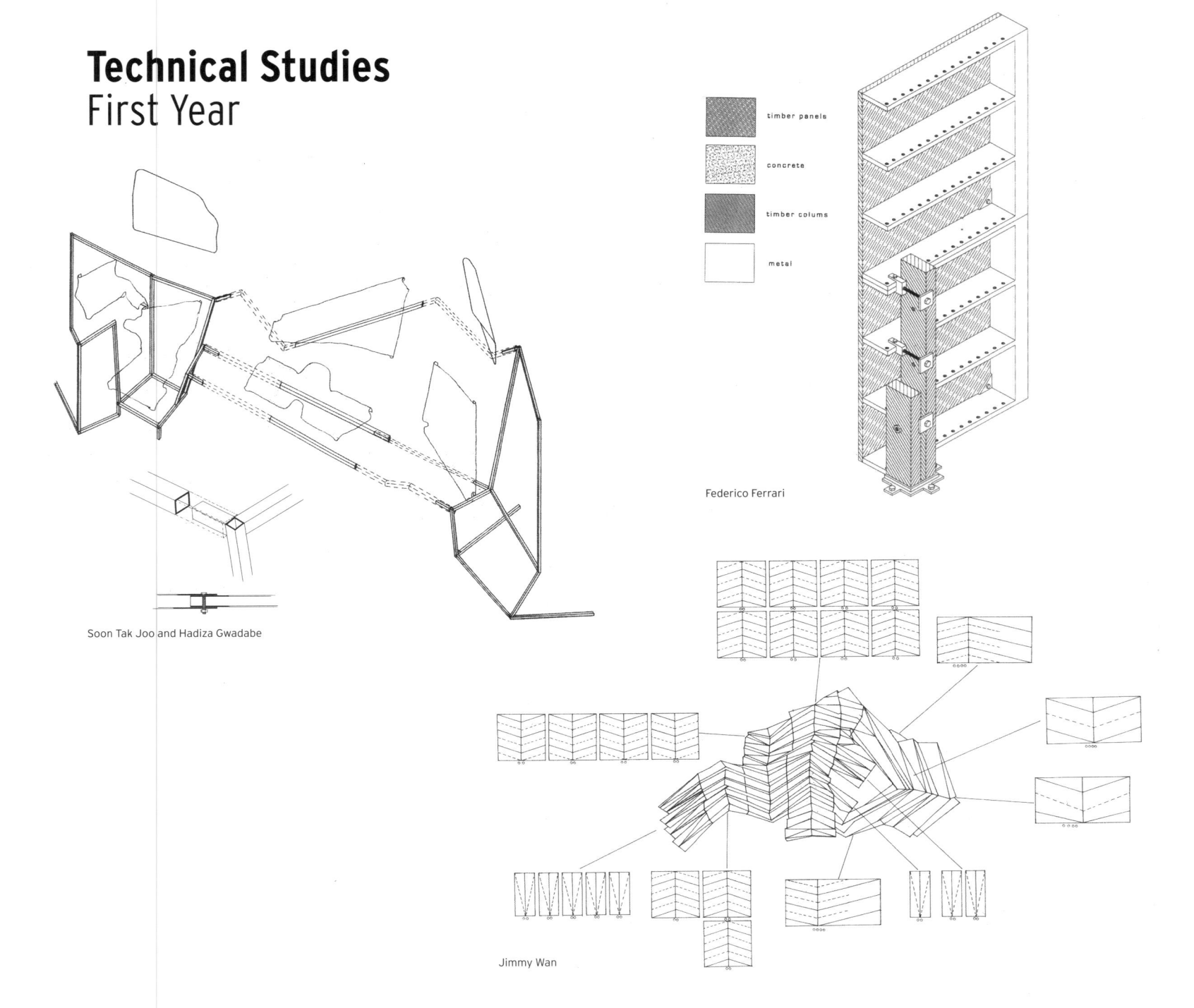

timber panels

concrete

timber colums

metal

Federico Ferrari

Soon Tak Joo and Hadiza Gwadabe

Jimmy Wan

The First Year Technical Studies programme sets out to provide a grounding in the understanding of structural principles, and in the relation between architectural detail and the overall conception of architectural space. This is encouraged through careful observation and analysis, as well the testing and resolution of architectural propositions. Technical Studies in the First Year calls for the actual making of objects, in conjunction with the varied intentions of the unit programmes, and, in particular, requires that the physical aspects of the work fulfil the concepts identified at the project's inception. Students are asked to think, in a critical way, about the choices made in design work: choices about how, and of what, things are made.

This year, the course began with a series of seminars introducing students to the principles of structure and the basic methods of

calculating forces. Allied to this was a series of visits to buildings that illustrated these principles, including the new Jubilee Line stations, Tobacco Dock, Stockwell Bus Garage, Lord's Media Centre and Peckham Library. A particularly successful pairing was a talk by Anderson Inge on the distribution of forces in a bicycle frame and wheel, followed by a visit to the London Eye (in effect a giant bicycle wheel). The term's work culminated in a competition to make a 'spaghetti' bridge which was tested to destruction. Each student produced a Building Visit Notebook recording their comments on, and understanding of, the structures visited, with particular emphasis on the relation between detail and overall conception.

In the second term a series of talks was arranged to introduce students to the various uses of materials in buildings – glass, timber, brick, concrete and steel – and to the concept

of integrated systems in design. These began with Jonathan Sakula and the structural use of glass, which was followed by a visit to Preedy's Glassworks, talks on the Maison de Verre and the Eames House, Dominic Cullinan describing the process of building his own house, before proceeding to Prasad and Penoyre's Ecology Centre and the use of ecologically sound materials.

Unit work develops the students' propositions – a very important component of which is the guidance given by the Workshop staff in the making of models. The Workshop continues to play a critical role in encouraging the students to think about and develop the techniques whereby they might realise their ideas in physical form.

First Year Master, Technical Studies
Brendan Woods

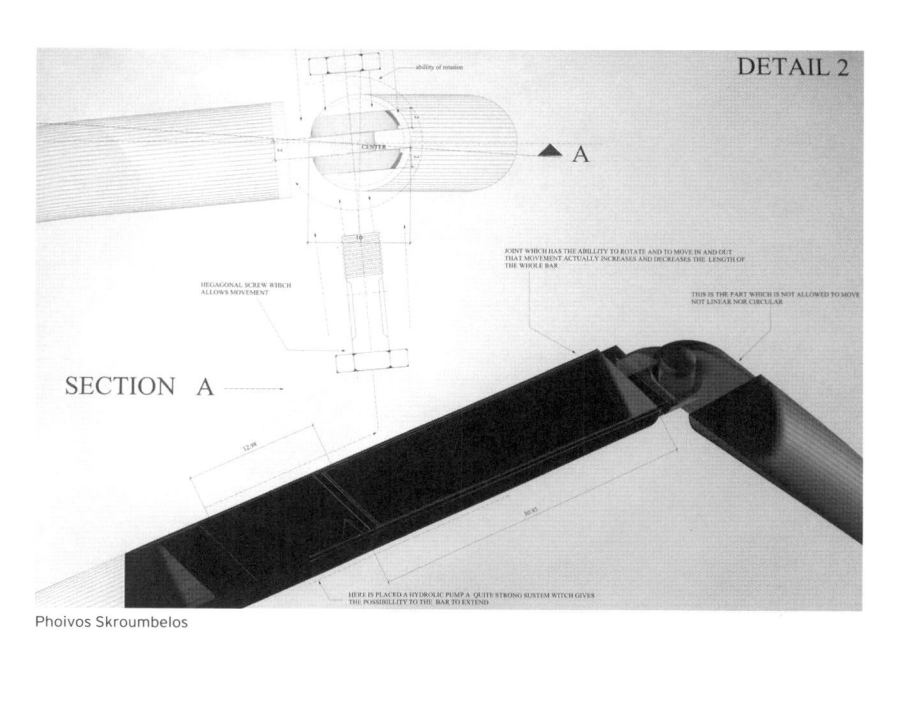

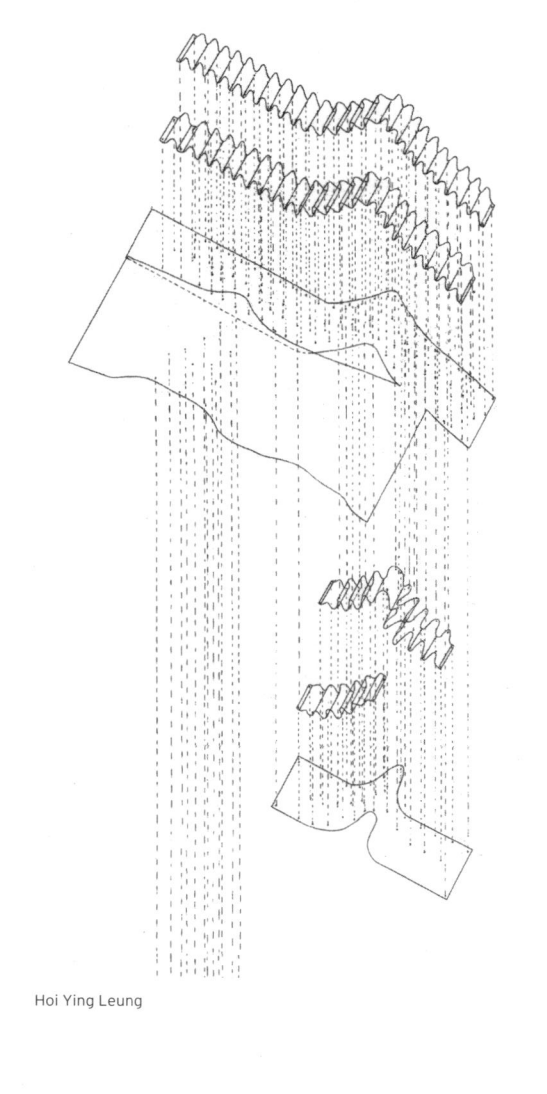

DETAIL 2

SECTION A

Phoivos Skroumbelos

Hoi Ying Leung

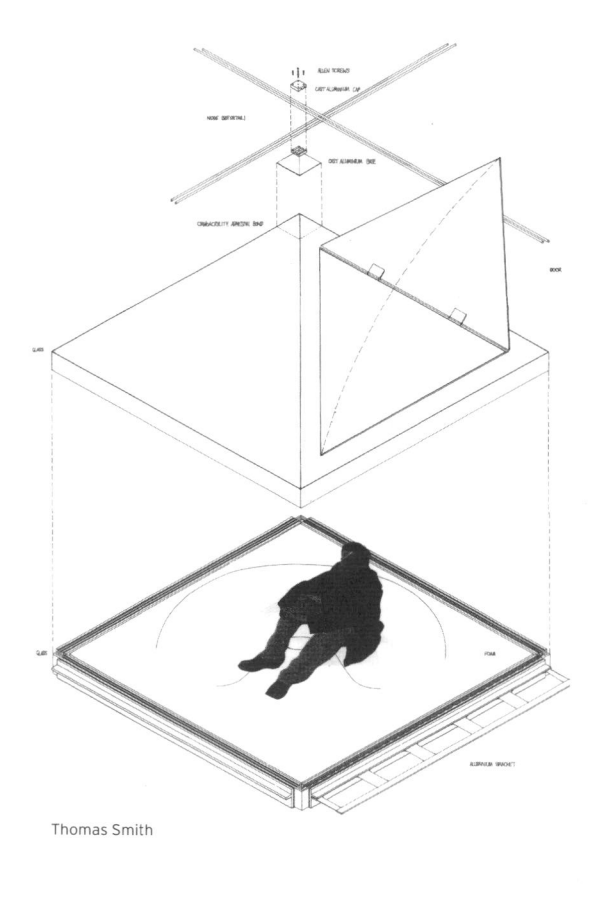

Thomas Smith

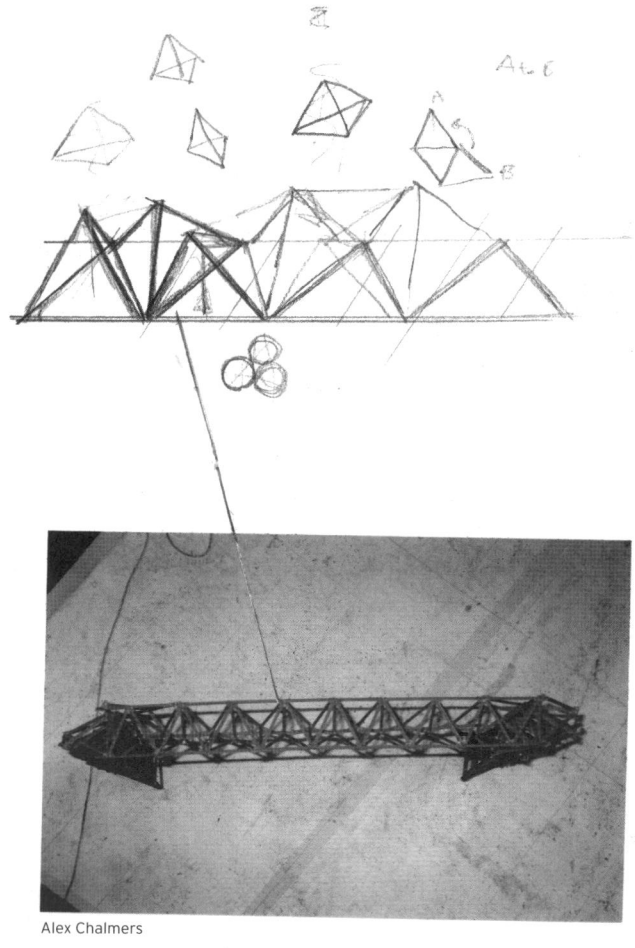

Alex Chalmers

Intermediate Technical Studies

In our ideal architectural world, all the work of a design project starts simultaneously; Technical Studies are so embedded within the proposition that they become inseparable from it, and the proposition is identifiable by its approach to its materialisation. The challenge for architecture is its demand that we both conceptualise and fabricate, thoroughly. It is within those investigations by students of techniques, that the opportunities exist to make personal explorations which individualise and colour their work. This year, the Intermediate Units have continued to develop their own technical investigations

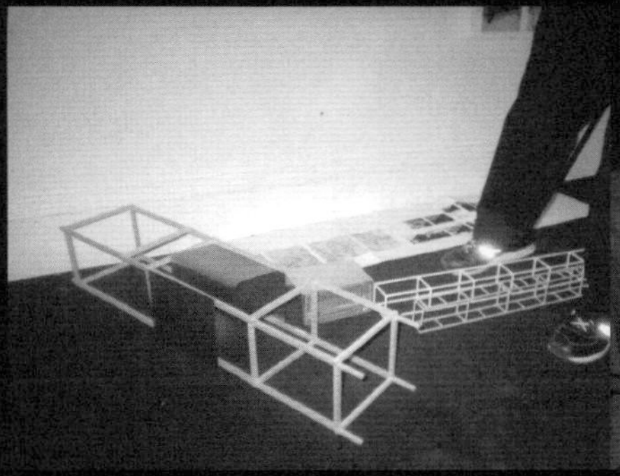

bridge Switzerland   Juan Pablo Trejo   Cecilia Ramirez Corzo   Juan Pablo Trejo   Paul La Tourelle

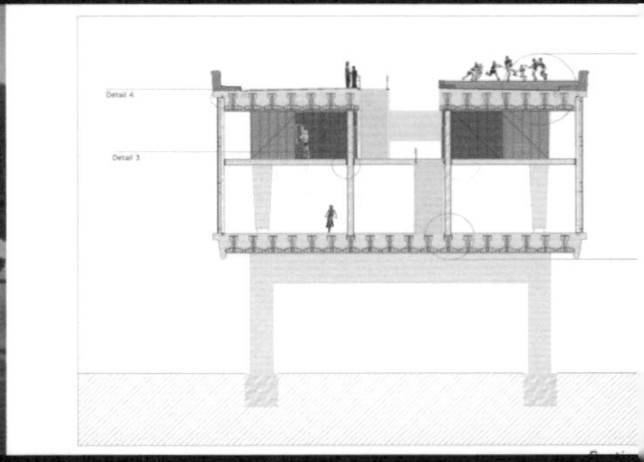

shanty site Lisbon   Phillipa Jelfs   Anna Ohlin   Charu Gandhi   Westway Guinness brand   Alex Catterall

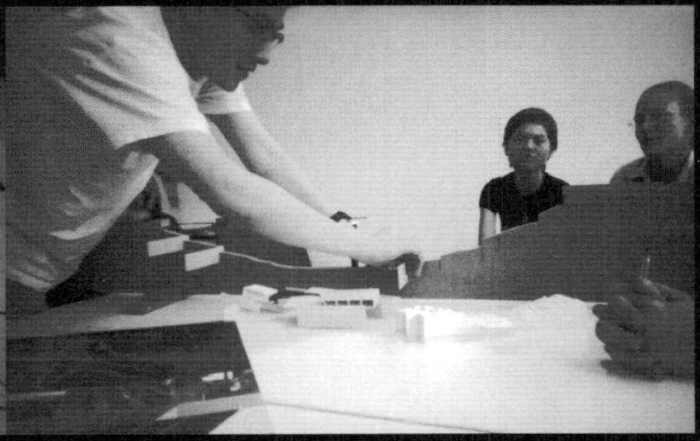

shanty site Lisbon   Jinbok Wee   interchange Holloway Road   Chihiro Nakagawa   shanty site Lisbon   Jinbok Wee   Land Terrain

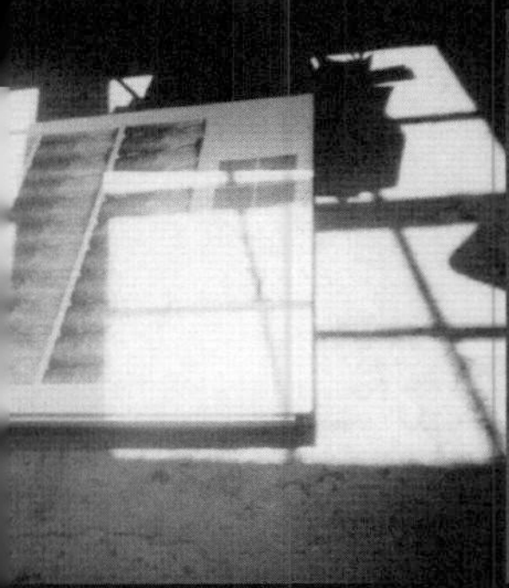

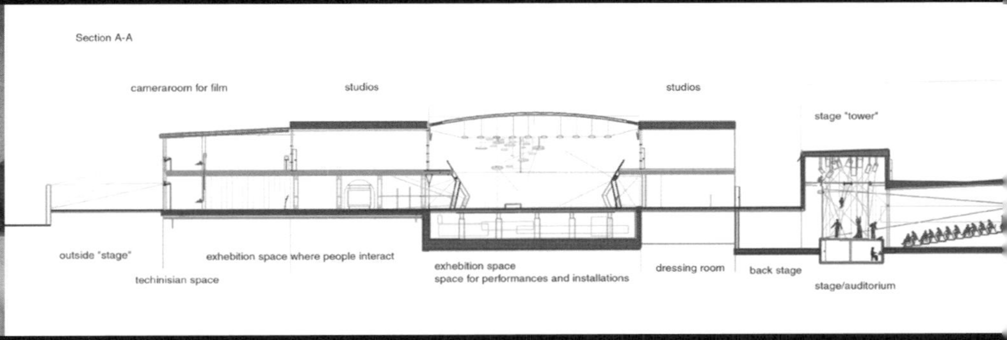

Section A-A

cameraroom for film   studios   studios   stage "tower"

outside "stage"   exhibition space where people interact   exhebition space space for performances and installations   dressing room   back stage   stage/auditorium

techinisian space

land terrain   Nazhila Maghzian   shanty site Lisbon   emerging structures Alexandra Jaeschke   southwark infoBox   Kristine Bisgaard
prototype test Igor Gottschalk

Construction: The eight lectures in the first term set the Construction Course goals for the rest of the year. The lecture course explored how design and construction are not two separate things but stages of one and the same process. During the second and third terms, the students were helped to search for solutions which would help them to 'materialise' their original design concept. The students were encouraged to produce an assignment, preferably on one of the projects on which they were currently working. Hiromasa Makino's

In the idiom of their projects, with the Technical Studies staff (with their hard hats and overalls) acting as external catalysts or irritants, to extract and challenge the outcomes. The range of Unit approaches reveals the School's diversity and the possibilities of current architectural practice:
Inter 5, fabrication manifested in large scale models; Inter 3, ingenious adaptations of existing buildings - Centrepoint Westway Trafalgar Square as 3D representations of brand; Inter 1, skins and surfaces as the edges of concepts; Inter 9, dynamic infrastructures; Inter 8, the imprint of technique on idea, Inter research into new kinds of materials, experiments developing components and a full size real construction of a living unit; Inter 7, extraction of ideas from process/material studies; Inter 10, bridging as a vehicle to investigate the physical manifestations of technique; Inter 6, reactive architecture of the enclosing skin; and Inter 2 enhanced descriptions of our environment through computer techniques which make critical use of the medium.

Javier Castanon and Ros Diamond with thanks to Carolina Bartram, Pat Brown, Aran Chadwick, Phil Cooper, Claire Devine, Belinda Flaherty, Max Fordham & Partners, Fenella Griffin, Anderson Inge, Wolf Mangelsdorf, Val Petrushechkin, Paul Swann, Neil Thomas, Mike Weinstock

Trafalgar Square absolut vodka brand   Bosmat Brants   Bridge Switzerland   Cecilia Ramirez Corz   Juan Pablo Trejo

Alex Catterall   shanty site Lisbon   Amanda Friedman   Amanda Friedman   Land Terrain jury   Fenella and Saul Griffin

erode Nazhila Maghzian   River Thames   floating auditorium Kyoko Kobayashi   interchange Holloway Road   Yeena Yoon   serpentine   flat earth society Alex Papadakis

ures testing dimensional analysis model project   ts jury prototype staircase

(Inter 4) study of folding panels showed a determination to succeed on the part of its author. The majority of the students chose to study a specific aspect of their project, which proved to be an excellent way to keep in touch with their development. In addition to simply providing technical support, it became our task to encourage the students to keep on trying when they ran aground. Aleksandra Jaeschke (Inter 8), for example, never gave up until the physical expression of her site analysis came through her design for the Lisbon Project

Some more spectacular results are to be found in Inter 10, where the Bridge Projects of Paul La Tourelle, Juan Pablo Trejo and Jordi Rafols were equally a result of never giving up the search, not only for a form and a material but also for a sequence and a method of construction. If the variety of the assignments made their assessment interesting, some of the texts were just as refreshing, as in the case of Beatriz Minguez de Molina (Inter 4), who wrote on the design and construction of the Third Capsule with great insight and yet with great simplicity.

Diploma Technical Studies

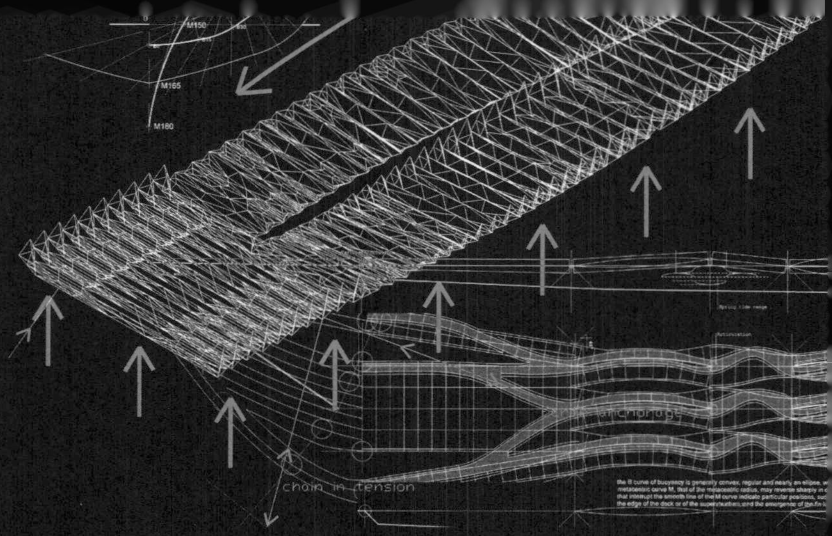

Michael Weinstock
Technical Studies Master

Diploma Technical Studies offers students a freedom of subjects –
from the strategic organisation of large constructions to detailed
design and fabrication. Fifth Year students follow their own research
or design studies in a field of their choice . Specific case studies of
current material processes, constructed artefacts and buildings are
followed by either critical reflection on these studies or
experimentation with the ideas and techniques revealed.
Among a number of excellent Research and Design Theses this year
are the following:

Miki Ando *Skin, surface and roofing*
Leire Asenio *Coastal structures*
Bhupinder Chawla *Low-cost housing and remediation strategies*
Mariano Ciccone *Differential space frame structures*
Rita Lambert *Excavation procedures and foundation strategies*
Philipp Misselwitz *Berlin sands*
Henry Ho Yin Ng *Forming complex curved surfaces in steel*
John O'Mara *Structural strategy for sequential occupation*
Aikari Paing *Puppet theatres*
Nathalie Rozencwajg *Wind energy and building form*
Irenie Sheehan *Glass flytower*
Sven Steiner *Adaptive building structures for subsidence*
Mark Tavener *Sheet moulding composites for low-cost housing*
Ty Tikari *Multi-phase pylon system for irregular loads*

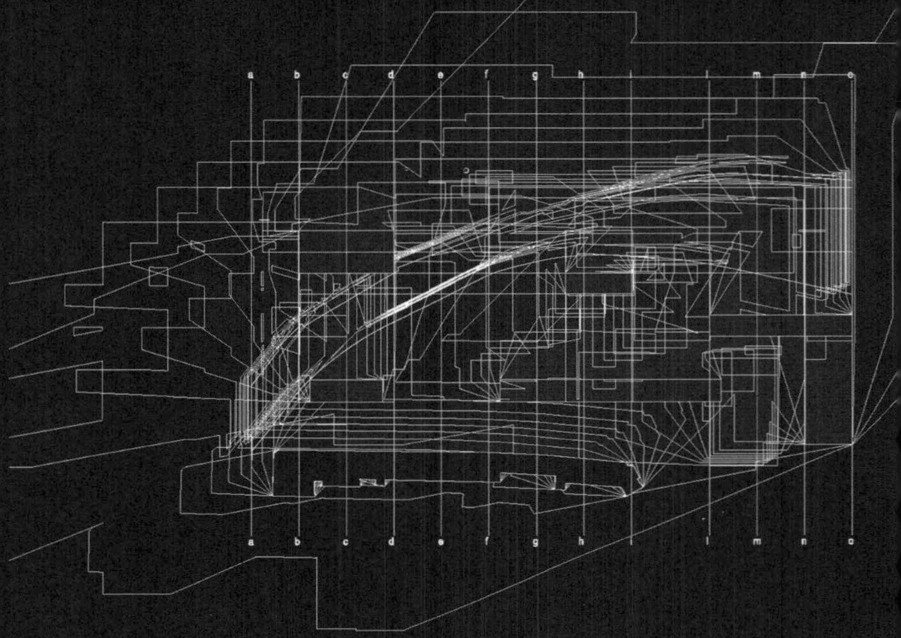

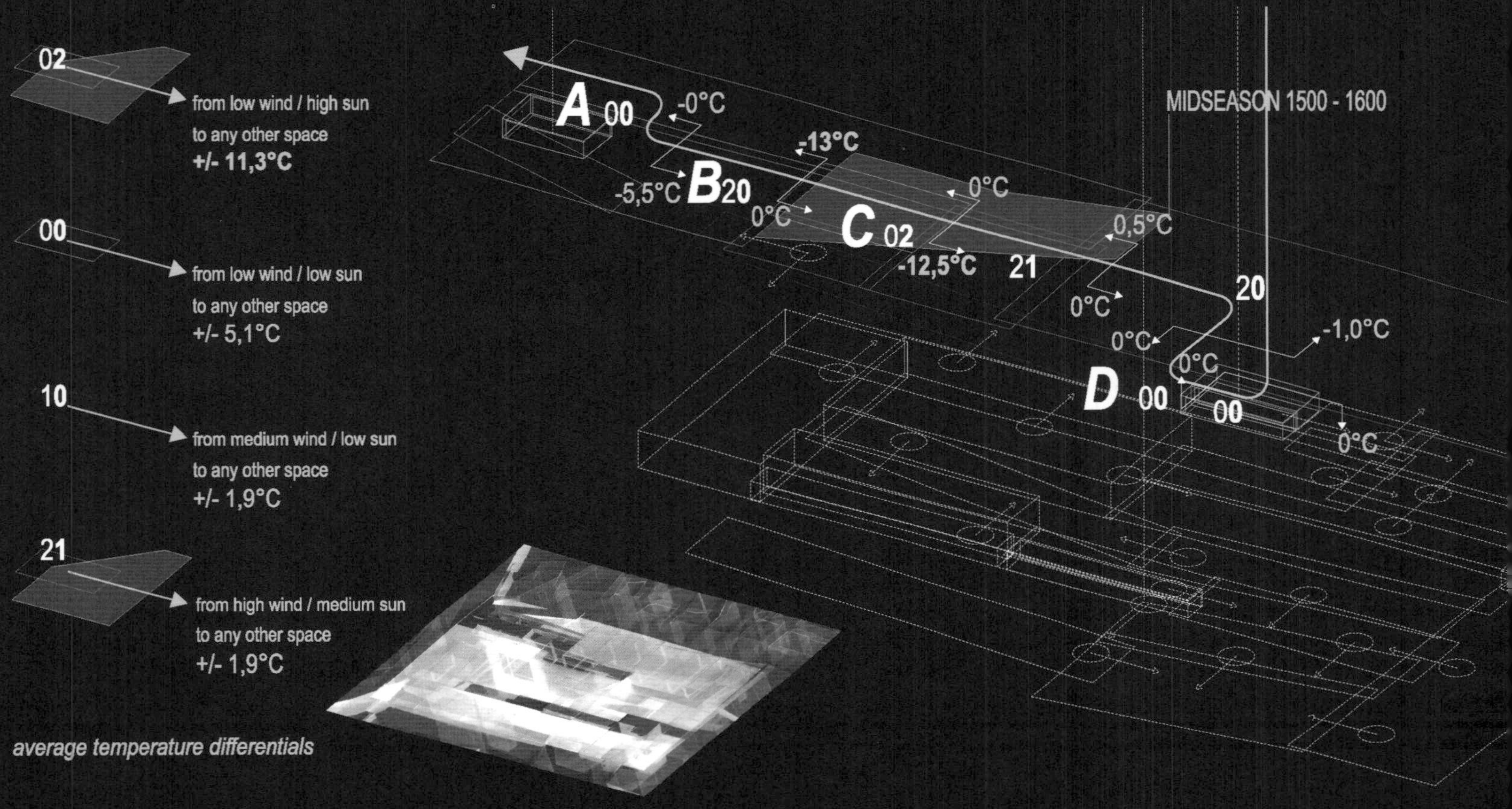

02
from low wind / high sun
to any other space
+/- 11,3°C

00
from low wind / low sun
to any other space
+/- 5,1°C

10
from medium wind / low sun
to any other space
+/- 1,9°C

21
from high wind / medium sun
to any other space
+/- 1,9°C

average temperature differentials

MIDSEASON 1500 - 1600

A 00 -0°C
-13°C
-5,5°C **B** 20 0°C
0°C **C** 02 0,5°C
-12,5°C 21
0°C 20
0°C -1,0°C
D 00 00 0°C
0°C

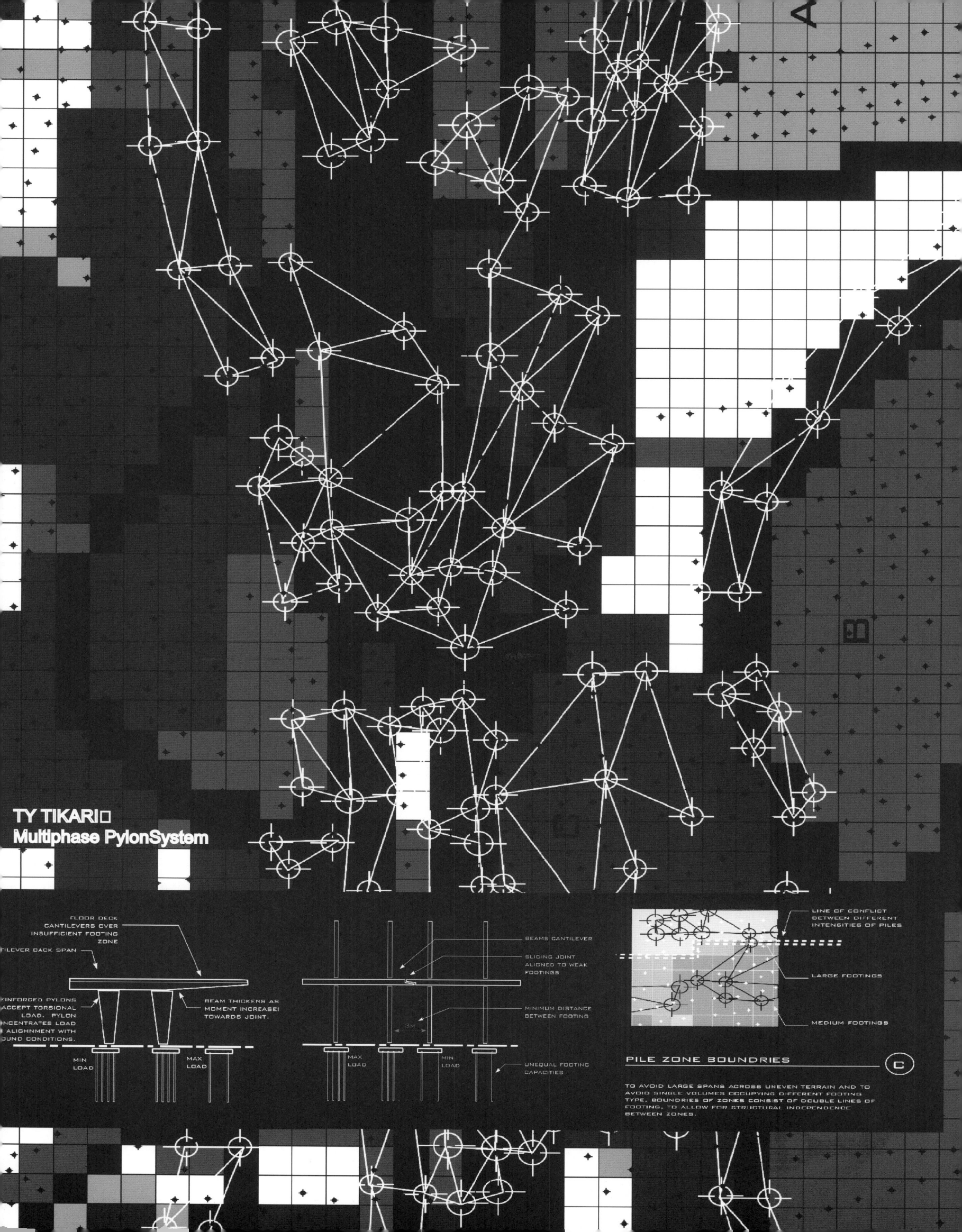

TY TIKARI□
Multiphase PylonSystem

FLOOR DECK
CANTILEVERS OVER
INSUFFICIENT FOOTING
ZONE

TILEVER BACK SPAN

EINFORCED PYLONS
ACCEPT TORSIONAL
LOAD. PYLON
ONCENTRATES LOAD
ALIGNMENT WITH
OUND CONDITIONS.

BEAM THICKENS AS
MOMENT INCREASE!
TOWARDS JOINT.

MIN
LOAD

MAX
LOAD

BEAMS CANTILEVER

SLIDING JOINT
ALIGNED TO WEAK
FOOTINGS

MINIMUM DISTANCE
BETWEEN FOOTING

3м

MAX
LOAD

MIN
LOAD

UNEQUAL FOOTING
CAPACITIES

LINE OF CONFLICT
BETWEEN DIFFERENT
INTENSITIES OF PILES

LARGE FOOTINGS

MEDIUM FOOTINGS

PILE ZONE BOUNDRIES ———— C

TO AVOID LARGE SPANS ACROSS UNEVEN TERRAIN AND TO
AVOID SINGLE VOLUMES OCCUPYING DIFFERENT FOOTING
TYPE, BOUNDRIES OF ZONES CONSIST OF DOUBLE LINES OF
FOOTING, TO ALLOW FOR STRUCTURAL INDEPENDENCE
BETWEEN ZONES.

Workshop

The workshop provides students with the opportunity to deal, at first hand, with a broad range of materials and techniques. The work produced, often in tandem with the model workshop, varies in scale and type – from small site models to large conceptual pieces.

The workshop provides a unique setting in which design and its application can be combined. Students are encouraged to explore the propoerties and application of materials in order to increase their capacity for lateral thinking and problem solving.

During the past year the workshop has engaged with twenty-first-century technology, following the introduction of a CNC routing machine that enables professional up-to-date production techniques to be married to traditional craft skills. A link has been created between the computer room and the workshop, which has given a new dimension to the process of model making.

The workshop epitomises the philosophy that order is achieved through chaos. Often hectic but always creative, the workshop has a unique atmosphere and is an essential resource within the AA.

Staff

Manager
Marcellus Letang

Assistant Manager
Trystrem Smith

Technician
Anthony Beckett

Object Fabrication (Model Workshop)
Chris Pauling

Workshop Tutors
Shin Egashira, Lucy Tilley

Workshop Assistance
Wei Tseng

Student Assistants
Yoichiro Akiba, Ran Ankory,
Takashi Nishibori

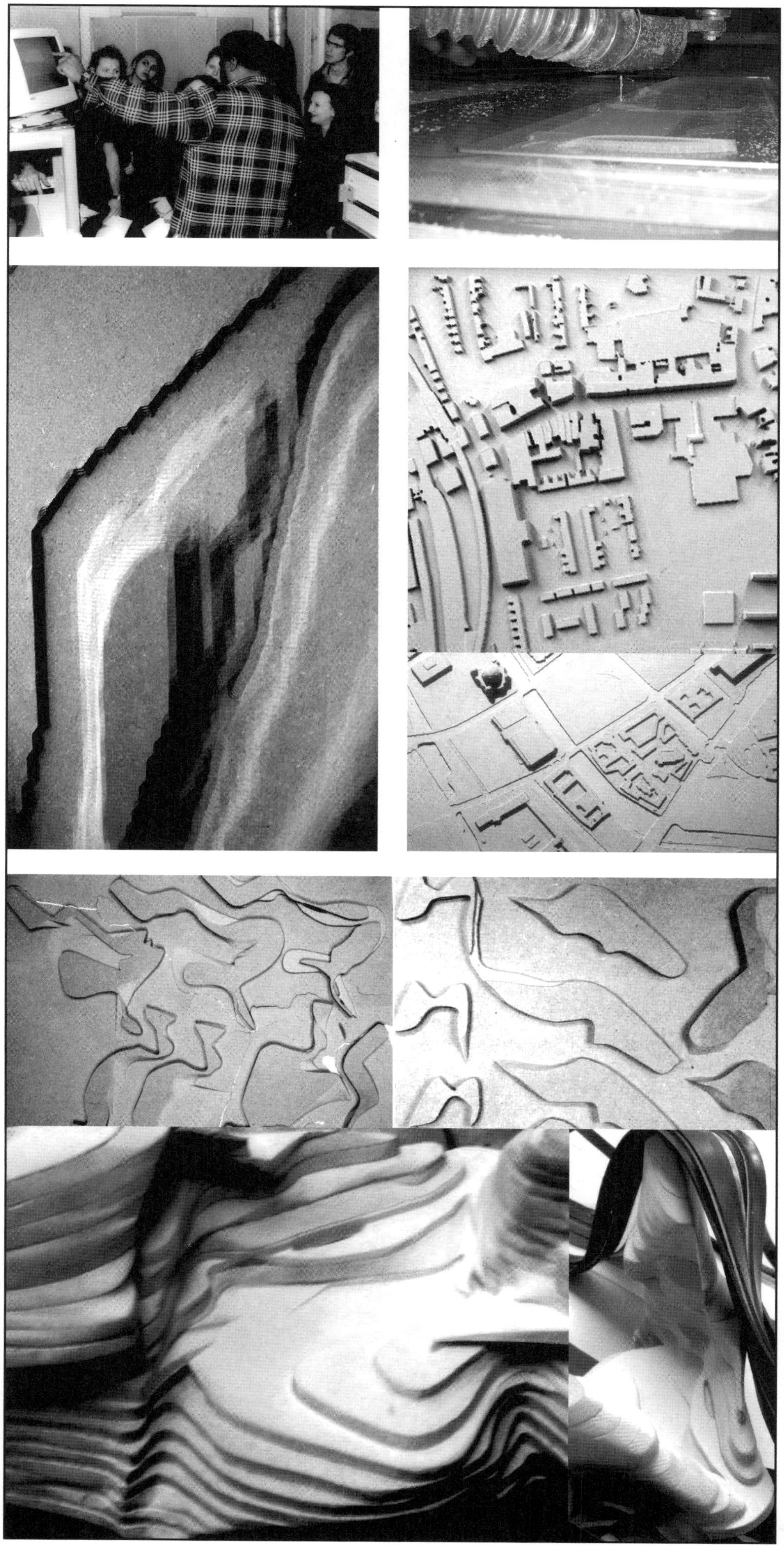

CNC

MODELSHOP

Image from Housing and Urbanism unit publication,
Transforming Cities: Design in the Favelas of Rio de Janeiro

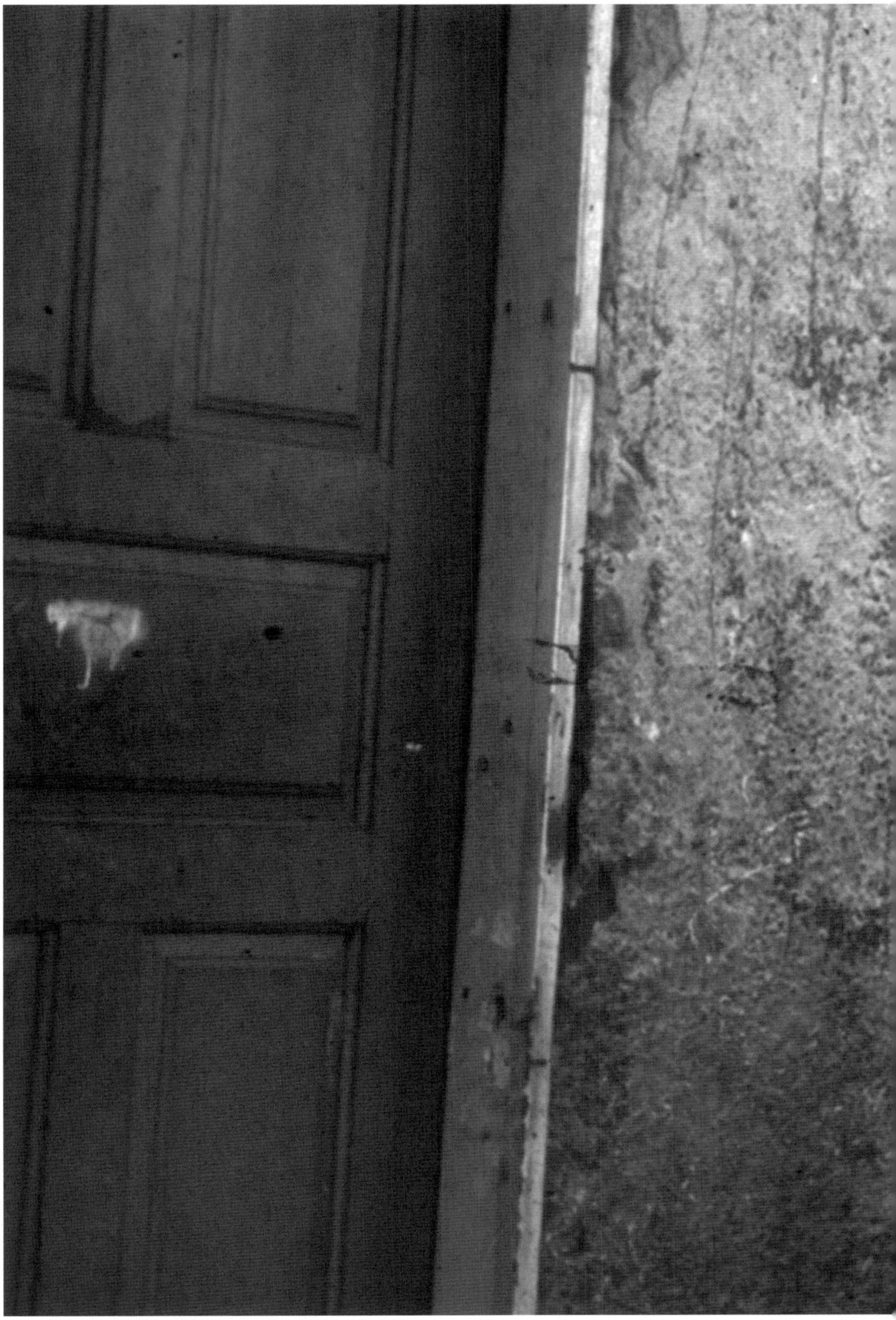

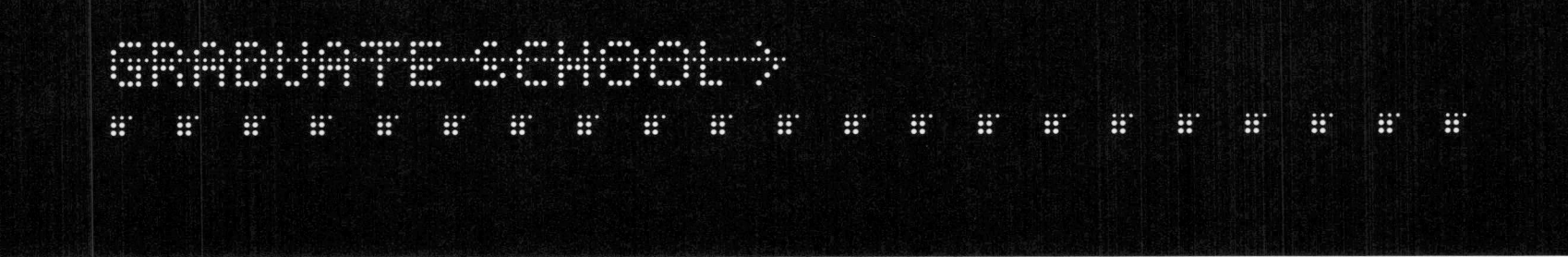

GRADUATE SCHOOL →

Graduate Design
DESIGN RESEARCH LAB

WWW.AADRL.COM

Visit the AADRL end-of-year exhibition online: WWW.AADRL.COM/ENDOFY
Project Archives, Model Photos, Presentations, Exhibitions, Animat
Courses, Syllab

AA Design Research Lab

The AADRL is a sixteen-month, post-professional course awarding a MArch (Masters of Architecture) Degree. The four-term course is divided into two phases; a first academic year during which students take design studio, workshop and seminar courses, and a final term during which teams complete a comprehensive thesis design project. The AADRL develops advanced skills and knowledge through the study and creation of design proposals that project new, alternative forms of architectural and urban space. All work within the AADRL is pursued within self-organised teams addressing a shared overall research agenda.

AADRL Agenda 00/01

Phase II Thesis Design Projects completed work begun last year on Corporate Fields (highly integrated working environments), BrandSpace™ (intensely commercialised product and selling domains) and an e.Hotel (providing a nomadic infrastructure for online and offline travel work space). Phase I teams completed workshops and studio research on nano-urbanism: small-scale, augmented environments designed to operate as intelligent systems and distributed urban installations. This year's research into this area of smart, scripted interiors will continue as the agenda for 2001-2002.

Courses 00/01

Phase II Studios included a new headquarters for Razorfish UK, led by Patrik Schumacher. Brett Steele's teams developed product installation spaces related to their earlier BrandSpace™ research. Tom Verebes's groups worked on major infrastructural nodes in London (including Paddington Station) as sites for transitory work spaces. Phase I Studios included: Patrik Schumacher and Christopher Hight on Auto.poesis, Brett Steele on teleMorph.one and Tom Verebes on Virgin.Living. During the autumn term Chris Hight's Infomatics Series introduced studio resarch and analysis techniques and Tom Verebes led a series of 'Material Trajectories' Workshops. Research by nine teams led to 1:1 prototypes and models, which were evaluated and later developed within three larger design teams that refined the final projects and built a full scale 1:1 installation that tested the workshop prototypes. Andrew Benjamin led an autumn term seminar and spring term workshop analysing three key twentieth-century houses. Brett Steele led a seminar during the autumn and spring terms titled 'Monography I', which examined the twentieth-century rise and transformation of the architectural book as a major media format for the development, circulation and promotion of ideas about architecture and space.

08.10.00 Phase II Teams

13.05.01 Phase I Studio Interim

18.11.00 Phase I Modelling

23 & 24.01.01 Phase II Thesis Design Presentations

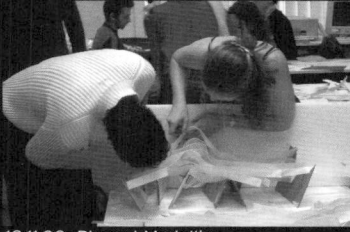

		Phase II Critics	Andrew Benjamin, Winka
Course Directors	Brett Steele		Dubbeldam, Detlef Mertins,
	Patrik Schumacher		Bob Lang, Bart Lootsma,
Course Master	Tom Verebes		Dagmar Richter, Lars Spybroek,
Course Tutors	Christopher Hight		Mohsen Mostafavi
	Andrew Benjamin		
External Tutor	Makato Saito	Phase I Critics	Juan Alayo, Francis Archer,
Workshop Tutors	Kenneth Bostock, Bob		Larry Barth, John Bell, Raoul
	Lang, Pablo Lazo, Theo		Bunschoten, Kenneth Bostock,
	Lorenz, Veronica Schmid,		Mark Cousins, Lucas Dietrich,
	Kivi Sotamaa, Caroline Voet		Thomas Duda, Helen Furjan,
Assistance	Margaret Marshall		Mark Hemel, Michael Hensel,
	(coordination), Sue Barr		Hilde Heynen, Hanif Kara,
	(darkroom), Valerie		Tom Kovacs, Bob Lang,
	Bennett (photography),		Pablo Lazo, David Lewis,
	Joel Newman (video)		George Liaropoulus- Legendre,
			Theo Lorenz, Mark Morris,
External Examiner	John Worthington		Mohsen Mostafavi, Ciro Najle,
			Chris Perry, Andreas Ruby,
			Veronica Schmid, Bob Somol,
			Kivi Sotamaa, Jeff Turko,
			Spela Videcnik, Caroline Voet,
			Bostjan Vuga, Mike Weinstock

With Thanks: Bostjan Vuga at Sadar & Vuga (Lubjiana); Benedetta Taglibue at Enric Miralles Architects (Barcelona); Archis magazine (Amsterdam); Architectural Design magazine (London); Future.com (Stockholm); Technical University (Monterrey); Bauhaus (Dessau); Departments of Architecture (University of North Carolina, Charlotte; University of Venice; University of Lubjana); Royal

GO AADRL .com

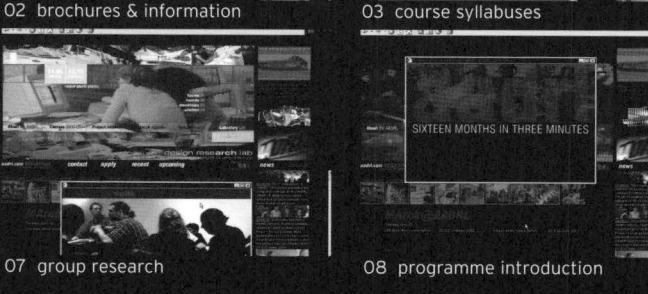

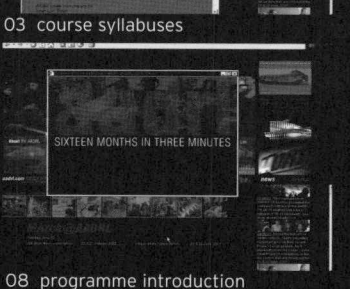

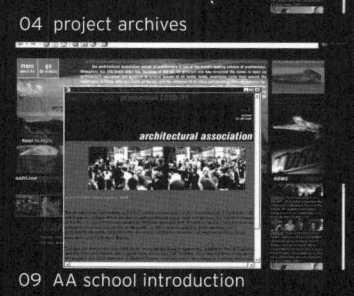

ab life   02 brochures & information   03 course syllabuses   04 project archives   05 presentations

study models   07 group research   08 programme introduction   09 AA school introduction   10 studio briefs

SIXTEEN MONTHS IN THREE MINUTES

architectural monography

seminar monography

architectural association

2.00 Phase II Interim

05.11.00 Material Trajectories Presentations

12.01.01 House Workshop Introduction

28.10.00 Material Trajectories Prototypes

09.03.01 Analogue Desktop

2.01 Studio Tutorials

13.10.00 Keyboard Density

25.02.01 Studio Tutorials

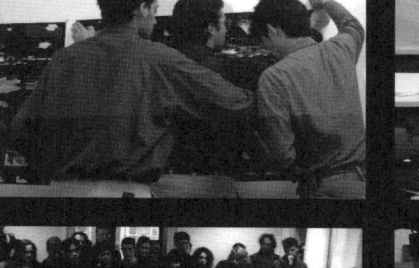

24.01.01 Phase II Thesis Design Presentations

15.01.01 Phase II CNC Model Production

01.12.00 1:1 Installation

02.02.01 Seminar Group Meeting

00 Material Operativity Workshop Presentation

22.03.01 Monography Seminar

10.10.00 Motion Capture Workshop

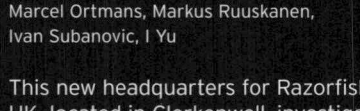

INTELLIGENT SPACE

Marcel Ortmans, Markus Ruuskanen,
Ivan Subanovic, I Yu

This new headquarters for Razorfis[h]
UK, located in Clerkenwell, investiga[tes]
the limits of using a company's dail[y]
organisational patterns as a form o[f]
complex, interactive, built environm[ent]
by embedding forms of artificial int[elli-]
gence into the space and artefacts [of]
the buildings interior. The project de[vel-]
oped a software tool for generating
descriptions of the organisational p[at-]
terns defining the company, which a[re]
used to guide the performance of p[lug-]
in, movable, intelligent furnishings.

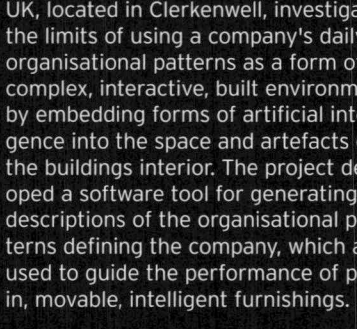

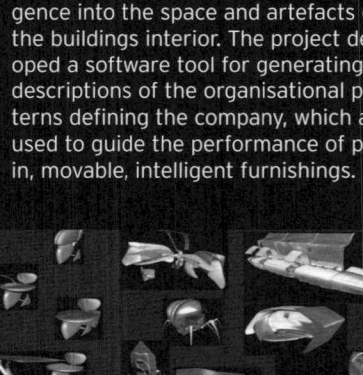

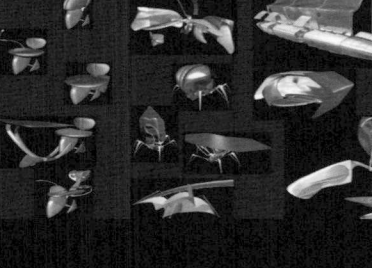

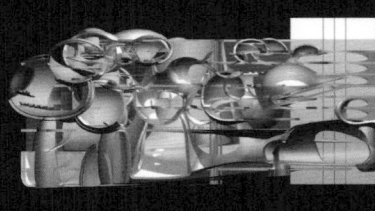

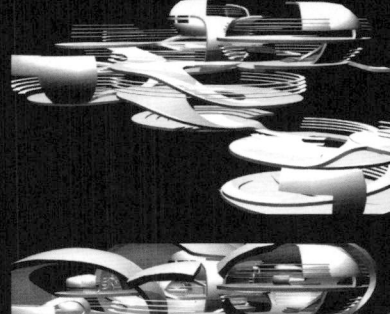

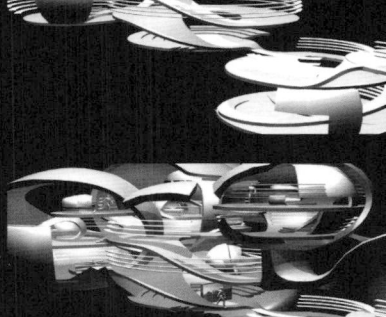

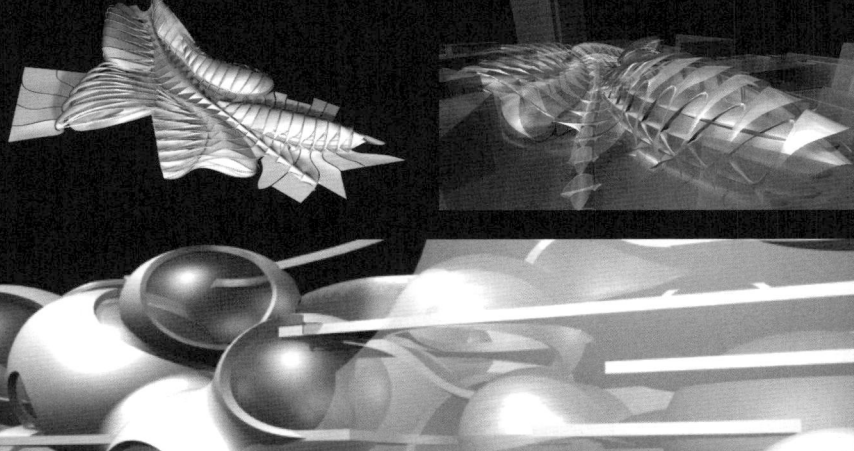

Fluid Networks
Changsu Ryu, Enrique Rojas Orta,
Hung-Kwon Ko, Chi-Son Lei

Built at the Holborn Viaduct in
London EC1, this project aligns building organisation, the construction
industry, and today's knowledge
industry by proposing a structure that
enables highly varied patterns of connectivity (built as well as organisational) relevant to the office needs of
Razorfish UK. The highly fluctuating
environment of today's corporate
organisation is addressed by a structure that enables continual re-config-
uration and non-linear organisation.

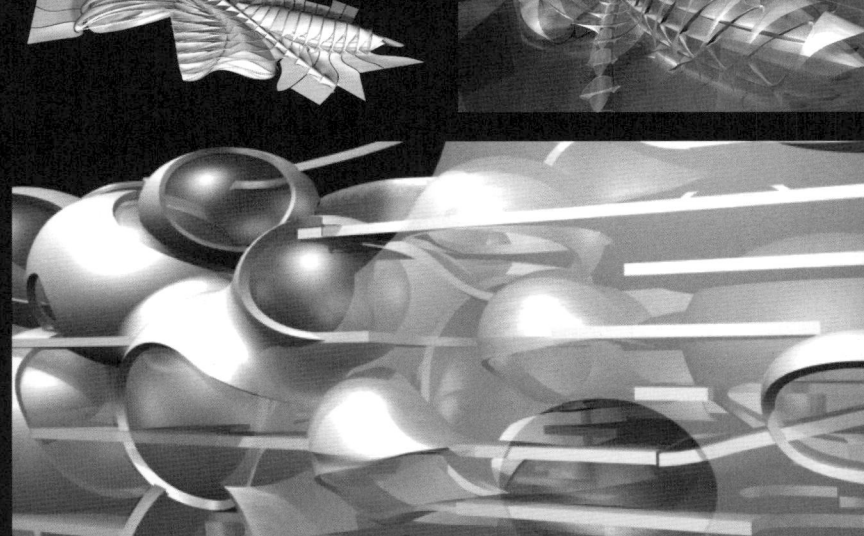

RAZOR_BIOS
Sonja Berthold, Jiin-Yi Hwang, Cedric Libert,
Anja Planiscek

This Clerkenwell headquarters for
Razorfish UK seeks to exchange
information and knowledge between
its urban and web users, by means
of an urban strategy that striates
the site into a field of discrete programmatic bands. The communication and social systems of the company are organised into an evolving
series of channels providing external as well as internal connections,
creating non-hierarchical, emergent,
topologies for the office.

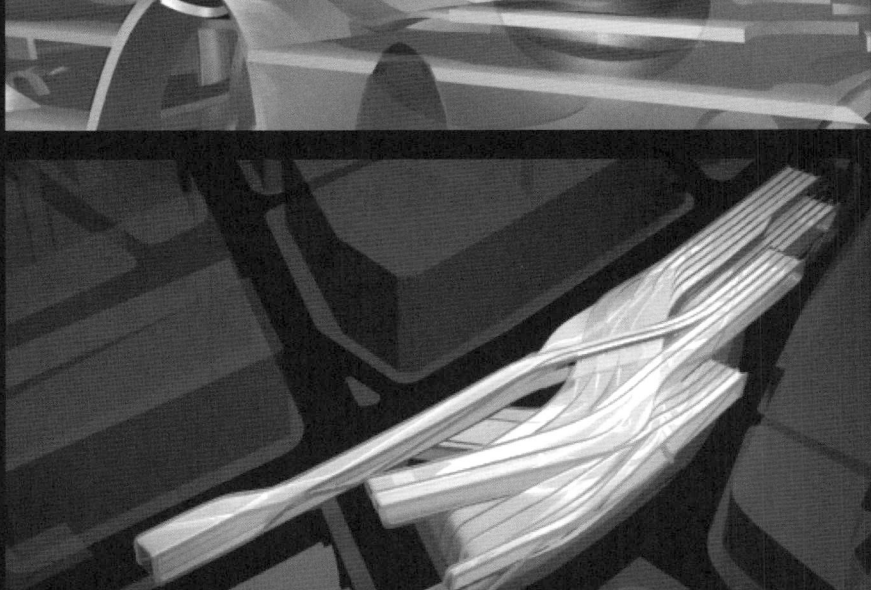

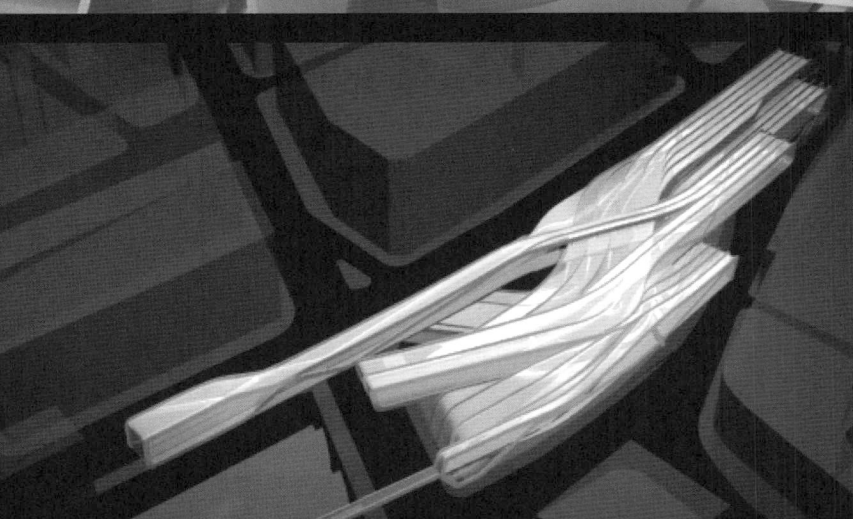

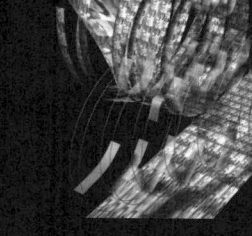

BRAND.SEGMENTS
Rasool al Khlaifat, Maisa al Mansoori

Utilising a system of smart surface segments, this installation targets the zone between the carpark and the entrance to Bluewater Shopping Mall, creating an interactive surface for display, information and promotion of Brand-name products. The system is based upon initial research into the speed of change characterising commercial retail space today, and is assembled as display devices and interactive surfaces that adjust quickly to the market change.

TRANS-IT
Beyit Ermiyagil, Iris Kaltenegger, Sofie Redele

Located atop and within existing buildings in London's West End, this project addresses the needs of a nomadic population of users requiring extreme flexibility, and change, in the spaces used during their daily routines. Following initial research into the global and local patterns of transit defining urban space today, Trans.it is assembled as flexible 3D frame spaces whose arrangement and configuration can be adjusted through pneumatic, inflatable mechanisms.

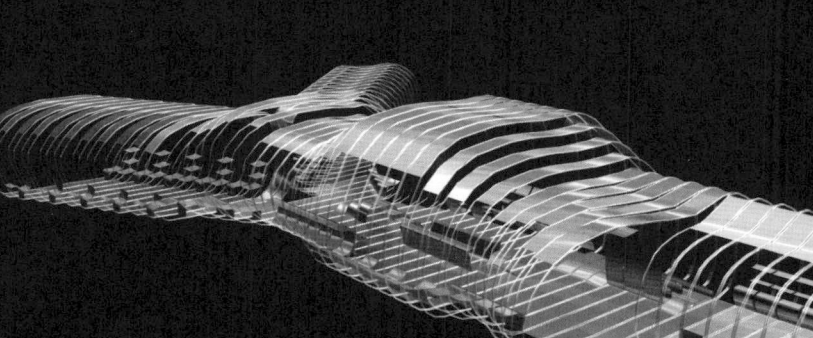

URBANETS
Praveen Bavadekar, Luis Pereira Miguel, Yosuke Nagumo, Vivek Shankar

Urbanets researches mobility, time and facilities in urban networks by projecting relevant environments able to respond to urban nomads. Ongoing socio-economic restructuring involves significant shifts in the organisational patterns that describe work and business relations, which this project captures as an installation of 'third spaces' at major existing infrastructural sites in London made into interconnected business facilities.

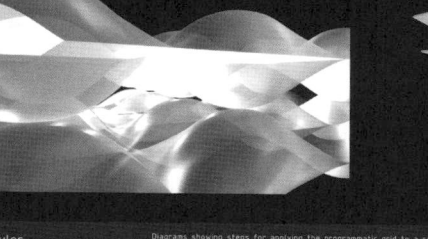
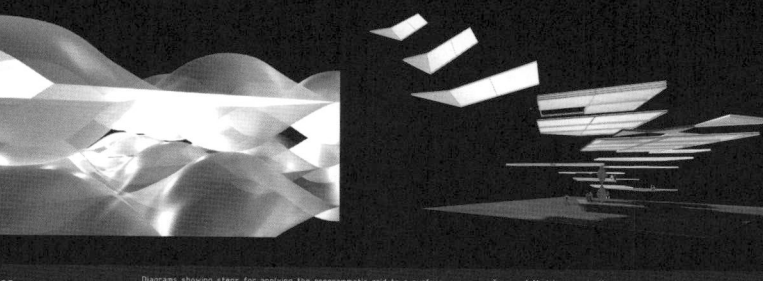
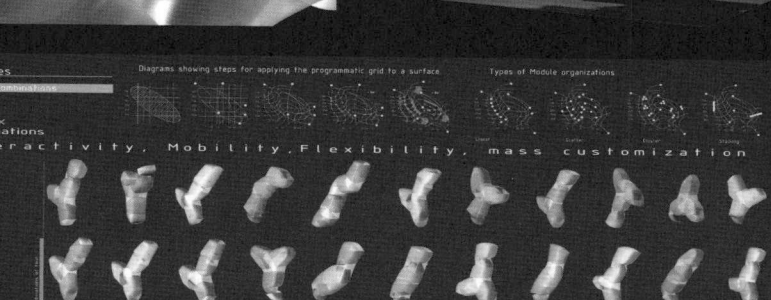

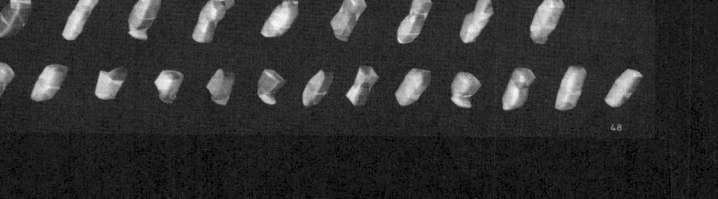

Trajectories, User Groups, Facilities, Surface

Interactivity, Mobility, Flexibility, mass customization

FISTULA

Masato Ashiya, Marcus Bergerheim, Jean Santelises, Theodore Spyropoulos

This project plays out its response to the saturation of media in the city by restricting itself to a strategic re-working of the interior facade line dividing the circulation and selling spaces of Bluewater, Europe's largest mall. Fistula reconfigures the principal selling surface of today's built space, the vertical planes upon which all forms of display and advertising operate. The existing forms of this condition are replaced with a fluid, interactive 'blankspace'.

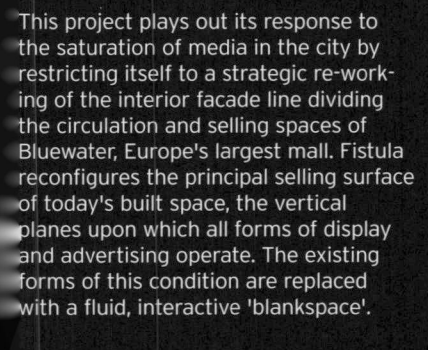

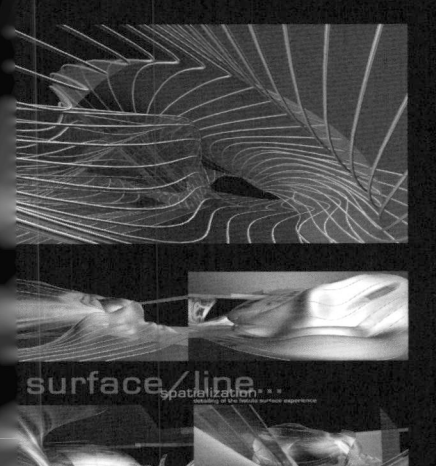

surface/line...
spatialization...

tranSTASIS

el Muchachito, el Rover, data Partida

Transit is becoming an overwhelmingly common human condition; one defined by movement, displacement and speed but as well by slowdown, sclerosis and stasis. The dichotomy of transit and stasis yields the notion of transtasis, which is the focus of this project: the uneven shifts and overlaps between networks visible at selected hubs in these systems. The forms of inhabitation at these locations evade normal definition and defy more familiar programmes.

facade extrusions 1   2   3   4

section lines 6   7   8   9

fistula line 11   13   14

fistula generation

fistula space 16   17   18   19

BRAND.NET

Jabali Chinai, Marina Mindlin Loeb, Chun-Shuo Hsiao

Based upon an analysis of lifestyle clusters organising the format of Out magazine, this project for a n installation surface in Bluewater M extends the ways in which space is used to brand lifestyles, products themes. The scripted, thematic, sh ping experiences of the city are tra formed by the installation of chan able surfaces that transform exist identities and products; a spatial r anism that test the capacity of int radicalisation of the shopping mal

SOUTHBANK ™

Joakim Dahlqvist, Sonja Strummerer,
Francesco Tiribelli

Located on the Southbank (one of
London's recently 're-branded' areas),
this multi-use facility investigates the
various ways in which all architectural
space today operates as a form of
media. The client for the project is
AOL Time-Warner, the world's largest
media conglomerate and the thesis for
the project investigates the ways in
which the viewing demands of a
media-saturated environment
re-configure the surfaces of that
environment.

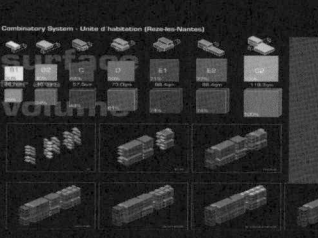

BOUNDARY NEGOTIATION

Aljosa Dekleva, Manuela Gatto, Tina Gregoric,
Robert Sedlak, Vasilis Stroumpakos

Research into existing design ecolo-
gies and contemporary social scenarios inform a parametric design
approach to 'domestic' space.
Territories are defined via interlocking
social envelopes rather than discrete
housing 'units'. Extreme spatial nego-
tiations between adjacent household
requirements, derived from ergonomic analysis, create performative
spaces that operate in section to
assemble larger, inter-connected,
neighbourhoods.

V.LIVING

Alan Furlong, Paul Loh, Lawrence Sassi,
Lorenzo Viola

V.Living investigates architectonic
interventions as a form of interface
between users and their urban environments. The thesis is tested in the
form of a programme for short-term
or temporary residents in a distributed
site in central London. This aims to
integrate accessibility to commercial
products and services into modulated
domestic facilities by a reformulation
of the transitional movements occur-
ring between the urban and the
domestic.

Specimen of social formation

[+ss]

Initial social structure are derived from
the introduced process of social
formation.
The illustrated formation to the left
demonstrates a possible arrangement
of social elements (units), forming
complex relations as they aggregate
into larger sets.
The result is a gradient of sub-
communities building up the overall
community of the complex.

But for the illustration of the closed
households the external links
intend to demonstrate the potential
or the aim of further social formations.

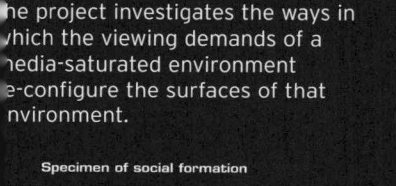

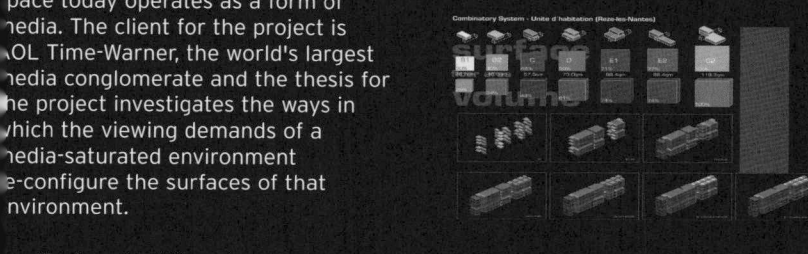

possible social formation

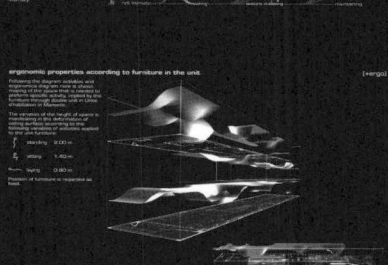

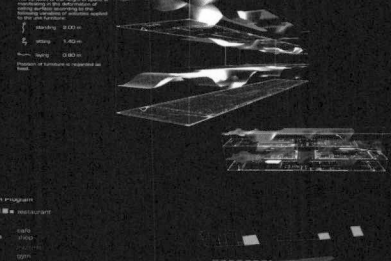

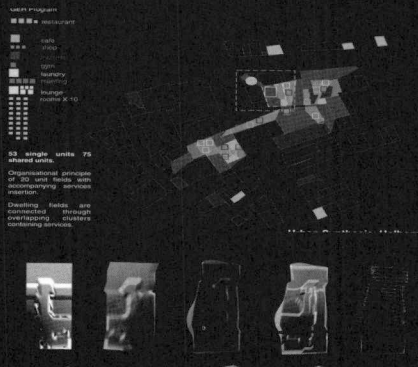

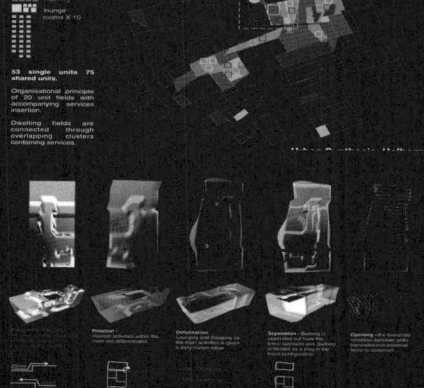

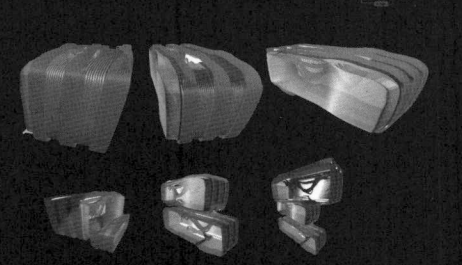

INTERIOR CONFIGURATION-3
ERGONOMIC DATUM
The Diagram reveals the ergonomic interface
of the body. Each datum denotes points on
which the body rested when performing the
activity.

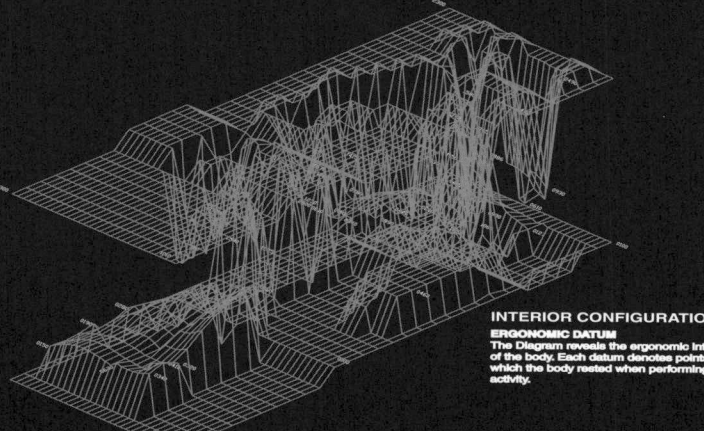

POSSIBLE COMBINATION ZONES

POSSIBLE COMBINATIONS

PRECINCT STRUCTURATION

POSSIBLE COMBINATION ZONES

	750 –	750 –	450 –	250 –	100 –

a Garden space
b Terrace space
c Direct entrance
d Indirect entrance through corridor
e Indoor staircase
  (Apartment on two different levels)

f - Private isolated cell unit
  (indirect visual access to context)
g - Semi-Public unit
  Direct and indirect visual access to context
h - Public unit
  (direct visual access to context)

SMART STRATA
Jeongsu Eun, Derek Renata Kawiti,
Jyong-Ki Min, Elke Stauber

This project employs cognitive and
social systems as design tools for
domestic prototypes. Globally, these
are configured into stratified organ
tions within existing urban fields.
These living spaces are distributed
along divergent trajectories of cos
and flexibility. Locally, this creates
gradient of spatial differentiation,
from mobile furnishings and partit
in fixed envelopes to fully dynamic
surfaces with scripted interactivity.

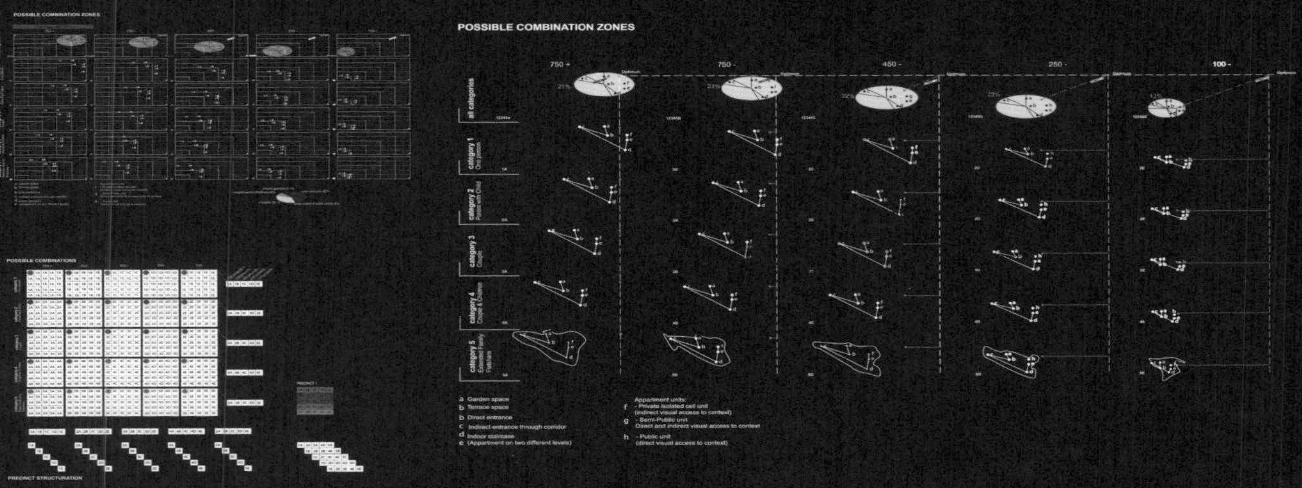

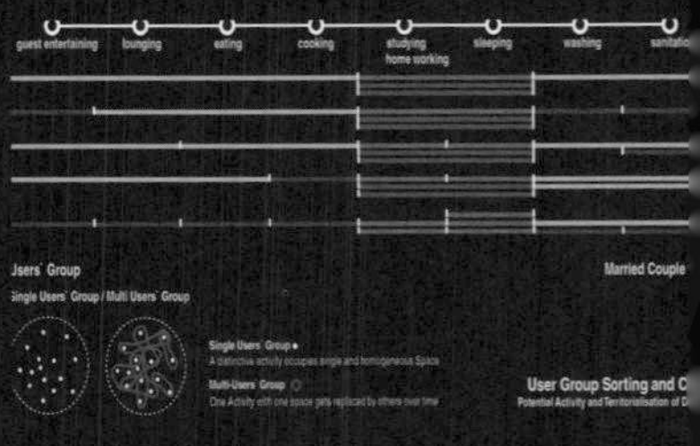

trajectory analysis

analysis/ proposal

possible trajectories
the **TATE**experience, *sponsored by* **orange**

	one *nine*	two *eight*	three *seven*	four *six*	five *five*	six *four*	seven *three*	eight *two*	nine *one*
check-in		V+nH / V+H	V+nH / V+H	platform					
check-in		H+nH / H+H	V+nH / V+H	V+nH / V+H	H+nH / H+H	platform			
check-in		V+nH / V+H	V+nH / V+H	H+nH / H+H	V+nH / V+H	V+nH / V+H	platform		
check-in		H+nH / H+H	V+nH / V+H	V+nH / V+H	V+nH / V+H	V+nH / V+H	V+nH / V+H	H+nH / H+H	platform
check-in		V+nH / V+H	V+nH / V+H	H+nH / H+H	V+nH / V+H	V+nH / V+H	H+nH / H+H	platform	
check-in		H+nH / H+H	V+nH / V+H	V+nH / V+H	H+nH / H+H	V+nH / V+H	V+nH / V+H	platform	
check-in		H+nH / H+H	V+nH / V+H	V+nH / V+H	platform				
check-in		V+nH / V+H	V+nH / V+H	H+nH / H+H	platform				

RECIPROCAL
RECIPROCAL
NON-RECIPROCAL

check-in / platform
& vice versa

all possible trajectories through ONE
vertical level transition ◀ 02'57"

all possible trajectories through TWO
vertical level transition ◀ 04'23"

TATE

23

orange

26

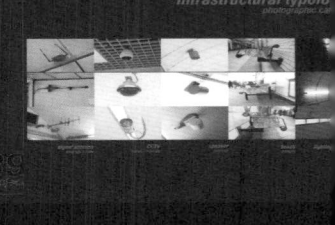

infrastructural typolo

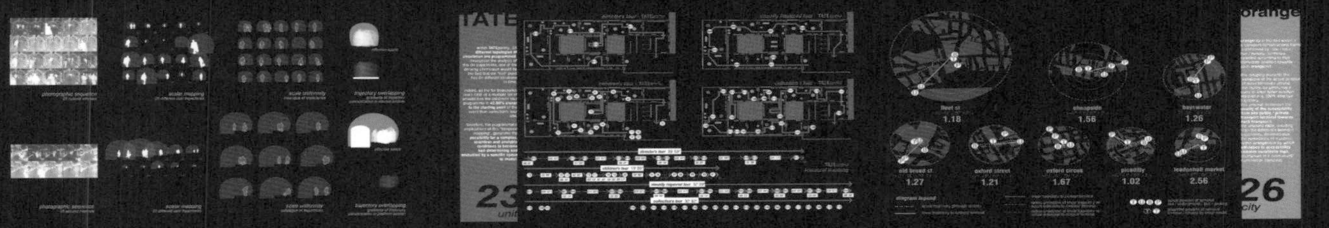

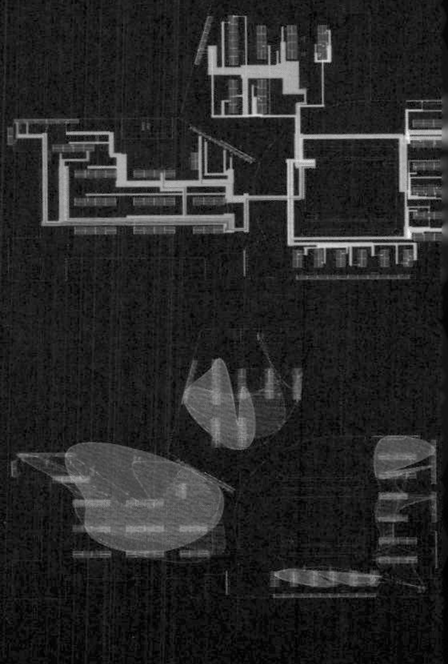

VIRGIN URBAN RESORT
C. Fernando Perez, Marco A. Velazquez,
Cesar Villarreal

The research investigates the organisational logic of music retail and
entertainment environments in
London, along with daily cyclical inter-
vals of resort complexes associated
with Virgin UK. The project deploys a
24-hour dynamic event structure of
music, travel and retail businesses as
a soft model of re-use, growth and
adaptability of the existing, disused
C&A buildings on the rooftops of
Oxford Street, which are accessed
through changeable urban lobbies.

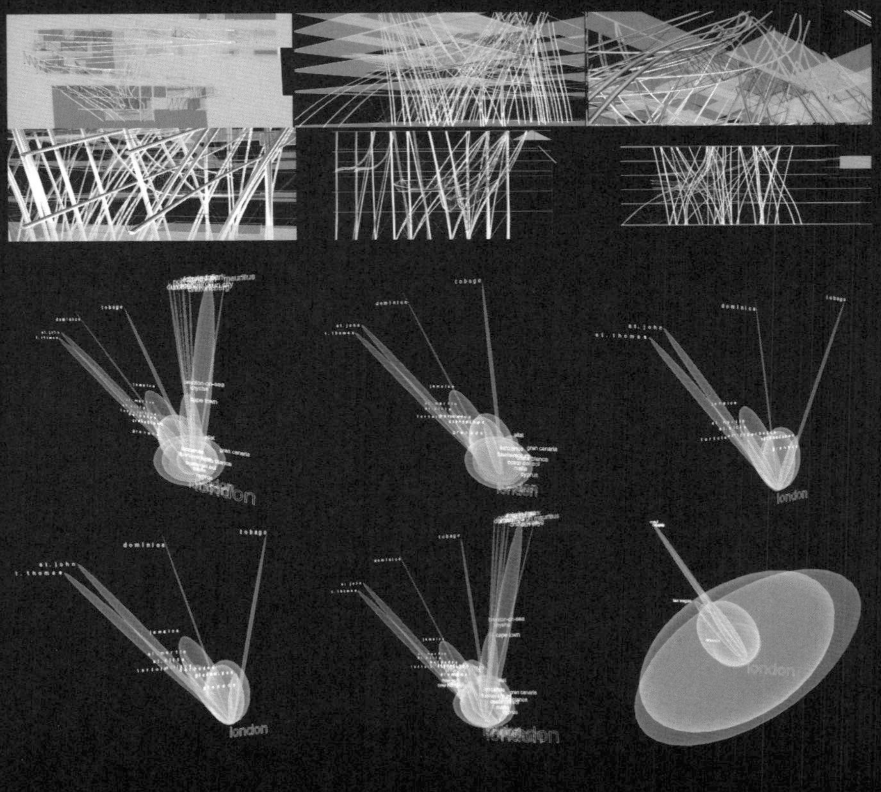

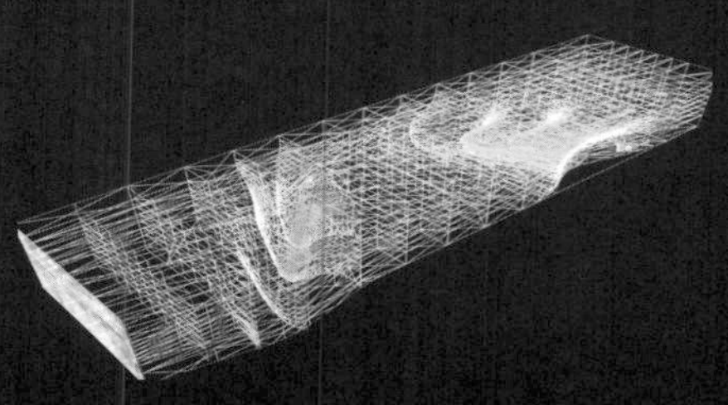

orienTATE
Marco Ortiz Perez, Jiann-Jyh Wu

TATE Modern's existing wireless m
ated tours are taken out of the bui
ing, unfolded and overlapped withi
specific mapped trajectories inside
underground station at Liverpool
Street. A differentiated spiral surfa
presents and displays the Tate, allo
ing commuters to interact through
visual and mobile phone forms of c
tact, through effects provoked by t
provisional form of architecture sit
ed in a highly controlled, self-con-
tained, urban environment.

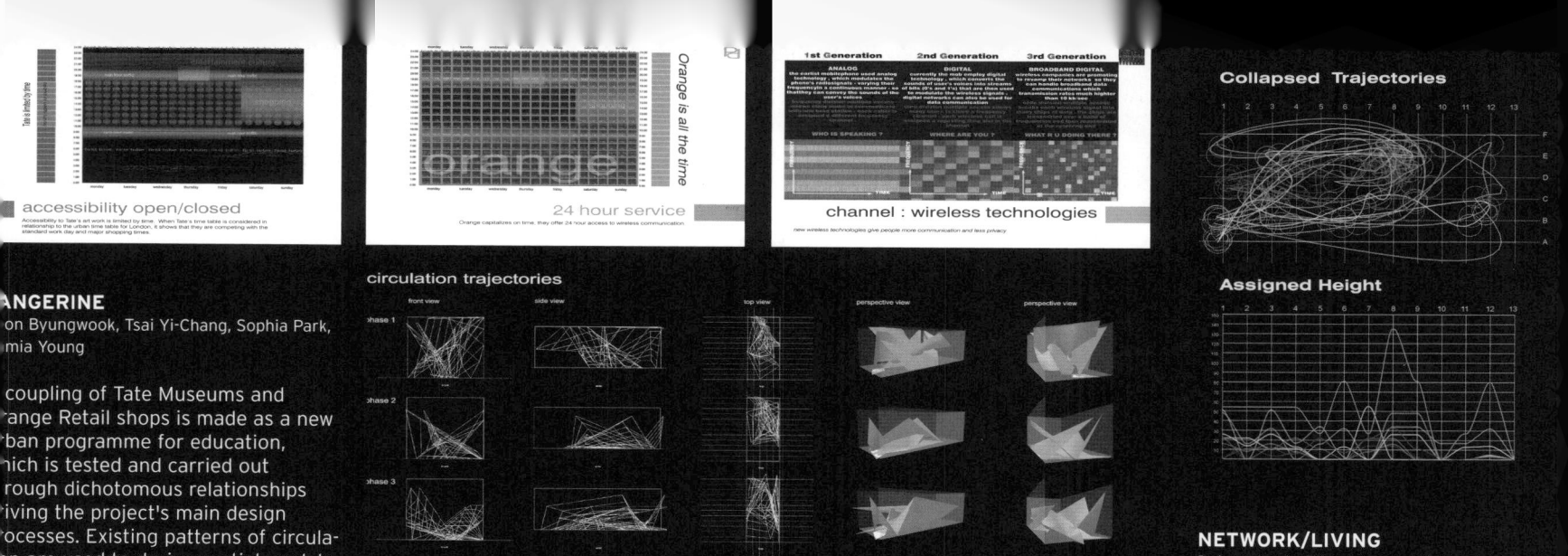

accessibility open/closed

Accessibility to Tate's art work is limited by time. When Tate's time table is considered in relationship to the urban time table for London, it shows that they are competing with the standard work day and major shopping times.

Orange is all the time

orange

24 hour service

Orange capitalizes on time, they offer 24 hour access to wireless communication

1st Generation	2nd Generation	3rd Generation
ANALOG	**DIGITAL**	**BROADBAND DIGITAL**

channel : wireless technologies

new wireless technologies give people more communication and less privacy

Collapsed Trajectories

TANGERINE

Jon Byungwook, Tsai Yi-Chang, Sophia Park, Mia Young

A coupling of Tate Museums and Orange Retail shops is made as a new urban programme for education, which is tested and carried out through dichotomous relationships driving the project's main design processes. Existing patterns of circulation are used to derive spatial models for a fluid, re-configurable, smart surface that works as an interactive form or image presentation able to respond to users' mobile network technologies.

circulation trajectories

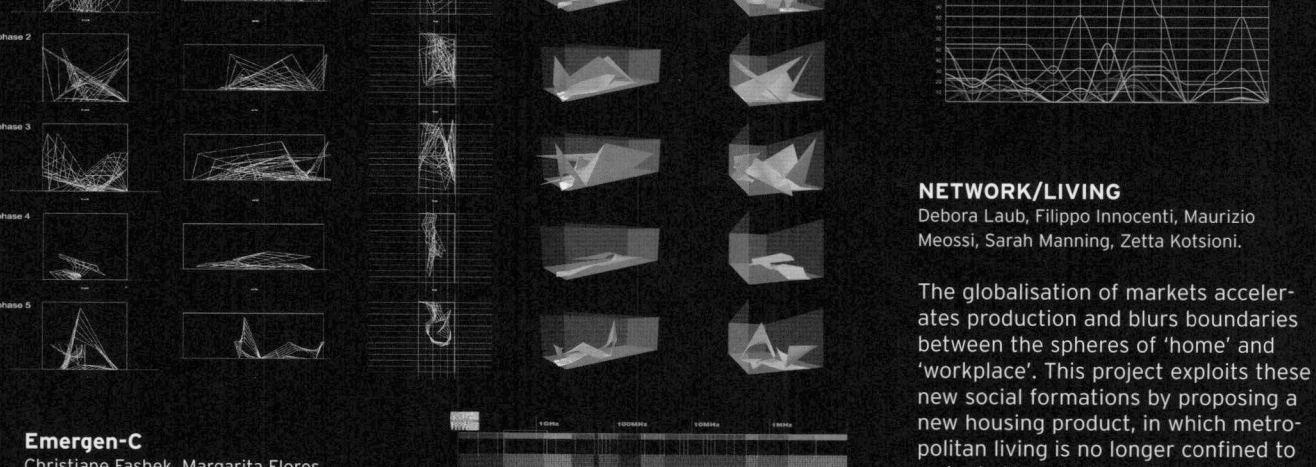

phase 1 / phase 2 / phase 3 / phase 4 / phase 5

front view — side view — top view — perspective view — perspective view

Assigned Height

NETWORK/LIVING

Debora Laub, Filippo Innocenti, Maurizio Meossi, Sarah Manning, Zetta Kotsioni.

The globalisation of markets accelerates production and blurs boundaries between the spheres of 'home' and 'workplace'. This project exploits these new social formations by proposing a new housing product, in which metropolitan living is no longer confined to a single locus but redefined as a network differentiated across four London sites. The live-work scenario thus encounters a richer field of interaction and new life-styles.

TATE ATTENTION SPAN | VISIBLE & AUDIBLE

VISI-TATE-TION

VISUAL ORIENTATION & EXHIBITS ENHANCE EXPERIENCE

ORANGE ATTENTION SPAN | VISIBLE & AUDIBLE

ORANGE EXCURSION

VISUAL & AUDIBLE BOMBARDMENT GRABS ATTENTION

Emergen-C

Christiane Fashek, Margarita Flores, Cesare Griffa, Yasha Grobman, Yanchuan Liu

The project integrates the mobile, clustered, technological nature of Orange telecommunications with the enclosed, cyclical environment of Tate Modern, through their schared cultural and commercial interests in display. The zone of overlap between these two territories in London highlights a field of intervention, entertainment entities in the urban fabric that amalgamate activities, branding and imagery present in the separate worlds.

channel : wavelength occupation

abstract e-scapes

the abstract e-escapes are 3d diagrams of the actual shapes that the final e-scapes will have. they are generated by the diagrams of action and the diagrams of flows. their utility is to inform and control the final shapes of the e-scapes according to the actions they accomplish.

24.5.01 — unit configurations

'villa' type: dwelling core / 'casbah' type: social core / 'loft' type: individual work core / 'office' type: collective work core

CORE UNITS

CORE CLUSTERS

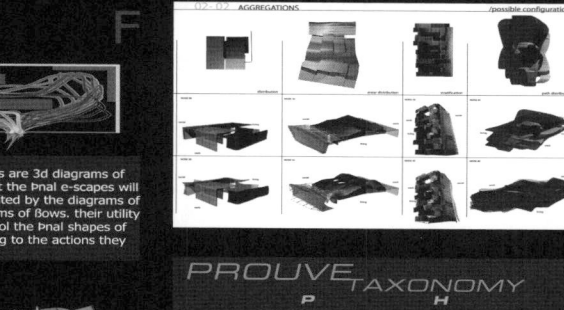

02-02 AGGREGATIONS /possible configurations

02-01 AGGREGATIONS /territorial catalogue

LWS

HOW LONG WILL YOU STAY AT THE TATE?

196 min

AVERAGE TIME IN THE TATE

HOW LONG WILL YOU STAY IN AN ORANGE SHOP?

51.5 min

AVERAGE TIME IN ORANGE SHOP

PROUVE TAXONOMY

P H Y L A

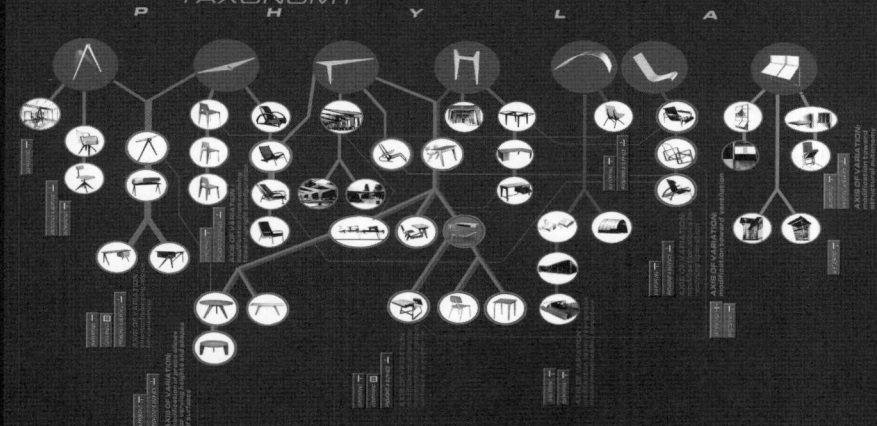

A D A P T I V E   T U N I N G

Phase I: Seon Byunghwook, Tsai Yi Chang, Aljosa Dekleva, Jeongsu Eun, Christiane Fashek, Margarita Flores, Alan Furlong, Manuela Gatto, Cesare Griffa, Tina Gregoric, Yasha Grobman, Filippo Innocenti, Renata Kawiti, Debora Laub, Paul Loh, Yanchuan Liu, Zetta Kotsioni, Sarah Manning, Maurizio Meossi, Jyong-Ki Min, C. Fernando Perez, Marco Ortiz Perez, Sophia Park, Lawrence Sassi, Robert Sedlak, Elke Sta... Vasilis Stroumpakos, Marco A. Velazquez, Cesar Villarreal, Lorenzo Viola, Jiann-Jyh Wu, Camia Young   **Phase II:** Masato Ashiya, Markus Bergerheim, Praveen Bavadekar, Sonja Berthold, Jabali Chinai, Jo...

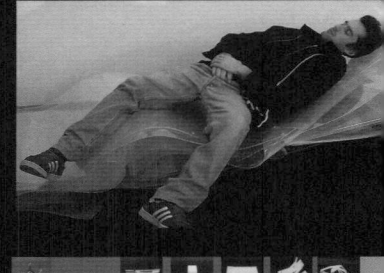

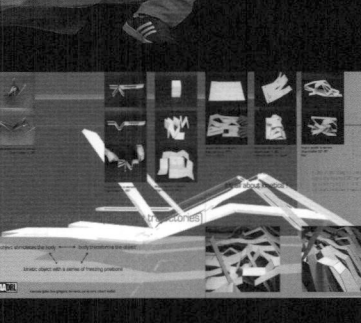

MATERIAL TRAJECTORIES
Modelling and Prototypes
Organised by Tom Verebes

During Autumn Term two series of workshops investigated analog and digital modelling techniques able to develop variable material organisations. During the first workshop, titled 'Mathematical Products', nine teams developed 1:1 prototypes at the scale of ergonomic products, while mapping the animated patterns of use/occupation each of the models projected. These simulations led to a re-grouping of the results into three 'superteams' during the second workshop, titled 'Material Operativity', during which initial results were evaluated and the most promising possibilities selected for further development. The workshop series concluded in a 1:1 installation that tested the spatial effects and material performance of the earlier prototypes.

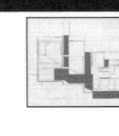
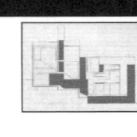
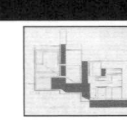
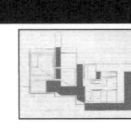
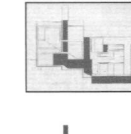

KNOTS: Stipps no. — crossing — loops

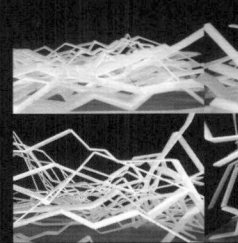

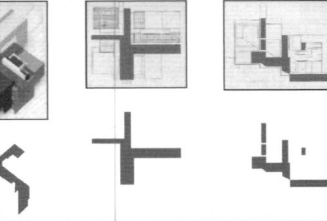

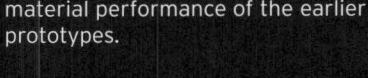

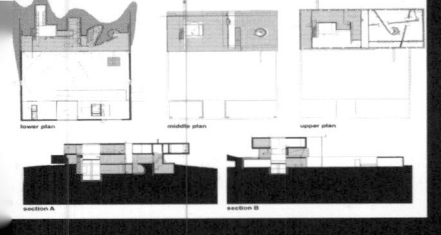

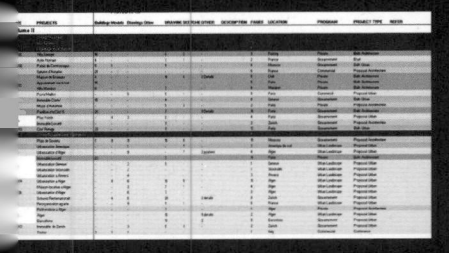

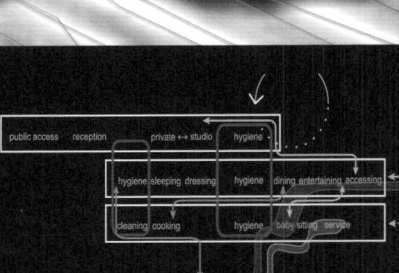

HOUSE
Analysis & Synthesis
Organised by Andrew Benjamin

During an autumn term AADRL seminar three teams each analys... one of three seminal houses: the Farnsworth House, by Mies van de... Rohe; House X, by Peter Eisenma... and the Bordeaux House, by OMA... Each of these three structures we... investigated alongside the theore... intentions of their architects and... within the evolving contemporary... courses of architecture. During a... week workshop in the spring term... results of these analyses were tes... by the teams in the form of a des... project that extended and synthe... the design techniques and theore... positions elaborated in the first te... research, concluding the research... project in a form that deliberately... bridged the gap between design a... theoretical work.

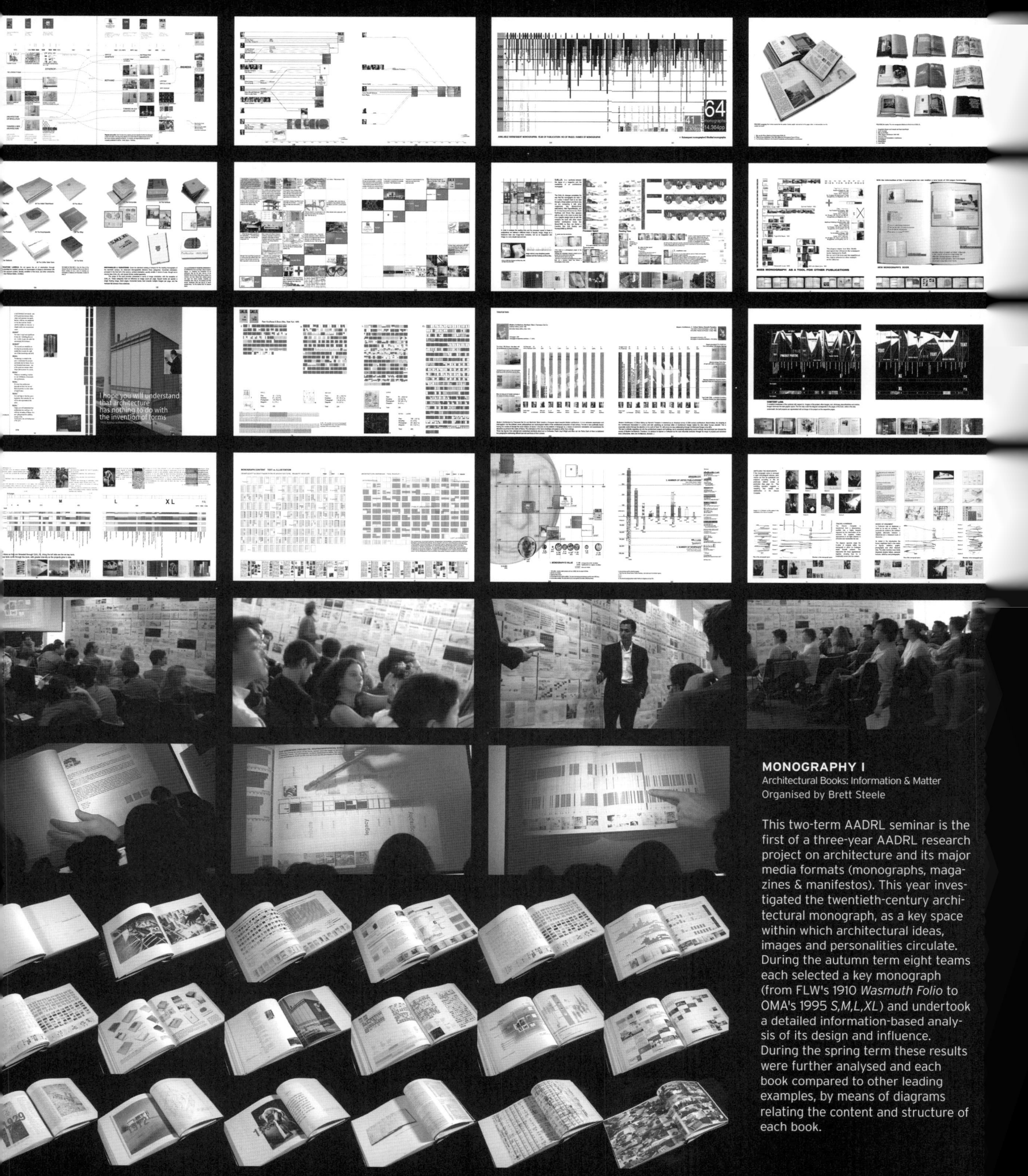

...vist, Fernando Doms, Jo, Al Ermiyagil, Chun Shuo Hsiao, Jinr Yi Hwang, Iris Kaltenegger, Rasool Al Khalifat, Hung Kwon Ko, Chi-Son Lei, Cedric Libert, Marina Minaini Loeb, ...a Al Mansoori, Luis Cabral Pereira Miguel, Yosuke Nagumo, Enrique Rojas Orta, Marcel Ortmans, Roberto Otero, Mara Partida, Anja Planiscek, Sofie Redele, Markus ...kanen, Changsu Ryu, Jean Santelises, Theodore Spyropoulos, Vivek Vijay Shankar, Sonja Stummerer, Ivan Subanovic, Francesco Tiribelli, I Yu

GO AADRL.com

MONOGRAPHY I

Architectural Books: Information & Matter
Organised by Brett Steele

This two-term AADRL seminar is the first of a three-year AADRL research project on architecture and its major media formats (monographs, magazines & manifestos). This year investigated the twentieth-century architectural monograph, as a key space within which architectural ideas, images and personalities circulate. During the autumn term eight teams each selected a key monograph (from FLW's 1910 *Wasmuth Folio* to OMA's 1995 *S,M,L,XL*) and undertook a detailed information-based analysis of its design and influence. During the spring term these results were further analysed and each book compared to other leading examples, by means of diagrams relating the content and structure of each book.

Landscape Urbanism

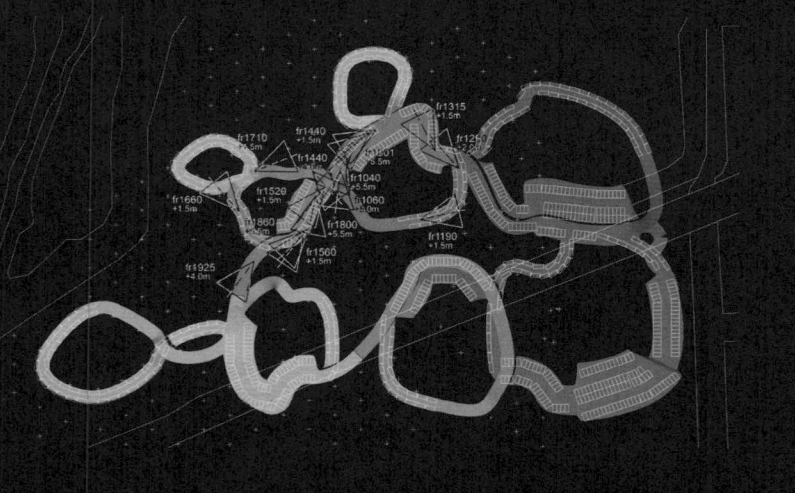

Julian Varas TOPOGRAPHY AS INFRASTRUCTURE: Accesibility and regimes of the public. As bundles of paths of infiltrate the site transversely, they define stripes of public and private land. Public areas slope at various angles allowing for diverse patterns of use and efficiency of circulation. By becoming permeable at several scales, Lower Lea Valley is irrigated with performative potential.

Fabian Hecker OVER-SATURATION: Productive Redundancies. A system of parking facilities infiltrates the existing fabric, deliberately causing redundancies that vary in time. Provisional and permanent sporting and leisure facilities populate them locally.

Armando Oliver Suinaga SITUATIONAL TOPOGRAPHY: Permeable housing strategies. The intervention redefines the landscape continuity through housing as a material for topographical permeability. The strategy links programmatically existing discontinuities between infrastructural systems, while reacting to situational conditions on the local scale.

Frven Lim LOOPfiPOOL: Co-evolutionary parking development. LOOPfiPOOL develops a system of looping as a technique to construct a temporal and spatial strategy. The application of casual algorithmic relations across scales is controlled by local concerns. The loops and pools co-exist within new typologies of urban outdoor space.

Jose Parral ARTLAND: Urban Curatorial Devices. A series of circulation loops at different speeds (from highway to pedestrian) used as tools to re-stratify existing urban conditions. Sensory, motion and economic parameters define circulation with the potential of a new exhibition system.

Julia Wessendorf FROM BROWNFIELD TO GREENWOOD: Excavation of the contaminated soil. Formation into mounds. Accommodation of programmes. Emergence of new pedestrian and bicycle circulatory systems. Conversion of the excavated areas into water bodies.

Nabeel Essa INFILTRATIONS: The un-private ground. Through a series of east and west infiltrations, the project injects catalytic development satellites. Along these trajectories material rhythms set an in-between urban armature of exteriority and interiority: the common ground between house and garden, work and leisure.

Rosalea Monacella COEXISTIVE TERRITORIES: The post consumer landscape. A farming and research center is constructed via the act of supply: the supply of products in the realm of farming, manufacturing, distribution and retail (the supermarket). Based on the internal organisation of Sainsbury's, the proposal constructs intense consumer corridors.

Simona Bencini WINDOWSCAPE: Between public and shopping domains. The exploration of collaboration between public and commercial domains proposes a field of windows: a free land of pedestrian circulation.

Santiago Bozzola CHANGING STRUCTURES: A system of changing structures produces a range of relationships between various scales and programmes, creating levels of material collaboration between urban and landscape operations. A deployment of commercial units is expanded into a set of artificial lakes and canals along the Lea Valley. The accumulation of structures accommodates leisure programs.

above: Frven Lim
Fabian Hecker
Armando Oliver Suinaga
Santiago Bozzola

Jose Parral
Armando Oliver Suinaga

Frven Lim
Santiago Bozzola

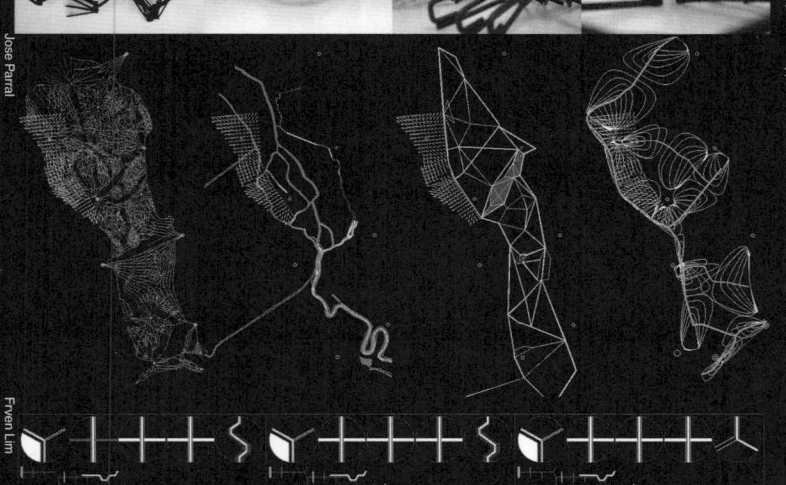

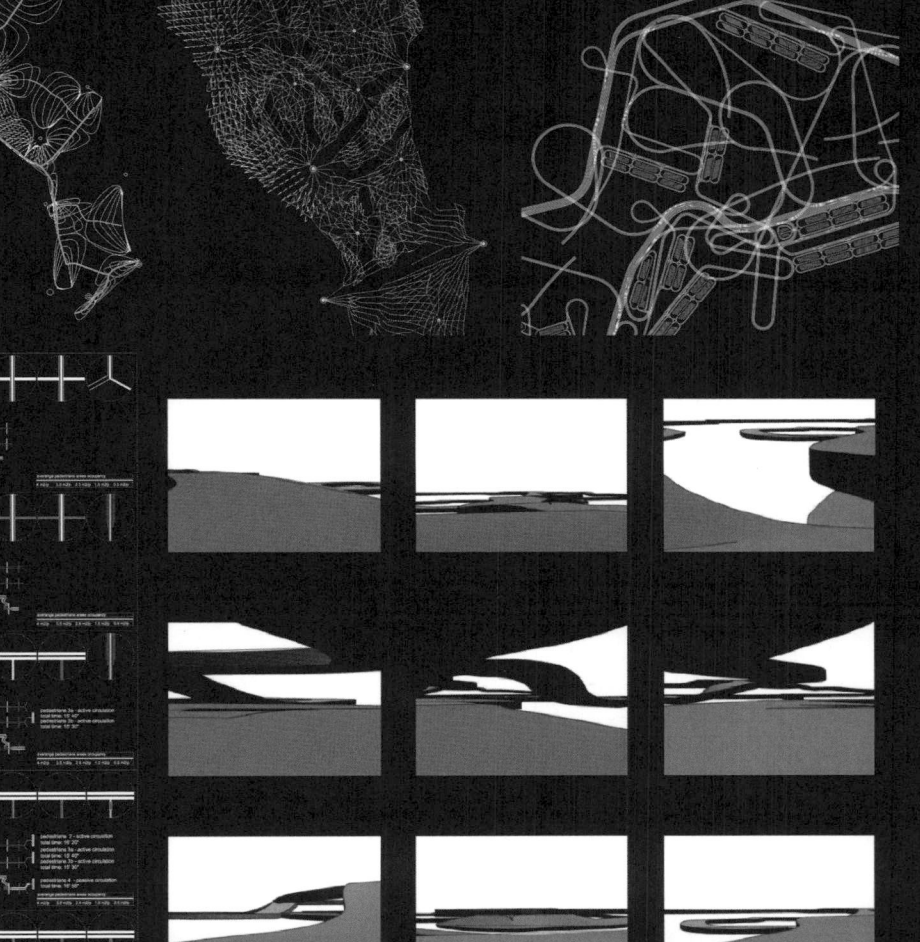

The AA Graduate School's Landscape Urbanism programme is a twelve-month studio-based course designed for students with prior academic and professional qualifications who are interested in integrating, within the domain of urbanism, the techniques and modes of operation historically described as Landscape Design. The programme's aim is to open up fields of exploration that move fluidly across disciplinary boundaries, in an attempt to develop inclusive paradigms and modes of practice which are able to transform broad territories, and to affect the organisation and coordination of complex systems.

The programme is structured around a full-time design studio in which students confront projects of increasing complexity and develop techniques and innovative design solutions. The studio is organised as a continuing design process, informed and supported by a series of seminars and workshops. Students are encouraged to attend other courses offered by the Graduate School and by General Studies.

The four terms of study are divided into two phases. The topics and objectives that serve as the programme's focus are introduced and elaborated in design studio projects, seminars and workshops during the first phase. Design Studio courses are pursued through all three

terms of this phase. Workshops and Seminars held during terms 1 and 2 expose students to a wide range of contemporary landscape theories and techniques, and introduce seminal projects. During the second phase – covering the summer period – students complete a comprehensive individual design thesis project which demonstrates the skills and knowledge acquired in the first three terms.

Staff
Ciro Najle, Mohsen Mostafavi, Sandra Morris, Chris Fannin

Lectures and workshop directors
Ian Carradice, Greg Haigh, Juan Herreros, Martina Juvara, Nate Kolbe, Sanda Lenzholzer, Benedict O'Looney, Lluis Ortega, Laurie Richards, Malcolm Smith, Clon Ulrick, Alex Wall

Guest Critics
Peter Beard, Florian Beigel, Jordi Bellmunt, David Buck, Phil Christou, Xavier Costa, Chris Hight, Hugo Hinsley, Sergio Forster, Sebastian Khourian, Sanda Lenzholzer, Theo Lorenz, Carles Muro, Chris Perry, Brett Steele, Victor Tenez, Tom Verebes, Spela Videcnik, Mike Weinstock

Students
Simona Bencini, Santiago Bozzola, Nabeel Essa, Fabian Hecker, Frven Lim, Rosalea Monacella, Armando Oliver Suinaga, Jose Parral, Touchapon Suntrajarn, Julian Varas, Julia Wessendorf

STUDIO
Sensitive Systems
Ciro Najle, Chris Fannin, Mohsen Mostafavi
The studio investigates new modes of practice by exploring urban organisations as the material evidence of divergent temporal processes. The aims of the studio are to construct a series of modalities of interference between information and formation, to constitute a sequentiality for apparently simultaneous processes of exchange of information, and to co-ordinate this sequentiality in a prototype able to network and to proliferate.

A first stage of the Studio involves the simulation of a series of urban dynamics through the reduction of variables and parameters, and through quantitative analysis. The focus of this stage is placed on the production of fields of information (a plane of performance where diverse logics of transformation coexist) and a notation system capable of systematizing and integrating those performances. A second stage involves the construction of an urban prototype

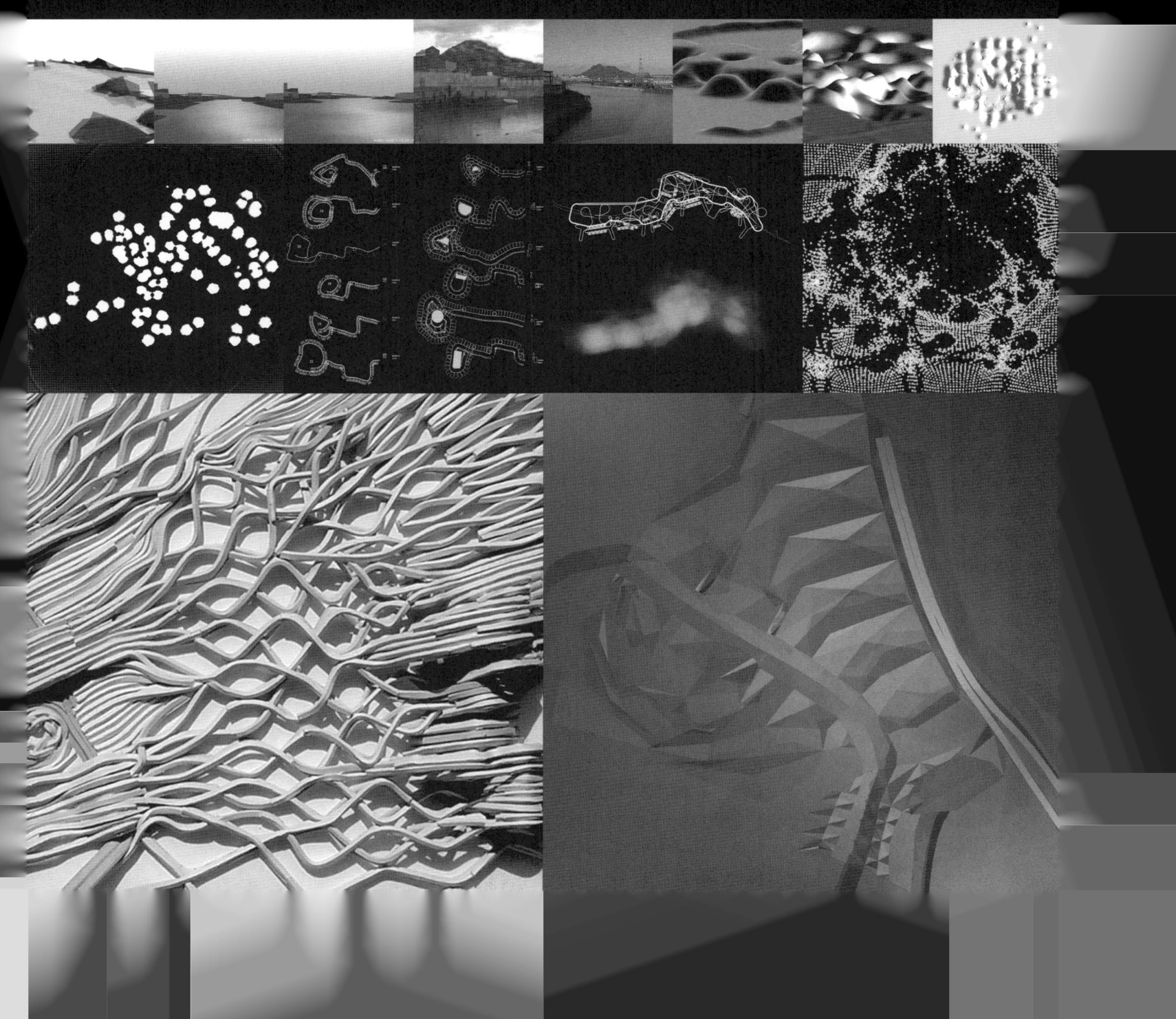

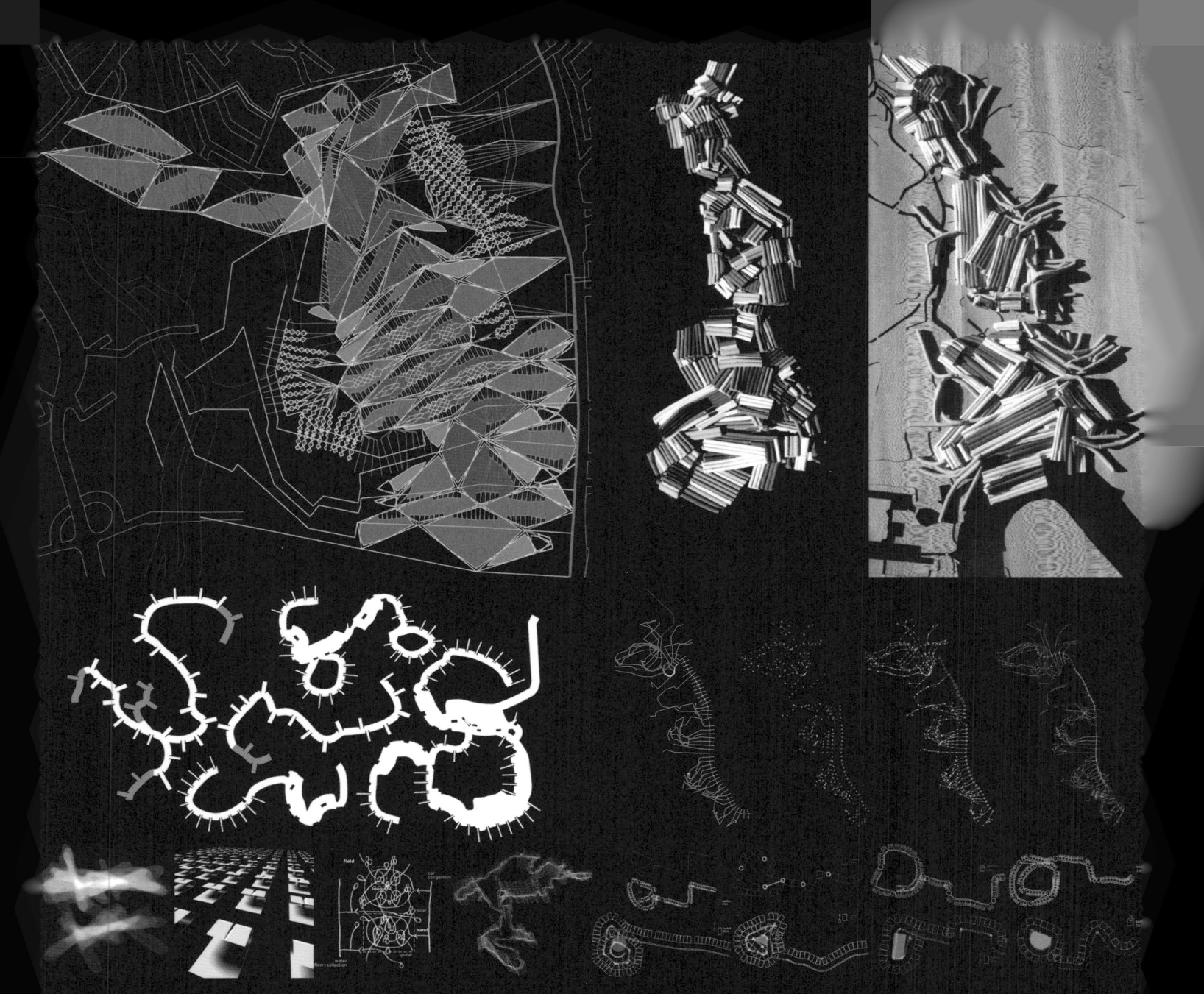

emerging out of a large strategy by differentiating its internal organization through the incorporation of information at many scales: raw materials with potentials (primitives) and the regulation of a series of internal modes of differentiation. During the third stage, a more specific system of transference of information across scales is developed as the project differentiates its material organisation. This involves the construction of a set of scales of time and space recognisable as instruments of a specified mode of development. The projects are developed materially, constructing specific modes of organisation, temporal strategies and new urban typologies. During the fourth stage, the work is aimed at constructing a complex argument about the implication of its modes of order in time and space. The temporalities in the development of the prototypical organisations are part of the proposals – if not as an explicit coordination of dynamics, then as a potential immanent in their organisation, or simply implicit in the procedure of their production. This is brought together into a Thesis which is presented, in public, during late September.

The Studio is currently developing a series of proposals for the Lea Valley corridor. Between Hackney Marsh and the Greenwich Peninsula,

between Stratford and the Dome, crossing the River Thames, along the Lea Valley, and between the A102m and the new Jubilee Line, a chain of abandoned or misfunctioning territories surrounds and inconsistently integrates a series of infrastructural corridors. This vast area is the size of Central Park, the length between Kensington and the City, is very sparsely populated, and is immediately adjacent to the most recent large urban developments in London: the Greenwich Peninsula, the two fast corridors to the Docklands and the City, the adjacent Canary Wharf development, and the rapidly growing Stratford transport node, that collects the Jubilee Line and the DLR, and is planned to become a 1km-long International Station on the way to King's Cross. Its local and global connectivity is being rapidly increased (Stansted and London City airports, the City, Canary Wharf, the DLR, the Jubilee Line, the A102m and Blackwall Tunnel, Eurostar, etc.). Through this area the river Lea collects small streams and its meanders fragment ground continuities and property. Its tidal rhythms expose the waste from old industries and frame a few local environments. This strip, although poor in its energetic exchanges and in its urban diversity, receives an influx from a wide variety of urban and natural forces, traditionally

overwhelmed by industrial production. New forces tend to negotiate for space amid the vast, newly freed territories. These forces carry the potential to develop the area quickly and tend to engender overwhelming occupations.

SEMINARS AND LECTURES
Seminars provide a means to examine theories and techniques of contemporary landscape architecture, including economic, sociological, planting and ecological issues. The evening lecture series, open to all members of the school community, exposes students to important examples of contemporary work in the field of landscape, architecture and urbanism. A river trip down the Thames to Greenwich, led by architect Benedict O'Looney, introduced students to the complex layering of London's history from Roman times to the present. A study trip to Europe introduced students to recent landscape projects.

Contemporary Landscape Projects
Sandra Morris TERM 1
Landscape has been used as a tool to create or regenerate public space in the city. Beginning with historical precedents, such as Cerdà's Ensanche in Barcelona and Haussmann's urban renewal of Paris, this course moves on to consider recent projects by leading European landscape architects, such as

Rosalea Monacella
José Parral
Julián Varas

Fiven Lim
Armando Oliver Suinaga
Simona Bencini

Santiago Bozzola
Nabeel Essa, Armando Oliver
Suinaga and Simona Bencini

Michel Desvigne and Christine Dalnoky, Claire and Michel Corajoud, Alexandre Chemetoff, and Jacqueline Osty in Paris; Peter and Anneliese Latz in Germany; Gustafson Porter in Amsterdam. This year a trip to Barcelona in Term 1 allowed students to assess the ongoing programme of urban regeneration, and to focus more closely on specific aspects of physical and material landscapes.

Models and Modalities
Ciro Najle and Mohsen Mostafavi TERMS 1 & 2
Nonlinear, unpredictable yet deliberate, impulsive but without a clear finality, machinic rather than mechanic - creative modalities of constituting material organisations are studied as components to be integrated into active fields of consistency. The seminars explore the potentials, relevance and functional operativity of models in the production of urban-environmental organisations. By analysing the systematicity, richness and constraints of artificial and deliberate processes of differentiation, by organising catalogues of raw materials, diagramming modalities and ranges of operational regimes, and by investigating discursive and material resonances, the seminars investigate consistencies in the mediation between processes and material components, and organisations.

Ecology and Environment
Ian Carradice TERMS 1 & 2
This lecture series by experts from the Ove Arup team introduces environmental concerns related to designing on or near the River Thames - an area severely contaminated by obsolete and abandoned industries. The aim is to provide of a technical background to urgent contemporary issues. It begins with a definition of 'sustainability' and its relation to the design process, and looks at the many parties involved in the planning and making of decisions. In the second term, students are introduced to the 'Thames Strategy' and are asked to focus on problems of soil remediation and the control of flooding and groundwater pollution.

WORKSHOPS
A series of workshops given by international architects, landscape architects and theoreticians serve to introduce alternative ideas and strategies, in order to ensure that a broad spectrum of approaches to landscape urbanism are engaged.

Systems and Systematicities
Ciro Najle, Lluis Ortega TERM 1
This introductory workshop aims at a study of techniques of organization able to operate across scales. Digital simulations are constructed through a set of rules in order to diagram the performance of one or many systems in a given project. This year, a series of primitives and protocols were abstracted from Central Park, in order to analyse their temporal regimes of differentiation.

Urban Devices
Juan Herreros TERM 2
Juan Herreros, of Abalos & Herreros, led a design workshop at the end of Term 2 and the beginning of Term 3. The series had a pragmatic approach, focusing on the relationship between material technologies and urban strategies, on questions of the image and identity of the city, and, particularly, on the eploitation of the opportunities offered by the sites. His intervention included lectures, meetings and a series of juries.

Direct Interventions
Chris Fannin TERM 2
This workshop aimed at making direct studies of the area through physical interventions that challenge previous understandings of place. By intervening, recording and representing the process, students were required to define a set of intentions of transformation of the site developed from a precise reading of its physical conditions.

Environment, Energy & Sustainable Design

The AA Graduate School's Environment and Energy programme explores the issues of sustainable environmental design at the level of the city and the individual building. The one-year MA programme combines training in environmental design research with field studies and design projects; it provides knowledge and skills for designing with little or no dependence on non-renewable energy, and introduces environmental criteria as creative parameters in the design process. The complex and contradictory issues of sustainability are explored through the critical study of theories and built examples, complemented by the use of analytic tools and environmental performance assessment techniques. Student work is project-based and carried out partly in teams. The MPhil and PhD programmes combine taught components with advanced research projects of two and three years' duration respectively.

MA PROGRAMME 00-01

This year's lecture courses ran in four interrelated thematic streams: theories, principles, tools, and practice. *Theories* looked at the politics of the environment and the criteria for environmentally sustainable architecture and urbanism. *Principles* covered the theory and practice of environmental design in an urban context, extending into issues beyond the scale of individual buildings. *Tools* dealt with the use of analytic tools in the course of design, introducing the application of computer modelling and simulation techniques for environmental design research and performance assessment. *Practice* focused on building case studies illustrating the processes of design, construction, post-occupation monitoring and environmental assessment; leading practitioners presented their recent work in the second term. The lecture courses provided the foundations for cross-course workshops, projects and field studies in London, Berlin and Santorini. Collaborations continued with research groups in other countries on natural cooling techniques for buildings in Europe, on tropical architecture and on roof design; lectures and workshops were organised on these topics. Student projects produced this year were presented at the Technical University of Berlin, the University of Dortmund, the Federal University of Rio de Janeiro, the National Technical University of Athens and at Kingston University. A Graduate Forum, held on a regular basis in the first two terms, brought together teaching staff and students from all of the post-graduate programmes to review work in progress and to engage in constructive criticism and debate. Started at the beginning of the third term, the MA dissertation projects are continued over the summer for submission in September.

Guest speakers 00-01

Grant Booker, Matthew Brundle, Paula Cadima, Peter Clegg, Jeffrey Cook, Tristan Couch, David Crowther, Bill Dunster, Giovanni Festa, Brian Ford, Jean-François Roger France, Nathan Gray, David Hirsch, Nigel Howard, David Lloyd Jones, Tim Lewers, Sonny Maesero, Andrew Marsh, Isaac Meir, Koen Steemers, Derek Taylor

Study trips and special events

Martina Albers, Servando Alvarez, Nicos Fintikakis, Theano Fotiou, Agnes Kouvela, Eduardo Maldonado, Mat Santamouris, Werner Sewing, Joachim Renner, Claus Steffan

For this year's London building studies. thanks to: Allies & Morrison Architects; Alsop & Störmer; Ove Arup & Partners; Battle McCarthy; Jon Broome, Architype; Canary Wharf and Finsbury Park station duty managers; Coin Street Community builders; Drake & Scull Rail Ltd consulting engineers; Bill Dunster Architects; Foster & Partners; Hampshire Architects Department; Michael Hopkins & Partners; Kelles family, Broadwall Housing Complex; Lifschutz Davidson; David Matzdorf; Kevin McCartney; Proctor Matthews Architects; Peckham Library staff; King Alfred School teachers and pupils; van Heyningen and Haward Architects; Whitby Bird & Partners consulting engineers; David Wild Architects.

MA Students

Alejandro Arizmendi, Sonal Bhide, Gayatri Dipotontro, Carla Garozzo, Styliani Giatili, Miliana Gruenberg, Maria Kalapanida, Tanya Keller, Poly Konsta, Ania Krenz, Anders Kristensen, Claudia Mercantini, Annette Schirber, Alfonso Senatore, Georgios Skourtis, Kem Fan To, Defne Ülgüray, Danny Wang

MPhil & PhD Students

Dulce Marques de Almeida, Gustavo Cantuaria, Luciano Dutra, Solange Goulart, Benito Jimenez Alcalá, Helena Massa, Carlos Miranda, Raul Moura, Guilherme Quintino

Staff

Simos Yannas, Susannah Hagan, Peter Sharratt

Workshop tutors and reviewers

Louisa Hutton, Barbara Muench, Heide Schuster, Thanos Stasinopoulos, Mark Hewitt, Nelly Marda

MA DISSERTATION PROJECTS

Alejandro Arizmendi *Sustainable geometries: a study of natural forces that maximise the environmental susceptibility of buildings*

Sonal Bhide *Passive cooling toward a sustainable India*

Gayatri Dipotontro *Building underground in hot climates*

Carla Garozzo *The architecture of historical hypogeal buildings and its application in contemporary practice*

Styliani Giatili *Adjustable facades in the Mediterranean*

Miliana Gruenberg *Text and design: comparison of four environmental architects*

Maria Kalapanida *Environmental aspects of ancient Greek buildings*

Tanya Keller *Toward a sustainable urban development: environmetal retrofitting of working units in London*

Poly Konsta *GEK Headquarters in Athens: an environmental approach*

Ania Krenz *The compact city: comfort, density and urban form*

Alfonso Senatore *Natural ventilation strategies in retrofitted office buildings*

Georgios Skourtis *Environmental retrofitting of mass housing with case study in Athens*

Kem Fan To *Transformations of our cities: new approaches in urbanism*

Defne Ülgüray *Environmental attributes of double facades*

Danny Wang *Sunny Side-up: building integrated photovoltaics on mixed-use urban housing in Los Angeles*

PHD PROJECTS

Dulce Marques de Almeida *Design guidelines for pedestrian areas*

Gustavo Cantuaria *Trees and microclimatic comfort (submitted 2001 awaiting viva)*

Luciano Dutra *Design process and environmental information*

Solange Goulart *Thermal inertia and natural ventilation*

Benito Jimenez Alcalá *Environmental aspects of Hispano-Islamic architecture*

PROJECTS AND WORKSHOPS

Building Studies *Term 1*

Using London as a laboratory the building studies provided a cross-course vehicle for applying the concepts and tools introduced in the taught programme, as well as exploring the city and its architecture. Recently built or renovated buildings were selected for study, focusing on their environmental attributes and performance. Occupants, architects and

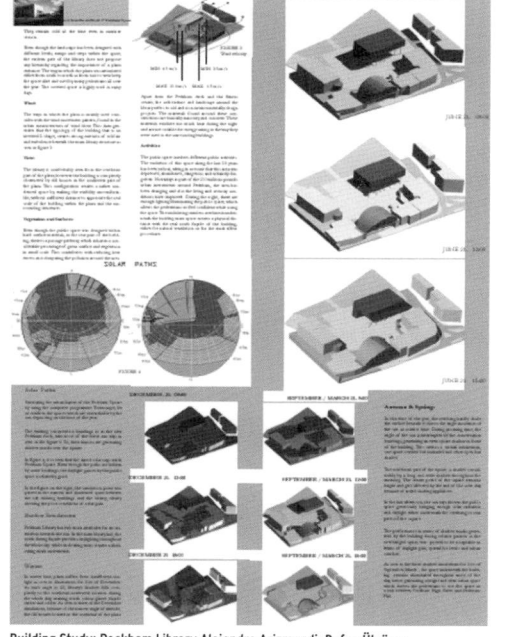

Building Study: Peckham Library Alejandro Arizmendi, Defne Ülgüray

Anders Kristensen *Sustainable building materials and environmental assessment methods*

Claudia Mercantini *Smart facades for mixed-use buildings in Northern Europe*

Annette Schirber *Toward intelligent temporary shelters*

Carlos Miranda *The house: energy efficiency and architectural expression*

Helena Massa *Urban aerodynamics*

Raul Vilaça e Moura *Thermal comfort and environmental quality in social housing*

Guilherme Quintino *Environmental aspects of traditional building techniques*

engineering consultants were interviewed; environmental conditions were measured over short periods; the physical fabric of the buildings was modelled and various aspects of their environmental performance were simulated on computer. Working in teams, participants then engaged in investigations of increasing specificity based on testable hypotheses arising from the fieldwork. One space in each building was chosen as the focus of more detailed observations that were followed by design proposals.

Berlin East *West Term 2*

Starting with a study trip to Berlin in January, this design workshop continued till the end of the second term with a two-stage project that combined exploration of urban design strategies with proposals for individual buildings. Working in teams of three or four, student groups divided between two sites, one in West Berlin adjacent to the Technical University, and the other a strip of land along the banks of the river Spree in the East. Following from the master plans developed in this first stage, the groups divided into smaller teams to proceed with design proposals for individual building programmes on their chosen sites. Twelve different schemes evolved, six for each site; some of these are illustrated on these pages.

Fire Earth Air Water Term 3

Term 3 started with a five-day workshop on the island of Santorini. Organised with the Department of Architecture of the National Technical University of Athens, the workshop focused on the island's distinctive landscape and architecture. Participants presented sketchbooks and impressions on the final day.

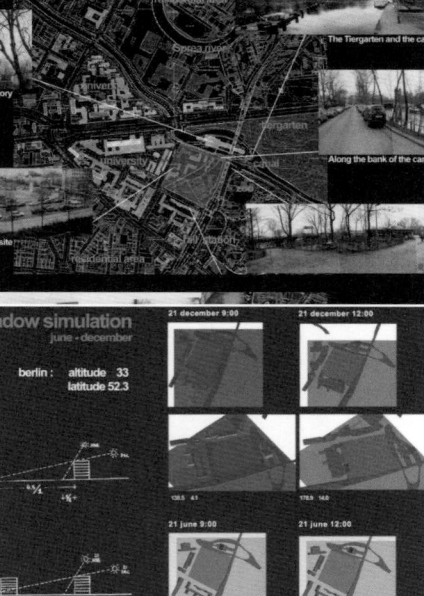
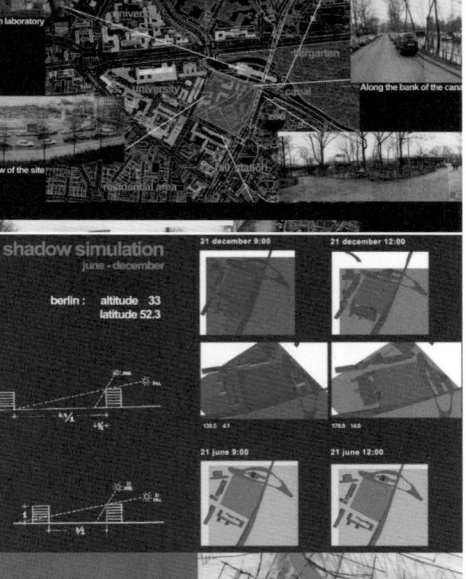
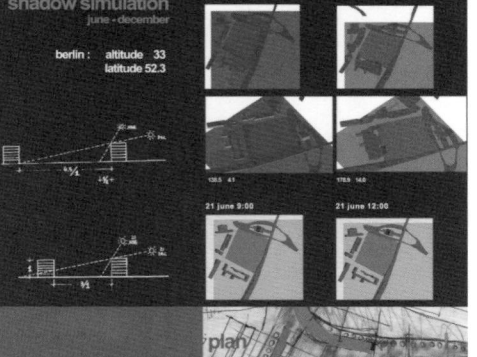
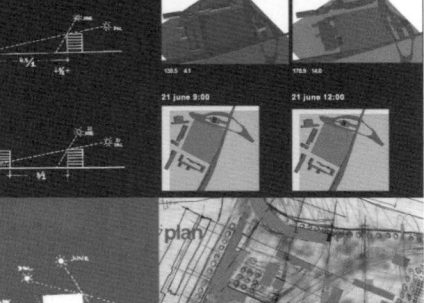
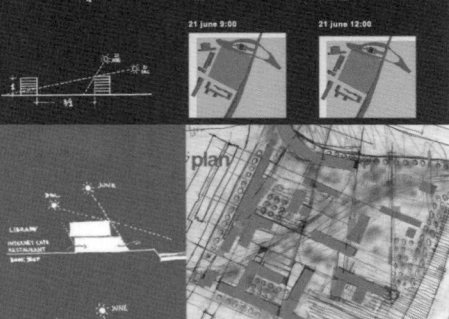
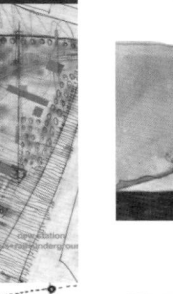
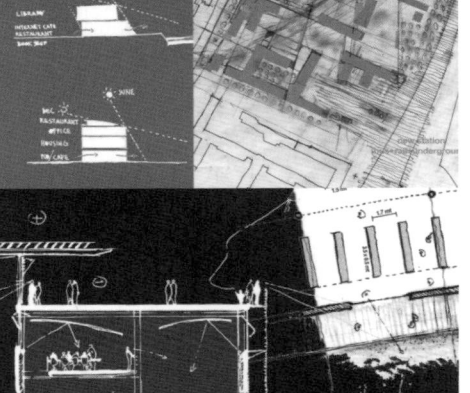

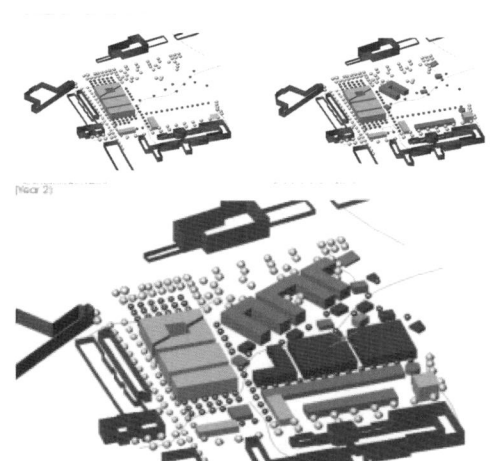
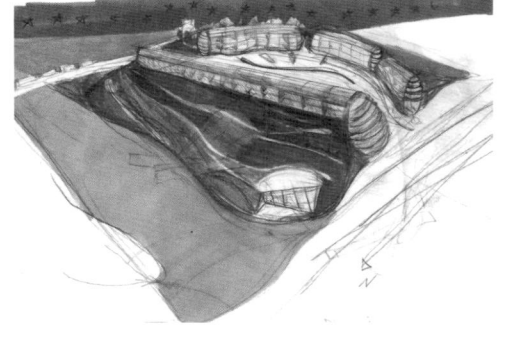

Above: Gayatri Dipotontro, Carla Garozzo
Left: Claudia Mercantini, Alfonso Senatore
Below: Tanya Keller, Annette Schirber

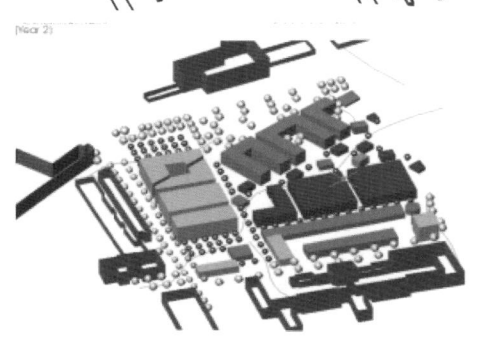

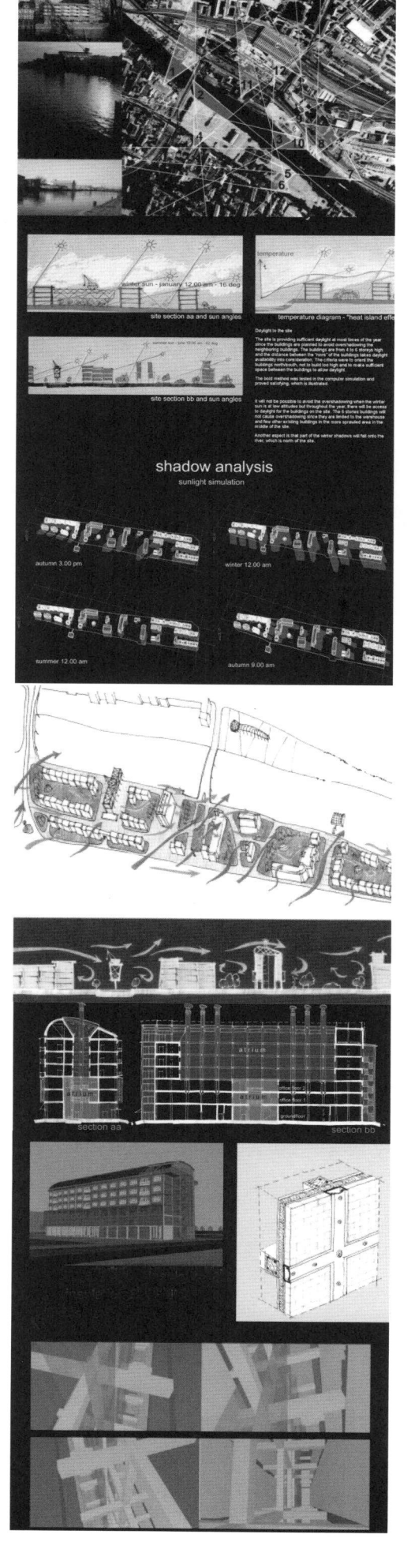

Left: Ania Krenz, Anders Kristensen
Right: Alejandro Arizmendi
Below: Sonal Bhide, Styllani Giatili, Poly Konsta, Defne Ügüray

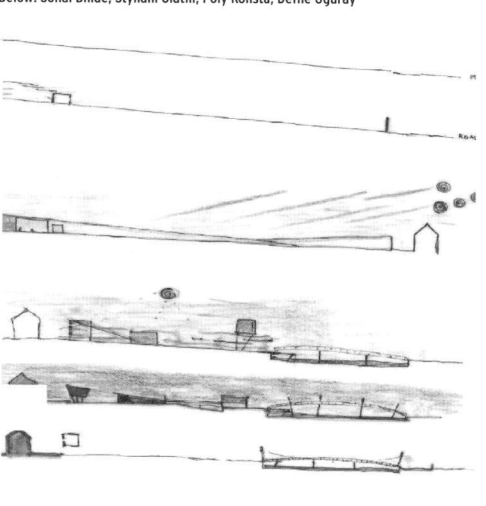
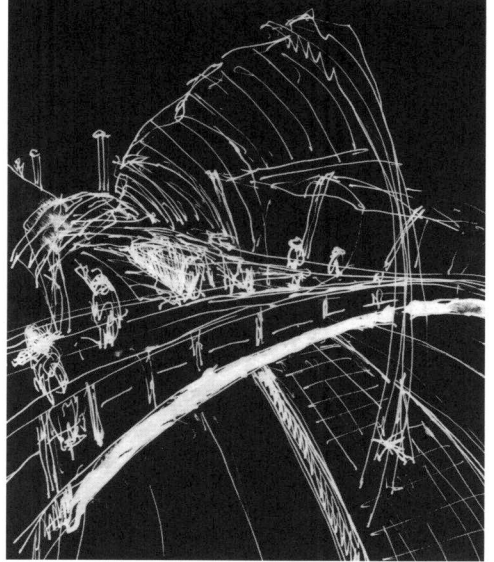
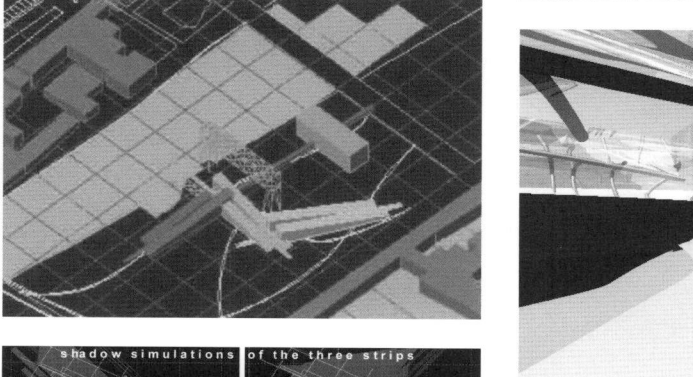

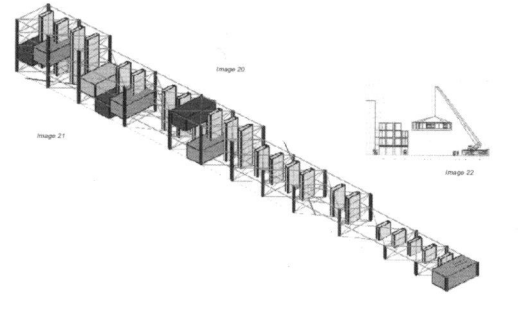

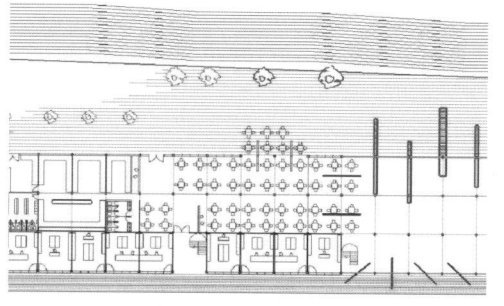

shadow analysis
sunlight simulation

shadow simulations of the three strips

Histories & Theories of Architecture

This year the Histories and Theories programme has begun a systematic process of academic and practical reconstruction. This is reflected in a major change in the staffing and the organisation of the course, partly dictated by the increasing numbers of Histories and Theories students as a whole, including a dramatic increase in the number of students doing PhDs. The MA in Histories and Theories and the PhD programme can be taken together. The MA programme, which is taken as an independent degree by many students, has the following focus – to equip students with a critical understanding of the history of modernism and of debates within it, such as art history and psychoanalysis, which will serve as a basis for their subsequent analysis of contemporary theory and practices. The PhD programme, now in a period of expansion, supervises a very wide range of issues, from the architectural concept of the hole, to the architectural protection against magic in the Thai vernacular house – but all our PhD students are required to bring their topics within the scope of what is needed to equip a graduate student with an adequate architectural and theoretical grasp of materials.

CORE COURSES

Architecture and Subjective Pleasure
Mark Cousins

This course is designed to provide students with a basis for dealing with arguments drawn from philosophy, aesthetics and social criticism that have been influential in defining the nature of architecture and architectural projects. It starts by looking at the nature of aesthetics and at how, within modern thought, the beautiful and the sublime were thought of as central categories. It then moves to a more historical and philosophical account of architecture in the writings of Hegel. These two strands are followed through the nineteenth century in the writings of Heinrich Wölfflin and August Schmarsow. The issues which are raised are brought into a contemporary dimension in the writings of Jacques Derrida and Michel Foucault.

Psyche and Space
Mark Cousins
Open Lecture Series
The lecture series directly engages with the question of the possible contribution of psychoanalysis to the study of space. In order to do this it seeks to establish why a theory of the subject's relation to space is a necessary component of architectural discourse and why other subjective theories of space might be seen to have failed. It establishes the concept of topography as a necessary element of conceptualising the psyche and investigates how it yields a theory of mental places. It continues by examining the issue of identification and its role in the mechanism of introjection and projection. It argues that spatial relations cannot be abstracted from the topics of sexuality, fantasy and desire.

Ideology in Architecture
Robert Maxwell

The aim of this course is to show how ideological currents invade architecture, so that, in spite of its supposedly factual basis in physical causality, it is not immune to the pressure of desire. To do this, architecture has to be defined as a discourse, and placed within cultural discourse: not the traditional discourse of architectural history, but the framing offered by modern cultural studies.

The course examines some of the historical factors contributing to the Post-Modern Condition: the semiological revolution stemming from the work of Ferdinand de Saussure and Claude Lévi-Strauss, its incorporation in French Structuralism, the consequent extension of relativism and loss of ontological certainty in language, the perception of knowledge as provisional and practical instead of absolute and ontological, modern rhetoric's expansion into the resulting void and its invasion of the visual fields of advertising, design and art, and finally the role of symbolism as the Universal Contaminator of meaning. Examples are drawn mainly from the fields of architecture and design.

Expression in Architecture
Robert Maxwell

The aim of this course is to show how the practice of architecture diverges from its theory. During the twentieth century architecture has claimed to proceed under the theory of functionalism, but this theory has been unable to account for the variety of practices that have unfolded. The course examines some of the notable instances where differences have occurred, and seeks to clarify both the pressure of desire within the architect's attempts to express ideas and the constraints of society in limiting or subverting the outcome. The course follows some key architectural movements through specific buildings, from the so-called classical Modernism of the Rietveld-Schroeder House and Le Corbusier's Villa Savoye to the work of Venturi, Graves and Eisenman. The works are investigated in relation to the desired theoretical context of their production.

Narratives of Modernism
Vittoria Di Palma

This course explores the construction and subsequent critique of early modernist architectural discourse. It looks both at the ways that ideas of the modern have been discussed over the course of the twentieth century, and at how these ideas were articulated within the context of the Modern Movement in architecture. Through the careful consideration of key architectural and theoretical texts, this course offers a forum for discussing the ways in which an identifiably modernist vocabulary and agenda were generated by the writings of architects and critics in the first half of the twentieth century, and considers how and why that discourse came to be challenged and dismantled.

Graduate School Forum
Combined Graduate Course
This course meets in the lecture hall five times each term. During each of the sessions one of the five Graduate Programmes presents selected examples of current work within the course (by a single student or small teams), addressing the specific terms by which members of the other courses would like to investigate it, including its content, techniques, or ways of working. The series provides a means for members of the Graduate School to come together regularly and sharpen their ongoing work by presenting, discussing and challenging it within a larger forum.

Space and Politics
Paul Hirst

This course examines how two kinds of ideals have interacted in the history of the West – political models of the self-governing community and conceptions of the ideal city. We consider the Greek ideal of the *polis*, which still shapes our vision of politics and the city,

together with Renaissance city republics, absolutist ideal cities, and the attempts to shape a stable relationship between democracy, industrialism and the city which began in the nineteenth century and continue today. Space and politics are closely interconnected, so are space and power. In the latter part of the course the relationship between buildings – churches, fortresses – and the governance of space and people is considered.

Diagrams and Drawing
Andrew Benjamin
The aim of this course is to provide part of the history for the current conception of the diagram within architectural theory and practice. This history will be one after the event. In other words, its project is to create the moments of continuity and discontinuity that allow the particularity of the diagram to emerge. The point of departure is the link between drawing and representation. The move to the diagram is not a move from the possibility of diagrams containing elements that are representational, but to the formulation of the diagram that cannot be understood in purely representational terms.

The first lectures are concerned with the conception of drawing that is evident in Pliny the Elder and Quintillian. What emerges from these early considerations is the way representation provides the interpretative frame within which drawing is to be interpreted. The point is not that drawing does not have a representational element, but that it is constrained to be interpreted as representational. The argument developed in the lectures is that the diagram emerges once the hold of representation is relinquished. In that release there is the need for the development of another theoretical understanding of the diagram and the drawing. The lectures are concerned to develop that understanding.

Critical Projects
Neil Leach
This course addresses a number of key concerns within contemporary architectural culture. The sessions are organised around broad themes: memory, place, identity, image, environment. The intention is to measure contemporary architectural discourse against broader cultural concerns. To this end, each session addresses specific building projects or

theoretical manifestos in the light of philosophical texts drawn primarily from *Rethinking Architecture*.

Advanced Research Degree Seminar
A weekly forum addressing the work of MPhil and PhD research students, organised as a series of candidates' presentations.

Architecture and Mass Culture
Xavier Costa
Modernism's disenchantment with historical structures initiated a process that approximated architecture to contemporary cultural processes of production and consumption. The lectures began by tracing this debate in the context of the Frankfurt School and the individuals and groups that followed it, before examining more recent efforts to articulate the relationship between architecture and mass culture. Lectures are supported by seminars based on the works of Eugène E. Viollet-le-Duc, Theodor Adorno, Walter Benjamin, Reyner Banham, the Independent Group, Guy Débord, Henri Lefèbvre, Jean Baudrillard, Robert Venturi, Michel de Certeau, Andreas Huyssen, Jacques Herzog, Rémy Zaug, Anthony Vidler, John Urry and Manuel Castells.

The City, Architecture and Gender
Hilde Heynen
This course explores the interrelation between architecture and the city from the perspective of gender. Lectures focus on: the gendering of the city; matrix of man; Sibyl Moholy-Nagy's critique of modern urbanism; places of the everyday; from the Smithsons to Koolhaas; gendered images and metaphors.

Spectacular Space
Helene Furján
The emergence of filmic, televisual, video, digital and laser image techniques, particularly combined with techniques of projection, have allowed electronic media in the latter part of the twentieth century to inflect and even create spatial practices, developing not only new kinds of viewing space but whole new experiences in public space.

Perspective and Architecture
Lorens Holm
The development of centrally organised perspective is usually treated as a historic

moment in the development of the pictorial and architectural representation. It is still thought of as a technique for representing 3D space within two dimensions. The course looks critically at this tradition of interpretation and shows that it is also a means by which space can be distorted and manipulated.

Size Matters
Mark Morris
This course examines the relationship between architecture and scale, considering objects from the colossal to the miniature to the non-dimensional. The sublime is found both in the telescopic and the microscopic as perceptions of measurement are challenged.

MA STUDENT THESES

Kuwait study
Haneen Al Rayes
From around 1950 the production of oil in Kuwait led this small, boat-building, pearl-diving and fishing country to redefine itself and its position within the modern world. Over a twelve-year period, through the recruitment of professional engineers, architects, technicians, white-collar workers and labourers, both from abroad and from within the region, the country exploded into a cosmopolitan, increasingly urban land. To make room for this modernisation, many of the historical districts were destroyed. These urban remains are evidence of the economic, political and social factors which shaped modern Kuwait.

Through exposure to the West and other parts of the world, new customs were adapted, which altered the way of living and thinking. Today Kuwait finds itself trying to regain the identity it lost through the urbanisation process of the 1950s, by returning to the built forms of the past as a real expression of a lost culture. Elements such as arches and domes are plastered onto buildings in order to make them more 'cultural' or 'Arabic'. There is no doubt that when these elements are skilfully used they can produce culturally authentic architectural creations. However, it is very easy to 'Islamise' Western architecture by relying on elements as superficial substitutes for a true interaction with the environment, its historical and cultural heritage, and its contemporary problems.

The 1:1 scale model
Maria Elena Ghersi

This thesis intends to explore the conditions inherent to the model as a representational object. Starting from a historical and conceptual definition, it will try to identify and question the conditions inherent in its nature.

The image of the 1:1 scale model will be used as a critical device for the deconstruction of the subject of study.

The 1:1 scale model, derived from the intersection point of two fundamental conditions of the model, shape and scale, would help to open up many pertinent issues such as place, representation, originality, temporality, etc., that are deeply engaged with the character of the model, yet very different.

Aware of the particular uses and roles, methods or approaches that the architectonic model could have, the notion of the model will be taken in general as a representational object that takes part in the design process. The core of the dissertation will be formalised by a series of independent yet connected paradigms, illustrated by case studies.

The dissertation intends to nourish the understanding of the development of the design process, as well as its growing fusion with other disciplines.

Transparency
Jiyeon Lew

I am investigating the notion of transparency in the context of twentieth-century architecture, especially how the idea is modified and practised in contemporary architecture. The concept of transparency varies in both its philosophical and architectural aspect, which makes it difficult to define. Today the idea of transparency is often associated with a transparent material such as glass; however, historically the notion of transparency was not an issue of visibility, it was rather the legibility or knowledge of space.

In analysing the Sendai Mediatheque by Toyo Ito, I aim to explore how the notion of transparency has been appropriated and

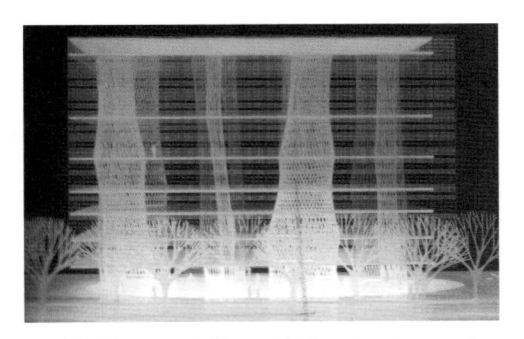

modified in association with the development of technology. These aspects are then analysed in relation to the notions of transparency put forward by Giedion, Rowe and Slutzky. Since architecture grows and changes with the development of culture and the perception of time, I wish to open another notion of transparency within the contemporary architectural context.

Athens project
Loraini Alimantiri

In an attempt to situate the particularity of Greece within issues concerning the development of the modern museum around the world, one is confronted with a different way of experiencing art – similar to an experience of the city and linked to the Greek definition of the art object, its location and relocation. Looking at the new Athens Metro as a contemporary interpretation of the site of the Greek experience of art – a place in between a museum and an archaeological void – an attempt is made to situate this example within the larger issue of the monument, its re-definition and the musealisation of urban space. How can one look at this space in relation to the modern city of Athens, its archaeological voids and museums? How can one situate this project within the larger debate of the spectacularised city-museum? Is it a mere beautification of the urban space? Is it a nostalgic aesthetisation of the city and its pasts? Is it a manipulated narrative of the city aimed at the establishment of new political relationships?

Writing a history of the unchanging: Sigfried Giedion and *The Eternal Present*
Albert Narath IV

This thesis concerns itself with an investigation of *The Eternal Present: The Beginnings of Architecture*, one of Sigfried Giedion's least-read but most wide-ranging works. Grounded in

a loose metaphysics, *The Eternal Present* arises as a lengthy fantasy reflecting Giedion's morose feelings towards the rise of an unchecked rationalism throughout modern civilisation. This situation stems from a disjunction between thinking and feeling, and between interior and exterior reality, resulting from the rise of mechanisation in the nineteenth century. Giedion's project becomes one of re-integration, arrived at through a re-connection to a notion of constancy that lies slumbering in the depths of the unconscious. Giedion believes that only through attention to the realm of emotion and spirituality can modern man return to the equipoise of being. The ideas set forth in this two volume project with regard to eighteenth- and nineteenth-century discourse into the origins of architecture will be considered together with the Giedion's late additions to *Space, Time, and Architecture*, in a rethinking of Giedion's position within the trajectory of writing about modern architecture. Ultimately, *The Eternal Present* becomes a summation of Giedion's position in the architectural middle ground, emerging as what one might call, a spiritual conservatism.

The courtyard life–a case study of Ju're Hutong in the Old City of Beijing
Sherlene Ting

Having survived revolution and turmoil over centuries, the Chinese capital Beijing is now facing a huge task. The increasing population and inadequate housing policy results in numerous high-rise apartments throughout the Old City, destroying the urban fabric that once symbolised the genius of Chinese city planning. Like many developing countries around the world, with unprecedented economic growth since the late 80s, Beijing is struggling between the process of modernisation and the protection of its traditional heritage. Starting with the analysis of 'critical regionalism' that has been widely discussed among architectural critics, I will investigate its conception and methodology.

The second part of the dissertation focuses on the Ju're Hutong project, which attempted to reinterpret life in the Old City. Opposing the overwhelming universalisation of the modern built environment, Wu Liangyong, its leading architect and urban planner, argues that 'organic renewal' is a way to achieve a balance between ancient values and modern concepts. By analysing and examining the project, I am questioning the method that was used in the project in the context of its social and cultural aspects, and proposing a more attentive continuation.

PhD STUDENT THESES

Fear as a cultural phenomenon in Thailand with special reference to the spatial relations of domestic architectures
Nuttinee Karnchanaporn
This research focuses on fear as a cultural phenomenon, and in particular the question of spatial fear in relation to Thai domestic architecture. In Thai popular culture, fear has animated the traditional belief in supernatural power, and this traditional belief is expressed spatially in the way the Thai house is configured and built. For Thai people, the house is recognised as the origin and the locus of the conscious recognition of ambiguity. Although spatial aspects of the traditional belief within the Thai household have changed, the belief in supernatural power is still strong. It is the purpose of this thesis to demonstrate how this belief relates to the spatial implication and articulation of Thai houses, and to discover the extent to which traditional spatial organisation, as a defence against fear, has been abandoned or reproduced within contemporary Thai architecture. The hypotheses of this research are: when the Thai traditional remedies and traditional spatial configuration have been eroded, the Thais lose their traditional defences against fear. Fear among the Thais may have increased in relation to architectural space: the remains and traces of these traditional aspects in contemporary Thai domestic architecture could culturally construct a 'fearful' environment among the modern Thais.

Total works of art
Nikolaos Koronis
This thesis concentrates on the twentieth-century practice of architecture, especially on the first period of modern architecture. It tries to investigate how Total Design has been manifested, what factors affected its manifestations and what influence it had on the overall practice of architecture. The

modernist approach of an architect being able, and sometimes obliged, to design everything (from a teaspoon to the city) is being questioned. Attention will be given to the selective puritive reduction of the early to show see how Total Design fitted within the 'less is more' motive. Several works of architecture from that period will be investigated, attempting to understand the way in which Total Design served the modernist Utopia; how instead of being a goal, it became a medium for achieving several other goals, and how it has been wrongly perceived by architects and designers of later generations.

The architecture of the hole – a modern view into holes
Marcelo Espinosa Martinez
A hole is there where something isn't. The theoretical analysis of the simplest architectural elements and events finds its basis in complex space. Often what seems most elemental turns into a problem of considerable complexity. A hole would seem to belong pre-eminently to a commonplace category of everyday life. The purpose of this research is to refer to this common-sense position and to reveal the hole as an issue which is inseparable from architecture, but resistant to the elemental terms of architectural analysis.

Holes are cognate entities, things that are together with, or in relation to something. Holes are superficial particulars or individuals, and in this sense dependent particulars – they cannot exist alone. A hole represents a formal and perceptual discontinuity on the architectural surface. Holes in the architectural field would introduce a qualitative discontinuity, a disturbance on the surface that can no longer be seen as an opening, but as something else, consuming space against space.

A (hi)story of distraction: Las Vegas and the imagination of anxiety
Armando Montilla, Jr
This thesis attempts to recreate an 'archaeological history' of Las Vegas, through its different and successive architectural layers of transformation and redefinition, in order to predict what the next stage of evolution of the themed-city will be. A new definition of the concept of entertainment and spectatorship is considered, in order to establish the position of architecture as a medium to convey distraction. Like the distraction process, the medium (architecture) loses its original function. It evolves into a series of cumulative historical strata, serving the redefined role and nature of the city (successively: trade post on the route to California, Mormon settlement, Hollywood-glamour enclave, war-time Government-subsidised Sun Belt location, casino-Mafia boostered-hyped town, mega-resort development site, Disneyfication and so on) During the process of redefinition of the urban strata, the conventional forces of history are manipulated and redefined, creating the sense of anti-history in the absence of a conventional historical development and the non-appropriation of landmark values. While other cities become commodified objects of tourism, Las Vegas recycles these commodities by destroying what exists, and creating the perfect *überhistorisch* city.

Staff
Mark Cousins, Director
Andrew Benjamin
Katharina Borsi
Vittoria Di Palma
Paul Hirst
Neil Leach
Robert Maxwell

Housing & Urbanism

www.aaschool.ac.uk/hu/website

The Housing and Urbanism programme pursues a strong practical and theoretical exploration of issues surrounding urban design and strategy, drawing together architecture, urbanism and critical human sciences. Students develop a deeper understanding of the connection between urban fabric and urban process, and a greater facility with the practical aspects of a critically informed urbanism.

The programme has a continuing interest in dynamic urban areas that must confront embedded contrasts and divisions in order to move forward. The problem of housing presents a recurring theme in the programme's investigations, both as a critical element within the pursuit of urbanism and as the occasion for reflection on issues of domesticity, identity, and public space. Study options include a one-year, post-graduate course awarding an MA degree, and a research programme leading to MPhil and PhD degrees.

Staff

Jorge Fiori
Lawrence Barth
Nicholas Bullock
Hugo Hinsley
Irénée Scalbert

Visiting Staff

Joan Busquets
Michael Hensel
Elizabeth Lebas
Chris Moller
Ed Robbins
Carlos Villanueva Brandt

MA COURSE

The MA course is structured around three primary types of student work: lectures and seminars, which explore current theoretical and historical approaches to housing and urbanism; workshops and the Design Seminar, which offer the opportunity to investigate urban areas and test design strategies; and thesis work, which allows students to develop an extended and focused study within the field. Theoretical reflection and the pursuit of practical design solutions are evenly balanced within the programme's work agenda, with design projects providing an arena to test ideas and illustrate current problems and strategies within urbanism. The aim is to develop continuity of research through an overlapping and exchange of different types of work.

The programme addresses itself to a terrain between politics and the building of cities, and we locate our work where there is the challenge of political dispute and the opportunity for significant change. This year, our main Design Seminar work in London was directed toward the issue of large-scale redevelopment, with attention focused on the analysis and critique of the Elephant & Castle area. This, together with a shorter project in Spitalfields, allowed us to explore the dynamics of urban change at different scales, and the potential of architectural and urban design in such situations. A different focus, on methodologies of intervention in areas of irregularity, was investigated through our two-week design workshop in Rio de Janeiro, working with the 'Favela-Bairro' programme. The main activities of the course were supplemented by a series of public events and by a study trip to the Netherlands.

MA COURSES
Design Seminar on Housing and the City
Terms 1 & 2

The Design Seminar provided a framework for linking the wide range of issues covered in the programme to questions of design intervention, and for exploring the interrelationship between theories and practices. There were two short design workshops run in collaboration with Diploma Units on specific London sites in order to investigate ideas about housing and urban conditions. The main design project, running over two terms, took a site of significant urban change with an innovative client, to explore strategies of intervention and design proposals for it. The main themes were the current discussions about urban regeneration, about density and mixed uses, about 'compact' cities, and about domestic and working space.

The course included two seminar series intended to promote an awareness of the gap between urban theory and design in which the Design Seminar operates. One took as its theme a contemporary enthusiasm in European urbanism for the formless and the transitory. The other, inter-linked, seminar series took a similar trend in housing as its starting point, pursuing the investigation through the theme of domesticity.

Cities in a Transnational World
Term 1

This course explored the social and economic context of housing and urbanism. It offered a comparative analysis of the changing nature of cities and housing in the context of globalisation, economic adjustment and political restructuring, placing strong emphasis on issues of policy and planning, and on current reforms in systems of urban governance.

The Reason of Urbanism
Term 1

This lecture and discussion series provided the foundations for an engagement with the urban as a problem-field in Western governmental reason. The course traced the twentieth-century development of urbanism so as to highlight the complex political issues inherent in its pursuit. It aimed at investigating the relationship of key political concepts to the generation of new urban spatialities.

Shaping the Twentieth-Century City
Term 1

This course explored the various national and local strategies evolved by the State to meet the challenge of urban expansion during the twentieth century. It looked at key events, projects or texts illustrating contemporary responses to the opportunities and problems created by growth, focusing on post-1945 housing and planning in a number of European and US cities.

Critical Urbanism
Term 2

This course explored urbanism's role as an instrument of diagnosis and critique. Each session included an introductory lecture followed by a seminar addressing an example of twentieth-century urbanism, with an emphasis on developing each student's facility with the critical analysis of urban projects.

Housing and the Irregular City
Term 2

This course used the extreme circumstances of irregularity and fragmentation of the cities of the developing world to reflect on the role of housing as a strategic vehicle to explore the connections between physical intervention, social processes, architectural design and the redesigning of new urban institutions.

Themes of Twentieth-Century Housing
Term 2

This course developed a debate about the forces that have shaped urban and housing spaces in European and US cities. It offered a vantage-point from which to consider critical issues such as density, regeneration, mix of uses and new working and living patterns, all of which are a key part of the debate in the Design Seminar.

Graduate School Forum
Terms 1 & 2

This series provided a dedicated forum for members of the Graduate School to meet regularly. During each of the sessions one of the five Graduate Programmes presented selected examples of current work for debate and investigation by the other courses.

Other Events

In addition to the above courses students are encouraged to attend complementary courses offered by other Graduate School programmes and General Studies. The programme also invites a number of academics and practitioners from around the world to contribute to its activities during the year. Recent visitors included Jordi Borja, Joan Busquets, Ed Robbins, Richard Rogers and Ed Soja.

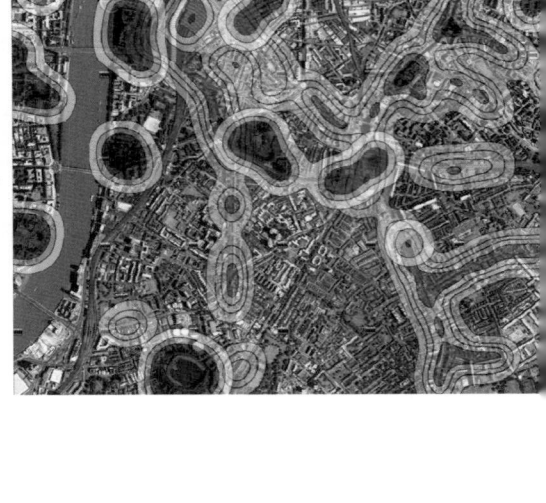

Design Seminar on Housing and the City

This seminar links the range of issues addressed by the programme to questions of project design and intervention in specific sites of urban change. Groups of students develop different strategies and proposals, which are compared and debated.

The main work this year has focused on the area of the Elephant & Castle in south London. Long neglected as a 'poor relation' of the north bank, there are now proposals for a large-scale redevelopment to put it on the map and to re-value this central urban space. What form should such development take, and who will benefit? Southwark Council has a programme of 'regeneration' and aims to produce significant physical and economic improvements for local people. Private investors see the site has great potential for up-market housing, offices and shopping. Can all parties win? What might be creative strategies for intervention and change in the area – in design terms and in programmatic terms? Three groups have developed proposals during Term 2, which are being discussed with Southwark Council, the development company and other consultants.

As a special workshop within the Elephant & Castle project we invited Prof. Joan Busquets from Barcelona to work with us on the issue of large-scale public space. The need for better public space is an element in many concepts of urban regeneration. If the aim of this regeneration is to put a 'new heart' into the area then how does the making of public space fit with other elements? This raised issues of context, connectivity, mix of surrounding uses, the creation of a destination, and quality.

Elephant and Castle

Stretching & Stitching

J. Brambila, K. Kang, B. Jansen, L. Lin, O. Rodriguez

Urban regeneration is understood as a process that runs along two lines. First, the slow and natural line of the existing social and economic structure and organisation. And second, the line that consists of visible, fast interventions in the physical fabric. Both must be backed by an awareness of and support for the need for change.

The strategy mapped a series of existing areas capable of channeling short and long term interventions. Through such areas of high connectivity, Stretching & Stitching extends, introduces and links activities, programmes and physical actions.

Stretching & Stitching is used as a tool that can direct the operation of the different levels of action (physical, social, local, global, etc.), allowing and stimulating complex associations, interactions, transgressions, and tensions among them during the process of regeneration. In the same manner the conceptual framework for physical intervention is embodied in the concept of Stretching & Stitching.

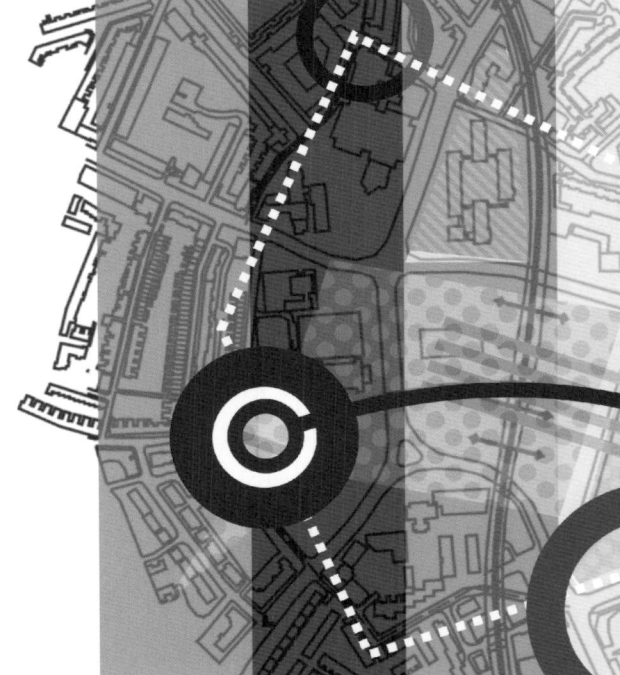

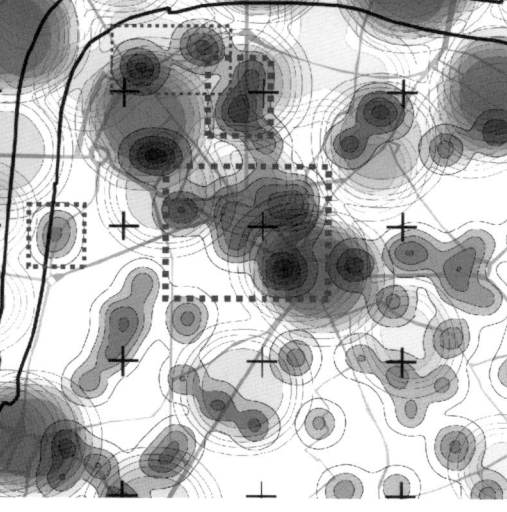
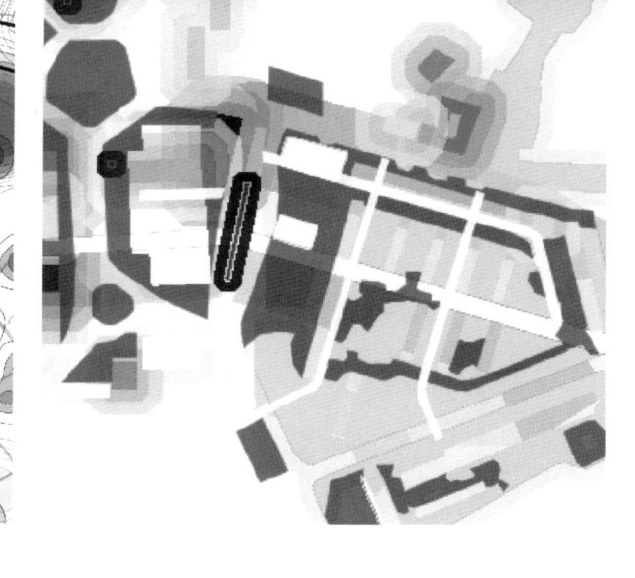

Incremental Planning

M. Bianconi, R. Boedi, E. Martinez de Velasco, E. Ortmann, P. Philippou

The starting point for the proposal was to challenge the present strategy of Southwark Council for the regeneration of the Elephant and Castle area, in which it has been designated a 'redevelopment area' with a selected regeneration 'partner'. Under this scheme, the Council has an excessive dependency on the developers to deliver the benefits, and little control over the regeneration process.

Instead of designing an alternative urban proposal, we propose a new framework of intervention, which instead of aspiring to a perfect final solution aims for a continuous and responsive process of regeneration.

The strategy operates by a series of tactical spatio-temporal interventions at neuralgic points which, incrementally implemented, trigger a continuous process which allows assessment, adaptation and participation of different actors at different scales of intervention.

Urban Regeneration, London

Greening Strategy

C. Bernini, T. Lopez, A. Olascoaga

This project approaches the Elephant & Castle's situation as a missing link in the larger urban fabric of London. Through a conceptual strategy, *greening* reclaims public space, streets and parks by intervening on a physical and social level.

The Greening Strategy could initiate a change in the urban fabric by means of subtle and time-elapsed interventions according to certain rules we believe are essential for reclaiming public space that is currently abandoned and deactivated.

By exploring and mapping the current status of the area we found a need for a more pedestrian-oriented landscape. The proposal would provide such a landscape by inverting the situation where the car dominates the terrain. As a result of *greening*, vehicle and pedestrian movement coexist, favouring the pedestrian whilst providing multi-modal permeability and accessibility to the area, creating a strong link with the city fabric.

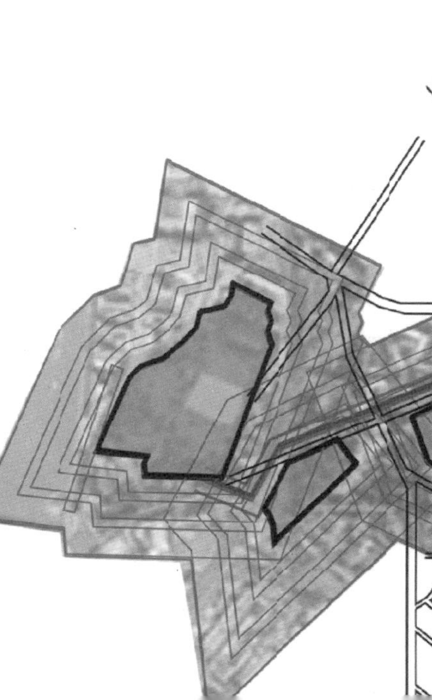

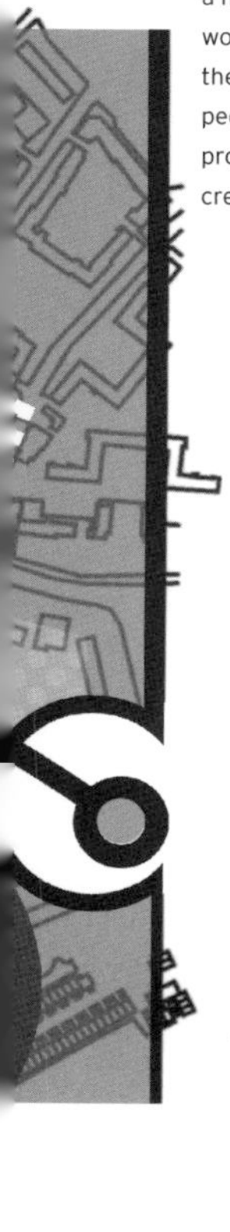

Favela Providencia and Docks, Rio de Janeiro

Rio de Janeiro
Term 2

For the past three years we have run this design workshop in collaboration with the Housing Department of Rio de Janeiro and the MA course in Urbanism of the Federal University. In April 2001 we returned to Rio along with members of Diploma Unit 4 to work on the formulation of general guidelines for a plan of intervention for the area of Gamboa, adjacent to Rio's docks and where Favela Providencia, the site of last year's workshop, is located. The aim was to address both the integration of Providencia and the surrounding area, and the relation of Gamboa to the redevelopment of the waterfront. Students worked in three groups to develop different proposals which were presented for debate. Our work was carried out in the context of the Favela-Bairro programme – a city-wide environmental and housing upgrading programme which aims to transform the favelas into neighbourhoods through the provision of public and social infrastructure, and through a multi-sectorial attack on poverty and social exclusion.

For further reference, see our publication:

'Transforming Cities - Design in the favelas of Rio de Janeiro'.

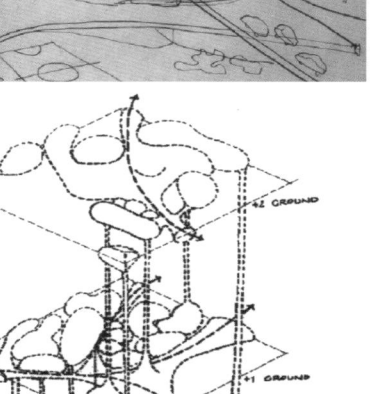

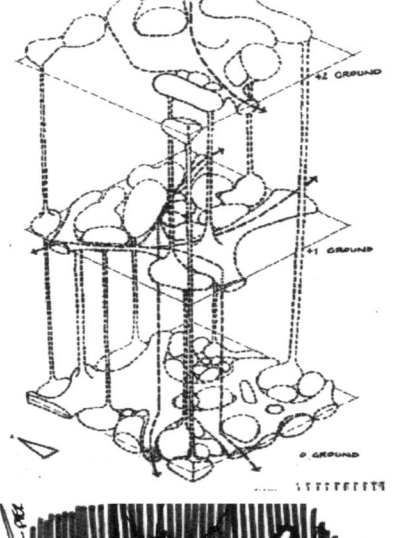

This team, working in a simulated planning process, developed and deployed a set of shared strategic tools that enabled a stronger integration of interests between the actors. The Super Dobra © [Super Fold] is a Federal Authority-initiated increase of the legislative and programmatic interface between the territories of the partners, a terrain for long-term coherent development of urban areas under supervision and with the subsidy of the federal government. The Atalhos Urbanos © [Urban Paths] replace exclusive zoning policies with the temporal distribution of diverse activities along selected and themed pathways. Porto Permeavel © [Permeable Port] entails the implementation of the urban paths in order to transform the waterfront into a highly accessible and attractive part of the city. Favela Bela © [Favela Beautiful] and Cidade Carnival © [Carnival City] aim at injecting elements born in the Favela and popular culture into the formal city to return its vitality.

Transforming Cities - Design in the Favelas of Rio de Janeiro

The favelas of Rio de Janeiro provide a rich and immensely challenging context to reflect on some of the most pressing issues of contemporary urbanism, beyond the metropolises of the developing world: questions of physical fragmentation, social exclusion, irregularity, citizenship, identity and political participation, are all posed in an extreme form. This is a context, moreover, which tests to the limit the role of design in the re-making of cities. It is a humbling experience exacerbated by the poverty of a design language to address such extreme circumstances. But it is also a learning experience that gives hope to the project of the city as a space of inclusion – a hope made more powerful and inspiring for having been cultivated within the most evident spaces of exclusion.

This publication documents the design workshop of April 2000 organised by the H&U programme in collaboration with the University of Rio, the City Government and the British Council. The workshop focused on the informal settlements of the city and was carried out in co-ordination with the City's Favela-Bairro programme. It sought to define the terms of reference and main components of a general plan of intervention in the oldest favela of Rio, Providencia. The publication summarises the work of the three groups which mixed students from the two academic institutions, and the views of the tutors involved, with the aim of raising politically relevant ideas and proposals.

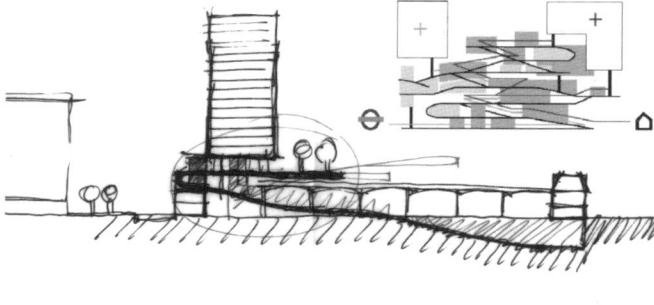

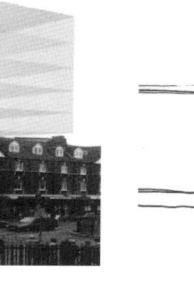

Spitalfields: Central and Marginal?

Term 1

This project investigated the forces of change and the conflicting needs of inner-city redevelopment. It used a case of dynamic change in central London to explore what might be appropriate design and policy responses to such forces. We worked as a joint design seminar with students and teachers from Diploma Unit 4 and the Federal University of Rio de Janeiro.

Through the disputed site of Spitalfields Market, a few minutes' walk from the Bank of England yet in an area with a long history of poverty and marginalisation, we explored the complexities of inner-city redevelopment. Six groups made proposals for the site that were both design and policy responses to the needs of the area and its urban landscape. The groups explored the tensions between the formal and the informal uses of space, between the needs and interests of rich and poor citizens, and between the existing buildings and spaces and the demand for new uses and built space.

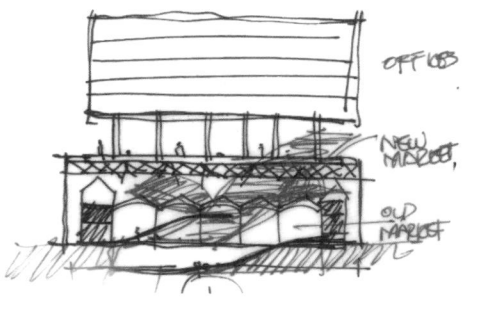

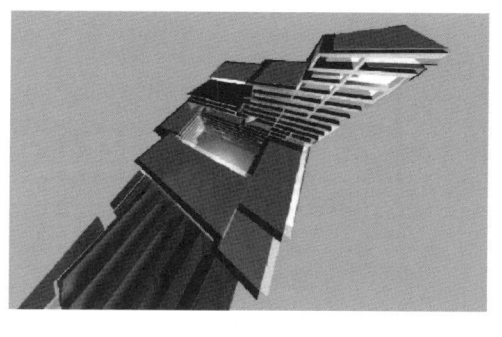

MA dissertation titles

Camila Bernini, *Critical ideas of the single-family house*

Marco Bianconi, *Architectural programming: considerations on the 'brief'*

Roy Boedi Utama, *'Global glamour' and mass tourism. The case of Ubud, Bali, Indonesia*

Jaime I. Brambila Corral, *The reinsertion of the dwelling in the new generation of non-conventional housing policy*

Bregit Jansen, *Excavating the future of master planning.*

Kun Wook Kang, *Regeneration of social housing estates in Britain: a programmatic approach to mixed use*

Da Chun Lin, *Technology and local identity in architecture*

Lin Lin, *Parochial autonomy and Chinese urban landscape - a study of 'Micro Residential District' planning*

Tania Lopez Winkler, *The house and its image*

Emilio Martinez de Valasco, *Liminal space and urban voids - addressing marginalisation in Mexico City*

Aurelio Olascoaga, *Retail planning policies in Cambridge: spatial and urban design implications*

Esther Ortmann, *Domesticity, privacy and house design*

Pavlos Philippou, *Organisation of (Dis)Appearances: an exercise at the intersection of space and politics*

Oscar Rodriguez, *Vague Network: a laboratory for public space*

Research Students

Completed in 2000/1

Themis Fagundes, Between masterplan and GIS applications: is there a site for Brazilian cities in the global network? (PhD)

Susana Gonzales, Recovering the city: ideology and the discourse of community in architectural practice (MPhil)

Andy Siswanto, Urban design and housing redevelopment in Indonesia (PhD)

Continuing research

Ludwig Abache, *The contested space of the highway: an inquiry into the transformation of public space* (MPhil)

Jose Brandao, *The role of urban design in strategic planning: the case of Rio de Janeiro* (PhD)

Jose Gomez Perez, *Fragmentary inner areas and urban development in Guadalajara, Mexico* (PhD)

Sarah Morgan, *Aroused by disturbance: community, conflict and socio-spatial disruption - the case of Harare, Zimbabwe* (PhD)

Elena Pascolo, *Scenario planning as an alternative urban planning strategy* (MPhil)

Gerardo Puente, *Min×Max/Mass: rationalisation and social housing architecture in Mexico* (PhD)

Paulo Rizzo, *Urban planning in the context of globalisation: the case of Florianopolis* (PhD)

Komson Teeraparbwong, *A mutual toleration? Socio-spatial relations in Chiang Mai City, Thailand* (PhD)

Jose Zavala, *State housing reform and structural adjustment policies in Argentina* (PhD)

Building Conservation

This course, intended for qualified architects, surveyors, engineers, conservation officers, planners, architectural historians and others who are (or who wish to be) professionally involved in the care and conservation of historic buildings in this country, was started in 1975 on the initiative of the RIBA and COTAC and is now well established as one of the leading courses of its kind. It maintains its position by continuing to attract the best lecturers and practitioners available to discuss current problems and their solutions with the course participants, who themselves are directly involved in these issues as part of their working lives. The course takes place on Fridays: lectures, seminars, visits to buildings in varying states of decay or under repair/conservation, craft workshops, studios and laboratories are brought together in a clearly defined order, and tailored as far as possible to keep up with continuing advances in practical and technological information and to meet the specific needs of the participants.

The chronological development of buildings and building types forms the basis of the course and an understanding of architectural history is assumed to be the best foundation for anyone involved in the care and repair of any historic building. The emphasis of the course has naturally evolved since its inception, but the first year continues to deal predominantly with basic attitudes to conservation; the recognition, diagnosis and repair of building faults; traditional building materials and crafts; building archaeology; historic buildings legislation; and building types from the early medieval period to the seventeenth century. The Second Year is broader in scope and deals with architectural development up to the present day, including the diverse building types that have emerged during the nineteenth and twentieth centuries. Other aspects examined include the introduction of services, the development of building crafts, historic interiors, environmental controls, the listing and repair of modern buildings, new design in the context of historic buildings, disasters that can befall historic buildings, and adaptations required to accommodate disabled people.

The course has increased its technical content, particularly in relation to nineteenth- and twentieth-century buildings, as practitioners of conservation are already involved in the repair of modern buildings.

While the main object of the course is to expose the participants to lectures and site visits conducted by experts, the knowledge that these provide is used throughout the course in the production of a number of written studies or exercises by each individual. These are directly linked to the lectures and visits in a definite development of the skills provided by the course, and culminate in the writing of a thesis during the Second Year. It is upon the quality of this thesis, backed up by an assessment of all the previous submissions, that the award of the Diploma depends. An outline of essay requirements follows.

Year One

Materials Essay
Each student writes a short essay either describing the medieval building materials of a specific locality, or contrasting the medieval materials with their modern equivalents. This acquaints the student with published literature on the subject, develops research and synthesis skills, and establishes a good reporting style. Sound academic practice is instilled by the need to provide references and bibliography.

Church Restoration Essay
To reinforce their current knowledge of architectural history and building archaeology, visual and surveying skills, self-discipline in research timing, and their ability to produce a well-rounded document, each student has to submit an illustrated essay (of about 500 words) describing the nineteenth-century 'restoration' carried out on a (preferably small) medieval church. This requires visual, documentary and archaeological research, and an examination of the selected church, including the original faculty documents, architect's drawings, builder and client correspondence, descriptions and illustrations of the church before restoration, and an assessment of the reasons for and the philosophy behind the restoration.

Structural Movement
The students each inspect the same small-scale building in poor structural repair, and submit a concise illustrated report suggesting a contemporary/short-term structural

Barn at Cressing Temple, Essex

Building Conservation study tour, Athens, led by Sue Blundell, June 2000.

consolidation. This tests the students' surveying and observational skills, as well as their understanding of the course lectures.

Dampness Exercise
A historic building affected by dampness from various sources is inspected, and each student submits a letter addressed to the building owner, thus honing their skills in making an appropriate written approach, as well as testing their ability to assess and appreciate the building's problems.

Dry Rot Exercise
Following the relevant lectures on the subject, a building infected with dry rot is inspected to assess its effects. This exercise, daunting for those who are neither architects nor engineers, is carried out in groups of three or four students, each group producing a joint report.

Timber-framed Building Study
After a number of lectures on various aspects of timber-framed buildings and their problems, a building in poor condition is visited in order that each student can study its condition, and suggest a hypothetical approach to its repair. Students then work on a report, illustrating the problems involved through drawings, plans, details and photographs.

Student Theses
During the Summer term of the first year students embark on the research which will culminate a year later in the submission of a thesis of between 15,000 and 20,000 words. Their brief is to produce an original piece of work in which source material relevant to the conservation of historic buildings is critically evaluated. Most of the completed projects have a strong historical perspective, but they also cover technical, aesthetic, philosophical, legal and policy concerns, often embracing the gamut of problems encountered when conservation issues are addressed.

Quinquennial Inspection
Students individually carry out the Quinquennial Inspection of a historic church, systematically inspecting the condition of the structure and decoration of a historic building. They then make recommendations for repair and set these into priorities.

Specification
Working in groups, students prepare tender documents for the repair of elements of a historic building. Submissions include contractual considerations and obligations as well as the preparation of technical repairs and their speculation.

Theses of 2001
Howard Allen The conservation of English modern movement houses

Marietta Balafouti
External colour schemes of neo-classical buildings in Athens

Belinda Bamber
Decorative interiors of modern movement houses

Russell Bateman
Retail developments in conservation areas

Rob Beynon
Post-Dayton recovery: conservation in Bosnia

Marcia Boys
A study of the depiction of evil in medieval wall paintings

Debbie Chiverton
Buildings containing shell decoration

James Gardner
Adopting cultural diversity in the protection of England's built heritage: will this lead to a crisis of authority?

Monica Harari
The White City, Tel Aviv: peeling cubes

Rachel James
Carlo Scarpa: a twentieth-century conservation architect?

Jane Lind
A conservation study of 15 Kensington Palace Gardens

Nick Marsh
'Watching the bathers': the conservation of lidos in the 'nautical moderne' style

Lindsay Nevin
A study of lakeland farm buildings and the effects of diversification

Paul Perry
Modern English hotels of the 1930s

Judith Roebuck
Harold Brakspear: architect and antiquarian

Andrew Shepherd
New churches and their repair in the diocese of Sheffield, 1913–62

Jane Stancliffe
Powell Moya's Churchill Gardens, Pimlico

Martin Caroe Memorial Scholarship
A new award has been generously endowed by Caroe & Partners in memory of their colleague the late Martin Caroe, a long-time supporter and adviser to the Building Conservation Course. The first holder of this award is Rob Beynon.

Staff
Academic Co-ordinator
Ian C. Bristow BArch DipArch (RWA) DPhil FSA ARIBA

Unit Masters
Second Year
John Redmill DipArch (Kingston) RIBA RIA
First Year
Alan Greening AADipl AADipArch RIBA

Academic Tutor
Sue Blundell BA PhD DipCont Ed

Course Co-ordinator
Rosemary Jury

Landscape & Garden Conservation

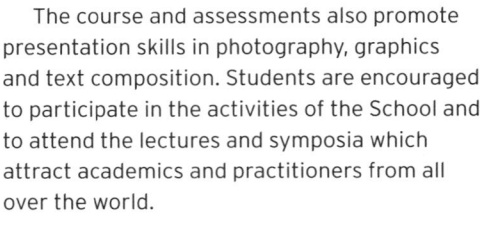

The course, which started in 1986, is the UK's leading postgraduate course in the conservation of historic landscapes and gardens. Graduates have taken up prominent roles in conservation and in historical research in the UK and abroad.

Validation was obtained from the Open University last year for postgraduate diplomas; in addition it is possible for qualified architects, planners, landscape architects and others to attend modules of the course as part of their Continuing Professional Development (CPD).

The Course
The course provides a solid foundation in historical skills and conservation. English and world garden and landscape history are an integral element of the course, with particular emphasis on linking ideas to practice. Students undertake essays and projects using historical surveys and research, and learn about the criteria for making assessments and recommending strategies for maintenance and conservation.

The principal areas of study were organised into the following modules of ten half-days each:

- The English landscape and its gardens up to the early Georgian period
- The English landscape garden and park
- Victorian landscape gardening to post-modernist landscape architecture
- European gardens: Italy, France, Germany, Russia, etc.
- Eastern and Western gardens: Eastern and Islamic, American and Australasian
- Aspects of garden history: historical planting, water features, and the English garden abroad
- Survey: methods, archaeology, and site description
- Historical research: sources, research and its interpretation, reports
- Evaluation: criteria, conditions and assessments of significance
- Management plans: from ethics and aims to prescription
- Protection, planning, presentation and interpretation
- Practical conservation at home and abroad, current professional work

Wherever appropriate, emphasis is placed on current issues, for example, urban parks and the holistic approach to conservation.

The course and assessments also promote presentation skills in photography, graphics and text composition. Students are encouraged to participate in the activities of the School and to attend the lectures and symposia which attract academics and practitioners from all over the world.

Structure of the Course
The course has a full programme of lectures, interspersed with day visits to gardens, parks and landscapes of particular interest and importance. In addition to attending the course on a regular basis, students are expected, by the end of the diploma, to complete four essays and projects, together with a 15,000-word thesis. The topic for the thesis is agreed with the tutors; it should involve original research and demonstrate both historical and practical skills.

Students are expected to attend organised field trips in their own time. These are seen as an essential part of the course - an opportunity for students to work in groups or individually on a specific site, bringing together all the skills that have been acquired in the preceding course work. On returning home, they are required to produce written and illustrated assessments which will be presented, together with projects and theses, to an external examiner.

Project on Site Description
The first year's project in the autumn term was on site description. This is a skill requiring knowledge of method and terminology together with powers of observation. The object was to provide a word picture of the place as it existed on the day of inspection, and as now routinely produced by English Heritage, Cadw and Historic Scotland for their various registers. A common format is desirable so that descriptions are easily digested by their readers and for this purpose English Heritage, the York database project and others have produced inspectors' manuals. In brief, the method is to conduct a tour as if for a tourist in the past (approach, house, garden, park, kitchen garden), and there are various conventions on site maps, terminology and categorisations. Site descriptions are supplemented by sketches, photographs and maps. Maps delimiting the extent of the designed landscape accompany the descriptions.

Students chose their own sites, generally ones of acknowledged historic interest and of medium complexity. They included some typical gentlemen's parks: Warlies Park in Essex, Shadben Park, and Cobham Park in Surrey, but also some unusual ones, like the gardens at Ingatestone Hall in Essex with their Tudor walls, and the town garden of Hall Place in Beaconsfield. There were two public parks: Brent Lodge Park and Kilburn Grange Park, and a cemetery in Kettering, Northamptonshire.

Essay on Historical Research
The theme of the spring term was historical research, and students were expected to prepare a historical report. Sites were chosen where a moderate amount of original research remained to be done to reveal its garden/landscape history. Advice on such a site is often obtained from a county gardens trust. Typically, a historical report starts with an introduction describing the location and physical characteristics of the site. It then progresses to accounts of the principal phases of change, and is completed by appendices that might include a list of owners, a chronology, a list of sources and/or any copies or transcripts containing especially interesting material. Emphasis was placed on the apparatus of scholarship, for example the use of bibliographies and footnotes.

The country seats chosen were Stratford Park, Stroud, Gloucestershire; Burwood Park, Surrey, which is now dismembered by housing estates; and Ascott House, Buckinghamshire, a Rothschild house where large quantities of Victorian material have recently come to light. Two sites with important Tudor phases were looked into: the gardens at Ingatestone Hall, Essex, and the Inner Temple Garden, London. The short-lived Botanical Gardens in Colchester were written up, as was Wicksteed Park, Kettering, Northamptonshire, perhaps the earliest 'theme park', and Severalls Hospital, Colchester, Essex, one of the largest and latest of the 'echelon' lunatic asylums.

Presentation on Evaluation
The summer term concentrated upon evaluation criteria, and the associated project was an oral presentation of an assessment employing the English Heritage criteria, with a final conclusion on the appropriate grade for the site. The presentation consists of visual evidence of both the site and historical material sufficient to give a clear picture of the

nature of the site and the particular components that have a bearing on grading assessments. The presentation was followed by feedback from the group.

The assessments under each criterion are justified by comparative studies that should highlight anything unusual about the site. This requires background research on comparative sites. Following this session, the students complete an 'inspector's report' consisting of a summary of no more than two sides, and the supporting evidence, visual and written.

Management Plan Project
Students in year two studied management planning. This activity is based around a skill in converting an assessment of the values of a place into a practical vision for how to nurture and enhance them into the future. The process is: Survey –> Analysis –> The Vision –> Outline proposals –> Costs and programme –> Consultation/Approval –>Implementation –> Monitoring –> Review.

Bearing in mind the time constraints, the project concentrated upon the stages Analysis –> The Vision –> Outline proposals. Students chose their own sites, preferably parks or gardens for which historical, archaeological, ecological, etc., values are already well understood.

Plans varied from a public park in London, West Heath and Golders Hill Park, to major country residences abroad, Le Domaine de Vizille en Dauphiné, France, and the Manor of Gronso, Sweden. Amongst the traditional English country houses were Rougham Hall, Norfolk, Heale House, Dorset, and Plumpton Rocks, Sussex. Villa landscapes included Fulham Palace, Holland Park and Marble Hill, all in London, and Highcliffe Castle, Dorset. One town garden, Burgh House, Hampstead, was selected, and also a former spa near Tunbridge Wells, now the Beacon Hotel, Rusthall. This diversity resulted in a wide variety of interesting issues arising.

Students
The intake of students comes from a range of disciplines including planning, landscape architecture, garden design, architecture and education. The mix is important to the success of the course, enlarging its scope and debate.

Dissertations
Dissertations were submitted in May/June 2001 on the following topics:

Catherine Durham, *Assessment and conservation of Ninian Niven Landscape: a case study at Massy's Wood*
Carolyn Bennett, *The early garden photograph: is it only black and white? What does the photograph tell us? What is its role in garden conservation?*
Robert Peel, *The historic impact of tree fruit & hops on the landscape of Kent and the role of conservation*
Lucy Scurfield, *A study of the Norwich playing fields and Open Spaces Society*
Barbara Simms, *Landscape conservation on span estates*
Kristina Taylor, *The park and gardens at Knole: conservation issues*
Fiona Webb, *Attitudes to open space and recreation in the Garden City Movement*

International Symposium
Getting it Right: landscape detailing for historic parks and gardens
Friday 8 June and Saturday 9 June 2001
This was the fourth in a series of symposia aimed at facilitating an international exchange of ideas and information, this time on the topical subject of conjectural detailing. We are particularly grateful to our speakers from abroad: Clemens Wimmer, Kim Legate and Ada Segre; and to Jan Woudstra, Brent Elliott, Edward Diestelkamp, Stephen Anderton, Stewart Harding, Peter Inskip and Hazel Conway who shared their experience gained in the UK. A special note of thanks is due to Ted Fawcett, the organiser.

Overseas Tours
A tour of the Veneto and the Trieste area has been arranged by Axel Griesinger for present students and alumni.

Tutors
Edward Fawcett OBE
Ken Fieldhouse DipLA DipTP MLI
Dr David Jacques PhD DipTP MIHT
(Course Director)
Sandra Morris BA (Oxon) GradDiplConsGardens (AA)
Dr Jan Woudstra PhD

Conservation Co-ordinator
Rosemary Jury – a special note of thanks is due to her for serving the programme so admirably for the last few years, and the AA's best wishes go with her to her new post at Hartwell House, Buckinghamshire.

ACADEMIC STAFF 00/01

Chairman
Mohsen Mostafavi

Foundation
Julia Wood, Valentin Bontjes van Beek,
Veronika Schmid

First Year
Academic Supervisor
Tony Swannell
Unit 1
Shin Egashira, Lucy Tilley
Unit 2
Mark Hemel, Denis Balent, Gianni Botsford
Unit 3
Teresa Stoppani, Rainer Hofmann
Unit 4
Katrin Lahusen, Shumon Basar
Unit 5
Pierre d'Avoine, Tom Emerson, Miraj Ahmed

Intermediate School
Academic Supervisor
Charles Tashima
Unit 1
Andrew Houlton, Stephen Taylor
Unit 2
Martha LaGess, Michael McNamara
Unit 3
Clive Sall, Kevin Rhowbotham, Kim Colin
Unit 4
Alex de Rijke, Philip Marsh, Sadie Morgan
Unit 5
Philippe Barthélémy, Mary Bowman, Neil Thomas
Unit 6
John Bell, Theo Lorenz
Unit 7
David Racz, Andreas Lang
Unit 8
Charles Tashima
Unit 9
Dominic Papa, Jonathan Woodroffe
Unit 10
Johannes Käferstein, Jamie Fobert

Diploma School
Academic Supervisor
Peter Beard
Unit 1
Jean Michel Crettaz, Takuro Hoshino
Unit 2
Peter Beard, Jim McKinney
Unit 3
Pascal Schöning
Unit 4
Michael Hensel, Ludo Grooteman

Unit 5
On sabbatical
Unit 6
Kevin Rhowbotham, Cedric Price
Unit 7
Nikolaus Hirsch, Makoto Saito
Unit 8
Mark Prizeman, Peter Thomas, Kevin Shepherd
Unit 9
Michael Weinstock
Unit 10
Carlos Villaneuva Brandt
Unit 11
Shin Egashira, David Greene
Unit 12
Raoul Bunschoten, Petra Marguc,
Christian Rogner
Unit 13
Götz Stöckmann, Jane Wernick
Unit 14
Ciro Najle, Hanif Kara
Unit 15
Christian Kieckens, Hélène Furján

Graduate School
Environment and Energy
Simos Yannas, Peter Sharratt, Susannah Hagan
Housing and Urbanism
Jorge Fiori, Hugo Hinsley, Nicholas Bullock,
Lawrence Barth, Irénée Scalbert
Histories and Theories
Mark Cousins, Paul Hirst, Robert Maxwell,
Andrew Benjamin, Neil Leach, Katharina Borsi,
Vittoria di Palma, Marina Lathouri, Hélène Furján
Graduate Design: Landscape Urbanism
Sandra Morris, Ciro Najle, Christopher Fannin
Graduate Design: AADRL
Brett Steele, Patrik Schumacher, Andrew Benjamin,
Chris Hight, Tom Verebes
Visiting Critics
Xavier Costa, Hilde Heynen

Professional Studies
Building Conservation
Ian Bristow, Alan Greening, John Redmill,
Sue Blundell
Garden Conservation
David Jacques, Ted Fawcett, Jan Woudstra,
Axel Griesinger, Sandra Morris, Ken Fieldhouse,
Hugh Prince
Professional Practice
Alastair Robertson

Visiting Teachers
Hugo Hinsley, Sandra Morris

Technical Studies
First Year
Brendan Woods
Intermediate
Rosamund Diamond, Javier Castañon
Diploma
Michael Weinstock, Wolf Mangelsdorf
Consultants
Carolina Bartram, Pat Brown, Ian Carradice
Ruth Conroy, Phil Cooper, Nick Dalton, Fenella Griffin,
Anderson Inge, Sophie Le Bourva, Chris Leubkeman,
Alvise Simondetti, Randall Thomas, Jane Wernick,
Mohsen Zikri

General Studies
Director
Mark Cousins
Academic Staff
Andrew Benjamin, Vittoria di Palma, Brian Hatton,
Andrew Higgott, Sarah Jackson, Marina Lathouri,
Neil Leach, Sandra Morris, Benedict O'Looney,
Diana Periton, Irénée Scalbert, Pascal Schöning
Consultants
Peter Blundell Jones, Paul Davies, Hélène Furjan,
Susannah Hagan, Lorens Holm, Mari Hvattum,
Guy Mannes Abbott, Mark Morris, Elizabeth Wilson

Communications
Course Master
Jean Michel Crettaz
Academic Staff
Sue Barr, Etienne Clement, Simon English,
Pete Gomes, Denise Hawrysio, Peter Lewis,
Anton Malinowski, Joel Newman,
Goswin Schwendinger, David Ward
Courses and Consultants
Martin Akpoveta, Enrico Benco, Christian Bodhi,
Nick Dalton, Max de Rosée, Julia Frazer,
Chris Woodward

Cover: Vessel for the city, tested in Hastings,
by Stefania Batoeva, Daniel Castella, Chloe Kobayashi
and Martin Wells, First Year Unit 1

Inside Cover: www.aaschool.ac.uk/projectsreview
Graphics by Ludwig Abache

Projects Review 00/01 has been produced through
the AA Print Studio by Nicola Bailey, Clare Barrett,
Chris Dell, Pamela Johnston, Allon Kaye, Mark Rappolt
and Marilyn Sparrow

© 2001 Architectural Association

Projects Review 00/01 and back issues are available from
AA Publications, 36 Bedford Square, London WC1B 3ES
publications@aaschool.ac.uk
www.aaschool.ac.uk/publications

Printed in England by Dexter Graphics

ISBN 1 902902 20 3/ ISSN 0265-4644